WESTERN CANADA SINCE 1870

WESTERN CANADA SINCE 1870

A SELECT BIBLIOGRAPHY AND GUIDE

Alan F.J. Artibise

UNIVERSITY OF BRITISH COLUMBIA PRESS
VANCOUVER

WESTERN CANADA SINCE 1870:
A SELECT BIBLIOGRAPHY AND GUIDE

©THE UNIVERSITY OF BRITISH COLUMBIA 1978
ALL RIGHTS RESERVED

Canadian Cataloguing in Publication Data

Artibise, Alan F.J., 1946-
  Western Canada since 1870

  Includes index.
  ISBN 0-7748-0090-9
  ISBN 0-7748-0091-7 pa.

  1. The West, Canadian* — Bibliography.
  2. The West, Canadian* — History — Bibliography. I. Title.
  Z1365.A78   016.971   C78-002011-1
  [FC3206]

International Standard Book Number 0-7748-0090-9 (cloth)
0-7748-0091-7 (paper)

Printed in Canada

Contents

Illustrations ix
Preface xi
Acknowledgements xiii
Directions for Users xv
Abbreviations xvi

1. *General*
   a) General — 1
   b) Immigration and Settlement — 8
   c) Indians and Ethnic Groups — 14
   d) Government and Politics — 21
   e) Railways — 27
   f) Agriculture and Rural Development — 32
   g) Economic Development and Labour — 42
   h) Education and Social and Cultural Development — 47
   i) Urban Development — 52
   j) Bibliographical and Methodological — 55

2. *Riel Rebellions*
   a) General — 62
   b) 1870 Rebellion — 64
   c) 1885 Rebellion — 66

3. *Northwest Territories to 1905* — 70

4. *Manitoba*
   a) General — 79
   b) The People — 83
   c) Government and Politics — 88
   d) Agriculture and Rural Development — 91
   e) Economic Development and Labour — 94
   f) Education and Social and Cultural Development — 97
   g) Urban Development
      i) General — 101
      ii) Winnipeg — 103
   h) Bibliographical — 116

5. *Saskatchewan*
   a) General . . . 117
   b) The People . . . 119
   c) Government and Politics . . . 122
   d) Agriculture and Rural Development . . . 129
   e) Economic Development and Labour . . . 133
   f) Education and Social and Cultural Development . . . 135
   g) Urban Development
      i) General . . . 139
      ii) Regina . . . 142
      iii) Saskatoon . . . 144
   h) Bibliographical . . . 146

6. *Alberta*
   a) General . . . 148
   b) The People . . . 151
   c) Government and Politics . . . 157
   d) Agriculture and Rural Development . . . 163
   e) Economic Development and Labour . . . 167
   f) Education and Social and Cultural Development . . . 170
   g) Urban Development
      i) General . . . 174
      ii) Calgary . . . 176
      iii) Edmonton . . . 184
   h) Bibliographical . . . 189

7. *British Columbia*
   a) General . . . 190
   b) The People . . . 197
   c) Government and Politics . . . 209
   d) Agriculture and Rural Development . . . 215
   e) Economic Development and Labour . . . 218
   f) Education and Social and Cultural Development . . . 226
   g) Urban development
      i) General . . . 229
      ii) Vancouver . . . 236
      iii) Victoria . . . 246
   h) Bibliographical . . . 250

A Brief Guide to Western Canadian Studies
   A. Newsletters and Journals . . . 253
   B. Archives and Libraries . . . 254
   C. Organizations and Societies . . . 259
   D. Specialized Series . . . 261

Select Subject Index
    i) Ethnic Groups   265
    ii) Political Parties and Politicians   266
    iii) Miscellaneous   267

Author Index   269

Organizations, Institutions, and Serial Index   293

Illustrations

Plate 1. Immigrants Arriving at the C.P.R. Station, Winnipeg.	9
Plate 2. Blackfoot Sun Dance Camp	18
Plate 3. Laying the C.P.R. Track near Castor, Alberta	30
Plate 4. Harvesting with a Steam Engine	37
Plate 5. Workers in the Clothing Industry, Winnipeg	44
Plate 6. Downtown Vancouver from Stanley Park	54
Plate 7. Settler's House with Sod Roof	77
Plate 8. Manitoba Department of Agriculture and Immigration Pamphlet, 1892	93
Plate 9. Winnipeg City Hall	110
Plate 10. T.C. Douglas and the Banner of the C.C.F., Weyburn	125
Plate 11. Grain Elevators on the C.P.R. Mainline, Lewvan, Saskatchewan	133
Plate 12. Bow River Ranch near Cochrane, Alberta	150
Plate 13. William Aberhart Broadcasting in the 1930's	162
Plate 14. Leduc Oil Well, Number One	169
Plate 15. Downtown Calgary across the Bow River	182
Plate 16. The Kwakiutl Village of Newitty in the Late 1870's	203
Plate 17. Parliament Buildings, Victoria, with One of the "Birdcages"	214
Plate 18. Logging Truck, Nanaimo Lakes, B.C.	223
Plate 19. Seiners with Their Nets Set in the Strait of Georgia	233

Photographic Credits

Plates 1, 5, 8, and 9 are from the Provincial Archives of Manitoba, Plate 10 is from the Provincial Archives of Saskatchewan, Plates 4 and 14 are from the Provincial Archives of Alberta, and Plates 16 and 17 are from the Provincial Archives of British Columbia. The Glenbow-Alberta Institute, Calgary, provided Plates 2, 3, 12, 13, and 15. Plate 6 is from the Photographic Division of the Vancouver *Sun*, and Plate 7 appears courtesy of the R.C.M.P. Museum, Regina. Plate 11 is from the collection of the NFB Photothèque (George Hunter). Plate 18 is courtesy of Crown Zellerbach and the Fisheries Association of British Columbia supplied Plate 19.

Preface

This bibliography is designed to provide students, teachers, researchers, librarians, and the general public with a ready and reliable guide to significant literature dealing with Western Canada. It attempts to steer a middle course between brief lists of references provided in most books and long, comprehensive bibliographies in which significant items are often lost in the sheer number of titles listed. *Western Canada Since 1870* does not, of course, replace such invaluable reference tools as Bruce B. Peel's *Bibliography of the Prairie Provinces to 1953* or the three-volume *Bibliography of British Columbia*. Instead, this select bibliography is meant to provide its users with ample references to undertake a study on almost any topic falling under the Western Canadian studies umbrella. Since most items listed here contain their own footnotes and bibliographies, this volume not only guides the reader directly to the references printed here, but also leads the inquirer to the much larger range of offerings cited in the individual references. Moreover, a special attempt has been made to include bibliographic items that will take the reader deeper into the wealth of material on the West that has become available recently.

While this bibliography does not completely replace previous works in the field, it does have several features that cannot be found in any other volume. First, it is the only bibliography that attempts to cover all four western provinces in a single volume. Second, it is an up-to-date study since it includes material completed as recently as 1977. Third, it contains not only books and pamphlets, but periodical articles and unpublished B.A. essays and M.A. and Ph.D. theses. The last two features are particularly important since anyone who has studied the region knows that the past two decades or so have been a time when there has been an extraordinary outpouring of material devoted to Canada's four western provinces and that a good portion of this material has appeared in either article or thesis form.

Western Canada Since 1870 is selective. The items contained in it are those the compiler judged to be essential to the study of the region. Inevitably, however, some important material has been either overlooked or misjudged. In these cases users are strongly encouraged to notify the compiler. It must also be noted that while the emphasis of this volume is on the historical development of Western Canada, it does not restrict itself to historical studies; it includes work completed in such diverse fields as political science, geography, economics, anthropology, sociology, and native, ethnic, urban and environmental studies. The bibliography does not attempt to cover in any detail fictional material or government publications. While a few of the more important works in both categories are cited, users are directed to the guides for this type of material listed in the appropriate sections of this volume for more detailed coverage. Finally, the compiler often faced difficult choices in deciding what to include and what to omit. The process of elimination was influenced not only by the relative significance of one item as compared to another, but also by the relative amount that has been written about any one topic. Where a subject has not been extensively studies, it was hard to refuse the inclusion of virtually all references that could be located.

The main objective of this work will have been achieved if the bibliography helps its users to find their way to the significant literature of Western Canada. It is also to be hoped, however, that *Western Canada Since 1870* will serve another purpose. Since it identifies the present state of research on western Canada, it should help to locate areas of insufficient research and, as a result, facilitate a more co-ordinated approach to the study of Canada's most diverse region.

Acknowledgements

This project began almost two years ago. Since then, the compilation of source material on Western Canada has consumed far more time than I ever intended. Yet, whatever the merits of this volume, I have found the experience gratifying because of the willing and able assistance I have received along the way.

Two people in particular have made this project more enjoyable than it might otherwise have been and deserve my deepest gratitude. My wife, Irene, took on the major task of compiling the author index. Given scholars' peculiar habit of using a different form of their names for almost every piece of work, this was a frustrating and time-consuming job. Jane C. Fredeman, Senior Editor, University of British Columbia Press, not only encouraged the publication of this volume, but made hundreds of revisions and corrections before the final version went to the printer. For the cheerful resourcefulness with which she handled these exacting duties, my thanks.

Several friends and colleagues read earlier drafts of the bibliography and made many useful suggestions. Among them are Pat Roy, Ian MacPherson, Bill Brennan, Rod McLeod, and Lewis H. Thomas. I must extend my thanks to them as well as to the staffs of the Provincial Archives of Manitoba, Saskatchewan, Alberta, and British Columbia, and the Glenbow-Alberta Archives. All the archives provided photographs for this volume on short notice. Finally, I want to mention the secretaries of the University of Victoria history department, particularly Puri Chadwick and June Belton. They completed an inordinate amount of typing skilfully and quickly.

Undertakings of this kind almost certainly contain some errors and I accept full responsibility for them. I hasten to add, however, that sins of omission and commission brought to my attention will be rectified as soon as the opportunity arises.

I dedicate this volume to all those who are cited in it—the vast number of people who, through their work, have made the understanding of a fascinating and complex region possible.

Alan F.J. Artibise
University of Victoria
December 1977

Directions for Users

1. The bibliography is best approached through the table of contents. There the reader will note that the volume has been organized into sixty-three categories and subdivisions. Under the various headings are listed the books, articles, and theses bearing on that particular topic.
2. The bibliography can also be approached through the author index. This index is a guide only to the authors of works cited here; it is neither a title nor a subject index.
3. For certain subjects, the bibliography can also be approached through the select subject index. This index is a complete listing of all works included in the bibliography on such topics as various ethnic groups, political parties, politicians, and the R.C.M.P. Subjects included in this index are those that did not seem to justify separate categories, or those that did not easily fit into the established categories.
4. Cross-referencing has been used in many cases to cope with such obvious questions as whether to list a work on ethnic politics under "Ethnic Groups" or "Government and Politics."
5. As a convenience to users, reprintings or new editions have been indicated whenever possible.
6. Edited collections of original papers have been listed both as individual volumes and as separate papers. Thus, for example, S.M. Trofimenkoff, ed., *The Twenties in Western Canada* is listed in the "General" section of part one, and the articles contained in the volume are cited under appropriate headings elsewhere in the bibliography. The only time this practice has not been followed is when edited volumes contain reprints of papers published elsewhere. In these cases, only the volume itself is cited.
7. The "General" categories are not restricted to items which deal exclusively with either Western Canada or a particular province. In many cases items not restricted to either the region or the province are listed since they contain material that is significant.
8. The heading "People" includes not only biographies and autobiographies, but work on ethnic groups as well.
9. The heading "Urban Development" includes not only urban studies but local and regional studies as well.

Abbreviations

A.H.R.	*Alberta Historical Review*
B.C.H.Q.	*British Columbia Historical Quarterly*
C.H.R.	*Canadian Historical Review*
C.J.E.P.S.	*Canadian Journal of Economics and Political Science*
H.S.S.M. *Transactions*	*Historical and Scientific Society of Manitoba Transactions*
Sask. Hist.	*Saskatchewan History*

1

General

a. General

1. **Allen, Richard, ed.** *A Region of the Mind: Interpreting the Western Canadian Plains.* Regina: Canadian Plains Research Center, 1973.
2. ———. *Man and Nature on the Prairies.* Regina: Canadian Plains Research Center, 1976.
2A. **Archer, John H.** "The Prairie Perspective in 1977." In Richard Simeon, ed. *Must Canada Fail?* (Montreal: McGill-Queen's University Press, 1977), pp. 73-84.
3. **Barr, John J., and Anderson, O., eds.** *The Unfinished Revolt: Some Views on Western Independence.* Toronto: McClelland and Stewart, 1971.
4. **Bennett, J.W.** "Adaptive Strategy and Processes in the Canadian Plains." In Richard Allen, ed. *A Region of the Mind* (Regina, 1973), pp. 181-200.
5. **Bercuson, David J., ed.** *Western Perspectives I: Papers of the Western Canadian Studies Conference.* Toronto: Holt, Rinehart and Winston, 1974.
6. ———. *Canada and the Burden of Unity.* Toronto: Macmillan, 1977.
7. **Berger, Carl, and Cook, Ramsay, eds.** *The West and the Nation: Essays in Honour of W.L. Morton.* Toronto: McClelland and Stewart, 1976.
8. **Bickersteth, J.B.** *The Land of Open Doors: Being Letters from Western Canada 1911-1913.* 1914. Reprint. Social History of Canada, vol. 29. Toronto: University of Toronto Press, 1976.
9. **Birrell, Andrew J.** "Classic Survey Photos of the Early West." *Canadian Geographical Journal* 91 (1975), pp. 12-19.

10. **Boam, Henry J., comp.** *The Prairie Provinces of Canada: Their History, People, Commerce, Industries, and Resources.* London: Sells, 1914.
11. **Breen, D.H.** "The Canadian West and the Ranching Frontier, 1875-1922." Ph.D. Thesis (University of Alberta, 1972).
12. **Brown, Lorne, and Brown, Caroline.** *An Unauthorized History of the R.C.M.P.* Toronto: James Lewis and Samuel, 1973.
13. **Brown, R. Craig.** "Canadian Nationalism in Western Newspapers." *A.H.R.* 10 (Summer 1962), pp. 1-7.
14. **Bruce, Jean.** *The Last Best West.* Toronto: Fitzhenry and Whiteside, 1976.
15. **Burmeister, K.H., ed.** *Western Canada 1909: Travel Letters by Wilhelm Cohnstaedt.* Regina: Canadian Plains Research Center, 1976.
16. **Burt, A.L.** *The Romance of the Prairie Provinces.* Toronto: Gage, 1930.
17. **Butler, W.F.** *The Great Lone Land.* London: Marston, Low, & Searle, 1872.
18. **Campbell, M.W.** *The Saskatchewan.* Toronto: Clarke, Irwin, 1950.
19. **Card, B.Y.** *The Canadian Prairie Provinces from 1870-1950: A Sociological Introduction.* Toronto: Dent, 1960.
20. **Cashman, Tony.** *An Illustrated History of Western Canada.* Edmonton: Hurtig, 1971.
21. **Creighton, Donald G.** "Sir John A. Macdonald, Confederation and the Canadian West." H.S.S.M. *Transactions* Series III, 23 (1966-67), pp. 5-14.
22. **Dempsey, Hugh A., ed.** *Men in Scarlet.* Calgary: Historical Society of Alberta and McClelland and Stewart West, 1974.
23. **Ebbutt, Frank.** "The Canoe in Western Canada." *Canadian Geographical Journal* 3 (1931), pp. 287-292.
24. **Eggleston, Wilfrid.** "The Short Grass Prairies of Western Canada." *Canadian Geographical Journal* 50 (1955), pp. 134-145.
25. **Elton, D.K., ed.** *One Prairie Province? Conference Proceedings and Selected Papers.* Lethbridge: University of Lethbridge and the Lethbridge *Herald*, 1970.
26. **England, Robert.** "The Emergent West." *Queen's Quarterly* 41 (1934), pp. 405-413.

27. **Ferguson, George V.** "The Outlook for the West." *Queen's Quarterly* 44 (1937), pp. 371-379.
28. ———. "The Prairie Provinces and Canadian Foreign Policy." *Foreign Affairs* 18 (October 1939), pp. 70-79.
29. ———. "The Prairie Provinces." *Think* 7, no. 9 (1941), pp. 51-72.
30. **Fetherstonhaugh, R.C.** *The Royal Canadian Mounted Police.* New York: Carrick and Evans, 1938.
31. **Friesen, Gerald.** "The Western Canadian Identity." Canadian Historical Association. *Historical Papers 1973*, pp. 13-20.
31A. ———. "Studies in the Development of Western Canadian Regional Consciousness, 1870-1925." Ph.D. Thesis (University of Toronto, 1973).
32. **Gagan, David P.**, ed. *Prairie Perspectives [1]: Papers of the Western Canadian Studies Conference.* Toronto: Holt, Rinehart and Winston, 1970.
33. **Gislason, I.** *Prairie Panorama: A Brief Study of the Prairie Provinces.* Calgary: Western Canada Institute, 1948.
34. **Gough, Barry M.**, "Sea Power and the History of Western Canada." *Journal of Canadian Studies* 8 (May 1973), pp. 50-59.
35. **Grant, George M.** *Ocean to Ocean: Sandford Fleming's Expedition through Canada in 1872.* 1873. Reprint. Edmonton: Hurtig, 1967.
36. **Hall, D.J.** "'The Spirit of Confederation': Ralph Heintzman, Professor Creighton, and the Bicultural Compact Theory." *Journal of Canadian Studies* 9 (November 1974), pp. 24-42.
37. **Harrington, L.** "The Dawson Route." *Canadian Geographical Journal* 43 (September 1951), pp. 136-143.
38. **Heintzman, Ralph.** "The Spirit of Confederation: Professor Creighton, Biculturalism, and the Use of History." *C.H.R.* 52 (1971), pp. 245-275.
39. **Higinbotham, John D.** *When the West Was Young: Historical Reminiscences of the Early Canadian West.* Toronto: Ryerson, 1933.
40. **Hill, Douglas.** *The Opening of the Canadian West.* London: Heinemann, 1967.
41. **Hourticq, L., and Jaray, G.-L.** *De Québec à Vancouver: A travers le Canada d'aujourd'hui.* Paris: Librairie Hachette, 1924.
42. **Howay, F.W.** "Some National Historic Sites in Western Canada." *Canadian Geographical Journal* 21 (1940), pp. 206-211.

43. **Hurd, W. Burton, and Grindley, T.W.** *Agriculture, Climate and Population of the Prairie Provinces of Canada.* Ottawa: F.A. Acland, 1931.
44. **Kelly, Nora.** "The Evolution of the R.C.M.P." *Canadian Geographical Journal* 86 (1973), pp. 168-181.
45. **Kelly, Nora, and Kelly, William.** *The Royal Canadian Mounted Police: A Century of History, 1873-1973.* Edmonton: Hurtig, 1973.
46. **Kizer, Benjamin, H.** *The U.S.-Canadian Northwest: A Demonstration Area for International Postwar Planning and Development.* Toronto: Ryerson, 1943.
47. **Klassen, H.C., ed.** *The Canadian West: Social Change and Economic Development.* Calgary: Comprint Publishing Co., 1977.
48. **Kuch, Peter.** "Arch Dale: The Pictorial Spokesman of the West." H.S.S.M. *Transactions* Series III, 19 (1962-63), pp. 44-49.
49. **Langstreth, T. Morris.** *The Silent Force: Scenes from the Life of the Mounted Police of Canada.* New York: Century Company, 1927.
50. **Leacock, Stephen B.** *My Discovery of the West: A Discussion of East and West in Canada.* Toronto: Thomas Allen, 1937.
51. **MacBeth, R.G.** *The Making of the Canadian West.* Toronto: William Briggs, 1898.
52. ———. *The Romance of Western Canada.* 1918. 2d. ed. Toronto: William Briggs, 1920.
53. **McCrossan, R.G., and Glaister, R.R.** *Geological History of Western Canada.* Calgary: Alberta Society of Petroleum Geologists, 1966.
54. **MacEwan, Grant.** *Fifty Mighty Men.* Saskatoon: Modern Press, 1958.
55. ———. *Portraits from the Plains.* Toronto: McGraw-Hill Ryerson, 1971.
56. ———. *. . . .And Mighty Women Too: Stories of Notable Western Canadian Women.* Saskatoon: Western Producer, 1975.
57. **MacEwan, Grant, and Foran, Maxwell.** *A Short History of Western Canada.* Toronto: McGraw-Hill Ryerson, 1968.
58. ———. *West to the Sea.* Toronto: McGraw-Hill Ryerson, 1968.
59. **MacGregor, James G.** *Blankets and Beads: A History of the Saskatchewan River.* Edmonton: Institute of Applied Art, 1949.
60. **Mackintosh, W.A.** "The Pioneer Problems of the Prairie Provinces of Canada: General Outline." *Pioneer Settlement.* American Geographical Society, Special Publication No. 14 (1932), pp. 1-11.

General 5

60A. MacPherson, Ian. *Each For All: A History of the Co-operative Movement in English Canada, 1900-1945.* Toronto: McClelland and Stewart, 1978.

61. **Mandel, E.** "Images of Prairie Man." In Richard Allen, ed. *A Region of the Mind* (Regina, 1973), pp. 201-209.

62. **Martin, Chester.** *"Dominion Lands" Policy.* Toronto: Macmillan, 1938.

63. **Mitchell, E.B.** *In Western Canada before the War: A Study of Communities.* London: John Murray, 1915.

64. **Mitchell, Ken, ed.** *Horizon: Writings of the Canadian Prairie.* Toronto: Oxford University Press, 1977.

65. **Morton, A.S.** *A History of the Canadian West to 1870-71: Being a History of Rupert's Land (the Hudson's Bay Company's Territory) and of the North-West Territory (including the Pacific Slope).* 1929. Reprint. Toronto: University of Toronto Press, 1973.

66. **Morton, W.L.** *The West and Confederation.* Canadian Historical Association Booklet 9. Ottawa: Canadian Historical Association, 1958.

67. ———. "A Century of Plain and Parkland." *A.H.R.* 17 (Spring 1969), pp. 1-10.

68. ———. "The West and the Nation, 1870-1970." In A.W. Rasporich and H.C. Klassen, eds. *Prairie Perspectives 2* (Toronto, 1973), pp. 8-24.

69. **Nelson, J.G.** "Canada's National Parks: Past, Present, Future." *Canadian Geographical Journal* 86 (March 1973), pp. 68-89.

70. ———. *Man's Impact on the Western Canadian Landscape.* Toronto: McClelland and Stewart, 1976.

71. **Nelson, John.** *The Canadian Provinces: Their Problems and Policies.* Toronto: Musson, 1924.

72. **Oliver, E.H.** "The Institutionalizing of the Prairies." Royal Society of Canada. *Proceedings and Transactions* 3d. ser. 31 (1937), sec. 2, pp. 1-21.

73. **Paul, A.H., and Dale, E.H., eds.** *Southern Prairies Field Excursion: Background Papers.* Regina: Department of Geography, University of Saskatchewan, Regina Campus, 1972.

74. **Rasmussen, Linda; Rasmussen, Lorna; Savage, Candace; and Wheeler, Anne.** *A Harvest Yet to Reap: A History of Prairie Women.* Toronto: Women's Press, 1976.

75. **Rasporich, A.W., and Klassen, H.C.**, eds. *Prairie Perspectives 2: Selected Papers of the Western Canadian Studies Conferences.* Toronto: Holt, Rinehart and Winston, 1973.

76. **Rasporich, A.W.**, ed. *Western Canada: Past and Present.* Calgary: McClelland and Stewart West, 1975.

77. **Rea, J.E.** "Images of the West." In David J. Bercuson, ed. *Western Perspectives I* (Toronto, 1974), pp. 4-9.

78. **Richards, J.H.** "The Prairie Region." In J. Warkentin, ed. *Canada: A Geographical Interpretation* (Toronto, 1968), pp. 396-437.

79. **Riddell, R.G.** "A Cycle in the Development of the Canadian West." *C.H.R.* 21 (1940), pp. 268-284.

80. **Robertson, Heather.** *Salt of the Earth: The Story of the Homesteaders of Western Canada, 1880-1914.* Toronto: James Lorimer, 1974.

81. **Roe, F.G.** "The Extermination of the Buffalo in Western Canada." *C.H.R.* 15 (1934), pp. 1-23.

82. ———. "The Old Log House in Western Canada." *A.H.R.* 5 (Spring 1958), pp. 1-9.

83. **Roy, R.H.** "West of the Mountains. . . and East." *A.H.R.* 17 (Spring 1969), pp. 16-22.

84. **Rutherford, P.F.W.** "The Western Press and Regionalism." *C.H.R.* 53 (1971), pp. 287-305.

85. **Sage, Walter N.** "Geographical and Cultural Aspects of the Five Canadas." Canadian Historical Association. *Annual Report 1937,* pp. 28-34.

85A. **Scace, R.C.** "Western Canadian Antecedents to Northern Conservation Reserves." *Contact: Journal of Urban and Environmental Affairs* 8, no. 4 (1976), pp. 3-29.

87. **Shortt, Adam**, ed. *Canada and Its Provinces.* Toronto: Glasgow, Brook, 1914-1917. [Volumes 19, 20, 21 and 22 are devoted to Western Canada.]

88. **Sloan, Robert W.** "The Canadian West: Americanization or Canadianization?" *A.H.R.* 16 (Winter 1968), pp. 1-7.

89. **Smith, Peter J.**, ed. *The Prairie Provinces: Studies in Canadian Geography.* Toronto: University of Toronto Press, 1972.

90. **Stacey, C.P.** "The Military Aspect of Canada's Winning of the West." *C.H.R.* 21 (1940), pp. 1-24.

91. **Stanley, George F.G.** "The Western Canadian Mystique." In David P. Gagan, ed. *Prairie Perspectives [1]* (Toronto, 1970), pp. 6-29.

91A. Stegner, Wallace. *Wolf Willow: A History, a Story, and a Memory of the Last Plains Frontier.* 1955. Reprint. New York: Viking Press, 1966.

92. Strayer, B.L. "One Prairie Province: The Constitutional Processes for Prairie Union." *Canadian Public Administration* 13 (1970), pp. 337-343.

93. Sutley, Zack T. *The Last Frontier.* Toronto, Macmillan, 1930.

94. Swainson, D., ed. *Historical Essays on the Prairie Provinces.* Toronto: McClelland and Stewart, 1970.

95. Thomas, Lewis H. "British Visitors' Perceptions of the West, 1885-1914." In A.W. Rasporich and H.C. Klassen, eds. *Prairie Perspectives 2* (Toronto, 1973), pp. 181-196.

96. Thomas, Lewis H., ed. *Essays on Western History.* Edmonton: University of Alberta Press, 1976.

97. Thompson, John H. *The Harvests of War: The Prairie West, 1914-1918.* Toronto: McClelland and Stewart, 1977.

98. Trofimenkoff, S.M., ed. *The Twenties in Western Canada.* Ottawa: National Museum of Man, History Division, 1972.

99. Voisey, P.L. "The Impact of the Frontier on Prairie Canada: Selected Themes, 1870-1916." M.A. Thesis (University of Calgary, 1975).

100. Wade, Mason, ed. *Regionalism in the Canadian Community, 1867-1967.* Toronto: University of Toronto Press, 1969.

101. Walnes, W.J. *Prairie Population Possibilities.* Ottawa: King's Printer, 1940.

102. Warkentin, J.H. "Western Canada in 1886." H.S.S.M. *Transactions* Series III, 20 (1963-64), pp. 85-116.

103. ———. *The Western Interior of Canada. A Record of Geographical Discovery, 1612-1917.* Toronto: McClelland and Stewart, 1964.

104. ———. "Time and Place in the Western Interior." *Arts Canada* 169/170/171 (1972), pp. 20-37.

105. Weir, T.R., and Matthews, G. *Atlas of the Prairie Provinces.* Toronto: Oxford University Press, 1971.

106. Wertenbaker, T.J. "The Molding of the Middle West." *Sask. Hist.* 1 (Spring 1948), pp. 25-26.

107. Wibois, Joseph. *Un Pays neuf: L'Ouest canadien.* Paris: Librairie Valois, 1931.

108. Wood, E.H. "Ralph Connor and the Canadian West." M.A. Thesis (University of Saskatchewan, 1975).

109. **Zimmerman, Carle C., and Moneo, G.W.** "The Total Community of the Canadian Wheat Prairies." *Canadian Journal of Agricultural Economics* 18, no. 3 (1970), pp. 6-28.

b. Immigration and Settlement

110. **Avery, Donald.** "Canadian Immigration Policy and the 'Foreign' Navvy, 1896-1914." Canadian Historical Association. *Historical Papers 1972,* pp. 135-156.
111. **Belkin, Simon.** *Through Narrow Gates: A Review of Jewish Immigration, Colonization and Immigrant Aid Work in Canada, 1840-1940.* Montreal: Eagle Publishing, 1966.
112. **Bennett, J.W., and Kohl, S.B.** "Characterological, Strategic, and Institutional Interpretations of Prairie Settlement." In A.W. Rasporich, ed. *Western Canada: Past and Present* (Calgary, 1975), pp. 14-27.
113. **Bicha, K.** *The American Farmer and the Canadian West, 1896-1914.* Lawrence, Kansas: Coronado Press, 1972.
114. **Bjork, K.O.** "Scandinavian Migration to the Canadian Prairie Provinces, 1893-1914." *North American Studies* 26 (1974), pp. 3-30.
115. **Breen, D.H.** "The Canadian Prairie West and the Harmonious Settlement Interpretation." *Agricultural History* 47 (1973), pp. 63-75.
116. **Broadfoot, Barry.** *The Pioneer Years, 1895-1914: Memories of Settlers Who Opened the West.* Toronto: Doubleday, 1976.
117. **Carter, D.J.** "Archbishops' Western Canada Fund." *A.H.R.* 16 (Winter 1968), pp. 10-17.
118. **Cheng, Tien-Fang.** *Oriental Immigration in Canada.* Shanghai: Commercial Press, 1931.
119. **Coates, Roy.** "To the Golden West, 1903: Part 1." *Sask. Hist.* 7 (Autumn 1954), pp. 104-109.
120. ———. "To the Golden West, 1904-08: Part II." *Sask. Hist.* 8 (Winter 1955), pp. 17-21.
121. **Corbett, D.C.** "A Study of Factors Governing Canada's Absorption of Immigrants, 1867-1914." M.A. Thesis (University of Toronto, 1949).
122. ———. *Canada's Immigration Policy.* Toronto: University of Toronto Press, 1957.

123. **Correll, Ernst, ed.** "The Debates in the Canadian House of Commons on the Mennonite Immigration from Russia in 1873-74." *Mennonite Quarterly Review* 20 (1946), pp. 255-275.

124. **Culliton, John T.** *Assisted Emigration and Land Settlement with Special Reference to Western Canada.* Montreal: Federated Press, 1928.

125. **Eggleston, Wilfrid.** "The Old Homestead: Romance and Reality." In H. Palmer, ed. *The Settlement of the West* (Calgary, 1977), pp. 114-129.

126. **Ehlers, E.** "The Expansion of Settlement in Canada: A Contribution to the Discussion of the American Frontier." *Geographische Rundschau* 18 (1966), pp. 327-337.

127. **England, Robert.** *The Central European Immigrant in Canada.* Toronto: Macmillan, 1929.

128. ———. "Land Settlement in Northern Areas of Western Canada." *C.J.E.P.S.* 1 (1935), pp. 578-587.

Plate 1. Immigrants Arriving at the C.P.R. Station, Winnipeg

129. ———. *The Colonization of Western Canada: A Study of Contemporary Land Settlement, 1896-1934.* Toronto: McClelland and Stewart, 1936.
130. **Galbraith, J.S.** "Land Policies of the Hudson's Bay Company, 1870-1913." *C.H.R.* 32 (1951), pp. 1-21.
131. **George, M.V.** *Internal Migration in Canada: Demographic Analyses.* 1961 Census Monograph. Ottawa: Dominion Bureau of Statistics, 1970.
132. **Gold, N.L.** "American Migration to the Prairie Provinces of Canada." Ph.D. Thesis (University of California, 1933).
133. **Green, Alan G.** *Immigration and the Postwar Canadian Economy.* Toronto: Macmillan, 1976.
134. **Hall, D.J.** "Clifford Sifton: Immigration and Settlement Policy, 1896-1905." In H. Palmer, ed. *The Settlement of the West* (Calgary, 1977), pp. 60-85.
135. **Hammer, Josiah Austin.** "Mormon Trek to Canada." *A.H.R.* 7 (Spring 1959), pp. 7-16.
136. **Hedges, J.B.** *Building the Canadian West: The Land and Colonization Policies of the Canadian Pacific Railway.* New York: Macmillan, 1939.
137. **Hill, Douglas.** *Great Emigrations I: The Scots to Canada.* London: Gentry Books, 1972.
138. **Hoffer, Clara, and Cahan, F.H.** *Land of Hope.* Saskatoon: Modern Press, 1960.
139. **Ignatiuk, G.P.** "Ukrainian Settlements in the Canadian West." In *Development of Agriculture on the Canadian Prairies: Proceedings of Seminar* (Regina, 1975), pp. 175-215.
140. **Kalbach, Warren E.** *The Impact of Immigration on Canada's Population.* 1961 Census Monograph. Ottawa: Dominion Bureau of Statistics, 1970.
141. **Kensit, H.E.M.** "The Centre of Population Moves West." *Canadian Geographical Journal* 9 (1934), pp. 263-269.
142. **Klippenstein, L., and Toews, J.G., eds.** *Mennonite Memories: Settling in Western Canada.* Winnipeg: Centennial Publications, 1977.
143. **Kovacs, M.L.** *Esterhazy and Early Hungarian Immigration to Canada.* Regina: Canadian Plains Research Center, 1974.

143A. Lehr, John C. "The Rural Settlement Behaviour of Ukrainian Pioneers in Western Canada, 1891-1914." In B.M. Barr, ed. *Western Canadian Research in Geography: The Lethbridge Papers* (Vancouver: B.C. Geographical Series, no. 21, 1975), pp. 51-66.

144. Lycan, Richard. "Interprovincial Migration in Canada: The Role of Spatial and Economic Factors." *Canadian Geographer* 13 (1969), pp. 237-254.

145. Macdonald, Norman. *Canadian Immigration and Colonization: 1841-1903.* Toronto: Macmillan, 1966.

146. Mackintosh, W.A. *Prairie Settlement: The Geographical Setting.* Toronto: Macmillan, 1934.

147. Martin, Chester, "Early History and Land Settlement of the Prairie Provinces of Canada." *Pioneer Settlement.* American Geographical Society, Special Publication No. 14 (1932), pp. 18-21.

148. Minifie, James M. *Homesteader: A Prairie Boyhood Recalled.* Toronto: Macmillan, 1972.

149. Morgan, E.C. "Soldier Settlement in the Prairie Provinces." *Sask. Hist.* 21 (Spring 1968), pp. 41-55.

150. Morrison, H.M. "The Background of the Free Land Homestead Law of 1872." Canadian Historical Association. *Annual Report 1935,* pp. 58-66.

151. Morton, A.S. *History of Prairie Settlement.* Toronto: Macmillan, 1938.

152. Morton, W.L. "The Significance of Site in the Settlement of the American and Canadian Wests." *Agricultural History* 25 (1951), pp. 97-104.

153. Norrie, K.H. "The Rate of Settlement on the Canadian Prairies, 1870-1911." *Journal of Economic History* 35 (1975), pp. 410-427.

154. Palmer, H., ed. *Immigration and the Rise of Multiculturalism.* Toronto: Copp Clark, 1975.

155. ———. *The Settlement of the West.* Calgary: Comprint Publishing Co., 1977.

156. Pollard, W.C. *Pioneering in the Prairie West.* London: Arthur H. Stockwell, c. 1926.

157. Rasporich, A.W. "Utopian Ideals and Community Settlements in Western Canada: 1880-1914." In H.C. Klassen, ed. *The Canadian West* (Calgary, 1977), pp. 37-62.

158. **Reid, Richard Gavin.** "From the Old Land to the New (Part 1)." *A.H.R.* 5 (Winter 1957), pp. 3-9.
159. ———. "From the Old Land to the New (Part 2)." *A.H.R.* 5 (Spring 1957), pp. 15-21.
160. **Richtik, James M.** "The Policy Framework for Settling the Canadian West, 1870-1880." *Agricultural History* 49 (1975), pp. 613-628.
161. **Robertson, Heather.** "Prairie Feudalism: Homesteading in the Nineteen-Seventies." In H.C. Klassen, ed. *The Canadian West* (Calgary, 1977), pp. 15-24.
162. **Russell, R.C.** "The Carlton Trail." *Sask. Hist.* 8 (Winter 1955), pp. 22-27.
163. **Seldon, J.** "Postwar Migration and the Canadian West: An Economic Analysis." In A.W. Rasporich and H.C. Klassen, eds. *Prairie Perspectives 2* (Toronto, 1973), pp. 154-170.
164. **Sharp, P.F.** "The American Farmer and the 'Last Best West.'" *Sask. Hist.* 1 (Winter 1948), pp. 18-20.
165. ———. "When Our West Moved North." *American Historical Review* 55 (1950), pp. 286-300.
166. ———. "Three Frontiers: Some Comparative Studies of Canadian, American and Australian Settlement." *Pacific Historical Review* 24 (1955), pp. 369-377.
167. **Simpson, G.W.** "The Blending of Traditions in Western Canadian Settlement." Canadian Historical Association. *Annual Report 1944*, pp. 46-52.
168. **Smith, W.G.** *A Study in Canadian Immigration.* Toronto: Ryerson, 1920.
169. **Spry, Irene.** "The Great Transformation: The Disappearance of the Commons in Western Canada." In Richard Allen, ed. *Man and Nature on the Prairies* (Regina, 1976), pp. 21-45.
170. **Stanley, George F.G.** "French Settlement West of Lake Superior." Royal Society of Canada. *Proceedings and Transactions* 3d ser. 48 (1954), pp. 107-118.
171. **Stead, Robert J.C.** "The Old Prairie Homestead." *Canadian Geographical Journal* 7 (1933), pp. 13-22.
172. **Stevens, R.C.** "Western Canadian Immigration in Sir Clifford Sifton's Time." M.A. Thesis (University of Western Ontario, 1963).
173. **Stich, K.P.** "Immigration and the Canadian West: From Propaganda to Fiction." Ph.D. Thesis (York University, 1974).

174. **Stone, Leroy O.** *Migration in Canada: Regional Aspects.* 1961 Census Monograph. Ottawa: Dominion Bureau of Statistics, 1969.
175. **Studness, C.M.** "Economic Opportunity and the Westward Migration of Canadians during the Late Nineteenth Century." *C.J.E.P.S.* 30 (1964), pp. 570-584.
176. **Swanson, W.W.** "The Immigration Problem in the Prairie Provinces." Canadian Society of Agricultural Economics. *Proceedings 1937*, pp. 68-74.
177. **Thomas, L.G.** "The Umbrella and the Mosaic: The French-English Presence and the Settlement of the Canadian Prairie West." In J.A. Carroll, ed. *Reflections of Western Historians* (Tucson: University of Arizona Press, 1969), pp. 135-152.
178. **Thomas, Lewis H.** "From Pampas to the Prairies: The Welsh Migration of 1902." *Sask. Hist.* 24 (Winter 1971), pp. 1-12.
179. **Timlin, M.F.** "Canada's Immigration Policy, 1896-1910." *C.J.E.P.S.* 26 (1960), pp. 517-532.
180. **Troper, Harold Martin.** *Only Farmers Need Apply: Official Canadian Government Encouragement of Immigration from the United States, 1896-1911.* Toronto: Griffin House, 1972.
181. ———. "Public Versus Private Land Promotion: The Western Canadian Immigration Association." In H. Palmer, ed. *The Settlement of the West* (Calgary, 1977), pp. 86-101.
182. **Tyman, John L.** "Patterns of Western Land Settlement." *H.S.S.M. Transactions* Series III, 28 (1971-72), pp. 117-136.
183. ———. *By Section, Township and Range: Studies in Prairie Settlement.* Brandon: Assiniboine Historical Society, 1972.
184. ———. "Prairie Settlement: The Legislative Framework." In A.H. Paul and E.H. Dale, eds. *Southern Prairies Field Excursion: Background Papers* (Regina, 1972), pp. 47-76.
185. **Vanderhill, B.G.** "Settlement in the Forest Lands of Manitoba, Saskatchewan and Alberta: A Geographic Analysis." Ph.D. Thesis (University of Michigan, 1956).
186. ———. "The Direction of Settlement in the Prairie Provinces of Canada." *Journal of Geography* 58 (1959), pp. 325-333.
187. ———. "The Decline of Land Settlement in Manitoba and Saskatchewan." *Economic Geography* 38 (1962), pp. 270-277.
188. **Warkentin, J.H.** "Water and Adaptive Strategies in Settling the Canadian West." *H.S.S.M. Transactions* Series III, 28 (1971-72), pp. 59-74.

189. **Whiteley, A.S.** "The Peopling of the Prairie Provinces of Canada." *American Journal of Sociology* 38 (1932), pp. 240-252.

190. **Woodsworth, J.S.** *Strangers within Our Gates, or Coming Canadians.* 1909. Reprint. Social History of Canada, vol. 7. Toronto: University of Toronto Press, 1972.

c. Indians and Ethnic Groups

191. **Anderson, Grace M., and Higgs, David.** *A Future to Inherit: The Portuguese Communities in Canada.* Toronto: McClelland and Stewart, 1976.

192. **Andrews, Isabel A.** "The Crooked Lake Reserves: A Study of Indian Policy in Practice from the Qu'Appelle Treaty to 1900." M.A. Thesis (University of Saskatchewan, Regina, 1972).

193. **Arnold, A.J.** "The Jewish Contribution to the Opening and Development of the West." H.S.S.M. *Transactions* Series III, 25 (1968-69), pp. 23-38.

194. ———. "Jewish Pioneer Settlements." *The Beaver* Outfit 306 (1975), pp. 20-26.

195. **Badoux, Maurice.** "Le Fait français dans l'ouest." *Le Canada français* 31 (1944), pp. 623-630.

196. **Barbeau, C.** *Indian Days on the Western Prairies.* Ottawa: National Museum of Man, 1960.

197. **Becker, A.** "The Germans in Western Canada: A Vanishing People." Canadian Catholic Historical Association. *Study Sessions 1975,* pp. 29-49.

198. **Bennett, J.W.** *Hutterian Brethren: The Agricultural Economy and Social Organization of a Communal People.* Stanford: Stanford University Press, 1967.

199. **Bowes, R.P., et al.** *The Indian: Assimilation, Integration or Separation?* Scarborough: Prentice-Hall, 1972.

200. **Bryce, P.H.** *The Story of a National Crime: An Appeal for Justice to the Indians of Canada.* Ottawa: James Hope and Sons, 1922.

201. **Buchanan, Donald W.** "The Mormons in Canada." *Canadian Geographical Journal* 2 (1931), pp. 255-270.

202. **Campbell, Maria.** *Halfbreed: A Proud and Bitter Canadian Legacy.* Toronto: McClelland and Stewart, 1973.

General 15

203. **Cardinal, Harold.** *The Unjust Society: The Tragedy of Canada's Indians.* Edmonton: Hurtig, 1969.
204. ———. *The Rebirth of Canada's Indians.* Edmonton: Hurtig, 1976.
205. **Chalmers, John W.** "Strangers in Our Midst." *A.H.R.* 16 (Winter 1968), pp. 18-23.
206. ———. "Treaty No. Six." *Alberta History* 25 (Spring 1977), pp. 23-27.
207. **Cohen, Zir, ed.** *Canadian Jewry: Prominent Jews of Canada.* Toronto: Canadian Jewish Historical Publishing Company, 1933.
208. **Dahlie, Jorgen.** "Scandinavian Experiences on the Prairies, 1890-1920: The Frederiksens of Nokomis." In H. Palmer, ed. *The Settlement of the West* (Calgary, 1977), pp. 102-113.
209. **Dahlie, Jorgen, ed.** "The Ethnic Voice: Eyewitness Accounts: Letters Home from a Danish Family on the Prairies." *Canadian Ethnic Studies* 8 (1976), pp. 93-95.
210. **Dawson, Carl A.** *Group Settlement: Ethnic Communities in Western Canada.* Toronto: Macmillan, 1936.
211. **Dempsey, Hugh A.** *Crowfoot: Chief of the Blackfeet.* Edmonton: Hurtig, 1972.
212. **Denny, Cecil.** "Indians of the Early West (Part 1)." *A.H.R.* 4 (Autumn 1956), pp. 22-26.
213. ———. "Indians of the Early West (Part 2)." *A.H.R.* 5 (Spring 1957), pp. 26-31.
214. **Dyck, Ruth.** "Ethnic Folklore in Canada: A Preliminary Survey." *Canadian Ethnic Studies* 7 (1975), pp. 90-101.
215. **Elliot, J.L., ed.** *Immigrant Groups: Minority Canadians 1.* Scarborough: Prentice-Hall, 1971.
216. ———. *Immigrant Groups: Minority Canadians 2.* Scarborough: Prentice-Hall, 1971.
217. **England, Robert.** *The Central European Immigrant in Canada.* Toronto: Macmillan, 1929.
218. ———. "Glimpses of Europe in Western Canada." *Canadian Geographical Journal* 5 (1932), pp. 3-20.
219. ———. "Ethnic Settlers in Western Canada: Reminiscences of a Pioneer." *Canadian Ethnic Studies* 8 (1976), pp. 18-33.
220. **Entz, W.** "The Suppression of the German Language Press in September 1918 (with Special Reference to the Secular German Language Papers in Western Canada)." *Canadian Ethnic Studies* 8 (1976), pp. 56-70.

221. **Epp, F.H.** *Mennonites in Canada, 1786-1920: The History of a Separate People.* Toronto: Macmillan, 1974.

222. **Epp, George K.**, ed. *Harvest: An Anthology of Mennonite Writing in Canada, 1874-1914.* Winnipeg: Centennial Publications, 1974.

223. **Falk, G.A.** "Missionary Education Work amongst the Prairie Indians, 1870-1914." M.A. Thesis (University of Western Ontario, 1973).

224. **Fisher, A.D.** "Cultural Conflict on the Prairies: Indian and White." *A.H.R.* 16 (Summer 1968), pp. 22-29.

225. **Flint, David.** *The Hutterites: A Study in Prejudice.* Toronto: Oxford University Press, 1975.

226. **Foster, W. Garland.** "Canadian Communists: The Doukhobor Experiment." *American Journal of Sociology* 41 (1935), pp. 327-340.

227. **Fowke, Edith.** "American Cowboy and Western Pioneer Songs in Canada." *Western Folklore* 21 (1962), pp. 247-256.

228. ———. *Folklore of Canada.* Toronto: McClelland and Stewart, 1976.

229. **Fowke, Edith, and Johnston, Richard.** *Folk Songs of Canada.* Waterloo: Waterloo Music, 1954.

230. ———. *More Folk Songs of Canada.* Waterloo: Waterloo Music, 1967.

231. **Francis, E.K.** "The Russian Mennonites: From Religious Group to Ethnic Group." *American Journal of Sociology* 54 (1950), pp. 101-107.

232. ———. "The Adjustment of a Peasant Group [The Mennonites] to a Capitalist Economy." *Rural Sociology* 17 (1952), pp. 218-228.

233. **Frémont, Donatien.** *Les Français dans l'ouest canadien.* Winnipeg: Editions de la liberté, 1959.

234. **Frideres, J.S.** "Discrimination in Western Canada." *Race* 15 (1973), pp. 213-222.

235. **Friedmann, Robert.** "Comprehensive Review of Research on the Hutterites, 1880-1950." *Mennonite Quarterly Review* 24 (1950), pp. 353-363.

236. ———. *Hutterite Studies.* Goshen, Ind.: Mennonite Historical Society, 1961.

237. **Friesen, I.I.** "The Mennonites of Western Canada with Special Reference to Education." M.Ed. Thesis (University of Saskatchewan, 1934).

238. **Gellner, John, and Smerek, John.** *The Czechs and Slovaks in Canada.* Toronto: University of Toronto Press, 1968.
238A. **Gibbins, Roger, and Ponting, J. Rick.** "Contemporary Prairie Perceptions of Canada's Native Peoples." *Prairie Forum* 2 (1977), pp. 57-82.
239. **Gibbon, J.M.** *Canadian Mosaic: The Making of a Northern Nation.* Toronto: McClelland and Stewart, 1938.
240. **Giraud, Marcel.** *Le Métis canadien: Son role dans l'histoire des provinces de l'ouest.* Paris: Institut d'Ethnologie, 1945.
241. ———. "Les Canadiens français dans les provinces de l'ouest." *Revue de l'Université Laval* 3 (1948), pp. 215-232.
242. ———. "The Western Métis after the Insurrection." *Sask. Hist.* 9 (Winter 1956), pp. 1-15.
243. **Graham-Cumming, G.** "Health of the Original Canadians, 1867-1967." *Medical Services Journal of Canada* 23 (1967), pp. 115-166.
244. **Gross, Paul S.** *The Hutterite Way: The Inside Story of the Life, Customs, Religion, and Traditions of the Hutterites.* Saskatoon: Freeman Publishing, 1965.
245. **Hamilton, L.** "Foreigners in the Canadian West." *Dalhousie Review* 17 (1938), pp. 448-460.
246. **Hatt, F.K.** "The Canadian Métis: Recent Interpretations." *Canadian Ethnic Studies* 3 (1971), pp. 1-16.
247. **Howay, F.W.** "Crowfoot: The Great Chief of the Blackfeet." Canadian Historical Association. *Annual Report 1930,* pp. 107-112.
248. **Huel, R.J.A.** "The French Language Press in Western Canada: Le Patriote de l'ouest, 1910-1941." *Revue de l'Université d'Ottawa* 46 (1976), pp. 476-499.
249. **Inglis, G.B.** "The Canadian Indian Reserve: Community, Population, and Social System." M.A. Thesis (University of British Columbia, 1971).
250. **Jenness, Diamond.** *The Indians of Canada.* Ottawa: National Museum of Man, 1932.
251. ———. *The Indian Background of Canadian History.* Ottawa: National Museum of Man, 1937.
252. **Jennings, John.** "The Plains Indian and the Law." In Hugh A. Dempsey, ed. *Men in Scarlet* (Calgary, 1974), pp. 50-65.
253. **Johnson, G.** "The Syrians in Western Canada." *Sask. Hist.* 12 (Winter 1959), pp. 31-32.

Plate 2. Blackfoot Sun Dance Camp

254. ———. "The Roumanians in Western Canada." *Sask. Hist.* 14 (Spring 1961), pp. 64-70.

255. **Klymasz, R.B.** *Folk Narrative among Ukrainian Canadians in Western Canada.* Ottawa: National Museum of Man, 1973.

256. ———. *Continuity and Change: The Ukrainian Heritage.* Ottawa: National Museum of Man, 1975.

257. **Kydd, M.W.** "Alien Races in the Canadian West." M.A. Thesis (McGill University, 1924).

258. **LaViolette, G.** "Notes on the Aborigines of the Prairie Provinces." *Anthropologica* 2 (1956), pp. 107-130.

259. **Leechman, J.D.** *Natives Tribes of Canada.* Toronto: Gage, 1956.

260. **Lehmann, Heinz.** *Das Deutschtum in Westkanada.* Berlin: Junker and Dünnhaupt Verlag, 1939.

261. **Lohrenz, Gerhard.** *The Mennonites of Western Canada.* Winnipeg: Centennial Publications, 1974.

262. **Lysenko, Vera.** *Men in Sheepskin Coats: A Study of Assimilation.* Toronto: Ryerson, 1947.

263. **MacEwan, Grant.** *Tatanga Mani: Walking Buffalo of the Stonies.* Edmonton: Hurtig, 1969.

264. ———. *Sitting Bull: The Years in Canada.* Edmonton: Hurtig, 1973.

265. **McKay, R.J.** "A History of Indian Treaty Number Four and Government Policies in Its Implementation, 1874-1905." M.A. Thesis (University of Manitoba, 1973).

266. **Makowski, W.B.** *History and Integration of Poles in Canada.* Niagara Peninsula: Canadian Polish Congress, 1967.

267. **Maranchuk, Michael H.** *The Ukrainian Canadians: A History.* Ottawa: Ukrainian Free Academy of Sciences, 1970.

268. **Morton, A.S.** "The New Nation, the Métis." Royal Society of Canada. *Proceedings and Transactions* 3d. ser. 33 (1939), sec. 2, pp. 137-145.

269. **Murray, Walter.** "Continental Europeans in Western Canada." *Queen's Quarterly* 38 (1931), pp. 53-75.

270. **Palmer, T.J.** "Ethnic Character and Social Themes in Novels about Prairie Canada in the Period from 1900 to 1940." M.A. Thesis (York University, 1972).

271. **Patterson, E. Palmer.** *The Canadian Indian: A History Since 1500.* Toronto: Collier-Macmillan, 1972.

272. **Paulsen, F.M.** *Danish Settlements on the Canadian Prairies: Folk Traditions, Immigrant Experiences, and Local History.* Ottawa: National Museum of Man, 1974.

273. **Peacock, Kenneth.** *A Survey of Ethnic Folk Music across Western Canada.* Ottawa: National Museum of Man, 1963.

274. ———. *Twenty Ethnic Songs from Western Canada.* Ottawa: National Museum of Man, 1966.

275. **Pennanen, Gary.** "Sitting Bull: Indian without a Country." *C.H.R.* 51 (1970), pp. 123-140.

276. **Peter, Karl.** "The Instability of the Community of Goods in the Social History of the Hutterites." In A.W. Rasporich, ed. *Western Canada: Past and Present* (Calgary, 1975), pp. 99-119.

277. **Peters, Victor J.** *All Things Common: The Hutterian Way of Life.* Minneapolis: University of Minnesota Press, 1965.

278. **Ponich, M.H.** "Wasyl Eleniak, Father of Ukrainian Settlers in Canada." *A.H.R.* 4 (Summer 1956), pp. 17-18.

279. **Radecki, Henry, and Heydenkorn, B.** *A Member of a Distinguished Family: The Polish Group in Canada.* Toronto: McClelland and Stewart, 1976.

280. **Rasporich, A.W., ed.** "The Ethnic Voice: Eyewitness Accounts: A Croatian Immigrant on the Frontier." *Canadian Ethnic Studies* 8 (1976), pp. 95-102.

281. **Ray, M.V.** "Sudeten Settlement in Western Canada." M.A. Thesis (University of Toronto, 1952).
282. **Reid, W. Stanford.** "The Scot and Canadian Identity." *Lakehead University Review* 4 (1971), pp. 1-25.
283. **Robertson, Heather.** *Reservations Are for Indians.* Toronto: James Lewis and Samuel, 1970.
284. **Royal Commission on Bilingualism and Biculturalism.** *The Cultural Contributions of Other Ethnic Groups.* Book IV. Ottawa: Government of Canada, 1970.
285. **Ryder, N.B.** "The Interpretation of Origin Statistics." *C.J.E.P.S.* 21 (1955), pp. 466-479.
286. **Sanderson, James F.** "Indian Tales of the Canadian Prairies." *A.H.R.* 13 (Summer 1965), pp. 7-21.
287. **Scott, W.L.** *The Ukrainians, Our Most Pressing Problem.* Toronto: Catholic Truth Society of Canada, 1931.
288. **Sealey, D.B., ed.** *Stories of the Métis.* Winnipeg: Manitoba Métis Federation, 1973.
289. **Sealey, D.B., and Lussier, A.S.** *The Métis: Canada's Forgotten People.* Winnipeg: Manitoba Métis Federation, 1975.
290. **Shipley, Nan.** "Twilight of the Treaties." *Queen's Quarterly* 75 (1968), pp. 314-329.
291. **Smillie, E.E.** "An Historical Survey of Indian Migration within the Empire." *C.H.R.* 4 (1923), pp. 217-257.
292. **Stanley, George F.G.** "The Métis and the Conflict of Cultures in Western Canada." *C.H.R.* 28 (1947), pp. 428-433.
293. ———. "The Indian Background of Canadian History." Canadian Historical Association. *Annual Report 1952*, pp. 14-21.
293A. ———. "French Settlement West of Lake Superior." Royal Society of Canada. *Proceedings and Transactions* 3d. ser. 48 (1954), sec. 2, pp. 107-115.
294. ———. "French and English in Western Canada." In M. Wade, ed. *Canadian Dualism: Studies of French-English Relations* (Toronto, 1960), pp. 311-330.
295. **Symington, Fraser.** *The Canadian Indian: The Illustrated History of the Great Tribes of Canada.* Toronto: McClelland and Stewart, 1969.
296. **Tarasoff, K.** *A Pictorial History of the Doukhobors.* Saskatoon: Western Producer, 1969.

297. **Tracie, C.J.** "Ethnicity and the Prairie Environment: Patterns of Old Colony Mennonite and Doukhobor Settlement." In Richard Allen, ed. *Man and Nature on the Prairies* (Regina, 1976), pp. 46-65.
298. **Trémaudon, A.H. de.** *Histoire de la nation métisse dans l'ouest canadien.* Montreal: Editions Albert Lévesque, 1936.
299. **Turner, C. Frank.** "Sitting Bull Tests the Mettle of the Redcoats." In Hugh A. Dempsey, ed. *Men in Scarlet* (Calgary, 1974), pp. 66-76.
300. **Vallee, F.G., and Shulman, N.** "The Viability of French Groupings outside Quebec." In M. Wade, ed. *Regionalism in the Canadian Community, 1867-1967* (Toronto, 1969), pp. 83-99.
301. **Willms, A.M.** "The Brethren Known as Hutterians." *C.J.E.P.S.* 24 (1958), pp. 391-405.
302. **Wolcott, H.F.** "Acculturation among the Indian Children of Western Canada: A Case Study." Ph.D. Thesis (Stanford University, 1963).
303. **Woodcock, George, and Avakumovic, Ivan.** *The Doukhobors.* Toronto: Oxford University Press, 1968.
304. **Woycenko, Ol'ha.** *The Ukrainians in Canada.* Winnipeg: Trident Press, 1968.
305. **Wright, J.F.C.** "Ukrainian-Canadians." *Canadian Geographical Journal* 25 (1942), pp. 74-87.
306. **Young, Charles H.** *The Ukrainian Canadians: A Study of Assimilation.* Toronto: Thomas Nelson & Sons, 1931.
307. **Young, Charles H.; Reid, Helen R.Y.; and Carrothers, W.A.** *The Japanese Canadians.* Toronto: University of Toronto Press, 1938.
308. **Zentner, H.** "The Impending Identity Crisis among Native Peoples." In D.P. Gagan, ed. *Prairie Perspectives [1]* (Toronto, 1970), pp. 78-91.

d. *Government and Politics*

309. **Avakumovic, Ivan.** "The Communist Party of Canada and the Prairie Farmer: The Interwar Years." In David J. Bercuson, ed. *Western Perspectives I* (Toronto, 1974), pp. 78-87.
310. **Baker, W.M.** "A Case Study of Anti-Americanism in English-Speaking Canada: The Election Campaign of 1911." *C.H.R.* 51 (1970), pp. 426-448.
311. **Beck, J. Murray.** *Pendulum of Power: Canada's Federal Elections.* Scarborough: Prentice-Hall, 1968.

312. **Bellamy, D.J.; Pammett, J.H.; and Rowat, D.C.**, eds. *The Provincial Political Systems: Comparative Essays.* Toronto: Methuen, 1976.

313. **Britnell, G.E.** "Public Ownership of Telephones in the Prairie Provinces." M.A. Thesis (University of Toronto, 1934).

314. **Carrigan, O.** *Canadian Party Platforms, 1867-1968.* Toronto: Copp Clark, 1968.

315. **Clark, A.B.** *An Outline of Provincial and Municipal Taxation in British Columbia, Alberta, and Saskatchewan.* Winnipeg: University of Manitoba, 1920.

316. **Cleverdon, Catherine L.** *The Woman Suffrage Movement in Canada.* 1950. Reprint. Social History of Canada, vol. 18. Toronto: University of Toronto Press, 1974.

317. **Cook, Ramsay.** "Dafoe, Laurier and the Formation of Union Government." *C.H.R.* 42 (1961), pp. 185-208.

318. **Cross, Michael S.**, ed. *The Decline and Fall of a Good Idea: CCF-NDP Manifestos, 1932-1969.* Toronto: New Hogtown Press, 1974.

319. **Dafoe, John W.** *Clifford Sifton in Relation to His Times.* Toronto: Macmillan, 1931.

320. **Diefenbaker, John G.** *One Canada—Volume 1: The Crusading Years, 1895-1956.* Toronto: Macmillan, 1975.

321. ———. *One Canada—Volume 2: The Years of Achievement, 1956-1962.* Toronto: Macmillan, 1976.

322. ———. *One Canada—Volume 3: The Tumultuous Years, 1962-1967.* Toronto: Macmillan, 1977.

323. **Ecroyd, L.G.** "The CCF Is Twenty-One." *Western Business and Industry* 27 (May 1953), pp. 24-25, 100-103.

324. **Fowke, Donald, and Fowke, V.C.** "Political Economy and the Canadian Wheat Grower." In N. Ward and D. Spafford, eds. *Politics in Saskatchewan* (Don Mills, 1968), pp. 207-220.

325. **Fowke, Edith**, ed. *Towards Socialism: Selections from the Writings of J.S. Woodsworth.* Toronto: Ontario Woodsworth Memorial Foundation, 1948.

326. **Friesen, Gerald.** "'Yours in Revolt': The Socialist Party of Canada and the Western Canadian Labour Movement." *Labour/Le Travailleur* 1 (1976), pp. 139-157.

327. **Gibbins, Roger.** "Models of Nationalism: A Case Study of Political Ideologies in the Canadian West." *Canadian Journal of Political Science* 10 (1977), pp. 341-373.

328. **Godfrey, W.G.** "The 1933 Regina Convention of the Co-operative Commonwealth Federation." M.A. Thesis (University of Waterloo, 1965).

329. **Graham, Roger.** *Arthur Meighen: A Biography.* 3 vols. Toronto: Clarke, Irwin, 1960-65.

―――. *Arthur Meighen.* Canadian Historical Association Booklet 16. Ottawa: Canadian Historical Association, 1965.

331. **Griezic, F.J.K.** "The Honourable Thomas Alexander Crerar: The Political Career of a Western Liberal Progressive in the 1920s." In S.M. Trofimenkoff, ed. *The Twenties in Western Canada* (Ottawa, 1972), pp. 107-137.

332. **Groome, A.J.** "M.J. Coldwell and C.C.F. Foreign Policy, 1932-1950." M.A. Thesis (University of Saskatchewan, Regina, 1967).

333. **Hall, D.J.** "The Political Career of Clifford Sifton, 1896-1905." Ph.D. Thesis (University of Toronto, 1974).

334. **Hart, J.E.** "William Irvine and Radical Politics in Canada." Ph.D. Thesis (University of Guelph, 1972).

335. **Heaps, Leo.** *The Rebel in the House: The Life and Times of A.A. Heaps, M.P.* London: Niccolo Publishing Company, 1970.

336. **Hedlin, Ralph.** "Edmund A. Partridge." H.S.S.M. *Transactions* Series III, 15 (1960), pp. 59-68.

337. **Hromnysky, Roman.** "The Western Canadian Regional Governments and the Federal System, 1900-1930." M.A. Thesis (University of British Columbia, 1965).

338. **Irvine, William.** *The Farmer in Politics.* Toronto: McClelland and Stewart, 1920.

339. ――――. *Co-operative Government.* Ottawa: Mutual Press, 1929.

340. **Irving, John A.** "A Prairie Ideals and Realities." *Queen's Quarterly* 63 (1956), pp. 188-200.

341. **Johnson, J.K.,** ed. *The Canadian Directory of Parliament, 1867-1967.* Ottawa: Public Archives of Canada, 1968.

342. **Knowles, Stanley.** *The New Party.* Toronto: McClelland and Stewart, 1961.

343. **McClung, Nellie.** *In Times Like These,* 1915. Reprint. Social History of Canada, vol. 5. Toronto: University of Toronto Press, 1972.

344. **McCormack, A.R.** *Reformers, Rebels, and Revolutionaries: The Western Canadian Radical Movement, 1899-1919.* Toronto: University of Toronto Press, 1977.

345. **McCutcheon, Brian R.** "The Birth of Agrarianism in the Prairie West." *Prairie Forum* 1 (1976), pp. 79-94.

346. **McHenry, D.E.** *The Third Force in Canada: The Cooperative Commonwealth Federation, 1932-1948.* Berkeley and Los Angeles: University of California Press, 1950.

347. **MacInnis, Grace.** *J.S. Woodsworth: A Man to Remember.* Toronto: Macmillan, 1953.

348. **Macleod, R.C.** "The Mounted Police and Politics." In Hugh A. Dempsey, ed. *Men in Scarlet* (Calgary, 1974), pp. 95-114.

349. **McNaught, K.** "J.S. Woodsworth and a Political Party for Labour, 1896-1921." *C.H.R.* 30 (1949), pp. 123-143.

350. ———"C.C.F.: Town and Country." *Queen's Quarterly* 61 (1954), pp. 213-219.

351. ———. *A Prophet in Politics: A Biography of J.S. Woodsworth.* Toronto: University of Toronto Press, 1959.

352. **Mallory, J.R.** *Social Credit and the Federal Power in Canada.* Toronto: University of Toronto Press, 1954.

353. **Martin, Chester.** *"The Natural Resources Question": The Historical Basis of Provincial Claims.* Winnipeg: King's Printer, 1920.

354. **Maxwell, J.A.** "The Dispute over the Federal Domain in Canada." *Journal of Political Economy* 41 (1933), pp. 777-805.

355. ———. *Federal Subsidies to Provincial Governments in Canada.* Cambridge, Mass.: Harvard University Press, 1937.

356. **Mitchener, E.A.** "William Pearce and Federal Government Activity in the West, 1874-1904." *Canadian Journal of Public Administration* 10 (1967), pp. 235-253.

357. ———."William Pearce and Federal Government Activity in Western Canada, 1882-1904." Ph.D. Thesis (University of Alberta, 1971).

358. **Morton, W.L.** "Direct Legislation and the Origins of the Progressive Movement." *C.H.R.* 25 (1944), pp. 279-288.

359. ———. "The Western Progressive Movement, 1919-1921." Canadian Historical Association. *Annual Report 1946,* pp. 41-55.

360. ———. "The Social Philosophy of Henry Wise Wood, the Canadian Agrarian Leader." *Agricultural History* 22 (1948), pp. 114-123.

361. ———. *The Progressive Party in Canada.* 1950. Reprint. Toronto: University of Toronto Press, 1967.

General 25

362. ———. "The Bias of Prairie Politics." Royal Society of Canada. *Proceedings and Transactions* 3d. ser. 49 (1955), sec. 2, pp. 57-66.
363. **Neatby, H. Blair.** *The Politics of Chaos: Canada in the Thirties.* Toronto: Macmillan, 1972.
364. **Newman, Peter C.** *Renegade in Power: The Diefenbaker Years.* 1963. Reprint. Toronto: McClelland and Stewart, 1973.
365. **Northrup, Minnie.** "Borden's Western Tour, A Personal Glimpse." *A.H.R.* 14 (Spring 1966), pp. 22-26.
366. **Partridge, E.A.** *A Farmers' Trade Union.* Winnipeg: Grain Growers' Grain Co., 1907.
367. **Patton, Harold S.** *Grain Growers'* Coöperation in Western Canada. Cambridge, Mass.: Harvard University Press, 1928.
368. **Robin, Martin, ed.** *Canadian Provincial Politics: The Party Systems of the Ten Provinces.* Scarborough: Prentice-Hall, 1972.
369. **Rodney, W.** *Soldiers of the International: A History of the Communist Party of Canada, 1919-1929.* Toronto: University of Toronto Press, 1968.
370. **Saywell, John T.** "Liberal Politics, Federal Policies, and the Lieutenant-Governor: Saskatchewan and Alberta, 1905." *Sask. Hist.* 8 (Autumn 1955), pp. 81-88.
371. ———. *The Office of the Lieutenant-Governor.* Toronto: University of Toronto Press, 1957.
372. **Sharp, P.F.** *The Agrarian Revolt in Western Canada: A Survey Showing American Parallels.* Minneapolis: University of Minnesota Press, 1948.
373. **Simeon, Richard.** *Federal-Provincial Diplomacy: The Making of Present Policy in Canada.* Toronto: University of Toronto Press, 1972.
374. **Sinclair, Peter R.** "Class Structure and Populist Protest: The Case of Western Canada." *Canadian Journal of Sociology* 1 (1975), pp. 1-17.
375. **Smith, David E.** "Interpreting Prairie Politics." *Journal of Canadian Studies* 7, no. 4 (1972), pp. 18-32.
376. ———. "Interpreting Prairie Politics." In Richard Allen, ed. *A Region of the Mind* (Regina, 1973), pp. 103-124.
377. ———. "Western Politics and National Unity." In David J. Bercuson, ed. *Canada and the Burden of Unity* (Toronto, 1977), pp. 143-168.

378. **Smith, Denis.** "Politics and the Party System in the Three Prairie Provinces, 1917-1958." B.Litt. Thesis (Oxford University, 1959).

379. ———. "Liberals and Conservatives on the Prairies, 1917-1968." In D.P. Gagan, ed. *Prairie Perspectives [1]* (Toronto, 1970), pp. 30-45.

379A. **Strong-Boag, Veronica.** "Canadian Feminism in the 1920s: The Case of Nellie L. McClung." *Journal of Canadian Studies* 12, no. 4 (1977), pp. 58-68.

380. **Thomas, Lewis H.** "Milton Campbell, Independent Progressive." In

381. **Thompson, John H.** "'The Beginnings of Our Regeneration': The Great War and Western Canadian Reform Movements." Canadian Historical Association. *Historical Papers 1972,* pp. 227-246.

382. **Tiveton, D.J.** "The Border Farmer and the Canadian Reciprocity Issue, 1911-1912," *Agricultural History* 37 (1963), pp. 235-241.

383. **Underhill, F.H.** *Canadian Political Parties.* Canadian Historical Association Booklet 8. Ottawa: Canadian Historical Association, 1956.

384. **Waddell, W.S.** "The Honourable Frank Oliver." M.A. Thesis (University of Alberta, 1950).

385. **Waines, W.J.** "Problems of Public Finance in the Prairie Provinces." *C.J.E.P.S.* 3 (1937), pp. 355-369.

386. **Ward, Norman.** "The Politics of Patronage: James Gardiner and Federal Appointments in the West, 1935-1957." *C.H.R.* 58 (1977), pp. 294-310.

387. **Warner, D.F.** "The Farmers' Alliance and the Farmers' Union: An American-Canadian Parallelism." *Agricultural History* 23 (1949), pp. 9-19.

388. **Westmacott, M.W.** "Western Canada and the National Transportation Act: A Case Study in Cooperative Federalism." Ph.D Thesis (University of Alberta, 1972).

389. **Wilbur, Richard.** *The Bennett Administration, 1930-1935.* Canadian Historical Association Booklet 24. Ottawa: Canadian Historical Association, 1969.

390. **Wood, Louis Aubrey.** *A History of Farmers' Movements in Canada: The Origins and Development of Agrarian Protest, 1872-1924.* 1924. Reprint. Social History of Canada, vol. 25. Toronto: University of Toronto Press, 1975.

391. **Woodward, J.S.** "Wheat and Politics on the Prairies." *Queen's Quarterly* 37 (1931), pp. 733-744.

392 **Young, Walter D.** *The Anatomy of a Party: The National C.C.F., 1932-1961.* Toronto: University of Toronto Press, 1969.

393. ———. *Democracy and Discontent: Progressivism, Socialism and Social Credit in the Canadian West.* Toronto: Ryerson, 1969.

394. **Zakuta, Leo.** *A Protest Movement Becalmed: A Study of Change in the C.C.F.* Toronto: University of Toronto Press, 1964.

395. **Ziegler, Olive.** *Woodsworth, Social Pioneer.* Toronto: Ontario Publishing, 1934.

e. Railways

396. **Berton, Pierre.** *The National Dream: The Great Railway, 1871-1881.* Toronto: McClelland and Stewart, 1970.

397. ———. *The Last Spike: The Great Railway, 1881-1885.* Toronto: McClelland and Stewart, 1971.

398. **Biggar, E.B.** *The Canadian Railway Problem.* Toronto: Macmillan, 1917.

399. **Bladen, M.L.** "Construction of Railways in Canada to the Year 1885." *Contributions to Canadian Economics* 5 (1932), pp. 43-60.

400. ———. "Construction of Railways in Canada from 1885 to 1931." *Contributions to Canadian Economics* 7 (1934), pp. 82-107.

401. **Bocking, D.H., ed.** "Documents of Western History: Railway Branch Lines." *Sask. Hist.* 20 (Spring 1967), pp. 64-70.

402. **Bone, P.T.** *When the Steel Went Through: Reminiscences of a Railroad Pioneer.* Toronto: Macmillan, 1947.

403. **Burpee, Lawrence J.** *Sandford Fleming: Empire Builder.* Toronto: Oxford University Press, 1915.

404. **Canada. Department of Transport.** *The Canadian National and Canadian Railway Systems: Origins and Growth with Statutory Authorities.* Ottawa: King's Printer, 1948.

405. **Charles, J.L.** "Railways March Northward." *Canadian Geographical Journal* 62 (1961), pp. 2-21.

406. **Chodos, Robert.** *The C.P.R.: A Century of Corporate Welfare.* Toronto: James Lewis and Samuel, 1973.

407. **Christenson, R.A.** "The Calgary and Edmonton Railway and the *Edmonton Bulletin.*" M.A. Thesis (University of Alberta, 1967.)

28 Western Canada Since 1870

408. **Coutts, R.M.** "The Railway Policy of Sir Wilfrid Laurier: The Grand Trunk Pacific—National Transcontinental." M.A. Thesis (University of Toronto, 1968).
409. **Currie, A.W.** "Freight Rates on Grain in Western Canada." *C.H.R.* 21 (1940), pp. 40-55.
410. ———. "Freight Rates and Regionalism." *C.J.E.P.S.* 14 (1948), pp. 427-440.
411. ———. *The Grand Trunk Railway of Canada.* Toronto: University of Toronto Press, 1957.
412. ———. *Economics of Canadian Transportation.* Toronto: University of Toronto Press, 1959.
413. **Davidson, J.W.** "The Canadian Northern Railway." *Queen's Quarterly* 13 (1906), pp. 97-108.
414. **Dorin, Patrick C.** *Canadian National Railway.* Saanichton, B.C.: Hancock House, 1975.
415. **Eagle, John A.** "Sir Robert Borden and the Railway Problem in Canadian Politics, 1911-1920." Ph.D. Thesis (University of Toronto, 1972).
416. ———."Sir Robert Borden, Union Government and Railway Nationalization." *Journal of Canadian Studies* 10, no. 4 (1975), pp. 59-66.
417. **Earl, L.** "The Hudson Bay Railway." H.S.S.M. *Transactions* Series III, 14 (1958-59), pp. 24-32.
418. **Fleming, H.A.** *Canada's Arctic Outlet: A History of the Hudson's Bay Railway.* Berkeley and Los Angeles: University of California Press, 1957.
419. **Fournier, Leslie T.** *Railway Nationalization in Canada: The Problem of the Canadian National Railways.* Toronto: Macmillan, 1935.
420. **Gibbon, J.M.** *Steel of Empire: The Romantic History of the Canadian Pacific, the North-West Passage of Today.* Indianapolis: Bobbs-Merrill, 1935.
421. **Glazebrook, G.P. de T.** *History of Transportation in Canada.* 2 vols. 1938. Reprint. Toronto: McClelland and Stewart, 1964.
422. **Greenberg, Dolores.** "A Study of Capital Alliances: The St. Paul & Pacific." *C.H.R.* 57 (1976), pp. 25-39.
423. **Harris, T.H.** *The Economic Aspects of the Crowsnest Pass Rates Agreement.* McGill University Economic Studies No. 13. National Problems of Canada. Toronto: Macmillan, 1930.

424. **Hedges, J.B.** *The Federal Railway Land Subsidy Policy of Canada.* Cambridge, Mass.: Harvard University Press, 1934.
425. **Henderson, G.F.** "Alexander Mackenzie and the Canadian Pacific Railway, 1871-1878." M.A. Thesis (Queen's University, 1964).
426. **Hewetson, H.W.** "The Railway Rate Problems of Western Canada." M.A. Thesis (University of British Columbia, 1925).
427. **Hodge, Gerald.** "Branch Line Abandonment: Death Knell for Prairie Towns?" *Canadian Journal of Agricultural Economics* 16, no. 1 (1968), pp. 54-70.
428. **Innis, Harold A.** "Transportation as a Factor in Canadian Economic History." Canadian Political Science Association. *Proceedings* 3 1931), pp. 166-184.
429. ———. *A History of the Canadian Pacific Railway.* 1923. Reprint. Toronto: University of Toronto Press, 1970.
430. **Irwin, L.B.** *Pacific Railways and Nationalism in the Canadian-American North-West, 1845-1873.* Philadelphia: L.B. Irwin, 1939.
431. **Jackman, W.T.** *Economics of Transportation.* Toronto: University of Toronto Press, 1926.
432. **Lamb, W. Kaye.** *History of the Canadian Pacific Railway.* New York: Macmillan, 1975.
433. **Lower, J.A.** "The Grand Trunk and British Columbia." M.A. Thesis (University of British Columbia, 1939).
434. **MacBeth, R.G.** *The Romance of the Canadian Pacific Railway.* Toronto: Ryerson, 1924.
435. **McDougall, J.L.** *Canadian Pacific: A Brief History.* Montreal: McGill-Queen's University Press, 1968.
436. **MacEwan, Grant.** *The Battle for the Bay: The Story of the Hudson Bay Railroad.* Saskatoon: Western Producer, 1975.
437. **MacGibbon, D.A.** *Railway Rates and the Canadian Railway Commission.* New York: Houghton Mifflin, 1917.
438. **Maclean, Hugh.** *Man of Steel: The Story of Sir Sandford Fleming.* Toronto: Ryerson, 1969.
439. **Martin, Chester.** "Our 'Kingdom for a Horse': The Railway Land Grant System in Western Canada." Canadian Historical Association. *Annual Report 1934,* pp. 13-19.
440. **Mika, Nick.** *Railways of Canada: A Pictorial History.* Toronto: McGraw-Hill Ryerson, 1972.
441. **Moore, W.H.** *Railway Nationalization and the Farmer.* Toronto: McClelland, Goodchild, and Stewart, 1917.

Plate 3. Laying the C.P.R. Track near Castor, Alberta

442. **Morris, Keith.** *The Story of the Canadian Pacific Railway.* London: William Stevens, 1920.
443. **Pollard, J.R.A.** "Railways and Settlement (1881-1891)." *Sask. Hist.* 1 (Spring 1948), pp. 16-19.
444. **Regehr, T.D.** "The Canadian Northern Railway: The West's Own Product." *C.H.R.* 51 (1970), pp. 177-186.
445. ———. "Serving the Canadian West: Policies and Problems of the Canadian Northern Railway." *Western Historical Quarterly* 3 (1972), pp. 283-298.
446. ———. "William Mackenzie, Donald Mann, and the Larger Canada." In A.W. Rasporich, ed. *Western Canada: Past and Present* (Calgary, 1975), pp. 69-83.
447. ———. "Contracting for the Canadian Pacific Railway." In Lewis H. Thomas, ed. *Essays on Western History* (Edmonton, 1976), pp. 113-128.
448. ———. *The Canadian Northern Railway: Pioneer Road of the Northern Prairies, 1895-1918.* Toronto: Macmillan, 1976.
449. ———. "Western Canada and the Burden of National Transportation Policies." In David J. Bercuson, ed. *Canada and the Burden of Unity* (Toronto, 1977), pp. 115-142.
450. **Reid, L.V.** "Railway Development in Canada, with Particular Reference to Regional Influences." M.A. Thesis (University of British Columbia, 1949).

451. **Roe, F.G.** "An Unsolved Problem of Canadian History [the Route of the C.P.R.]." Canadian Historical Association. *Annual Report 1936,* pp. 65-77.
452. **Rowntree, G.M.** *The Railway Worker: A Study of the Employment and Unemployment Problems of the Canadian Railways.* Toronto: Oxford University Press, 1936.
453. **Savage, R.L.** "American Concern over Canadian Railway Competition in the North-West, 1885-1900." Canadian Historical Association. *Annual Report 1942,* pp. 82-93.
454. **Secretan, J.H.E.** *Canada's Great Highway from the First Stake to the Last Spike.* Toronto: Longmans, Green, 1924.
455. **Sindlinger, T.L.** "Railway Freight Rate Discrimination in Relation to Western Canada." M.A. Thesis (University of Calgary, 1969).
456. **Skelton, O.D.** *The Railway Builders.* Toronto: Glasgow and Brooke, 1916.
457. **Stephenson, G.P.** "The West, the Railways and Change." *Manitoba Centre for Transportation Studies Proceedings* (1968-69), pp. 43-60.
458. **Stevens, G.R.** *Canadian National Railways.* 2 vols. Toronto: Clarke, Irwin, 1960-1962.
459. ———. *History of the Canadian National Railways.* Toronto: Collier-Macmillan, 1973.
460. **Talbot, F.A.** *The Making of a Great Canadian Railway: The Story of the Search for and Discovery of the Route, and the Construction of the Nearly Completed Grand Trunk Pacific Railway.* London: Seeley, Service & Co., 1912.
416. **Thompson, L.R.** *The Canadian Railway Problem: Some Economic Aspects of Canadian Transportation and a Suggested Solution for the Railway Problem.* Toronto: Macmillan, 1938.
462. **Thompson, N., and Edgar, J.H.** *Canadian Railway Development from the Earliest Times.* Toronto: Macmillan, 1933.
463. **Vaughan, W.** *The Life and Work of Sir William Van Horne.* New York: Century Company, 1920.
464. **Wade, G.M.** "The Hudson Bay Railway." M.A. Thesis (University of Manitoba, 1927).
465. **Westmacott, M.W.** "Western Canada and the National Transportation Act: A Case Study in Cooperative Federalism." Ph.D. Thesis (University of Alberta, 1972).

466. **Wilgus, W.J.** *The Railway Interrelations of the United States and Canada.* 1937. Reprint. New York: Russell & Russell, 1970.
467. **Zahradnitzky, G.L.** "The Development and Application of Prairie Railway Policy." M.A. Thesis (University of Regina, 1974).

f. Agriculture and Rural Development

468. **Anderson, C.H.** *History of Soil Erosion by Wind in the Palliser Triangle of Western Canada.* Ottawa: Agriculture Canada, 1975.
469. **Anderson, J.A.** "Canadian Agriculture and Its Supporting Research." *Canadian Geographical Journal* 83 (1971), pp. 2-17.
470. **Anderson, W.J.** "The Basis of Economic Policy for Canadian Agriculture." *Canadian Journal of Agricultural Economics* 11, no. 2 (1963), pp. 19-28.
471. **Archibald, E.S.** "Prairie Farm Rehabilitation." *Canadian Geographical Journal* 21 (1940), pp. 158-172.
472. **Armstrong, P.C., and Swanson, W.W.** *Wheat.* Toronto: Macmillan, 1930.
473. **Auld, F.H.** *Canadian Agriculture and World War II.* Ottawa: Canada Department of Agriculture, 1953.
474. **Bandrowski, S.** "Some Demographic, Social and Economic Aspects of Prairie Farmers." M.A. Thesis (University of Ottawa, 1961).
475. **Barton, G.S.H.** "The Historical Background of Canadian Agriculture." *Canada Year Book.* Ottawa: King's Printer, 1939.
476. **Bennett, J.W.** *Northern Plainsmen: Adaptive Strategy and Agrarian Life.* Chicago: Aldine Publishing Co., 1969.
477. **Booth, J.F.** *Canadian Agriculture and Agricultural Policies since the First World War.* Ottawa: King's Printer, 1944.
478. **Boulding, K.E.** "Economic Analysis and Agricultural Policy." *C.J.E.P.S.* 13 (1947), pp. 436-446.
479. **Boyd, C.F.** *A Consolidation of Field Reports on the Combine Reaper-Thresher in Saskatchewan.* Regina: Department of Agriculture, 1926.
480. **Boyd, Hugh.** *New Breaking: An Outline of Co-operation among the Western Farmers of Canada.* Toronto: Dent, 1938.
481. **Bracken, John.** *Crop Production in Western Canada.* Winnipeg: Grain Growers Guide, Ltd., 1920.
482. ———. *Dry-Farming in Western Canada.* Winnipeg: Grain Growers Guide, Ltd., 1921.

483. **Breen, D.H.** "The Canadian West and the Ranching Frontier, 1875-1922." Ph.D. Thesis (University of Alberta, 1972).
484. **Britnell, G.E.** "The Rehabilitation of the Prairie Wheat Economy." *C.J.E.P.S.* 3 (1937), pp. 508-529.
485. ———. "The Rehabilitation of Prairie Farms." *Canadian Banker* 47 (October 1939), pp. 18-31.
486. ———. *The Wheat Economy.* Toronto: University of Toronto Press, 1939.
487. ———. "Dominion Legislation Affecting Western Agriculture, 1939." *C.J.E.P.S.* 6 (1940), pp. 275-282.
488. ———. "The War and Canadian Wheat." *C.J.E.P.S.* 7 (1941), pp. 397-413.
489. ———. "The Implications of United States Policy for the Canadian Wheat Economy." *C.J.E.P.S.* 22 (1956), pp. 1-16.
490. **Britnell, G.E., and Fowke, V.C.** *Canadian Agriculture in War and Peace, 1935-1950.* Stanford: Stanford University Press, 1962.
491. **Buller, A.H.R.** *Essays on Wheat.* New York: Macmillan, 1919.
492. **Burton, F.W.** "Wheat in Canadian History." *C.J.E.P.S.* 3 (1937), pp. 210-217.
493. **Burton, G.L.** "The Farmer and the Market." *C.J.E.P.S.* 15 (1949), pp. 495-504.
494. **Butlin, J.A.** "The Effect of Canadian Business Cycles on the Adoption of Technological Innovations in Canadian Agriculture, 1926-27." *Canadian Journal of Agricultural Economics* 19, no. 2 (1971), pp. 61-71.
495. **Caplan, Joseph.** "Towards a Market-Oriented Canadian Grain Economy." *Canadian Journal of Agricultural Economics* 18, no. 1 (1970), pp. 20-35.
496. **Cavert, W.L.** "The Technological Revolution in Agriculture, 1910-1955." *Agricultural History* 30 (1956), pp. 18-27.
497. **Chakravarti, A.K.** "Precipitation Deficiency Patterns in the Canadian Prairies, 1921 to 1970." *Prairie Forum* 1 (1976), pp. 95-110.
498. **Church, G.C.** "Dominion Government Aid to the Dairy Industry in Western Canada, 1890-1906." *Sask. Hist.* 16 (Spring 1963), pp. 41-58.
499. ———. "Farm Organizations on the Prairies." In *Development of Agriculture on the Prairies: Proceedings of Seminar* (Regina, 1975), pp. 43-49.

500. Coleman, G.P. "Innovation and Diffusion in Agriculture." *Agricultural History* 42 (1968), pp. 173-187.
501. Correll, Ernst. "Canadian Agricultural Records on Mennonite Settlements, 1875-77." *Mennonite Quarterly Review* 21 (1947), pp. 34-46.
502. Currie, A.W. "Freight Rates on Grain in Western Canada." *C.H.R.* 21 (1940), pp. 40-55.
503. Dale, E.H. "The General Problem of Western Canada's Small Rural Towns." In J.E. Spenser, ed. *Saskatchewan Rural Themes* (Regina, 1977), pp. 87-100.
504. Danielson, R.S. "Three Studies in Canadian Agriculture: I. Output and Input Data for Canadian Agriculture, 1926-1970. II. Productivity Growth in Canadian Agriculture, 1946-1970. III. A Canadian Agricultural Transformation Function, 1946-1970." M.A. Thesis (University of British Columbia, 1975).
505. Davisson, Walter P. *Pooling Wheat in Canada*. Ottawa: Graphic Publishers, 1927.
506. Denison, Merrill. *Harvest Triumphant: The Story of Massey-Harris*. Toronto: McClelland and Stewart, 1948.
507. Drummond, W.G. "Transportation and Canadian Agriculture." In H.A. Innis, ed. *Essays in Transportation in Honour of W.T. Jackman* (Toronto, 1941), pp. 71-84.
508. Drummond, W.M. "The Role of Agricultural Marketing Boards." In J.J. Deutsch; B.S. Keirstead; K. Levitt; and R.M. Will, eds. *The Canadian Economy: Selected Readings* (Toronto, 1965), pp. 246-256.
509. Drummond, W.M., and Mackenzie, W. *Progress and Prospects of Canadian Agriculture*. Ottawa: Queen's Printer, 1957.
510. Dunlop, J.S. "Changes in the Canadian Wheat Belt, 1931-1969." *Geography* 55 (1970), pp. 156-168.
511. Easterbrook. W.T. "Agricultural Debt Adjustment," *C.J.E.P.S.* 2 (1936), pp. 390-403.
512. ———. *Farm Credit in Canada*. Toronto: University of Toronto Press, 1938.
513. Edwards, E.E. "Agricultural History as a Field of Research." Canadian Historical Association. *Annual Report 1941*, pp. 15-24.
514. *Farms and Farmers in Western Canada*. Ottawa: Department of the Interior, 1904.

515. **Fowke, V.C.** "Dominion Aids to Wheat Marketing, 1929-1939." *C.J.E.P.S.* 6 (1940), pp. 390-402.
516. ———."Introduction to Canadian Agricultural History." *C.J.E.P.S.* 8 (1942), pp. 56-68.
517. ———. "An Introduction to Canadian Agricultural History." *Agricultural History* 16 (1942), pp. 79-90.
518. ———. *Canadian Agricultural Policy: The Historical Pattern.* Toronto: University of Toronto Press, 1946.
519. ———. *An Introduction to Canadian Agricultural History.* Toronto: University of Toronto Press, 1947.
520. ———. "Royal Commissions and Canadian Agricultural Policy." *C.J.E.P.S.* 14 (1948), pp. 163-175.
521. ———. *The National Policy and the Wheat Economy.* Toronto: University of Toronto Press, 1957.
522. **Furniss, I.F.** "Productivity Trends in Canadian Agriculture, 1935-1965." In R.M. Irving, ed. *Readings in Canadian Geography* (Toronto, 1968), pp. 205-215.
523. **Good, W.C.** *Farmer Citizen: My Fifty Years in the Canadian Farmers' Movement.* Toronto: Ryerson, 1958.
524. **Gray, James H.** *Men against the Desert.* Saskatoon: Western Producer, 1967.
525. **Grest, E.G.** "Comments on Depreciation and Repairs of Combine Harvesters and Tractors on the Canadian Prairies." *Scientific Agriculture* 13 (1932), pp. 26-35.
526. **Griffin, H.L.** "Public Policy in Relation to the Wheat Market." *C.J.E.P.S.* 1 (1934), pp. 482-500.
527. ———. "The Basis of the Wheat Problem." *Canadian Banker* 49 (1942), pp. 79-93.
528. **Grimes, W.E.** "The Effect of the Combined Harvester-Thresher in a Wheat Growing Region." *Scientific Agriculture* 9 (1929), pp. 773-782.
529. **Grindley, T.W.** "Wheat in the Canadian West." *Queen's Quarterly* 37 (1930), pp. 370-385.
530. **Gunn, R.R.** "Capitalization of the Agricultural Industry in Western Canada." M.A. Thesis (University of Manitoba, 1931).
531. **Hardy, E.A.** "The Combine-Harvester in Western Canada." *Scientific Agriculture* 12 (1933), pp. 121-129.
532. **Hargreaves, M.W.M.** "Dry Farming Alias Scientific Farming." *Agricultural History* 22 (1948), pp. 56-63.

533. **Hays, James.** "The Role of Federal Research in Prairie Agriculture." In *Development of Agriculture on the Canadian Prairies: Proceedings of Seminar* (Regina, 1975), pp. 50-63.

534. **Haythorne, G.V.** "Harvest Labor in Western Canada: An Episode in Economic Planning." *Quarterly Journal of Economics* 47 (1933), pp. 533-544.

535. **Herbert, W.B.** "Wheat Pool Prospects." *Co-operative Review* 5 (1931), pp. 222-229.

536. **Hiemstra, Mary.** *Gully Farm.* Toronto: McClelland and Stewart, 1955.

537. **Hind, E. Cora.** "A Story of Wheat." *Canadian Geographical Journal* 2 (1931), pp. 89-114.

538. **Hope, E.C.** "Weather and Crop History in Western Canada." *Canadian Society of Technical Agriculture Review* 16 (1938), pp. 347-358.

539. **Hopkins, E.S., and Baines, S.** *Crop Rotations and Soil Management for the Prairie Provinces.* Ottawa: Department of Agriculture, 1928.

540. **Hopkins, E.S., et al.** *Soil Drifting in the Prairie Provinces.* Ottawa: Department of Agriculture, 1935.

541. **Hurd, W. Burton.** *Contemporary Demographic Movements Underlying Canadian Agricultural Development.* Hamilton: Dominion Advisory Committee on Reconstruction, 1943.

542. **Ingles, Ernest B.** "Some Aspects of Dry-Land Agriculture in the Canadian Prairies to 1925." M.A. Thesis (University of Calgary, 1973).

543. **Innis, Harold A., ed.** *The Dairy Industry in Canada.* Toronto: Ryerson, 1937.

544. ———. *The Diary of Alexander James McPhail.* Toronto: University of Toronto Press, 1940.

545. **Jackson, Gilbert E.** "Wheat and the Trade Cycle." *C.H.R.* 3 (1922), pp. 256-271.

546. **Johnson, A.N.** "The Impact of Farm Machinery on the Farm Economy." *Agricultural History* 24 (1950), pp. 58-61.

547. **Johnson, Charles W.** "Relative Decline of Wheat in the Prairie Provinces of Canada." *Economic Geography* 24 (1948), pp. 209-216.

548. **Johnston, A.** "A History of the Rangeland of Western Canada." *Journal of Range Management* 23 (1970), pp. 3-8.

549. **Jones, H.I.** "Canadian Federation of Agriculture." M.A. Thesis (Queen's University, 1954).

General 37

Plate 4. Harvesting with a Steam Engine

550. **Kelly, L.V.** *The Rangemen.* Toronto: William Briggs, 1913.
551. **Kirk, D.W.** "A Study of the Prairie Farm Rehabilitation Administration." M.A. Thesis (University of Saskatchewan, Regina, 1939).
552. **Laing, Hamilton M.** "Our Canadian Deserts." *Canadian Geographical Journal* 8 (1934), pp. 135-142.
553. **Lattimer, J.E.** "The Economic Aspects of the Agricultural Problem." Canadian Political Science Association. *Proceedings* 3 (1931), pp. 135-144.
554. **Laughland, A.** "Some Aspects of Grain Handling in the Prairies." In *Development of Agriculture on the Prairies: Proceedings of Seminar* (Regina, 1975), pp. 124-135.
555. **Lee, Lawrence B.** "The Canadian-American Irrigation Frontier, 1884-1914." *Agricultural History* 40 (1966), pp. 271-284.
556. **Lonergan, S.G.** "Agricultural Organization and Canadian Grain Marketing Policy, 1935-1955." M.A. Thesis (University of Saskatchewan, 1957).
557. **Long, P.S.** *The Great Canadian Range.* Vancouver: Cypress Publishing, 1970.

558. **MacDonald, R.I.** "Monopoly Capitalism and Prairie Agriculture in Canada: A Study in Political Economy." M.A. Thesis (University of Alberta, 1974).

559. **MacEwan, Grant.** *The Sodbusters.* Toronto: Thomas Nelson & Sons, 1948.

560. ———. *Agriculture on Parade: The Story of the Fairs and Exhibitions of Western Canada.* Toronto: Thomas Nelson & Sons, 1950.

561. ———. *Between the Red and the Rockies.* Toronto: University of Toronto Press, 1952.

562. ———. *Blazing the Old Cattle Trail.* Saskatoon: Modern Press, 1962.

563. ———. *Hoofprints and Hitchingposts.* Saskatoon: Modern Press, 1964.

564. ———. *Harvest of Bread.* Saskatoon: Western Producer, 1969.

565. ———. *Power for Prairie Plows.* Saskatoon: Western Producer, 1971.

566. ———. *Memory Meadows: Horse Stories from Canada's Past.* Saskatoon: Western Producer, 1976.

567. **MacGibbon, D.A.** *The Canadian Grain Trade, 1931-1951.* Toronto: University of Toronto Press, 1952.

568. **MacKenzie, J.K.** *The Combine-Reaper-Thresher in Western Canada.* Ottawa: Department of Agriculture, 1927.

569. **Mackintosh, W.A.** *Agricultural Co-operation in Western Canada.* Toronto: Ryerson, 1924.

570. **MacLeod, W.B.** "The Farm Machinery Industry in Canada." M.A. Thesis (University of Western Ontario, 1937).

571. **McPherson, W.J.** "The Canadian Wheat Pool: An Analysis of Aims, Policies and Results." M.Sc. Thesis (University of Saskatchewan, 1937).

572. **Mahaffy, A.W.** "The Machine Process in Agriculture, with Special Reference to Western Canada," M.A. Thesis (University of Saskatchewan, 1923).

573. **Menzies, M.W.** "The Canadian Wheat Board: A Study in the Development of Canadian Agricultural Policy." M.A. Thesis (University of Saskatchewan, 1949).

574. **Mills, J.C.** "A Study of the Canadian Council of Agriculture, 1910-1930." M.A. Thesis (University of Manitoba, 1949).

575. **Mitchell, H.** "The Problem of Agricultural Credit in Canada." *Queen's Quarterly* 21 (1914), pp. 328-351.

576. **Morman, James B.** *Farm Credits in the United States and Canada.* New York: Macmillan, 1924.
577. **Morrison, J.W.** "Marquis Wheat—A Triumph of Scientific Endeavor." *Agricultural History* 34 (1960), pp. 182-187.
578. **Murchie, R.W.** "The Sociological Aspects of the Agricultural Problem." Canadian Political Science Association. *Proceedings* 3 (1931), pp. 145-152.
579. **Murchie, R.W.; Allen, William; and Booth, J.F.** *Agricultural Progress of the Prairie Frontier.* Toronto: Macmillan, 1936.
580. **Oddie, Emmie.** "Western Women in Agriculture." In *Development of Agriculture on the Prairies: Proceedings of Seminar* (Regina, 1975), pp. 30-34.
581. **Patton, Harold S.** *Grain Growers' Co-operation in Western Canada.* Cambridge, Mass.: Harvard University Press, 1928.
582. ———. "The Canadian Grain Pool." *Pacific Affairs* 3 (1930), pp. 165-180.
583. ———. "Observations on Canadian Wheat Policy since the World War." *C.J.E.P.S.* 3 (1937), pp. 218-233.
584. **Peterson, C.W.** *Wheat: The Riddle of Market.* Calgary: Farm and Ranch Review, 1930.
585. **Phillips, B.** "Farmers, Government, and Public Policy for Agriculture." In *Development of Agriculture on the Canadian Prairies: Proceedings of Seminar* (Regina, 1975), pp. 64-123.
586. **Piper, C.B.** *Principles of the Grain Trade of Western Canada.* Winnipeg: Empire Elevator Co., 1915.
587. **Pomeroy, E.M.** *William Saunders and His Five Sons: The Story of the Marquis Wheat Family.* Toronto: Ryerson, 1956.
588. **Regina, University of.** *Development of Agriculture on the Prairies: Proceedings of Seminar.* Regina, 1975.
590. **Roe, F.G.** "Early Opinions on the Fertile Belt of Western Canada." *C.H.R.* 27 (1946), pp. 131-149.
591. ———. "Early Agriculture in Western Canada in Relation to Climatic Stability." *Agricultural History* 26 (1952), pp. 104-123.
592. **Roehle, R.G.** "An Econometric Analysis of Farmland Values in Western Canada." M.Sc. Thesis (University of Manitoba, 1971).
593. **Rollins, Philip Ashton.** *The Cowboy: His Characteristics, His Equipment, and His Part in the Development of the West.* New York: Charles Scribner, 1922.

594. **Rutherford, J.C.** *The Cattle Trade of Western Canada.* Ottawa: King's Printer, 1909.

595. **Sharp, P.F.** "The American Farmer and the 'Last Best West!'" *Agricultural History* 21 (1947), pp. 65-75.

596. **Shutt, F.T.** *Western Prairie Soils: Their Nature and Composition.* Ottawa: Department of Agriculture, 1910.

597. **Spector, David.** *Field Agriculture in the Canadian Prairie West, 1870-1940, with Emphasis on the Period 1870-1920.* Ottawa: Manuscript Report No. 205, National Historic Parks and Sites, 1977.

598. **Spencer, L.O.** "Development and Planning of the Small Prairie Community in an Era of Rural Change." M.C.P. Thesis (University of Manitoba, 1974).

599. **Stahl, John.** "Prairie Agriculture: A Prognosis." In D.F. Gagan, ed. *Prairie Perspectives [1]* (Toronto, 1970), pp. 58-77.

600. **Stewart, A.** "A Prairie Farm Rehabilitation Programme." *C.J.E.P.S.* 5 (1939), pp. 310-324.

601. **Stewart, George.** *Alfalfa Growing in the United States and Canada.* New York: Macmillan, 1926.

602. **Stock, A.B.** *Ranching in the Canadian West.* London: Macmillan, 1912.

603. **Strange, H.G.L.** *A Short History of Prairie Agriculture.* Winnipeg: Searle Grain Company, 1954.

604. **Stuart, Duncan.** *The Canadian Desert.* Toronto: Ryerson, 1938.

605. ———. *Our Creeping Desert: Its Causes and Cures.* Calgary: Alberta Book and Novelty Co., 1942.

606. **Swanson, W.W., and Armstrong, P.C.** *Wheat.* Toronto: Macmillan, 1930.

607. **Symes, O.** "Agricultural Technology and Changing Life on the Prairies." In *Development of Agriculture on the Prairies: Proceedings of Seminar* (Regina, 1975), pp. 35-43.

608. **Taggart, J.G., and MacKenzie, J.K.** *Seven Years Experience with the Combined Reaper-Thresher, 1922-1928.* Ottawa: Department of Agriculture, 1929.

609. **Thair, P.J.** "Agricultural Development on the Prairies." In *Development of Agriculture on the Prairies: Proceedings of Seminar* (Regina, 1975), pp. 136-148.

610. **Thiessen, H.W.** "Rural Land Use Conflicts with Particular Reference to the Prairie Provinces." In W. Bell, ed. *Rural Land Use Conflicts: Some Solutions* (Winnipeg, 1977), pp. 7-18.
611. **Thomas, Lewis H.** "History of Agriculture on the Prairies." In *Development of Agriculture on the Prairies: Proceedings of Seminar* (Regina, 1975), pp. 1-15.
612. **Thompson, John H.** "Permanently Wasteful but Immediately Profitable: Prairie Agriculture and the Great War." Canadian Historical Association. *Historical Papers 1976,* pp. 193-206.
613. **Tiessen, Hugo.** "Old Style Prairie Ranching Gives Way to Intensive Crop and Cattle Farming." *Canadian Geographical Journal* 88 (April 1974), pp. 4-11.
614. **Tremblay, M.-A., and Anderson, W.J., eds.** *Rural Canada in Transition: A Multidimensional Study of the Impact of Technology and Urbanization on Traditional Society.* Ottawa: Agricultural Economics Research Council of Canada, 1966.
615. **Trotter, B.** *A Horseman and the West.* Toronto: Macmillan, 1925.
616. **Tyler, E.J.** "The Farmer as a Social Class in the Prairie Region." In M.-A. Tremblay and W.F. Anderson, eds. *Rural Canada in Transition* (Ottawa, 1966), pp. 228-340.
617. **Van Vliet, H.** "The Prairie Agricultural Region." In *Resources for Tomorrow: Conference Background papers.* Vol. 1 (Ottawa, 1961), pp. 527-537.
618. **Waterson, E.** *Pioneers in Agriculture: Massey, MacIntosh, Saunders.* Toronto: Clarke, Irwin, 1957.
619. **West, Edward.** *Homesteading: Two Prairie Seasons.* London: T.F. Unwin, 1918.
620. **Wheeler, S.** *Book on Profitable Grain Growing.* Winnipeg: Grain Growers Guide, Ltd., 1919.
621. **Widstoe, John A.** *Dry Farming: A System of Agriculture.* New York: Macmillan, 1911.
621A. **Willmott, Donald E.** *Organizations and Social Life of Farm Families in a Prairie Municipality.* Saskatoon: University of Saskatchewan, Centre for Community Studies, 1964.
622. **Yackulic, G.A.** "Modern Magic In Palliser's Triangle." *Western Business and Industry* 24 (November 1950), pp. 64-77.

g. Economic Development and Labour

623. **Abella, Irving M.** *Nationalism, Communism and Canadian Labour: The C.I.O., the Communist Party, and the Canadian Congress of Labour, 1935-1956.* Toronto: University of Toronto Press, 1973.

624. ———. *The Canadian Labour Movement, 1902-1960.* Canadian Historical Association Booklet 28. Ottawa: Canadian Historical Association, 1975.

625. **Allan, D.D.** "The Effect of the Panama Canal on Western Canada." M.A. Thesis (University of British Columbia, 1938).

626. **Ambrose, Peter.** "Patterns of Growth in the Canadian Labour Force, 1951-1969." *Canadian Geographer* 14 (1970), pp. 139-157.

627. **Anderson, K.** "The Organization of Capital for the Development of the Canadian West." M.A. Thesis (University of Regina, 1974).

627A. **Barr, B.M.** "Western Canadian Regional Experience as an Aid to Developing Commercial Relations with the U.S.S.R." In B.M. Barr, ed. *Western Canadian Research in Geography: The Lethbridge Papers* (Vancouver: B.C. Geographical Series, no. 21, 1975), pp. 43-50.

628. **Bercuson, David J.** "Western Labour Radicalism and the One Big Union: Myths and Realities." In S.M. Trofimenkoff, ed. *The Twenties in Western Canada* (Ottawa, 1972), pp. 32-49.

629. ———. "Western Labour Radicalism and the One Big Union: Myths and Realities." *Journal of Canadian Studies* 9 (May 1974), pp. 3-11.

630. ———. "Labour Radicalism and the Western Industrial Frontier, 1897-1919." *C.H.R.* 58 (1977), pp. 154-175.

631. **Bliss, Michael.** "The Ideology of Domination: An Eastern Big-Shot Businessman Looks at Western Canada." In H.C. Klassen, ed. *The Canadian West* (Calgary, 1977), pp. 181-196.

632. **Bradwin, E.W.** *The Bunkhouse Man: A Study of Work and Pay in the Camps of Canada, 1903-1914.* 1928. Reprint. Social History of Canada, vol. 4. Toronto: University of Toronto Press, 1972.

632A. **Cadden, P.G.** "Multi-plant Firms and Commodity Flows: The Case of the Western Canadian Flour-milling Industry." In B.M. Barr, ed. *Western Canadian Research in Geography: The Lethbridge Papers* (Vancouver: B.C. Geographical Series, no. 21, 1975), pp. 11-20.

633. **Canada. Department of the Interior.** *Natural Resources of the Prairie Provinces: A Brief Compilation Respecting the Development of Manitoba, Saskatchewan, and Alberta.* Ottawa: King's Printer, 1923.

634. **Caves, R.E., and Holton, R.H.** *The Canadian Economy: Prospect and Retrospect.* Cambridge, Mass.: Harvard University Press, 1959.
635. "Construction in Western Canada." *Western Business and Industry* 23 (June 1949), pp. 71-135. [A continuing feature.]
636. **DeMille, George.** *Oil in Canada West: The Early Years.* Calgary: Northwest Printing, 1969.
637. **Economic Council of Canada.** *Living Together: A Study of Regional Disparities.* Ottawa, 1977.
638. **Fellows, C.M.** "Factors Influencing the Marketing of Western Canadian Coking Coal." M.A. Thesis (University of Calgary, 1972).
639. **Forsey, Eugene A.** "A History of the Labour Movement." *Canada Year Book.* Ottawa: Queen's Printer, 1967.
640. ―――. *The Canadian Labour Movement: The First Ninety Years, 1812-1902.* Canadian Historical Association Booklet 27. Ottawa: Canadian Historical Association, 1974.
641. **Fowke, V.C.** "Economic Effects of the War on the Prairie Economy." *C.J.E.P.S.* 11 (1945), pp. 373-387.
642. ―――. "National Policy and Western Development in North America." *Journal of Economic History* 14 (1956), pp. 461-479.
643. **Friesen, Gerald.** "'Yours in Revolt': The Socialist Party of Canada and the Western Canadian Labour Movement." *Labour/Le Travailleur* 1 (1976), pp. 139-157.
644. "Fruit and Vegetables in Western Canada." *Western Business and Industry* 24 (September 1950), pp. 71-92. [A continuing feature.]
645. **Green, Alan G.** "Regional Inequality, Structural Change, and Economic Growth in Canada, 1890-1956." *Economic Development and Cultural Change* 17 (1969), pp. 567-583.
646. ―――. *Regional Aspects of Canada's Economic Growth.* Toronto: University of Toronto Press, 1971.
647. ―――. *Immigration and the Postwar Canadian Economy.* Toronto: Macmillan, 1976.
648. **Harris, T.H.** *The Economic Aspects of the Crowsnest Pass Rates Agreement.* Toronto: Macmillan, 1930.
649. **Innis, Harold A.** "Industrialism and Settlement in Western Canada." International Geographical Congress, Cambridge. *Report of Proceedings* (1930), pp. 369-376.
650. ―――. *Essays in Canadian Economic History.* 1956. Reprint. Toronto: University of Toronto Press, 1973.

Plate 5. Workers in the Clothing Industry, Winnipeg

651. **Jamieson, Stuart Marshall.** *Times of Trouble: Labour Unrest and Industrial Conflict in Canada, 1900-1966.* Ottawa: Information Canada, 1971.
652. **Kennedy, D.R.** *The Knights of Labor in Canada.* London: University of Western Ontario, 1956.
653. **Lang, A.H.** "Dawson and the Economic Development of Western Canada." *Canadian Public Administration* 14 (1971), pp. 236-255.
654. **Lipton, Charles.** *The Trade Union Movement of Canada, 1827-1959.* Montreal: Canadian Social Publications, 1967.
655. **Logan, H.A.** *Trade Unions in Canada.* Toronto: Macmillan, 1948.
656. **McCormack, A.R.** "The Industrial Workers of the World in Western Canada, 1905-1914." Canadian Historial Association. *Historical Papers 1975,* pp. 167-190.
657. ———. *Reformers, Rebels, and Revolutionaries: The Western Canadian Radical Movement, 1899-1919.* Toronto: University of Toronto Press, 1977.

658. **MacGibbon, D.A.** "Economic Factors Affecting the Settlement of the Prairie Provinces." *Pioneer Settlement.* American Geographical Society, Special Publication No. 14 (1932), pp. 31-36.

659. **Mackintosh, W.A., et al.** *Economic Problems of the Prairie Provinces.* Toronto: Macmillan, 1935.

660. **MacLeod, W.B.** "The Farm Machinery Industry in Canada." M.A. Thesis (University of Western Ontario, 1927).

661. **MacPherson, Ian.** *The Story of Co-operative Insurance Services Ltd.* Saskatoon: C.I.S. Ltd., 1974.

661A. ———. "The Origins of Co-operative Insurance on the Prairies." In Paul Uselding, ed. *Business and Economic History: Papers Presented at the Twenty-Second Annual Meeting of the Business History Conference* (Urbana, 1976), pp. 76-87.

661B. ———. *A History of Co-op Trust.* Saskatoon: Modern Press, 1978.

662. **McQueen, R.** "Economic Aspects of Federalism: A Prairie View." *C.J.E.P.S.* 1 (1935), pp. 352-367.

663. "Mining in Western Canada." *Western Business and Industry* 19 (November 1945), pp. 96-134. [A continuing feature.]

664. **Myers, Gustavus.** *A History of Canadian Wealth.* 1914. Reprint. Toronto: James Lewis and Samuel, 1972.

665. **Naylor, Tom.** *The History of Canadian Business, 1867-1914. I: The Banks and Finance Capital. II: Industrial Development.* Toronto: James Lorimer, 1975.

666. **Nordegg, Martin.** *The Possibilities of Canada Are Truly Great: Memoirs, 1906-1924.* Toronto: Macmillan, 1971. [Edited by T.D. Regehr.]

667. **Norrie, K.H.** "Some Comments on Prairie Economic Alienation." *Canadian Public Policy/Analyse de politiques* 2 (1976), pp. 211-224.

668. ———. "Agricultural Implement Tariffs, the National Policy, and Income Distribution in the Wheat Economy." *Canadian Journal of Economics* 7 (1974), pp. 449-462.

669. **Peck, D.** "Western Canada-Japan Trade." *Western Business and Industry* 37 (February 1963), pp. 24-43.

670. **Peet, J. Richard.** "Natural Gas Industries in Western Canada." *Canadian Geographer* 7 (1963), pp. 23-32.

671. **Pentland, H.C.** "Labour and the Development of Industrial Capitalism in Canada." Ph.D. Thesis (University of Toronto, 1969).

672. **Peterson, C.W.** *Wake Up, Canada! Reflections on Vital National Issues.* Toronto: Macmillan, 1919.
673. **Phillips, P.A.** "Structural Change and Population Distribution in the Prairie Region, 1911-1961." M.A. Thesis (University of Saskatchewan, 1963).
674. ———. "The National Policy and the Development of the Western Canadian Labour Movement." In A.W. Rasporich and H.C. Klassen, eds. *Prairie Perspectives 2* (Toronto, 1973), pp. 41-62.
675. ———. "National Policy, Continental Economics, and National Disintegration." In David J. Bercuson, ed. *Canada and the Burden of Unity* (Toronto, 1977), pp. 19-43.
676. **Porritt, E.** *The Revolt in Canada against the New Feudalism: Tariff History from the Revision of 1907 to the Uprising in the West in 1910.* London: Cassell, 1911.
677. **Reid, R.L.** "The First Bank in Western Canada." *C.H.R.* 7 (1926), pp. 294-301.
678. **Robin, Martin.** *Radical Politics and Canadian Labour, 1880-1930.* Kingston: Industrial Relations Centre, Queen's University, 1968.
679. **Sealey, G.D.** "History of the Hudson's Bay Company, 1870-1900." M.A. Thesis (University of Western Ontario, 1970).
680. **Shearer, Ronald A.** "Nationality, Size of Firm, and Exploration for Petroleum in Western Canada, 1946-1954." *C.J.E.P.S.* 30 (1964), pp. 211-227.
681. **Stewart, Keith J.** "Minerals and Canada's Prairie Provinces." *Canadian Geographical Journal* 84 (1972), pp. 104-115.
682. "The Fisheries of Western Canada." *Western Business and Industry* 23 (July 1949), pp. 53-83. [A continuing feature.]
683. "The Forest Industries of Western Canada." *Western Business and Industry* 24 (August 1950), pp. 55-100. [A continuing feature.]
684. "The Grain Trade in Western Canada." *Western Business and Industry* 22 (October 1948), pp. 69-101. [A continuing feature.]
685. "The Petroleum Industry in Western Canada." *Western Business and Industry* 24 (May 1950), pp. 73-174. [A continuing feature.]
686. **Thomas, J.J.** "The West's Big Building Boom." *Western Business and Industry* 27 (June 1953), pp. 37-95.
687. **Warrian, P.** "The Challenge of the One Big Union Movement in Canada, 1919-1921." M.A. Thesis (University of Waterloo, 1971).

688. **Westcott, F.J.** "An Approach to the Problem of Tariff Burdens on Western Canada." *C.J.E.P.S.* 4 (1938), pp. 209-218.
689. "Western Canada." *Industrial Canada* 28 (1927), pp. 1-140. [Special issue.]
690. **Wheatley, J.** "Economic Development in Western Canada." *Western Business and Industry* 29 (January 1955), pp. 31-70.
691. **Wright, J.F.C.** *Prairie Progress: Consumer Co-operation in Saskatchewan.* Saskatoon: Federated Co-operatives Ltd., 1956.

h. Education and Social and Cultural Development

692. **Allen, Richard.** "Salem Bland and the Social Gospel in Canada." M.A. Thesis (University of Saskatchewan, 1961).
693. ———. "The Crest and the Crisis of the Social Gospel in Canada, 1916-1927." Ph.D. Thesis (Duke University, 1967).
694. ———. *The Social Passion: Religion and Social Reform in Canada, 1914-1928.* Toronto: University of Toronto Press, 1971.
695. ———. "The Social Gospel as the Religion of the Agrarian Revolt." In Carl Berger and Ramsay Cook, eds. *The West and the Nation* (Toronto, 1976), pp. 174-186.
696. **Allen, Richard, ed.** *Religion and Society in the Prairie West.* Regina: Canadian Plains Research Center, 1974.
697. ———. *The Social Gospel in Canada.* Ottawa: National Museum of Man, History Division, 1975.
698. **Anderson, J.T.M.** *The Education of the New Canadian.* Toronto: Dent, 1919.
699. **Armstrong, W.H.G.** *Separate Schools: Introduction of the Dual System into Eastern Canada and Its Subsequent Extension to the West.* [Saskatoon?]: Grand Orange Lodge of Saskatchewan, 1918.
700. **Benham, M.L.** *Nellie McClung (1873-1951).* Toronto: Fitzhenry and Whiteside, 1975.
701. **Bland, Salem.** *The New Christianity, or the Religion of the New Age.* 1920. Reprint. Social History of Canada, vol. 12. Toronto: University of Toronto Press, 1973.
702. **Boon, T.C.B.** *The Anglican Church from the Bay to the Rockies: A History of the Ecclesiastical Province of Rupert's Land and Its Dioceses, 1820-1950.* Toronto: Ryerson, 1962.

703. **Boudreau, Joseph A.** "Western Canada's Enemy Aliens in World War One." *A.H.R.* 12 (Winter 1964), pp. 1-9.
704. ———. "The Enemy Alien Problem in Canada, 1914-1921." Ph.D. Thesis (University of California, Los Angeles, 1965).
705. **Brooks, W.H.** "Methodism in the Canadian West in the Nineteenth Century." Ph.D. Thesis (University of Manitoba, 1972).
706. **Card, B.Y.** *The Canadian Prairie Provinces from 1870-1950: A Sociological Introduction.* Toronto: Dent, 1960.
707. **Carpenter, David C.** "Petrified Mummies and Mummified Daddies: A Study of Matriarchs and Patriarchs in Canadian Prairie Fiction." In H. Palmer, ed. *The Settlement of the West* (Calgary, 1977), pp. 153-173.
708. **Carrington, Philip.** *The Anglican Church in Canada: A History.* Toronto: Collins, 1963.
709. **Chalmers, John W.** "Schools for Our Other Indians: Education of Western Canadian Métis Children." In H.C. Klassen, ed. *The Canadian West* (Calgary, 1977), pp. 93-109.
710. **Chapman, T.L.** "'The Drug Problem' in Western Canada, 1900-1920." M.A. Thesis (University of Calgary, 1976).
711. **Chown, S.D.** *The Story of Church Union in Canada.* Toronto: Ryerson, 1930.
712. **Clark, S.D., et al.** *Prophecy and Protest: Social Movements in Twentieth-Century Canada.* Toronto: Gage, 1975.
713. **Cook, Ramsay.** "Francis Marion Beynon and the Crisis of Christian Reformism." In Carl Berger and Ramsey Cook, eds. *The West and the Nation* (Toronto, 1976), pp. 187-208.
714. **Cook, Ramsay, and Mitchinson, Wendy,** *The Proper Sphere: Woman's Place in Canadian Society.* Toronto: Oxford University Press, 1976.
715. **Dahlie, Hallvard.** "Frederick Philip Grove and Social Change." In H.C. Klassen, ed. *The Canadian West* (Calgary, 1977), pp. 25-36.
716. **Dahlie, Jorgen.** "Learning on the Frontier: Scandinavian Immigrants and Education in Western Canada." *Canada and International Education* 1 (December 1972), pp. 56-66.
717. **Daly, George Thomas.** *Catholic Problems in Western Canada.* Toronto: Macmillan, 1921.
718. **Dawson, Carl A., and Younge, Eva B.** *Pioneering in the Prairie Provinces: The Social Side of the Settlement Process.* Toronto: Macmillan, 1940.

General 49

719. **Djwa, S.A.** "Biblical Archetype in Western Canadian Fiction." In A.W. Rasporich, ed. *Western Canada: Past and Present* (Calgary, 1975), pp. 193-203.

720. **Durkin, Douglas.** *The Magpie.* 1923. Reprint. Social History of Canada, vol. 23. Toronto: University of Toronto Press, 1974.

721. **Dyck, B.** "Attitudes and Actions of C.A.S.W. Members in the Prairies towards Political Involvement." M.S.W. Thesis (University of Calgary, 1972).

722. **Emery, George N.** "Methodism on the Canadian Prairies, 1896-1914: The Dynamics of an Institution in a New Environment." Ph.D. Thesis (University of British Columbia, 1970).

723. ———. "Ontario Denied: The Methodist Church on the Prairies, 1896-1914." In F.H. Armstrong; H.A. Stevenson; and J.D. Wilson, eds. *Aspects of Nineteenth-Century Ontario* (Toronto, 1974), pp. 312-326.

724. **Gale, D.T.** "Belief and the Landscape of Religion: The Case of the Doukhobors." M.A. Thesis (Simon Fraser University, 1973).

725. **Grant, H.C.** "The Co-operative Movement." *C.J.E.P.S.* 3 (1937), pp. 406-420.

726. **Gray, James H.** *The Winter Years: The Depression on the Prairies.* Toronto: Macmillan, 1966.

727. ———. *Red Lights on the Prairies.* Toronto: Macmillan, 1971.

728. ———. *Booze: The Impact of Whisky on the Prairies.* Toronto: Macmillan, 1972.

729. ———. *The Roar of the Twenties.* Toronto: Macmillan, 1975.

730. **Gresko, J.** "White 'Rites' and Indian 'Rites': Indian Education and Native Responses in the West, 1870-1910." In A.W. Rasporich, ed. *Western Canada: Past and Present* (Calgary, 1975), pp. 163-182.

731. **Gunn, Angus M.** *Inequalities within Canada.* Toronto: Oxford University Press, 1974.

732. **Harper, J.R.** *A People's Art: Primitive, Native, Provincial and Folk Painting in Canada.* Toronto: University of Toronto Press, 1974.

733. **Harrison, Richard.** *Unnamed Country: The Struggle for a Canadian Prairie Fiction.* Edmonton: University of Alberta Press, 1977.

734. **Horn, M.**, ed. *The Dirty Thirties: Canadians in the Great Depression.* Toronto, Vancouver, Montreal: Copp Clark, 1972.

735. **Huel, R.J.A.** "French-Speaking Bishops and the Cultural Mosaic in Western Canada." In R. Allen, ed. *Religion and Society in the Prairie West* (Regina, 1974), pp. 53-64.

736. **Hutchinson, Gerald.** "Early Wesleyan Missions." *A.H.R.* 6 (Autumn 1958), pp. 1-6.
737. **Jaenen, C.J.** "Ruthenian Schools in Western Canada, 1897-1919." *Paedagogica Historica* 10 (1970), pp. 517-541.
738. **Jameson, Sheilagh S.** "Women in the Southern Alberta Ranch Community: 1881-1914." In H.C. Klassen, ed. *The Canadian West* (Calgary, 1977), pp. 63-78.
739. **King, George B.** "Presbyterianism in Western Canada." Committee on Archives of the United Church of Canada. *Bulletin* 9 (1956), pp. 15-24.
740. **Lautt, M.L.** "Sociology and the Canadian Plains." In Richard Allen, ed. *A Region of the Mind* (Regina, 1973), pp. 125-152.
741. **Liversedge, Ronald,** ed. *Recollections on the On To Ottawa Trek.* Toronto: McClelland and Stewart, 1973.
742. **McClung, Nellie.** *In Times Like These.* 1915. Reprint. Social History of Canada, vol. 5. Toronto: University of Toronto Press, 1972.
743. ———. *Clearing in the West: My Own Story.* Toronto: Thomas Allen, 1935.
744. **McCourt, E.A.** *The Canadian West in Fiction.* Toronto: Ryerson, 1949.
745. **MacEwan, Grant.** *Entrusted to My Care.* Saskatoon: Modern Press, 1966.
746. **McLaurin, C.C.** *Pioneering in Western Canada: A Story of the Baptists.* Calgary: The Author, 1939.
747. **MacPherson, Ian.** "The Co-operative Union of Canada and the Prairies, 1919-1939." In S.M. Trofimenkoff, ed. *The Twenties in Western Canada* (Ottawa, 1972), pp. 50-74.
748. **Mandel, E.** "Romance and Realism in Western Canadian Fiction." In A.W. Rasporich and H.C. Klassen, eds. *Prairie Perspectives 2* (Toronto, 1973), pp. 197-211.
749. **Minifie, James M.** *Homesteader: A Prairie Boyhood Recalled.* Toronto: Macmillan, 1972.
750. **Mitchell, Ken.** "The Universality of W.O. Mitchell's *Who Has Seen the Wind.*" In R. Allen, ed. *Religion and Society in the Prairie West* (Regina, 1974), pp. 99-110.
751. **Moir, John S.** *Enduring Witness: A History of the Presbyterian Church in Canada.* Toronto: Presbyterian Publications, 1974.
752. **Morice, A.G.** *History of the Catholic Church in Western Canada.* 2 vols. Toronto: Musson, 1910.

753. ———. *The Catholic Church in Western Canada.* Winnipeg: Canadian Publishers, Ltd., 1931.

754. **Morrow, E.L.** *Church Union in Canada: Its History, Motives, Doctrine and Governance.* Toronto: Thomas Allen, 1923.

755. **Mozersky, K.A.** "Structural Differentiation of Community: An Analysis of Western Canadian Communities Undergoing Change." Ph.D. Thesis (Cornell University, 1970).

756. **Nicholson, B.J.** "Feminism in the Prairie Provinces to 1916." M.A. Thesis (University of Calgary, 1974).

757. **Oliver, E.H.** *The Liquor Traffic in the Prairie Provinces.* Toronto: Board of Home Missions and Social Service, Presbyterian Church in Canada, 1923.

758. **Oster, J.E.** "The Image of the Teacher in Canadian Prairie Fiction: 1921-1971." Ph.D. Thesis (University of Alberta, 1972).

759. **Page, Donald M.** "The Development of a Western Canadian Peace Movement." In S.M. Trofimenkoff, ed. *The Twenties in Western Canada* (Ottawa, 1972), pp. 75-106.

760. **Painchaud, Robert.** "Les Exigences linguistiques dans le recrutement d'un clergé pour l'ouest canadien: 1818-1920." La Société canadienne d'histoire de l'église catholique. *Sessions d'étude 1975,* pp. 43-64.

761. **Peel, Bruce.** "English Writers in the Early West." *A.H.R.* 16 (Spring 1968), pp. 1-4.

762. **Rasmussen, Linda; Rasmussen, Lorna; Savage, Candace; and Wheeler, Anne.** *A Harvest Yet to Reap: A History of Prairie Women.* Toronto: Women's Press, 1976.

763. **Rea, J.E.** "The Roots of Prairie Society." In D.G. Gagan, ed. *Prairie Perspectives [1]* (Toronto, 1970), pp. 46-57.

764. **Ricou, L.R.** "From King to Interloper: Man on the Prairie in Canadian Fiction, 1920-1929." In S.M. Trofimenkoff, ed. *The Twenties in Western Canada* (Ottawa, 1972), pp. 5-31.

765. ———. *Vertical Man/Horizontal World: Man and Landscape in Canadian Prairie Fiction.* Vancouver: University of British Columbia Press, 1973.

766. **Robinson, M.Z.** "Frontier College: Reminiscences of the Camps in the Early 1900s." *Sound Heritage* 3, no. 2 (1976), pp. 1-17.

767. **Royce, Marion V.** "The Contribution of the Methodist Church to Social Welfare in Canada." M.A. Thesis (University of Toronto, 1940).

768. **Shook, L.K.** *Catholic Post-Secondary Education in English-Speaking Canada.* Toronto: University of Toronto Press, 1971.

769. **Stephens, D.G.** *Writers of the Prairies.* Vancouver: University of British Columbia Press, 1973.

769A. **Strong-Boag, Veronica.** "Canadian Feminism in the 1920s: The Case of Nellie L. McClung." *Journal of Canadian Studies* 12, no. 4 (1977), pp. 58-68.

770. **Thompson, M.E.** *The Baptist Story in Western Canada.* Calgary: Baptist Union of Western Canada, 1974.

778. **Trosky, O.S.** *The Ukrainian Greek Orthodox Church in Canada.* Winnipeg: Bulman Brothers, 1968.

779. **Tyler, E.J.** "The Farmer as a Social Class in the Prairie Region." In M.A. Tremblay and W.J. Anderson, eds. *Rural Canada in Transition* (Ottawa, 1966), pp. 228-340.

780. **Weir, G.M.** "Evolution of the Separate School Law in the Prairie Provinces." E. Ph.D. Thesis (Queen's University, 1917).

781. ———. *The Separate School Question in Canada.* Toronto: Ryerson, 1934.

782. **Wilson, J.Donald; Stamp, R.M.; and Audet, L.P.** *Canadian Education: A History.* Toronto: Prentice-Hall, 1970.

783. **Zentner, H.** "The Study of Social Change in Western Canada: A Centra-Marxian Approach." In H.C. Klassen, ed. *The Canadian West* (Calgary, 1977), pp. 110-126.

784. **Ziegler, Olive.** *Woodsworth: Social Pioneer.* Toronto: Ontario Publishing, 1935.

i. Urban Development

785. **Appleton, John.** "After-War Financial Problems of Western Municipalities." *Journal of the Canadian Bankers' Association* 27 (1920), pp. 162-167.

786. **Barrow, G.T.** "A Factoral Ecology of Three Cities: Edmonton, Regina and Winnipeg, 1961." M.A. Thesis (University of Calgary, 1972).

787. **Careless, J.M.S.** "Aspects of Urban Life in the West, 1870-1914." In Gilbert A. Stelter and Alan F.J. Artibise, eds. *The Canadian City: Essays in Urban History* (Toronto, 1977), pp. 125-141.

788. **Clark, A.B.** *An Outline of Provincial and Municipal Taxation in British Columbia, Alberta, and Saskatchewan.* Winnipeg: University of Manitoba, 1920.

789. **Davies, W.K.D., and Barrow, G.T.** "A Comparative Factorial Ecology of Three Canadian Prairie Cities." *Canadian Geographer* 17 (1973), pp. 327-353.

790. **Gerecke, K., et al.** "Influence on Land Policy Development in the Prairie Provinces: State of the Art," *Urban Forum* 2, no. 2 (1976), pp. 17-29.

791. **Gyuse, T.T.I.** "Service Centre Change in Metropolitan Hinterlands: A Case Study of Calgary and Saskatoon, 1951-1971." M.A. Thesis (University of Calgary, 1974).

792. **Higgs, R.L.** "Location Theory and the Growth of Cities in the Western Prairie Region, 1870-1900." Ph.D. Thesis (Johns Hopkins University, 1968).

793. **Howard, Henry.** *Canada, The Western Cities: Their Borrowings and Assets.* London: Investors' Guardian, Ltd., 1914.

794. **Lenz, K.** "Large Urban Places in the Prairie Provinces: Their Development and Location." In R.C. Gentilcore, ed. *Canada's Changing Albertan Geographer* 5 (1969), pp. 65-74.

795. **McCann, L.D.** "Urban Growth in Western Canada, 1880-1960." *Alberton Geographer* 5 (1969), pp. 65-74.

796. **McCormack, A.R., and MacPherson, Ian, eds.** *Cities in the West: Papers of the Western Canada Urban History Conference.* Ottawa: National Museum of Man, History Division, 1975.

797. **Mitchell, F.B.** *In Western Canada before the War: A Study of Communities.* London: John Murray, 1915.

798. **Mozersky, K.A.** "Structure Differentiation of Community: An Analysis of Western Canadian Communities Undergoing Change." Ph.D. Thesis (Cornell University, 1970).

799. **Murray, O.B.** "Urban Growth and Population Shifts in the Prairie Region." *Canadian Library Journal* 78 (1971), pp. 344-350.

800. **Nader, G.A.** "Some Aspects of the Recent Growth and Distribution of Apartments in Prairie Metropolitan Areas." *Canadian Geographer* 15 (1971), pp. 307-17.

801. **Rutherford, P.F.W.** "Tomorrow's Metropolis: The Urban Reform Movement in Canada, 1880-1920." In Gilbert A. Stelter and Alan F.J. Artibise, eds. *The Canadian City: Essays in Urban History* (Toronto, 1977), pp. 368-392.

Plate 6. Downtown Vancouver from Stanley Park

802. **Smith, Peter J.** "Changing Forms and Patterns in the Cities." In Peter J. Smith, ed. *The Prairie Provinces* (Toronto, 1972), pp. 99-117.

802A. **Stabler, J.C.** "The Future of Small Communities in the Canadian Prairie Region." *Contact: Journal of Urban and Environmental Affairs* 9, no. 1 (1977), pp. 145-173.

803. **Stalker, A.** *Taxation of Land Values in Western History.* History and Economics, No. 4. Montreal: McGill University, 1914.

804. **Stelter, Gilbert, and Artibise, Alan F.J., eds.** *The Canadian City: Essays in Urban History.* Toronto: McClelland and Stewart, 1977.

805. **Taylor, John H.** "Urban Social Organization and Urban Discontent: The 1930s." In David J. Bercuson, ed. *Western Perspectives I* (Toronto, 1974), pp. 33-44.

806. ———. "The Urban West: Public Welfare and a Theory of Urban Development." In A.R. McCormack and Ian MacPherson, eds. *Cities in the West* (Ottawa, 1975), pp. 286-307.

807. **Voisey, P.L.** "The Urbanization of the Canadian Prairies, 1871-1916." *Histoire sociale/Social History* 8 (1975), pp. 77-101.

808. **Wade, F.C.** *Experiments with the Single Tax in Western Canada.* Denver: National Tax Association, 1914.

809. **Weaver, John C.** "Elitism and the Corporate Ideal: Businessmen and Boosters in Canadian Civic Reform, 1890-1920." In A.R. McCormack and Ian MacPherson, eds. *Cities in the West* (Ottawa, 1975), pp. 48-73.

810. ———. "'Tomorrow's Metropolis' Revisited: A Critical Assessment of Urban Reform in Canada, 1890-1920." In Gilbert A. Stelter and Alan F.J. Artibise, eds. *The Canadian City: Essays in Urban History* (Toronto, 1977), pp. 393-418.

811. **Weir, Thomas K.** "Road back from the Prairie: Canadian Pioneers Settle in Cities." *Geographical Magazine* 45 (1973), pp. 506-511.

812. **Whetten, N.L.** "The Social and Economic Structure of the Trade Center in the Canadian Prairie Provinces with Special References to Its Change, 1910-1930." Ph.D. Thesis (Harvard University, 1932).

813. **Woodsworth, J.S.** *My Neighbour: A Study of City Conditions, A Plea for Justice.* 1911. Reprint. Social History of Canada, vol. 3. Toronto: University of Toronto Press, 1972.

814. **Zimmerman, C.C., and Mones, G.W.** *The Prairie Community System.* Ottawa: Agricultural Economics Research Council of Canada, 1971.

j. Bibliographical and Methodological

815. **Abler, T.S.; Sanders, D.; and Weaver, S.M.** *A Canadian Indian Bibliography, 1960-1970.* Toronto: University of Toronto Press, 1974.

815A. **Andrews, Margaret W.** "Review Article: Attitudes in Canadian Women's History, 1945-1975." *Journal of Canadian Studies* 12, no. 4 (1977), pp. 69-78.

816. **Archer, John H.** "Resources and Perspectives for Canadian Plains Research." In Richard Allen, ed. *A Region of the Mind* (Regina, 1973), pp. 3-13.

816A. "Archives: A Retrospective Bibliography." *Archivaria: The Journal of the Association of Canadian Archivists* 1 (Winter 1975/1976), pp. 131-142. [Continued in subsequent issues.]

817. **Artibise, Alan F.J.** "Canadian Urban Studies." *Communique: Canadian Studies* 3 (April 1977), pp. 1-130.

818. **Barr, B.M.,** ed. *The Lethbridge Papers: Western Canadian Research in Geography.* Vancouver: Tantalus Research, 1975.

818A. Barr, B.M., ed. *New Themes in Western Canadian Geography: The Langara Papers.* Vancouver, B.C. Geographical Series, no. 22, 1976.

819. Bercuson, David J. "Recent Developments in Prairie Historiography." *Acadiensis* 4 (1974), pp. 138-148.

820. Berger, Carl. "William Morton: The Delicate Balance of Region and Nation." In Carl Berger and Ramsay Cook, eds. *The West and the Nation* (Toronto, 1976), pp. 9-32.

821. ———. *The Writing of Canadian History: Aspects of English Canadian Historical Writing, 1900-1970.* Toronto: Oxford University Press, 1976.

821A. Binsfield, Edmund L. "Church Archives in the United States and Canada: A Bibliography." *American Archivist* 21 (1958), pp. 311-332.

822. Bowsfield, Hartwell. "Writing Local History." *A.H.R.* 17 (Summer Look at the Ranching Frontier." In Lewis H. Thomas, ed. *Essays on*

823. ———. "The West." In J.L. Granatstein and Paul Stevens, eds. *Canada Since 1867: A Bibliographical Guide* (Toronto, 1974), pp. 87-108.

824. Breen, D.H. "The Turner Thesis and the Canadian West: A Closer Look at the Ranching Frontier." In Lewis H. Thomas, ed. *Essays on Western History* (Edmonton, 1976), pp. 147-158.

825. ———. "The Ranching Frontier in the Prairie West: An Historiographical Comment." In *Development of Agriculture on the Canadian Prairies, Proceedings of Seminar* (Regina, 1975), 11 pp. [Attached.]

826. Brooks, I.R. *Native Education in Canada and the United States: A Bibliography.* Calgary: Office of Educational Development, University of Calgary, 1976.

827. Camponi, L., and Oppen, W., comps. *A Catalogue of Maps Relating to Indian Reserves in Manitoba, Saskatchewan and Alberta, 1817-1967.* Ottawa: Public Archives of Canada, National Map Collection, 1976.

828. Canadian Council on Urban and Regional Research. *Urban and Regional References, 1945-1969.* Ottawa, 1970. [Supplements annually.]

829. Careless, J.M.S. "Frontierism, Metropolitanism and Canadian History." In Carl Berger, ed. *Approaches to Canadian History* (Toronto, 1967), pp. 63-83.

830. ———. "Localism or Parochialism in Canadian History?" *B.C. Perspectives* 2 (1972), pp. 4-14.

831. **Child, Alan H.** "The History of Canadian Education: A Bibliographical Note." *Histoire sociale/Social History* 8 (1971), pp. 105-117.
832. *Citizenship, Immigration and Ethnic Groups in Canada: A Bibliography of Research Published and Unpublished Sources, 1920-1958.* Ottawa: Department of Citizenship and Immigration, 1960. [Supplements periodically.]
833. **Cook, G.L.** "Some Uses of Local and Regional History as an Introduction to the Study of History." *B.C. Perspectives* 2 (1972), pp. 15-24.
834. **Cook, Ramsay.** "Frontier and Metropolis." In Ramsay Cook. *The Maple Leaf Forever* (Toronto, 1971), pp. 166-175.
835. **Cowan, Ann S., and Corcoran, F.** "Museums and Canadian Studies." *Communique: Canadian Studies* 2 (May 1976), pp. 9-97.
836. **Dempsey, Hugh A.** "Local Histories as Source Materials for Western Canadian Studies." In A.W. Rasporich and H.C. Klassen, eds. *Prairie Perspectives 2* (Toronto, 1973), pp. 171-180.
837. **Doughty, H.** "Industrial Relations and Labour History." *Communique: Canadian Studies* 1 (March 1975), pp. 2-26.
838. **Duke, Mary D.** *Agricultural Periodicals Published in Canada, 1836-1960.* Ottawa: Department of Agriculture, 1962.
839. **Easterbrook, W.T.** "Recent Contributions to Economic History: Canada." *Journal of Economic History* 19 (1959), pp. 76-102.
840. **Fowke, Edith; Henderson, C.; and Brooks, J.** *A Bibliography of Canadian Folklore in English.* Downsview: York University, 1976.
841. **Gillis, P.; Hume, D.; and Armstrong, R.** *Records Relating to Indian Affairs.* Ottawa: Public Records Division, Public Archives Canada, 1975.
842. **Granatstein, J.L., and Steven, Paul, eds.** *Canada Since 1867: A Bibliographical Guide.* 1974. 2d. ed. Toronto: Hakkert, 1977.
843. **Hann, R.G.; Kealey, G.S.; Kealey, L.; and Warrian, P.** *Primary Sources in Canadian Working Class History, 1860-1930.* Kitchener: Dumont Press, 1973.
844. **Harris, R.C.** "Historical Geography." *Canadian Geographer* 11 (1967), pp. 235-240.
845. **Harrison, Richard.** "The Mounted Police in Fiction." In Hugh A. Dempsey, ed. *Men in Scarlet* (Calgary, 1974), pp. 163-174.
846. **Heggie, Grace F.** *Canadian Political Parties, 1867-1968: A Historical Bibliography.* Toronto: Macmillan, 1977.

847. **Horvath, Maria.** *A Doukhobor Bibliography. Part I: Books and Periodical Articles. Part II: Government Publications.* Vancouver: U.B.C. Library, 1968. Supplement, 1970.

848. **Hostetler, John A.** "A Bibliography of English Language Materials on the Hutterian Brethren." *Mennonite Quarterly Review* 44 (1970), pp. 106-113.

849. **Innis, Harold A.** "Canadian Frontiers of Settlement: A Review." *Geographic Review* 25 (1935), pp. 92-106.

850. **Isbester, A.F.; Coates, D.; and Williams, C.B.** *Industrial and Labour Relations in Canada: A Selected Bibliography.* Kingston: Industrial Relations Centre, Queen's University, 1965.

851. **Kaye, B., and Moodie, D.W.** "Geographical Perspectives on the Canadian Plains." In Richard Allen, ed. *A Region of the Mind* (Regina, 1973), pp. 17-46.

852. **Klassen, H.C.** "The Mounties and the Historians." In Hugh A. Dempsey, ed. *Men in Scarlet* (Calgary, 1974), pp. 175-186.

853. **Klinck, Carl F., ed.** *Literary History of Canada: Canadian Literature in English.* 2d ed. 3 vols. Toronto: University of Toronto Press, 1976.

854. **Klymasy, R.B.** *Bibliography of Ukrainian Folklore in Canada, 1902-1964.* Ottawa: National Museum of Man, 1969.

855. **Knight, Rolf.** *Work Camps and Company Towns in Canada and the U.S.: An Annotated Bibliography.* Vancouver: New Star Books, 1975.

856. **Koester, Charles B., comp.** *A Bibliography of Selected Theses in the Library of the University of Alberta (Edmonton) Relating to Western Canada, 1915-1965.* Edmonton: Western Canada Research Project, 1965.

856A. **Leigh, R., ed.** *Contemporary Geography: Western Viewpoints.* Vancouver: B.C. Geographical Series, no. 12, 1971.

857. **Lochhead, Douglas, comp.** *Bibliography of Canadian Bibliographies.* Toronto: University of Toronto Press, 1972.

858. **Lunn, Jean.** "Bibliography of the History of the Canadian Press." *C.H.R.* 22 (1941), pp. 416-433.

859. **McCourt, E.A.** "Prairie Literature and Its Critics." In Richard Allen, ed. *A Region of the Mind* (Regina, 1973), pp. 153-164.

860. **McDougall, J.L.** "The Frontier School and Canadian History." Canadian Historical Association. *Annual Report 1929,* pp. 121-126.

861. **Mallea, J.R., and Philip, L.** "Canadian Cultural Pluralism and Education: A Select Bibliography." *Canadian Ethnic Studies* 8 (1976), pp. 81-88.

862. **Malycky, A., ed.** "Bibliographies of Ten Canadian Ethnic Groups." *Canadian Ethnic Studies* 1 (1969), pp. 1-163.

863. ———. "Bibliographies of Twenty-Five Canadian Ethnic Groups." *Canadian Ethnic Studies* 2 (1970), pp. 1-249.

864. ———. "Bibliographies of Twenty-Eight Canadian Ethnic Groups." *Canadian Ethnic Studies* 5 (1976), pp. 1-426.

865. **Marken, Jack W.** *The Indians and Eskimos of North America: A Bibliography of Books in Print through 1972.* Vermillion: Dakota Press, 1972.

866. **Minter, Ella S.G., comp.** *Publications of the Canada Department of Agriculture, 1867-1959.* Ottawa: Queen's Printer, 1963.

867. **Morton, W.L.** "Clio in Canada: The Interpretation of Canadian History." In Carl Berger, ed. *Approaches to Canadian History* (Toronto, 1967), pp. 42-49.

868. ———. "The Historiography of the Great West." Canadian Historical Association. *Historical Papers 1970,* pp. 46-59.

869. **Osborne, K., ed.** *The Prairies: Selected Historical Sources.* Toronto: McClelland and Stewart, 1969.

870. **Page, James.** "Native Studies: Resources for Curriculum Development." *Communique: Canadian Studies* 1 (October 1974), pp. 5-22.

871. **Peel, Bruce.** *A Bibliography of the Prairie Provinces to 1953, with Biographical Index.* 1956. 2d. ed. Toronto: University of Toronto Press, 1973.

872. **Pentland, H.C.** "Recent Developments in Economic History: Some Implications for Local and Regional History." H.S.S.M. *Transactions* Series III, 24 (1967-68), pp. 7-16.

873. **Poulin, J.** *Records of the Royal Canadian Mounted Police.* Ottawa: Public Records Division, Public Archives Canada, 1975.

874. **Preston, R.A.** "Is Local History Really History?" *Sask. Hist.* 10 (Autumn 1957), pp. 97-103.

875. **Regehr, T.D.** "Historiography of the Canadian Plains after 1870." In Richard Allen, ed. *A Region of the Mind* (Regina, 1973), pp. 87-102.

876. **Ryder, Dorothy E., ed.** *Canadian Reference Sources: A Selective Guide.* Ottawa: Canadian Library Association, 1973.

877. **Sharp, P.F.** "Three Frontiers: Some Comparative Studies of Canadian, American and Australian Settlement." *Pacific Historical Review* 24 (1953), pp. 369-377.
878. **Smith, David E.** "Interpreting Prairie Politics." *Journal of Canadian Studies* 7, no. 4 (1972), pp. 18-32.
879. **Smith, Dwight L.**, ed. *Indians of the United States and Canada: A Bibliography.* Santa Barbara: American Bibliographical Center, 1974.
879A. **Spector, David.** "A Bibliographic Study of Field Agriculture in the Canadian Prairie West, 1870-1940." National Historic Parks and Sites Branch. *Research Bulletin* 46 (1977), pp. 1-23.
879B. ———. "An Annotated Bibliography for the Study of Animal Husbandry in the Canadian Prairie West, 1880-1925: Part A— Sources Available in Western Canada and the United States." National Historic Parks and Sites Branch. *Research Bulletin* 77 (1978), pp. 1-50.
879C. ———. "An Annotated Bibliography for the Study of Animal Husbandry in the Canadian Prairie West, 1880-1925: Part B— Sources Available in Ottawa." National Historic Parks and Sites Branch. *Research Bulletin* 78 (1978), pp. 1-18.
880. **Stanley, George F.G.** "Western Canada and the Frontier Thesis." Canadian Historical Association. *Annual Report 1940,* pp. 105-117.
881. **Stelter, Gilbert A.** "A Sense of Time and Place: The Historian's Approach to Canada's Urban Past." In Gilbert A. Stelter and Alan F.J. Artibise, eds. *The Canadian City: Essays in Urban History* (Toronto, 1977), pp. 420-441.
882. **Stelter, Gilbert A., and Artibise, Alan F.J.** "Urban History Comes of Age: A Review of Current Research." *City Magazine* 3, no. 1 (1977), pp. 22-35.
883. **Sutyla, C.** "Multicultural Studies in Canada: A Bibliography with Introductory Comments." *Communique: Canadian Studies* 3 (October 1976), pp. 4-65.
884. **Swyripa, F.A.** "Ukrainian-Canadian Historiography in the English Language: A Survey." M.A. Thesis (University of Alberta, 1976).
885. **Tanghe, R.**, comp. *Bibliography of Canadian Bibliographies.* Toronto: Bibliographical Society of Canada, 1960.
886. **Thibault, Claude**, comp. *Bibliographia Canadiana.* Toronto: Longman, 1973.
887. **Thomas, L.G.** "Historiography of the Fur Trade Era." In Richard Allen, ed. *A Region of the Mind* (Regina, 1973), pp. 73-86.

888. **Thomas, Lewis H.** "Documentary Sources for Teaching Western Canadian History." *A.H.R.* 17 (Autumn 1969), pp. 23-25.
889. **Walker, J.W.** "The Indian in Canadian Historical Writing." Canadian Historical Association. *Historical Papers 1971,* pp. 21-51.
890. **Whiteside, Dan.** *Aboriginal People: A Selected Bibliography Concerning Canada's First People.* Ottawa: National Indian Brotherhood, 1973.
891. **Winnipeg, Public Library.** *A Select Bibliography of Canadiana of the Prairie Provinces: Publications Relating to Western Canada by English, French, Icelandic, Mennonite, and Ukrainian Authors.* Winnipeg: Public Library, 1949.
892. **Wood, W.D.; Kelly, L.A.; and Reimer, P.** *Canadian Graduate Theses, 1919-1967: An Annotated Bibliography.* Kingston: Industrial Relations Centre, Queen's University, 1970.
893. **Zaslow, M.** "The Frontier Hypothesis in Recent Historiography." *C.H.R.* 29 (1948), pp. 153-167.

2

Riel Rebellions

a. General

894. **Anderson, F.W.** "Louis Riel's Insanity Reconsidered." *Sask. Hist.* 3 (Autumn 1950), pp. 104-110.
895. **Bowsfield, Hartwell.** "Documents of Western History: Louis Riel's Letter to President Grant, 1875." *Sask. Hist.* 21 (Spring 1968), pp. 67-75.
896. ———. *Louis Riel: The Rebel and the Hero.* Toronto: Oxford University Press, 1971.
897. **Bowsfield, Hartwell,** ed. *Louis Riel: Rebel of the Western Frontier or Victim of Politics and Prejudice?* Toronto: Copp Clark, 1969.
898. **Charlebois, Peter.** *The Life of Louis Riel.* Toronto: New Canada Press, 1975.
899. **Clark, C.K.** "A Critical Study of the Case of Louis Riel." *Queen's Quarterly* 12 (1905), pp. 379-391; 13 (1905), pp. 14-17.
900. **Clark, D.** "A Psycho-Medical History of Louis Riel." *American Journal of Insanity* (1887), pp. 35-51.
901. **Davidson, W.M.** *The Life and Times of Louis Riel.* Calgary: The Albertan, 1951.
902. ———. *Louis Riel, 1844-1885.* Calgary: Alberta Publishing Co., 1955.
903. **Dhand, H.,** et al. *Louis Riel: An Annoted Bibliography.* Saskatoon: Research Resources Centre, College of Education, University of Saskatchewan, 1972.
904. **Dunlevy, Ursula.** "The Canadian Halfbreed Rebellions of 1870 and 1885: The Origin of the Métis, or Halfbreeds, of Western Canada." *North Dakota Quarterly* 9 (1942), pp. 86-113, 137-166.

905. **Flanagan, Thomas E.** "Catastrophe and the Millennium: A New View of Louis Riel." In Richard Allen, ed. *Religion and Society in the Prairie West* (Regina, 1974), pp. 35-52.
906. ———. "Louis 'David' Riel: Prophet, Priest-King, Infallible Pontiff." *Journal of Canadian Studies* 9, no. 3 (1974), pp. 15-25.
907. ———. "Louis Riel's Religious Beliefs: A Letter to Bishop Taché." *Sask. Hist.* 27 (Winter 1974), pp. 15-28.
908. ———. "The Mission of Louis Riel." *Alberta History* 23 (Winter 1975), pp. 1-12.
909. ———. "Louis Riel: Insanity and Prophecy." In H. Palmer, ed. *The Settlement of the West* (Calgary, 1977), pp. 15-36.
910. **Flanagan, Thomas E., ed.** *The Diaries of Louis Riel.* Edmonton: Hurtig, 1976.
911. **Frégault, Guy.** "Louis Riel, patriote persécuté." *L'Action nationale* 25 (1945), pp. 15-22.
912. **Greenland, C.** "The Life and Death of Louis Riel—Part II: Surrender, Trial, Appeal and Execution." *Canadian Psychiatric Association Journal* 10 (1965), pp. 253-264.
913. **Hall, D.J.** "The Half-Breed Claims Commission." *Alberta History* 25 (Spring 1977), pp. 1-8.
914. **Howard, Joseph Kinsey.** *Strange Empire: A Narrative of the Northwest.* New York: William Morrow, 1952.
915. ———. *Strange Empire: Louis Riel and the Métis People.* Toronto: James Lewis and Samuel, 1974. [Reprint of 1952 edition, with introduction by Martin Robin.]
916. **Jonasson, J.A.** "The Background of the Riel Rebellions." *Pacific Historical Review* 3 (1934), pp. 270-279.
917. ———. "The Riel Rebellions." Ph.D. Thesis (Stanford University, 1936).
918. ———. "The Red River Amnesty Question." *Pacific Historical Review* 6 (1937), pp. 58-66.
919. **Lamb, R.E.** *Thunder in the North: Conflict over the Riel Risings, 1870, 1885.* New York: Pageant Press, 1957.
920. **Lusty, Terrance.** *Louis Riel: Humanitarian.* Calgary: Northwest Printing and Lithographing Ltd., 1973.
921. **Markson, E.R.** "The Life and Death of Louis Riel: A Study in Forensic Psychiatry—Part I: A Psychoanalytic Commentary." *Canadian Psychiatric Association Journal* 10 (1965), pp. 246-252.

922. **Neering, Rosemary.** *Louis Riel.* Toronto: Fitzhenry & Whiteside, 1977.
923. **Osler, E.B.** *The Man Who Had to Hang: Louis Riel.* Toronto: Longmans, Green, 1961.
924. **Pearl, Stanley.** *Louis Riel: A Volatile Legacy.* Toronto: Maclean-Hunter Learning Materials Co., 1972.
925. **Silver, A.I.** "French Quebec and the Métis Question, 1869-1885." In Carl Berger and Ramsay Cook, eds. *The West and the Nation* (Toronto, 1976), pp. 91-113.
926. **Stanley, George F.G.** *The Birth of Western Canada: A History of the Riel Rebellions.* 1936. Reprint. Toronto: University of Toronto Press, 1960.
927. ———. "The Half-Breed 'Rising' of 1875." *C.H.R.* 17 (1936), pp. 399-412.
928. ———. "Riel's Petition to the President of the United States, 1870." *C.H.R.* 20 (1939), pp. 421-428.
929. ———. "The Métis and the Conflict of Culture in Western Canada." *C.H.R.* 27 (1947), pp. 428-433.
930. ———. "A Footnote to History: Was Louis Riel an American Citizen?" *C.H.R.* 29 (1948), pp. 40-43.
931. ———. *Louis Riel: Patriot or Rebel?* Canadian Historical Association Booklet 2. Ottawa: Canadian Historical Association, 1956.
932. ———. *Louis Riel.* Toronto: Ryerson, 1963.
933. ———. "Louis Riel." *Revue d'histoire de l'Amérique française* 18 (1964), pp. 14-26.
934. **Thomas, Lewis H.** "A Judicial Murder—The Trial of Louis Riel." In H. Palmer, ed. *The Settlement of the West* (Calgary, 1977), pp. 37-59.
935. **Woodcock, George.** "Riel, Defender of the Past." *The Beaver* Outfit 290 (1960), pp. 24-30.

b. *1870 Rebellion*

936. **Begg, Alexander.** *The Creation of Manitoba; or, A History of the Red River Troubles.* Toronto: A.H. Hovey, 1871.
937. **Boissonnault, C.-M.** "L'Expédition du nord-ouest: Le Rapport Wolseley." Royal Society of Canada. *Proceedings and Transactions* 4th ser. 8 (1970), pp. 123-132.

938. **Bowsfield, Hartwell,** ed. *James Wickes Taylor Correspondence, 1859-1870.* Altona: Manitoba Record Society, 1968.
939. **Dorge, L.** "Bishop Taché and the Confederation of Manitoba (1869-1870)." H.S.S.M. *Transactions* Series III, 29 (1972-73), pp. 93-110.
940. **Glueck, A.C.** *Minnesota and the Manifest Destiny of the Canadian Northwest.* Toronto: University of Toronto Press, 1965.
941. **Groulx, Lionel.** *Louis Riel et les événements de la Rivière-Rouge.* Montréal: Ligue d'action nationale, 1945.
942. **Huyshe, G.L.** *The Red River Expedition.* London: Macmillan, 1871.
943. **Kreutzweiser, Erwin E.** *The Red River Insurrection: Its Causes and Events.* Gardenvale: Garden City Press, 1936.
944. **McDougall, John.** *In the Days of the Red River Rebellion: Life and Adventure in the Far West of Canada, 1868-1872.* Toronto: William Briggs, 1903.
945. **Martin, Chester.** "The First New Province of the Dominion." *C.H.R.* 1 (1920), pp. 534-578.
946. **Morice, A.G.** *A Critical History of the Red River Insurrection after Official Documents and Non-Catholic Sources.* Winnipeg: Canadian Publishers, 1935.
947. **Morton, W.L.,** ed. *Alexander Begg's Red River Journal and Other Papers Relative to the Red River Resistance of 1868-1870.* Toronto: Champlain Society, 1956.
947A. ———. "Two Young Men, 1869: Charles Mair and Louis Riel." H.S.S.M. *Transactions* Series III, 30 (1973-74), pp. 33-43.
948. **Puchniak, S.A.** "Riel's Red River Government: A Legitimate Government, 1869-1870." M.A. Thesis (University of Ottawa, 1931).
949. **Ridd, John E.** "The Red River Insurrection, 1869-1870." M.A. Thesis (University of Manitoba, 1934).
950. **Robertson, R.W.W.** *The Execution of Thomas Scott.* Toronto: Burns and MacEachern, 1968.
951. **Stanley, George F.G.** *Manitoba 1870: A Métis Achievement.* Winnipeg: University of Manitoba Press, 1972.
952. **Todd, J.B.** "Sir John Schultz and the Canadian Expansionist Agitation at Red River, 1862-1871." M.A. Thesis (University of Toronto, 1933).
953. **Trémaudan, A.H. de.** "Louis Riel and the Fenian Raid of 1871." *C.H.R.* 4 (1923), pp. 132-144.

954. **Trémaudan, A.H. de, ed.** "Louis Riel's Account of the Capture of Fort Garry, 1870." *C.H.R.* 5 (1924), pp. 146-159.
955. ———. "The Execution of Thomas Scott." *C.H.R.* 6 (1925), pp. 222-235.
956. ———. "Letter of Louis Riel and Ambroise Lepine to Lieutenant-Governor Morris, January 3, 1873." *C.H.R.* 7 (1926), pp. 137-160.
957. **Warner, D.F.** "Drang nach Norden: The United States and the Riel Rebellion." *Mississippi Valley Historical Review* 39 (1953), pp. 693-712.

c. 1885 Rebellion

958. **Ahenakeu, Edward** (with Foreword by Alex. E. Peterson). "An Opinion of the Frog Lake Massacre." *A.H.R.* 8 (Summer 1960), pp. 9-15.
959. **Allan, Iris, ed.** "A Riel Rebellion Diary." *A.H.R.* 12 (Summer 1964), pp. 15-25.
960. **Anderson, F.W.** "Gabriel Dumont." *A.H.R.* 7 (Summer 1959), pp. 1-6.
961. ———. *1885, the Riel Rebellion.* High River: *High River Times,* 1961.
962. **Bartley, George.** "Jubilee Year of Loyalists' Victory, Riel's Second Rebellion in 1885." *Scarlet and Gold* 17 (1935), pp. 78-97.
963. ———. "The Trial and Sentence of Louis Riel." *Scarlet and Gold* 17 (1935), pp. 71-75.
964. **Bingaman, S.E.** "The Northwest Rebellion Trials of 1885." M.A. Thesis (University of Saskatchewan, Regina, 1971).
965. ———. "The Trials of the 'White Rebels,' 1885." *Sask. Hist.* 25 (Spring 1972), pp. 41-54.
966. ———. "The Trials of Poundmaker and Big Bear, 1885." *Sask. Hist.* 27 (Autumn 1975), pp. 81-94.
967. **Boulton, Charles A.** *Reminiscences of the North-West Rebellions.* Toronto: Grip Printing, 1886.
968. **Breen, D.H.** "'Timber Tom' and the North-West Rebellion." *A.H.R.* 19 (Summer 1971), pp. 1-7.
969. **Brown, D.H.** "The Meaning of Treason, 1885." *Sask. Hist.* 28 (Spring 1975), pp. 65-73.
970. **Cameron, William Bleasdell.** *The War Trail of Big Bear.* Toronto: Ryerson, 1926.

971. ———. *Blood Red the Sun.* Calgary: Kenway Publishing Co., 1950.
972. **Cornish, F.C.** "The Blackfeet and the Rebellion Experiences of an Agency Clerk in 1885." *A.H.R.* 6 (Spring 1958), pp. 20-26.
973. **Dempsey, Hugh A.** "Fort Ostell and the Riel Rebellion." *A.H.R.* 2 (Summer 1954), pp. 24-33.
974. **Denney, C.D.** "In Memory of Mary Rose (Pritchard) Sayers, the Last Witness [to the Frog Lake Massacre]." *Sask. Hist.* 24 (Spring 1971), pp. 63-72.
975. **Department of Indian Affairs and Northern Development.** *Batoche: National Historic Site.* Ottawa: Queen's Printer, 1970.
976. **Dunlop, Allan C.** "Letter from a Soldier Tourist." *Alberta History* 23 (Summer 1975), pp. 24-29.
977. **Fergusson, C.B.** "A Glimpse of 1885." *Sask. Hist.* 21 (Winter 1968), pp. 24-29.
978. **Forin, John A.** "Riel Rebellion of 1885." *Scarlet and Gold* 17 (1935), pp. 3-6.
979. **Fraser, W.B.** "Big Bear, Indian Patriot." *A.H.R.* 14 (Spring 1966), pp. 1-13.
980. **Harrington, L.** "Prairie Battlefield." *Canadian Geographical Journal* 66 (1963), pp. 28-37.
981. **Hicks, Joseph.** "With Hatton's Scouts in Pursuit of Big Bear." *A.H.R.* 18 (Summer 1970), pp. 14-23.
982. **Hitsman, J.M.** "Near Disaster at Cut Knife Hill, 1885." *Canadian Army Journal* 13 (1959), pp. 62-73.
983. **Hughes, S., ed.** *The Frog Lake 'Massacre': Personal Perspectives on Ethnic Conflict.* Toronto: McClelland and Stewart, 1976.
984. **Jamieson, F.C., ed.** *The Alberta Field Force of 1885.* Battleford: Canadian North West Historical Society, 1931.
985. **Kennedy, Howard Angus.** *The North-West Rebellion.* Toronto: Ryerson, 1928.
986. ———. "Memories of '85." *Canadian Geographical Journal* 11 (1935), pp. 55-64.
987. ———. "Memories of '85." *Canadian Geographical Journal* 70 (1965), pp. 154-161.
988. **Kinnaird, G.J.** "Recollections and Reminiscences: An Episode of the North-West Rebellion, 1885." *Sask. Hist.* 20 (Spring 1967), pp. 71-75.

989. **Lalonde, André.** "The North-West Rebellion and Its Effects on Settlers and Settlement in the Canadian West." *Sask. Hist.* 27 (Autumn 1974), pp. 95-102.

990. **Langton, H.H.**, ed. "The Commission of 1885 to the North-West Territories." *C.H.R.* 25 (1944), pp. 38-53.

991. **Larmour, J.** "Edgar Dewdney and the Aftermath of the Rebellion." *Sask. Hist.* 23 (Autumn 1970), pp. 105-116.

992. **Le Chavellier, Jules.** *Batoche, les missionaires du nord-ouest pendant les troubles de 1885.* Montreal: Presse Dominicaine, 1941.

993. **McCourt, E.A.** *Revolt in the West: The Story of the Riel Rebellion.* Toronto: Macmillan, 1958.

994. **McLean, W.J.** "Tragic Events at Frog Lake and Fort Pitt during the North West Rebellion." *Manitoba Pageant* 17 (Winter 1972), pp. 2-9. [Continued in subsequent issues.]

995. **Mika, Nick, comp.** *The Riel Rebellion of 1885.* Belleville: Mika Publishing, 1971.

996. **Miller, C.** "Lord Melgund and the North-West Campaign." *Sask. Hist.* 22 (Autumn 1969), pp. 81-108.

997. **Morton, Desmond.** "Des canadiens errants: French Canadian Troops in the North-West Campaign of 1885." *Journal of Canadian Studies* 5, no. 3 (1970), pp. 28-39.

998. ———. *The Last War Drum: The North West Campaign of 1885.* Toronto: Hakkert, 1972.

999. ———. *The Queen v Louis Riel.* Social History of Canada, vol. 19. Toronto: University of Toronto Press, 1974.

1000. **Morton, Desmond, and Roy, R.H.**, eds. *Telegrams of the North-West Campaign, 1885.* Toronto: Champlain Society, 1972.

1001. **Mulvaney, C.P.** *The History of the North-West Rebellion of 1885.* Toronto: A.H. Hovey, 1885.

1002. **Needler, G.H.** *Suppression of Rebellion in the North-West Territories.* Toronto: University of Toronto Press, 1948.

1003. ———. *Louis Riel: The Rebellion of 1885.* Toronto: Burns and MacEachern, 1957.

1004. **Normandeau, Louis.** "65th Mount Royal Regiment and the Riel Rebellion." *A.H.R.* 9 (Autumn 1961), pp. 22-26.

1005. **Pearce, William.** "Causes of the Riel Rebellion, A Personal View." *A.H.R.* 16 (Autumn 1968), pp. 19-26.

1006. **Preston, J.A.V.** "The Diary of Lieut. J.A.V. Preston, 1885." *Sask. Hist.* 8 (Autumn 1955), pp. 95-107.
1007. **Ridd, D.G.** "The Second Riel Insurrection." M.A. Thesis (University of Manitoba, 1934).
1008. **Rowand, Evelyn.** "The Rebellion at Lac La Biche." *A.H.R.* 21 (Summer 1973), pp. 1-9.
1009. **Roy, R.H.** "The Diary of Rifleman Forin." *Sask. Hist.* 21 (Autumn 1968), pp. 100-111.
1010. **Shera, John W.** "Poundmaker's Capture of the Wagon Train in the Eagle Hills, 1885." *A.H.R.* 1 (Spring 1953), pp. 16-20.
1011. **Stacey, C.P.** "The North-West Campaign, 1885." *Canadian Army Journal* 8 (1954), pp. 10-20.
1012. **Stanley, George F.G.** "Gabriel Dumont's Account of the North-West Rebellion, 1885." *C.H.R.* 30 (1949), pp. 249-269.
1013. ———. "General Middleton's Account of the Suppression of the North-West Rebellion, 1885." *Sask. Hist.* 2 (Spring 1949), pp. 30-34.
1014. ———. "The Campaign of 1885: A Contemporary Account." *Sask. Hist.* 13 (Autumn 1960), pp. 100-107.
1015. **Stanley, George F.G., and Peterson, Alex. E.** "An Account of the Frog Lake Massacre." *A.H.R.* 4 (Winter 1956), pp. 23-29.
1016. **Thomas, Lewis H., ed.** "Documents of Western History: Louis Riel's Petition of Rights, 1884." *Sask. Hist.* 23 (Winter 1970), pp. 16-26.
1017. **Woodcock, George.** *Gabriel Dumont: The Métis Chief and His Lost World.* Edmonton: Hurtig, 1975.

3

Northwest Territories to 1905

1018. **Andrews, Isabel A.** "Indian Protest against Starvation: The Yellow Calf Incident of 1884." *Sask. Hist.* 28 (Spring 1975), pp. 41-51.

1019. **Atkin, Ronald.** *Maintain the Right: The Early History of the North West Mounted Police, 1873-1900.* London: Macmillan, 1973.

1020. **Auld, F.H.** "Farmers' Institutes in the North-West Territories." *Sask. Hist.* 10 (Spring 1957), pp. 41-54.

1021. **Battleford Historical Society Publications.** *The Cree Rebellion of 1884, or Sidelights on Indian Conditions Subsequent to 1876.* Battleford: *Saskatchewan Herald*, 1926.

1022. **Begg, Alexander.** *The Great Canadian North West.* Montreal: Lovell, 1881.

1023. ———. *History of the North-West.* 3 vols. Toronto: Hunter, Rose, 1894-95.

1024. **Benoist, Charles.** *Les Français et le nord-ouest canadien.* Bar-le-Duc: Imprimerie de l'oeuvre de Saint-Paul, 1895.

1025. **Berry, Gerald L.** "Fort Whoop-Up and the Whisky Traders." *A.H.R.* 1 (Summer 1953), pp. 6-11.

1026. **Bocking, D.H.** "Political Ambitions and Territorial Affairs." *Sask. Hist.* 17 (Spring 1965), pp. 63-75.

1027. ———. "Political Manoeuvring in the Territorial Executive, 1895." *Sask. Hist.* 24 (Winter 1971), pp. 29-32.

1028. **Bocking, D.H., ed.** "Documents of Western History: Homestead Venture, 1883-1892, An Ayrshire Man's Letters Home." *Sask. Hist.* 14 (Autumn 1961), pp. 98-109.

1029. ———. "Documents of Western History: The Greenfell Mechanic's and Literary Institute, Minute Book, 1892-95." *Sask. Hist.* 17 (Autumn 1964), pp. 105-110.

1030. ———. "Politics and Patronage, 1894." *Sask. Hist.* 18 (Winter 1965), pp. 30-31.

1031. ———. "The Gilchrist Diaries [Fort Qu'Appelle, 1883-93, 1895-96]." *Sask. Hist.* 20 (Autumn 1967), pp. 108-113.

1032. **Brooks, W.H.** "The Primitive Methodists in the North-West." *Sask. Hist.* 29 (Winter 1976), pp. 26-37.

1033. **Callihoo, Victoria.** "Early Life in Lac Ste. Anne and St. Albert in the 1870s." *A.H.R.* 1 (Autumn 1953), pp. 21-26.

1034. **Chambers, Ernest J.** *The Royal North-West Mounted Police: A Corps History.* Montreal: Mortimer Press, 1906.

1035. **Choquette, Robert.** "Adélard Langevin et les questions scholaires du Manitoba et du nord-ouest, 1895-1915." *Revue de l'Université d'Ottawa* 46 (1976), pp. 324-344.

1036. **Church, H.E.** *An Emigrant in the Canadian Northwest.* London: Methuen, 1929.

1037. **Clinskill, J.** "Experiences of Starting and Conducting a Store in Saskatchewan in the Early 1880s." *Sask. Hist.* 17 (Winter 1964), pp. 12-23.

1038. ———. "Recollections and Reminiscences: Member of the Territorial Assembly for Battleford, 1888." *Sask. Hist.* 22 (Winter 1969), pp. 29-33.

1039. **Dempsey, Hugh A.** "Donald Graham's Narrative of 1872-73." *A.H.R.* 4 (Winter 1956), pp. 10-19.

1040. **Dempsey, Hugh A.,** ed. *Men in Scarlet.* Calgary: McClelland and Stewart West, 1974.

1041. **Den Otter, A.A.** "Sir Alexander T. Galt and the Northwest: A Case Study of Entrepreneurialism on the Frontier." Ph.D. Thesis (University of Alberta, 1975).

1042. **Dowse, Thomas.** *Manitoba and the Canadian Northwest.* St. Paul: The Author, 1879.

1043. **Drake, Earl G.** "The Territorial Press in the Region of Present Day Saskatchewan, 1878-1905." M.A. Thesis (University of Saskatchewan, 1951).

1044. ———. "Pioneer Journalism in Saskatchewan, 1878-1887. Part I: The Founding of the Territorial Press." *Sask. Hist.* 5 (Winter 1952), pp. 17-27.

1045. ———. "Pioneer Journalism in Saskatchewan, 1878-1887. Part II: Some Characteristics of the Territorial Press." *Sask. Hist.* 5 (Spring 1952), pp. 41-54.

1046. **Duncan, D.M.** *A History of Manitoba and the Northwest Territories.* Toronto: Gage, 1902.

1047. **Dyck, N.E.** "The Administration of Federal Indian Aid in the Northwest Territories, 1879-1885." M.A. Thesis (University of Saskatchewan, 1970).

1048. **Eager, E., ed.** "Documents of Western History: Minutes of the North-West Council, 1873-1874." *Sask. Hist.* 13 (Winter 1960), pp. 25-30.

1049. **Edmonds, W.E.** "The Establishment of the North-West Mounted Police in Northern Alberta." *A.H.R.* 2 (Autumn 1954), pp. 3-27.

1050. ———. "F.W.G. Haultain, Premier of the North-West Territories." *A.H.R.* 5 (Autumn 1957), pp. 11-16.

1051. **Essar, D.** "A Letter from an Early Saskatchewan Settler." *Sask. Hist.* 29 (Spring 1976), pp. 65-72.

1052. **Fitzpatrick, J.F.E.** *Sergeant 331: Personal Recollections of a Member of the Canadian North-West Mounted Police from 1879-1885.* New York: The Author, 1921.

1053. **Getty, I.A.L.** "The Failure of the Native Church Policy of the CMS in the North West." In Richard Allen, ed. *Religion and Society in the Prairie West* (Regina, 1974), pp. 19-34.

1054. **Giraud, Marcel.** "Métis Settlement in the North-West Territories." *Sask. Hist.* 7 (Winter 1954), pp. 1-16.

1055. **Goldring, P.** "The Cypress Hills Massacre: A Century's Retrospect." *Sask. Hist.* 26 (Autumn 1973), pp. 81-102.

1056. **Graham, W.R.** "Indian Treaties and the Settlement of the North-West." *Sask. Hist.* 2 (Winter 1949), pp. 19-22.

1057. **Hall, D.J.** "A Divergence of Principle: Clifford Sifton, Sir Wilfrid Laurier and the North West Autonomy Bills, 1905." *Laurentian University Review* 7 (1974), pp. 3-24.

1058. **Hardy, John.** *Farming in the Canadian North-West.* London: Henry J. Drove, 1906.

1059. **Harris, Charles Edward.** "My Trip to the Canadian West in 1882." *A.H.R.* 2 (Winter 1954), pp. 23-28.

1060. **Harvey, Horace.** "The Early Administration of Justice in the North West." *Alberta Law Quarterly* 1 (1934), pp. 1-15.

1061. ———. "Some Notes on the Early Administration of Justice in Canada's Northwest." *A.H.R.* 1 (Autumn 1953), pp. 5-20.

1062. **Haydon, A.L.** *The Riders of the Plains, A Record of the Royal North-West Mounted Police of Canada, 1873-1910.* 1910. Reprint. Edmonton: Hurtig, 1971.

1063. **Hill, Douglas.** *The Opening of the Canadian West.* London: Heinemann, 1967.

1064. **Horrall, S.W.** "Sir John A. Macdonald and the Mounted Police Force for the Northwest Territories." *C.H.R.* 53 (1972), pp. 201-225.

1065. ———. "The March West." In Hugh A. Dempsey, ed. *Men in Scarlet* (Calgary, 1974), pp. 13-26.

1065A. ———. "The Mounted Police and Prohibition in the North-West Territories, 1874-1891." H.S.S.M. *Transactions* Series III, 30 (1973-74), pp. 5-16.

1066. **Hunter, A.T.** *Chronicle of Alcoholic Beverages in the North West Territories and Saskatchewan.* Regina: Commercial Printers Ltd., n.d.

1067. **Jameson, G.B.** "Vocational Education in the N.W.T. from 1870-1905, Saskatchewan from 1905-1950." M.Ed. Thesis (University of Saskatchewan, 1955).

1068. **Johnson, G.** "Wolverine House." *Sask. Hist.* 1 (Autumn 1948), pp. 18-20.

1069. **Kaye, V.J.** *Early Ukrainian Settlements in Canada, 1895-1900: Dr. Josef Oleslow's Role in the Settlement of the Canadian Northwest.* Toronto: University of Toronto Press, 1964.

1070. **Kemp, V.A.M.** *Scarlet and Stetson: The Royal North-West Mounted Police on the Prairies.* Toronto: Ryerson, 1964.

1071. **Koester, Charles B.** "The Agitation for Parliamentary Representation of the North-West Territories, 1879-1887." *Sask. Hist.* 26 (Winter 1973), pp. 11-23.

1072. **Lalonde, André.** "Colonization Companies in the 1880s." *Sask. Hist.* 24 (Autumn 1971), pp. 101-114.

1073. ———. "Settlement in the North-West Territories by Colonization Companies, 1881-1891." Ph.D. Thesis (Laval University, 1971).

1074. **Larmour, J.** "Edgar Dewdney, Commissioner of Indian Affairs and Lieutenant-Governor of the North-West Territories, 1879-1888." M.A. Thesis (University of Saskatchewan, Regina, 1969).

1075. **Lingard, C.C.** *Territorial Government in Canada: The Autonomy Question in the Old North-West Territories.* Toronto: University of Toronto Press, 1946.

1076. **Lunsden, J.** *Through Canada in Harvest Time: A Study of Life and Labour in the Golden West.* London: T.F. Unwin, 1903.

1077. **Lupul, M.R.** "Relations in Education between the State and the Roman Catholic Church in the Canadian North-West with Special Reference to the Provisional District of Alberta, 1880-1905." Ph.D. Thesis (Harvard University, 1963).

1078. ―――. *The Roman Catholic Church and the North-West School Question: A Study in Church-State Relations in Western Canada, 1875-1905.* Toronto: University of Toronto Press, 1974.

1079. **Lyle, G.R.** "Eye Witness to Courage [the Barr Colonists]." *Sask. Hist.* 20 (Autumn 1967), pp. 81-107.

1080. **MacBeth, R.G.** *Policing the Plains, Being the Real-Life Record of the Famous North-West Mounted Police.* Toronto: Hodder and Stoughton, 1921.

1081. **McDonald, R.J.** "The Presbyterian Church in Saskatchewan in the Nineteenth Century." *Sask. Hist.* 14 (Autumn 1951), pp. 93-101.

1082. **McLeod, D.M.** "Liquor Control in the North-West Territories: The Permit System, 1870-1891." *Sask. Hist.* 16 (Autumn 1963), pp. 81-89.

1083. **McLeod, R.C.** *The North-West Mounted Police and Law Enforcement, 1873-1905.* Toronto: University of Toronto Press, 1975.

1084. ―――. "Canadianizing the West: The North-West Mounted Police as Agents of the National Policy, 1873-1905." In Lewis H. Thomas, ed. *Essays on Western History* (Edmonton, 1976), pp. 101-112.

1085. **Macoun, J.** *Manitoba and the Great North-West.* Guelph: World Publishing Co., 1882.

1086. **Mitchener, E.A.** "The North Saskatchewan River Settlement Claims, 1883-84." In Lewis H. Thomas, ed. *Essays on Western History* (Edmonton, 1976), pp. 129-146.

1087. **Morgan, E.C.** "The Bell Farm [N.W.T.]." *Sask. Hist.* 19 (Spring 1966), pp. 41-60.

1088. ―――. "The North West Mounted Police, 1873-1883." M.A. Thesis (University of Saskatchewan, Regina, 1970).

1089. ―――. "The North West Mounted Police: Internal Problems and Public Criticism, 1874-1883." *Sask. Hist.* 26 (Spring 1973), pp. 41-62.

1090. **Morice, A.G.** *The Catholic Church in the Canadian Northwest.* Winnipeg: The Author, 1936.

1091. **Morrison, W.R.** "The North-West Mounted Police and the Klondike Gold Rush." *Journal of Contemporary History* 9 (1974), pp. 93-105.

1092. **Motherwell, W.R.** "The Territorial Grain Growers' Association." *Sask. Hist.* 8 (Autumn 1955), pp. 108-112.
1093. **Murray, L.H.** "St. John's College, Qu'Appelle, 1885-1894." *Sask. Hist.* 11 (Winter 1958), pp. 1-17.
1094. **Neatby, Hilda.** "The Medical Profession in the North-West Territories." *Sask. Hist.* 2 (Spring 1949), pp. 1-15.
1095. **Nicholson, L.H.** "North-West Mounted Police 1873-1885: 'Highlights of the First Years.'" *Canadian Geographical Journal* 86 (1973), pp. 142-154.
1096. **Oliver, E.H.** "The Beginning of White Settlement in the Provincial District of Saskatchewan, 1870-1891." Royal Society of Canada. *Proceedings and Transactions* 3d ser. 19 (1925), sec. 2, pp. 83-129.
1097. ———. *The Canadian North West: Its Early Development and Legislative Records.* 2 vols. Ottawa: King's Printer, 1915.
1098. **Parley, K.** "Moffat, Assiniboia, North-West Territories." *Sask. Hist.* 20 (Winter 1967), pp. 32-36.
1099. **Poelzer, Irene A.** "The Catholic Normal School Issue in the North-West Territories, 1884-1900." Canadian Catholic Historical Association. *Study Sessions 1975*, pp. 5-28.
1100. **Raby, S.** "Prairie Fires in the North-West." *Sask. Hist.* 19 (Autumn 1966), pp. 81-99.
1101. **Reid, A.N.** "Local Government in the North-West Territories: I. The Beginnings of Rural Local Government, 1883-1905." *Sask. Hist.* 2 (Winter 1949), pp. 1-13.
1102. ———. "Local Government in the North-West Territories: II. The Rural Municipalities." *Sask. Hist.* 2 (Autumn 1949), pp. 1-14.
1103. ———. "Local Government in the North-West Territories: III. The Villages." *Sask. Hist.* 4 (Spring 1951), pp. 41-56.
1104. ———. "Urban Municipalities in the North-West Territories: Their Development and Machinery of Government." *Sask. Hist.* 9 (Spring 1956), pp. 41-62.
1105. ———. "Functions of Urban Municipalities in the North-West Territories: Public Works and Public Utilities." *Sask. Hist.* 10 (Autumn 1957), pp. 81-96.
1106. **Saskatchewan Archives Board.** *Directory of Members of Parliament and Federal Elections for the North-West Territories and Saskatchewan, 1887-1966.* Regina and Saskatoon, 1967.
1107. ———. *Directory of the Council and Legislative Assembly of the North-West Territories, 1876-1905.* Regina and Saskatoon, 1970.

1108. **Sharp, P.F.** "Massacre at Cypress Hills," *Sask. Hist.* 7 (Autumn 1954), pp. 81-99.

1109. **Shortt, Adam.** "Some Observations on the Great North-West." *Queen's Quarterly* 2 (1894), pp. 183-197.

1110. ———. "Some Observations on the Great Northwest: Social and Economic Conditions." *Queen's Quarterly* 3 (1895), pp. 11-22.

1111. **Silver, A.I.** "French-Canadian Attitudes Towards the North-West and North-West Settlement, 1870-1890." M.A. Thesis (McGill University, 1966).

1112. **Spector, David.** "The 1883 Locomotive Engineers' Strike in the Canadian North West." *Manitoba Pageant* 22 (Autumn 1976), pp. 1-4.

1113. **Stabler, J.C.** "Factors Affecting the Development of a New Region: The Canadian Great Plains, 1870-1889." Regional Science Association. *Annals* 7 (1973), pp. 75-87.

1114. **Stanley, George F.G.** "The Man Who Sketched the Great March." In Hugh A. Dempsey, ed. *Men in Scarlet* (Calgary, 1974), pp. 27-49.

1115. **Steele, S.B.** *Forty Years in Canada: Reminiscences of the Great North-West.* London, 1915.

1116. **Stewart, W.R.** "The Americanization of the Canadian Northwest." *The Cosmopolitan* 34 (1903), pp. 603-610.

1117. **Stuart, K.** "The Scottish Crofter Colony, Saltcoats, 1889-1904." *Sask. Hist.* 24 (Spring 1971), pp. 41-51.

1118. **Thomas, Jean McC.** "Homesteading at Indian Head." *Sask. Hist.* 4 (Spring 1951), pp. 68-71.

1119. **Thomas, L.G., ed.** *The Prairie West to 1905: A Canadian Sourcebook.* Toronto: Oxford University Press, 1975.

1120. **Thomas, Lewis H.** "The Constitutional Development of the North-West Territories, 1870-1888." M.A. Thesis (University of Saskatchewan, 1941).

1121. ———. "The Annual Reports of the Lieutenant-Governor of the North-West Territories." *Sask. Hist.* 1 (Spring 1948), pp. 10-15.

1122. ———. "The Lieutenant-Governor's Proclamations and Minutes." *Sask. Hist.* 1 (Autumn 1948), pp. 9-13.

1123. ———. "The Territorial Public Service." *Sask. Hist.* 2 (Spring 1949), pp. 14-18.

1124. ———. "Early Territorial Hospitals." *Sask. Hist.* 2 (Winter 1949), pp. 16-20.

Plate 7. Settler's House with Sod Roof

1125. ———. "Lloyd George's Visit to the North-West, 1899." *Sask. Hist.* 3 (Winter 1950), pp. 17-22.

1126. ———. *The Struggle for Responsible Government in the North-West Territories, 1870-1897.* Toronto: University of Toronto Press, 1956.

1127. ———. *The North-West Territories, 1870-1905.* Canadian Historical Association Booklet 26. Ottawa: Canadian Historical Association, 1970.

1128. Thomas, Lewis H., ed. "Documents of Western History: The Edwin J. Brooks Letters, Part II [1883]." *Sask. Hist.* 11 (Winter 1958), pp. 30-37.

1129. Thompson, W.T. "Adventures of a Surveyor in the Canadian North-West, 1880-1883 [Introduction by Lewis H. Thomas]." *Sask. Hist.* 3 (Autumn 1950), pp. 81-98.

1130. Turner, Allan R. "The Letters of P.G. Laurie [Editor, *Saskatchewan Herald*, 1878-1903]." *Sask. Hist.* 14 (Spring 1961), pp. 41-63.

1131. Turner, John Peter. "When the Mounted Police Went West—Part 1." *Canadian Geographical Journal* 10 (1935), pp. 53-62.

1132. ———. "When the Mounted Police Went West—Part 2." *Canadian Geographical Journal* 10 (1935), pp. 107-114.

1133. ———. *The North-West Mounted Police, 1873-1893.* 2 vols. Ottawa: King's Printer, 1950.

1134. **Ward, W. Peter.** "The Administration of Justice in the North-West Territory, 1870-1887." M.A. Thesis (University of Alberta, 1968).

1135. **Wickett, S.M.** "Municipal Home Rule in the North-West Territories." *Canadian Magazine* 26 (1905), pp. 67-69.

1136. ———. "Municipal Government in the North-West Territories." In S.M. Wickett, ed. *Municipal Government in Canada* (Toronto, 1907), pp. 149-164.

1137. **Wood, Kerry.** *The Queen's Cowboy.* Toronto: Macmillan, 1960.

4

Manitoba

a. General

1138. **Alexander, Mary H.T.** *Fort Prince of Wales.* Toronto: Ryerson, 1930.
1139. **Begg, Alexander.** *The Creation of Manitoba.* Toronto: Hunter, Rose, 1871.
1140. **Bonenfant, J.-C.** "La Dualité linguistique au Manitoba." Royal Society of Canada. *Proceedings and Transactions* 4th ser. 8 (1970), pp. 133-140.
1141. **Bryce, George.** *Manitoba: Its Infancy, Growth and Present Condition.* London: Marston, Searle & Rivington, 1882.
1142. ———. *A History of Manitoba: Its Resources and People.* Toronto: Canada History Co., 1906.
1143. **Canada Press Club.** *The Multilingual Press in Manitoba.* Winnipeg, 1974.
1144. **Carlyle, W.J.** "The Relationships between Settlement and the Physical Environment in Part of the West Lake Area of Manitoba, 1878-1963." M.A. Thesis (University of Manitoba, 1965).
1145. **Chorney, Harold.** "The Political Economy of Provincial Economic Development Policy: A Case Study of Manitoba." M.A. Thesis (University of Manitoba, 1970).
1146. **Cole, Douglas L.** "John S. Ewart and Canadian Nationalism." Canadian Historical Association. *Historical Papers 1969,* pp. 62-73.
1147. **Constantin-Weyer, M.** *Manitoba.* Paris: F. Rieder, 1923.
1148. **Dorge, L.** *Le Manitoba, reflets d'un passé.* Saint-Boniface: Editions du Blé, 1976.

1149. **Dowse, Thomas.** *Manitoba and the Canadian Northwest.* St. Paul: The Author, 1879.
1150. **Duncan, D.M.** *A History of Manitoba and the Northwest Territories.* Toronto: Gage, 1902.
1151. **Elias, P.D.** *Metropolis and Hinterland in Northern Manitoba.* Winnipeg: Manitoba Museum of Man and Nature, 1975.
1152. **Ewart, John S.** *The Manitoba School Question, Being a Compilation of the Legislation, the Legal Proceedings before the Governor General-in-Council. An Historical Account of the Red River Outbreak in 1869 and 1870, Its Causes, and Its Successes as Shown in the Treaty— The Manitoba Act—and a Short Summary of Protestant Promises.* Toronto: Copp Clark, 1894.
1153. **Frémont, Donatien.** *Mgr. Taché et la naissance du Manitoba.* Winnipeg: La Liberté, 1930.
1154. ———. "Archbishop Taché and the Beginnings of Manitoba." *North Dakota Historical Quarterly* 6 (1932), pp. 107-146.
1155. **Friesen, John.** "Expansion of Settlement in Manitoba, 1870-1890." H.S.S.M. *Transactions* Series III, 20 (1963-64), pp. 35-48.
1156. **Gibson, Dale, and Gibson, Lee.** *Substantial Justice: Law and Lawyers in Manitoba, 1670-1970.* Winnipeg: Peguis, 1970.
1157. **Gill, C.B.** "Manitoba's Northland Rediscovered." *Canadian Geographical Journal* 63 (1961), pp. 148-157.
1158. **Hall, Frank.** "How Manitoba Got Its Name." *Manitoba Pageant* 15 (Winter 1970), pp. 3-24.
1159. **Harrington, E.D.** *Manitoba Roundabout.* Toronto: Ryerson, 1951.
1160. **Hill, Robert B.** *Manitoba: History of Its Early Settlement, Development and Resources.* Toronto: William Briggs, 1890.
1161. **Hunter, B.F.C.** "The Development of New Manitoba, 1912-1930." M.A. Thesis (Western University, 1974).
1162. **Jackson, James A.** "The Disallowance of Manitoba Railway Legislation in the 1880s." M.A. Thesis (University of Manitoba, 1945).
1163. ———. *The Centennial History of Manitoba.* Toronto: McClelland and Stewart, 1970.
1164. **Jahn, H.E.** "Immigration and Settlement in Manitoba, 1870-1881: The Beginnings of a Pattern." M.A. Thesis (University of Manitoba, 1968).
1165. **Jones, R.L.** "The Ontario-Manitoba Boundary Dispute." M.A. Thesis (Queen's University, 1928).

1166. **Kavanagh, Martin.** *The Assiniboine Basin: A Social Study of the Discovery, Exploration, and Settlement of Manitoba.* Brandon: The Author, 1946.

1167. **Kemp, H.D.** "Land Grants under the Manitoba Act." H.S.S.M. *Transactions* Series III, 9 (1954), pp. 33-52.

1168. **Kitto, F.H.** *Manitoba, Canada: Its Resources and Development.* Ottawa: Department of the Interior, 1931.

1169. **Knox, H.C.** "Lake Winnipeg." *Canadian Geographical Journal* 13 (1936), pp. 31-36.

1170. **Lamb, J.E.** "Some Aspects of the Settlement Geography of Southern Manitoba." M.A. Thesis (University of Manitoba, 1970).

1171. **Legge, A.O.** *Sunny Manitoba: Its People and Its Industries.* London: T.F. Unwin, 1893.

1172. **Leslie, W.R.** "The Pembina Pocket: Manitoba's Garden Spot." *Canadian Geographical Journal* 63 (1961), pp. 76-83.

1173. **Lloyd, Trevor.** "Mapping Western Canada—The Red River Valley." *Canadian Geographical Journal* 26 (1943), pp. 230-239.

1174. **MacFarlane, R.O.** "Manitoba." *Canadian Geographical Journal* 35 (1947), pp. 124-152.

1175. **McIntyre, A.** *The Canadian West: A Geography of Manitoba and the Northwest Territories.* Toronto: Morang, 1904.

1176. **Mackie, Victor J.** "Manitoba—Province of Industry." *Canadian Geographical Journal* 41 (1950), pp. 166-181.

1177. **McWilliams, Margaret.** *Manitoba Milestones.* Toronto: Dent, 1928.

1178. **Macoun, J.** *Manitoba and the Great North-West.* Guelph: World Publishing Co., 1882.

1179. **Manitoba, University of.** *Manitoba Essays.* Toronto: Macmillan, 1937.

1180. **Megill, William J.** "Manitoba 1870-1970." *Canadian Geographical Journal* 81 (1970), pp. 38-47.

1181. **Moir, G., et al.** *Early Buildings of Manitoba.* Winnipeg: Peguis, 1973.

1182. **Morris, J.L.** "Old Fort Garry in 1881 and 1939." *Canadian Geographical Journal* 24 (1942), pp. 52-56.

1183. **Morton, W.L.** "Winnipeg and Manitoba, 1874-1922." *Manitoba Arts Review* 1 (Winter 1939), pp. 29-41.

1184. ———. *Northern Manitoba.* Winnipeg: Government of Manitoba, 1950.

1185. ———. *Manitoba: A History.* 1957. 2d. ed. Toronto: University of Toronto Press, 1967.
1186. ———. "Manitoba's Historic Role." H.S.S.M. *Transactions* Series III, 19 (1962-63), pp. 50-57.
1187. ———. "Raw Country." *Red River Valley Historian* (Summer 1974), pp. 3-7.
1188. **Morton, W.L.**, ed. *Manitoba: The Birth of a Province.* Altona: Manitoba Record Society, 1965.
1189. **Nelles, H.V.** "Public Ownership of Electrical Utilities in Manitoba and Ontario, 1906-1930." *C.H.R.* 57 (1976), pp. 461-484.
1190. **Pratt, A.M.** "Early Manitoba Rural Newspapers." H.S.S.M. *Transactions* Series III, 14 (1958-59), pp. 11-23.
1191. **Pritchett, John P.** "The Origin of the So-called Fenian Raid on Manitoba in 1871." *C.H.R.* 10 (1929), pp. 23-42.
1192. **Redikopp, H.I.** "An Analysis of the Social and Economic Problems of Four Small Communities in Northern Manitoba: Wabowden, Thicket Portage, Norway House, and Oxford House." M.A. Thesis (University of Manitoba, 1958).
1193. **Regehr, T.D.** "The National Policy and Manitoba Railway Legislation, 1879-1888." M.A. Thesis (Carleton University, 1963).
1193A. **Richtik, James M.** "A Historical Geography of the Interlake Area of Manitoba from 1871 to 1921." M.A. Thesis (University of Manitoba, 1964).
1194. **Richtik, James M.** "Manitoba Settlement: 1870-1886." Ph.D. Thesis (University of Minnesota, 1971).
1195. **Roscoe, A.A.** "The Manitoba Act in Transition, 1870-1896: The Transformation of Manitoba's French Canadian Politico-Cultural Institutions." M.A. Thesis (University of Manitoba, 1968).
1196. **Rudnychyj, J.B.** *Manitoba Mosaic of Place Names.* Winnipeg: Trident Press, 1970.
1197. **Russell, N.C.H.** "Photographic Highlights of the Architectural Historical Survey of Manitoba." *Manitoba Pageant* 14 (Winter 1969), pp. 4-23.
1198. **Schofield, Frank Howard.** *Manitoba, Pictorial and Biographical.* 2 vols. Winnipeg: S.J. Clark, 1913.
1199. **Seaman, H.S.** *Manitoba, Landmarks and Redletter Days, 1610-1920.* Winnipeg: The Author, 1920.

1200. **Spence, Thomas.** *Manitoba and the North-West of the Dominion.* Toronto: Hunter, Rose, 1871.
1201. **Stanley, George F.G.** "L'Invasion fénienne au Manitoba—un journal contemporain." *Revue d'histoire de l'Amérique française* 17 (1963), pp. 258-268.
1202. **Stuart, J.A.D.** *The Prairie W.A.S.P.: A History of the Rural Municipality of Oakland, Manitoba.* Winnipeg: Prairie Publishing Co., 1969.
1203. **Thomas, C.T.** "Birth Pangs of a National Park [Riding Mountain National Park]." *Manitoba Pageant* 15 (Autumn 1969), pp. 2-17.
1204. **Tyrrell, J.B.**, ed. *Report on North-Western Manitoba.* Ottawa: Queen's Printer, 1892.
1205. **Vanderhill, B.G.** "The Success of Government Sponsored Settlement in Manitoba." *Journal of Geography* 61 (1962), pp. 152-162.
1206. **Wallace, R.C.** "The New North in Manitoba." *Canadian Geographical Journal* 3 (1931), pp. 393-409.
1207. **Warkentin, J.H.** "Manitoba Settlement Patterns." H.S.S.M. *Transactions* Series III, 16 (1961), pp. 62-77.
1208. **Warkentin, J.H., and Ruggles, R.I.**, eds. *Manitoba Historical Atlas.* Winnipeg: Manitoba Historical Society, 1970.
1209. **Watson, Robert.** *Lower Fort Garry: A History of the Stone Fort.* Winnipeg: Hudson's Bay Company, 1928.
1210. ———. "The Story of Norway House." *Canadian Geographical Journal* 1 (1930), pp. 291-303.
1211. ———. "One Hundred Years of Lower Fort Garry." *Canadian Geographical Journal* 3 (1931), pp. 199-211.
1212. **Wright, Norman E.** *In View of Turtle Hill: A Survey of the History of Southwestern Manitoba to 1900.* Deloraine: Deloraine *Times*, 1951.
1213. **Young, George.** *Manitoba Memories, Leaves from My Life in the Prairie Province, 1868-1884.* Toronto: William Briggs, 1897.

b. The People

1214. **Arnold, A.J.** "Earliest Jews in Winnipeg, 1874-1882." *The Beaver* Outfit 304 (1974), pp. 4-12.

1215. **Backeland, L.L.** "The Franco-Manitobans: A Study in Cultural Loss." M.A. Thesis (University of Manitoba, 1971).

1215A. **Backeland, L.L., and Frideres, J.S.** "Franco-Manitobans and Cultural Loss: A Fourth Generation." *Prairie Forum* 2 (1977), pp. 1-8.

1216. **Benoit, D.P.** *Vie de Monseigneur Taché, archévêque de St. Boniface.* 2 vols. Montreal: Librairie Beauchemin, 1904.

1217. **Bilash, B.N.** "Bilingual Public Schools in Manitoba, 1897-1916." M.Ed Thesis (University of Manitoba, 1960).

1218. **Bonenfant, J.-C.** "La Dualité linguistique au Manitoba." Royal Society of Canada. *Proceedings and Transactions* 4th ser. 8 (1970), pp. 133-140.

1219. **Canadian Association of Social Workers.** *The Métis of Manitoba.* Winnipeg: Winnipeg Foundation, 1949.

1220. **Chiel, Arthur A.** *Jewish Experiences in Early Manitoba.* Winnipeg: Manitoba Jewish Publications, 1955.

1221. ———. *The Jews in Manitoba.* Toronto: University of Toronto Press, 1961.

1222. **Cook, Ramsay.** "John W. Dafoe: Conservative Progressive." Canadian Historical Association. *Annual Report 1961,* pp. 75-85.

1223. **Correll, Ernst.** "Mennonite Immigration into Manitoba: Sources and Documents, 1872, 1873." *Mennonite Quarterly* 11 (1937), pp. 196-227.

1224. ———. "Mennonite Immigration into Manitoba: Sources and Documents, 1872, 1873." *Mennonite Quarterly* 11 (1937), pp. 267-283.

1225. ———. "Mennonite Immigration into Manitoba: Documents and Sources, 1873-1874." *Mennonite Quarterly* 22 (1948), pp. 43-57.

1226. **Davidson, C.B.** *Population of Manitoba.* Winnipeg: King's Printer, 1938.

1227. **Dorge, L.** *Introduction à l'étude des Franco-Manitobains: Essai historique et bibliographique.* Saint-Boniface: La Société historique de Saint-Boniface, 1973.

1228. **Drache, H.M.** *The Challenge of the Prairies: Life and Times of Red River Pioneers.* Fargo: North Dakota Institute for Regional Studies, 1970.

1229. **Emery, George N.** "The Methodist Church and the 'European Foreigners' of Winnipeg: The All Peoples Mission, 1889-1914." H.S.S.M. *Transactions* Series III, 28 (1971-72), pp. 85-100.

1230. **Entz, W.** "German Language Newspapers of Manitoba before World War I." *Canadian Ethnic Studies* 2 (1970), pp. 59-66.

1230A. **Epp, O.J.** "The Manitoba Mennonite Brethern Population: Migration and Distribution." M.A. Thesis (University of North Dakota, 1968).

1231. **Ferguson, George V.** *John W. Dafoe.* Toronto: Ryerson, 1948.

1232. **Fowke, Edith.** "Songs of a Manitoba Family." *Canadian Folk Music Journal* 3 (1975), pp. 35-46.

1233. **Francis, E.K.** "The Origins of Mennonite Institutions in Early Manitoba." H.S.S.M. *Transactions* Series III, 2 (1945-46), pp. 56-71.

1234. ———. "Mennonite Institutions in Early Manitoba: A Study on Their Origins." *Agricultural History* 22 (1948), pp. 144-155.

1235. ———. *In Search of Utopia: Mennonites in Manitoba.* Altona: D.W. Friesen and Sons, 1955.

1236. **Giraud, Marcel.** "A Note on the Half-Breed Problem in Manitoba." *C.J.E.P.S.* 3 (1937), pp. 541-549.

1237. **Gordon, A.** "The Winnipeg Jewish Community: Patterns of Leadership in an Ethnic Subcommunity." M.A. Thesis (University of Manitoba, 1972).

1237A. **Haig, Kennethe M.** *Brave Harvest: The Life Story of E. Cora Hind, L.L.D.* Toronto: Thomas Allen, 1945.

1238. **Harvey, Robert.** *Pioneers of Manitoba.* Winnipeg: Prairie Publishing Company, 1970.

1239. **Herstein, Harvey H.** "The Growth of the Winnipeg Jewish Community and the Evolution of Its Educational Institutions." M.Ed. Thesis (University of Manitoba, 1964).

1240. ———. "The Growth of the Winnipeg Jewish Community and the Evolution of Its Educational Institutions." H.S.S.M. *Transactions* Series III, 22 (1965-66), pp. 27-66.

1241. **Hofer, Peter.** *The Hutterite Brethren and Their Beliefs.* Starbuck: Hutterite Brethren of Manitoba, 1955.

1242. **Hubicz, E.** *Polish Churches in Manitoba.* Winnipeg: Vatra, 1962.

1243. **Iutcovich, M.J.** "A Comparative Study of the Process of Acculturation among Certain Groups of Immigrants in the Province of Manitoba." M.A. Thesis (University of Manitoba, 1962).

1243A. **Jahn, H.E.** "Immigration and Settlement in Manitoba, 1871-1881: The Beginnings of a Pattern." M.A. Thesis (University of Manitoba, 1968).

1244. **Kirkconnell, Watson.** "Ukrainian Literature in Manitoba." *Mosaic* 3 (Spring 1970), pp. 39-47.
1245. **Klippenstein, L., ed.** "A Visit to Manitoba in 1873: The Russian Mennonite Delegation." *Canada* 3 (1975), pp. 48-61.
1246. **Krawchuk, P.** *The Ukrainians in Winnipeg's First Century.* Toronto: Kobzar Publishing Company, 1974.
1247. **Kristjanson, W.** *The Icelandic People in Manitoba: A Manitoba Saga.* Winnipeg: Wallingford Press, 1965.
1248. **Legasse, Jean H.** "The Métis in Manitoba." H.S.S.M. *Transactions* Series III, 15 (1960), pp. 39-58.
1249. **Legasse, Jean H., ed.** *A Study of the Population of Indian Ancestry Living in Manitoba.* Winnipeg: Social and Economic Research Office, Department of Agriculture and Immigration, 1959.
1250. **Landa, M.J.** "Easterville: A Case Study in the Relocation of a Manitoba Native Community." M.A. Thesis (University of Manitoba, 1969).
1251. **Lecompte, Edouard.** *Un Grand Chrétien, Sir Joseph Dubuc, 1840-1914.* Montreal: Imp. du Messager, 1923.
1252. **Levadie, M.** "John W. Dafoe and the Evolution of Canadian Autonomy, 1918-1926." M.A. Thesis (University of Manitoba, 1952).
1253. **MacBeth, R.G.** *Sir Augustus Nanton: A Biography.* Toronto: Macmillan, 1931.
1254. **MacFarlane, R.O.** "A Law-Abiding Rebel: John Christian Schultz." *Manitoba Arts Review* 1 (Spring 1939), pp. 21-26.
1255. **McRaye, W.J.** *Pioneers and Prominent People of Manitoba.* Winnipeg: Canadian Publicity Co., 1925.
1256. **Manitoba Library Association.** *Pioneers and Early Citizens of Manitoba: A Dictionary of Manitoba Biography from the Earliest Times to 1920.* Winnipeg: Peguis, 1971.
1257. **Marunchak, M.H.** *Studies in the History of Ukrainians in Canada. Vol. 2. History of Socio-Cultural Development of Ukrainians in Manitoba: Pioneer Era, Pt. 1.* Winnipeg: Ukrainian Free Academy of Science, 1966.
1258. **Medovy, H.** "Early Jewish Physicians in Manitoba." H.S.S.M. *Transactions* Series III, 29 (1972-73), pp. 23-40.
1258A. **Merrill, L.I.** "Population Distribution in the Riding Mountains and Adjacent Plains of Manitoba and Saskatchewan, 1879-1946." M.A. Thesis (McGill University, 1953).

1259. **Mott, M.K.** "The 'Foreign Peril': Nativism in Winnipeg, 1916-1923." M.A. Thesis (University of Manitoba, 1970).
1260. **Pelletier, Emile.** *A Social History of the Manitoba Métis.* Winnipeg: Manitoba Métis Federation Press, 1974.
1261. **Penny, N.L.** "Marriage Patterns in an Ethnic Community in Rural Manitoba, 1896-1970." M.A. Thesis (University of Manitoba, 1972).
1262. **Percira, C.P.** "East Indians in Winnipeg: A Study of the Consequences of Immigration for an Ethnic Group in Canada." M.A. Thesis (University of Manitoba, 1971).
1263. **Peters, Victor J.** "The Hutterians." H.S.S.M. *Transactions* Series III, 17 (1964), pp. 6-14.
1264. ———. *All Things Common: The Hutterian Way of Life.* Minneapolis: University of Minnesota Press, 1965.
1265. **Pettipas, K.,** ed. *The Diary of the Reverend Henry Budd, 1870-1875.* Winnipeg: Manitoba Record Society, 1974.
1266. **Reece, J.** "The Dynamics of Population Change in Manitoba and Some Implications for Planning." M.C.P. Thesis (University of Manitoba, 1973).
1267. **Richtik, James M.** "Manitoba: Population and Settlement in 1870." In A.H. Paul and E.H. Dale, eds. *Southern Prairies Field Excursion: Background Papers* (Regina, 1972), pp. 29-44.
1268. **Rosenberg, L.** *The Jewish Community in Winnipeg.* Montreal: Canadian Jewish Congress, 1946.
1269. **Rowan, M.L.** "Saint-Claude, Manitoba: A Demographic Analysis." M.A. Thesis (University of Manitoba, 1973).
1270. **Ryan, John.** "The Economic Significance of Hutterite Colonies in Manitoba." In A.H. Paul and E.H. Dale, eds. *Southern Prairies Field Excursion: Background Papers* (Regina, 1972), pp. 21-28.
1271. ———. *The Agricultural Economy of Manitoba Hutterite Colonies.* Toronto: McClelland and Stewart, 1977.
1272. **Sawchuk, J.** "The Métis of Manitoba: Reformulation of an Ethnic Identity." M.A. Thesis (University of Manitoba, 1973).
1273. **Sawatsky, H.L.** "Viability of Ethnic Group Settlement, with Reference to Mennonites in Manitoba." *Canadian Ethnic Studies* 2 (1970), pp. 147-160.
1274. **Schimnowski, F.M.** "Douze années d'immigration française au Manitoba." M.A. Thesis (Université d'Ottawa, 1950).

1275. Sharp, E.F., and Kristjanson, G.A. *The People of Manitoba, 1951-1961.* Ottawa: Queen's Printer, 1966.
1276. Stanton, J.B. *Métis in Manitoba.* Winnipeg: Manitoba Museum of Man and Nature, 1971.
1277. Toews, J.G., and Klippenstein, L., ed. *Manitoba Mennonite Memories: A Century Past but Not Forgotten.* Altona and Steinbach: Manitoba Mennonite Centennial Committee, 1974.
1278. Turek, Victor. *Poles in Manitoba.* Toronto: Polish Alliance Press, 1967.
1279. Warkentin, J.H. "Mennonite Agricultural Settlements of Southern Manitoba." *Geographical Review* 49 (1959), pp. 342-368.
1280. ———. "The Mennonite Settlements of Southern Manitoba." Ph.D. Thesis (University of Toronto, 1960).
1281. Weir, T.R. "Pioneer Settlement of Southwest Manitoba, 1879-1901." *Canadian Geographer* 8 (1964), pp. 64-71.
1282. Willows, A. "A History of the Mennonites, Particularly in Manitoba." M.A. Thesis (University of Manitoba, 1924).
1283. Wong, W.H. "A Statistical Analysis of Selected Population Characteristics for Ninety Settlements in Manitoba." M.A. Thesis (University of Manitoba, 1971).
1284. Woolworth, Nancy L. "Gingras, St. Joseph and the Métis in the Northern Red River Valley: 1843-1873." *North Dakota History* 42 (1975), pp. 16-27.
1285. Yuzyk, Paul. *The Ukrainians in Manitoba: A Social History.* Toronto: University of Toronto Press, 1953.

c. Government and Politics

1286. Bowles, R.S. "Adams George Archibald: First Lieutenant-Governor of Manitoba." H.S.S.M. *Transactions* Series III, 25 (1968-69), pp. 75-88.
1286A. Beaulieu, Paul. "The Transfer of Electoral Allegiance in Ethnic Politics: A Study of the Voting Behaviour of Franco-Manitobans, 1969-1974." M.A. Thesis (University of Manitoba, 1976).
1287. Bray, R.M. "The Role of Clifford Sifton in the Formulation of the Editorial Policy of the *Manitoba Free Press,* 1916-1921." M.A. Thesis (University of Manitoba, 1968).

1288. **Chisisk, E.** "The Development of Winnipeg's Socialist Movement, 1900 to 1915." M.A. Thesis (University of Manitoba, 1972).

1289. **Clague, R.E.** "The Political Aspects of the Manitoba School Question, 1890-1896." M.A. Thesis (University of Manitoba, 1939).

1290. **Clark, W.L.R.** "Politics in Brandon City, 1899-1946." Ph.D. Thesis (University of Alberta, 1976).

1291. **Cooke, E.** "The Federal Election of 1896 in Manitoba." M.A. Thesis (University of Manitoba, 1943).

1292. **Creighton, Donald G.** "Macdonald and Manitoba." *The Beaver* Outfit 287 (1957), pp. 12-17.

1293. **Crunican, P.E.** "The Manitoba School Question and Canadian Federal Politics, 1890-1896." Ph.D. Thesis (University of Toronto, 1968).

1294. ———. *Priests and Politicians: Manitoba Schools and the Election of 1896.* Toronto: University of Toronto Press, 1974.

1295. **Donnelly, M.S.** "Parliamentary Government in Manitoba." *C.J.E.P.S.* 23 (1957), pp. 20-32.

1296. ———. *The Government of Manitoba.* Toronto: University of Toronto Press, 1963.

1297. **Eyler, Philip.** "Public Ownership and Politics in Manitoba, 1900-1915." M.A. Thesis (University of Manitoba, 1972).

1298. **Fisher, M.** "Local Government Reorganization." H.S.S.M. *Transactions* Series III, 17 (1964), pp. 15-23.

1299. **Fisk, Larry J.** "Controversy on the Prairies: Issues in the General Provincial Elections of Manitoba, 1870-1969." Ph.D. Thesis (University of Alberta, 1975).

1300. **Griezic, F.J.K.** "The Honourable Thomas Alexander Crerar, Marquette Riding, and the Union Government Election of 1917." H.S.S.M. *Transactions* Series III, 28 (1971-72), pp. 101-116.

1301. **Guest, H.J.** "The Old Man's Son—Sir Hugh John Macdonald." H.S.S.M. *Transactions* Series III, 29 (1972-73), pp. 49-68.

1302. **Hicks, D.C.** "An Evaluation of Provincial Planning Services to Local Governments in Manitoba." M.A. Thesis (University of Manitoba, 1974).

1303. **Holmes, J.L.** "Factors Affecting Politics in Manitoba: A Study of Provincial Elections, 1870-1899." M.A. Thesis (University of Manitoba, 1939).

1304. **Hutchings, C.J.** "Municipal Taxation in Manitoba." M.A. Thesis (University of Manitoba, 1927).

1305. **Inglis, A.I.** "Some Political Factors in the Demise of the Roblin Government, 1915." M.A. Thesis (University of Manitoba, 1968).

1306. **Jackson, James A.** "Disallowance of Manitoba Railway Legislation in the 1880s: Railway Policy as a Factor in the Relations of Manitoba with the Dominion." M.A. Thesis (University of Manitoba, 1945).

1307. **King, T.P.** "Taxation in Manitoba, Provincial and Municipal." M.A. Thesis (University of Manitoba, 1926).

1308. **McAllister, J.** "Ethnic Participation in Canadian Legislatures: The Case of Manitoba." *Canadian Ethnic Studies* 3 (1971), pp. 77-94.

1309. **MacBeth, M.E.** "Life and Work of the Honourable John Norquay." M.A. Thesis (University of Manitoba, 1925).

1310. **McCormack, A.R.** "Arthur Puttee and the Liberal Party: 1899-1904." *C.H.R.* 51 (1970), pp. 141-163.

1311. ———. "Radical Politics in Winnipeg, 1899-1915." H.S.S.M. *Transactions* Series III, 29 (1972-73), pp. 81-98.

1312. **McCormick, David.** "The Dissolution of the Coalition—Roblin's Rise to Leadership." H.S.S.M. *Transactions* Series III, 28 (1971-72), pp. 5-36.

1313. **McCutcheon, Brian R.** "The Patrons of Industry in Manitoba, 1890-1898." H.S.S.M. *Transactions* Series III, 22 (1965-66), pp. 7-26.

1314. ———. "The Economic and Social Structure of Political Agrarianism in Manitoba, 1870-1900." Ph.D. Thesis (University of British Columbia, 1974).

1315. **McKillop, A.B.** "Citizen and Socialist: The Ethos of Political Winnipeg, 1919-1935." M.A. Thesis (University of Manitoba, 1970).

1316. **Macleod, G.P.** "Sir Hugh John Macdonald." H.S.S.M. *Transactions* Series III, 14 (1958-59), pp. 24-32.

1317. **Maxwell, J.A.** "Financial Relations between Manitoba and the Dominion, 1870-86." *C.H.R.* 15 (1934), pp. 376-389.

1318. **Miller, J.R.** "D'Alton McCarthy, Equal Rights, and the Origins of the Manitoba School Question." *C.H.R.* 54 (1973), pp. 369-392.

1319. **Milligan, Frank A.** "The Lieutenant-Governorship in Manitoba, 1870-1882." M.A. Thesis (University of Manitoba, 1948).

1319A. **Ogmundson, Rick.** "A Social Profile of Members of the Manitoba Legislature, 1950, 1960, 1970." *Journal of Canadian Studies* 12, no. 4 (1977), pp. 79-84.

1320. **Orlikow, L.** "The Reform Movement in Manitoba, 1910-1915." H.S.S.M. *Transactions* Series III, 16 (1961), pp. 50-61.
1321. **Peterson, T.** "Manitoba: Ethnic and Class Politics in Manitoba." In M. Robin, ed. *Canadian Provincial Politics* (Scarborough, 1972), pp. 69-115.
1322. **Province of Manitoba.** *Manitoba's Case: A Submission Presented to the Royal Commission on Dominion-Provincial Relations by the Government of the Province of Manitoba.* Winnipeg: King's Printer, 1937.
1323. **Rea, J.E.** "The Politics of Conscience: Winnipeg after the Strike." Canadian Historical Association. *Historical Papers 1971*, pp. 276-288.
1324. ————. "Parties and Power: An Analysis of Winnipeg City Council, 1919-1975." Appendix IV. *Report and Recommendations.* Committee of Review, City of Winnipeg Act. Winnipeg: Department of Urban Affairs, 1976.
1325. ————. "The Politics of Class: Winnipeg City Council, 1919-1945." In Carl Berger and Ramsay Cook, eds. *The West and the Nation* (Toronto, 1976), pp. 232-249.
1326. **Ready, W.G.** "Political Factors Affecting the Manitoba School Question, 1896-1916." M.A. Thesis (University of Manitoba, 1948).
1327. **Ross, Hugh R.** *Thirty-Five Years in the Limelight: Sir Rodmond P. Roblin and His Times.* Winnipeg: *Farmer's Advocate,* 1936.
1328. **Stinson, L.** *Political Warriors: Recollections of a Social Democrat.* Winnipeg: Queenston House, 1975.
1329. **Turenne, R.E.** "The Minority and the Ballot Box: A Study of the Voting Behaviour of the French-Canadians of Manitoba, 1898-1967." M.A. Thesis (University of Manitoba, 1970).
1330. **Wilson, J.** "The Decline of the Liberals in Manitoba Politics." *Journal of Canadian Studies* 10 (February 1975), pp. 24-41.
1331. **Wiseman, Nelson.** "The CCF and the Manitoba 'Non-partisan' Government of 1940." *C.H.R.* 54 (1973), pp. 175-193.

d. *Agriculture and Rural Development*

1332. **Beddone, H.C.J.** "Labor and Mechanization on Manitoba Farms." M.Sc. Thesis (University of Manitoba, 1970).
1333. **Dauphin Historical Society.** *Dauphin Valley Spans the Years.* Dauphin: The Society, 1970.

1333A. **De Lisle, D.** "The Spatial Organization and Intensity of Agriculture in the Mennonite Villages of Southern Manitoba." Ph.D. Thesis (McGill University, 1975).

1334. **Drache, H.M.** "Bonanza Farming in the Red River Valley." H.S.S.M. *Transactions* Series III, 24 (1967-68), pp. 53-64.

1335. **Dugald Women's Institute.** *Springfield: First Rural Municipality in Manitoba, 1873-1973.* Dugald: The Institute, 1974.

1336. **Fahrni, M., and Morton, W.L.** *Third Crossing: A History of the First Quarter Century of the Town and District of Gladstone, Manitoba.* Winnipeg: W.L. Morton, 1946.

1337. **Fordham, R.C.** "The Structure of Manitoba's Agricultural Geography, 1951-1964." M.A. Thesis (University of Manitoba, 1966).

1338. **Friesen, John.** "The Manitoba Sugar Beet Industry—A Geographical Study." M.A. Thesis (University of Manitoba, 1962).

1339. **Garrioch, A.C.** *First Furrows: A History of the Early Settlement of Red River Country, Including That of Portage la Prairie.* Winnipeg: The Author, 1923.

1340. **Gilson, J.C., et al.** *The Report of the Manitoba Commission on Farm Organizations.* Winnipeg: Public Press Ltd., 1962.

1341. **Gordon, J.G.** "An Analysis of the Economic Policies of Farm Organizations in Manitoba, 1945-1962." M.A. Thesis (University of Manitoba, 1964).

1342. **Grant, H.C.** *Agricultural Income and Rural Municipal Government in Manitoba.* Winnipeg: Economic Survey Board, Province of Manitoba, 1939.

1343. **Guertin, E.K.** "A Geographic Study of Farm Depopulation in the Municipality of Ericsdale, 1941-1961." M.A. Thesis (University of Manitoba, 1968).

1344. **Hambley, G.H.** *Historical Records and Accounts of the Early Pioneers of the District of Swan Lake, Manitoba, 1873-1950.* Altona: D.W. Friesen and Sons, 1953.

1344A. **Lamb, James E.** "Some Aspects of the Settlement Geography of Southern Manitoba." M.A. Thesis (University of Manitoba, 1970).

1345. **Murray, S.N.** *The Valley Comes of Age: A History of Agriculture in the Valley of the Red River of the North, 1812-1920.* Fargo: North Dakota Institute for Regional Studies, 1967.

1346. **Newman, J.F.** "The Impact of Technology upon Rural Southwestern Manitoba, 1920-1930." M.A. Thesis (Queen's University, 1971).

Plate 8. Manitoba Department of Agriculture and Immigration Pamphlet, 1892

1347. **Panting, G.E.** "A Study of the United Farmers of Manitoba to 1928." M.A. Thesis (University of Manitoba, 1954).

1348. ———. "The Role of the United Farmers of Manitoba: 1920-1928." *Red River Valley Historian* (Summer 1974), pp. 8-14.

1349. **Quigley, Leo B.** "Agriculture, Fisheries, and Forestry in Manitoba." *Canadian Geographical Journal* 81 (1970), pp. 48-53.

1350. **Richtik, James M.** "Manitoba Settlement: 1870 to 1886." Ph.D. Thesis (University of Minnesota, 1971).

1351. ———. "Prairie Woodland and the Manitoba Escarpment: Settlement and Agricultural Development in Carlton Municipality to 1887." *Red River Valley Historian* (Summer 1976), pp. 16-26.

1352. **Robertson, Heather.** *Sugar Farmers of Manitoba.* Winnipeg: Manitoba Beet Grower's Association, 1968.

1353. **Rose, W.J.** "Early Minnedosa: The Crossing, the Town, and the Railway." H.S.S.M. *Transactions* Series III, 15 (1960), pp. 69-79.

1354. **Ryan, John.** *Mixed Farming near Carman, Manitoba.* Toronto: Ginn, 1968.

1355. ———. *The Agricultural Economy of Manitoba Hutterite Colonies.* Toronto: McClelland and Stewart, 1977.

1356. **Smith, C.E.** *The Swan River Valley, 1898-1958.* Minnedosa: The Author, 1958.

1357. **Somuyiwa, M.O.** "The Impact of Agricultural Credit Use on the Financial Progress of the Farm Firm in Western Manitoba, 1961-69." M.Sc. Thesis (University of Manitoba, 1974).

1358. **Stewart, A.** "The Dauphin District." M.A. Thesis (University of Manitoba, 1932).

1359. **Stuart, J.A.D.** *The Prairie W.A.S.P.: A History of the Rural Municipality of Oakland, Manitoba.* Winnipeg: Prairie Publishing, 1969.

1360. **Théoret, A.E.** *Sainte Rose-du-Lac.* Winnipeg: G.C. Murray, 1948.

1361. **Vanderhill, B.G.** "Post War Agricultural Settlement in Manitoba." *Economic Geography* 35 (1959), pp. 259-268.

1362. **Warkentin, J.H.** "The Geography of the Dauphin Area." M.A. Thesis (University of Toronto, 1954).

1363. ———. "The Dauphin Area—An Example of Regional Differentiation in the Canadian West." *Canadian Geographer* 1 (1955), pp. 71-83.

1364. ———. "Mennonite Agricultural Settlement of Southern Manitoba." *Geographical Review* 49 (1959), pp. 242-268.

1365. **Weir, T.R.** "Pioneer Settlement of Southwest Manitoba, 1879-1901." *Canadian Geographer* 8 (1964), pp. 64-71.

e. Economic Development and Labour

1366. **Avery, Donald.** "The Radical Alien and the Winnipeg General Strike of 1919." In Carl Berger and Ramsay Cook, eds. *The West and the Nation* (Toronto, 1976), pp. 209-231.

1367. **Balawyder, T., ed.** *The Winnipeg General Strike.* Problems in Canadian History Series. Vancouver, Toronto, and Montreal: Copp Clark, 1967.

1368. **Balian, O.S.** *The Caisse Populaire: A French-Canadian Economic Institution in Manitoba.* Winnipeg: University of Manitoba, 1975.

1369. **Bercuson, David J.** "The Winnipeg General Strike, Collective Bargaining, and the One Big Union Issue." *C.H.R.* 51 (1970), pp. 164-176.

1370. ———. "Labour in Winnipeg: The Great War and the General Strike." Ph.D. Thesis (University of Toronto, 1971).

1371. ———. *Confrontation at Winnipeg: Labor, Industrial Relations, and the General Strike.* Montreal: McGill-Queen's University Press, 1974.

1372. ———. "The Winnipeg General Strike." In Irving M. Abella, ed. *On Strike: Six Key Labour Struggles in Canada, 1919-1949.* (Toronto, 1974), pp. 1-32.

1373. **Careless, J.M.S.** "The Development of the Winnipeg Business Community." Royal Society of Canada. *Proceedings and Transactions* 4th ser. 8 (1970), pp. 239-254.

1373A. **Chorney, Harold.** "The Political Economy of Provincial Economic Development Policy: A Case Study of Manitoba." M.A. Thesis (University of Manitoba, 1970).

1373B. **Cline, John A.** "The Nelson River Hydro-Electric Development: A Public Utility Investment affecting Both Regional and national Development." M.A. Thesis (University of Manitoba, 1968).

1374. **Cowan, J.G.** "Manitoba's Black Gold." *Canadian Geographical Journal* 53 (1956), pp. 84-93.

1375. **Davidson, C.B.** *Employment in Manitoba.* Winnipeg: Economic Survey Board, Province of Manitoba, 1938.

1376. **Dillabough, J.V.** *Transportation in Manitoba.* Winnipeg: Economic Survey Board, Province of Manitoba, 1938.

1377. **Douglas, William.** *The House of Shea: The Story of a Pioneer Industry.* Winnipeg: Bulman Brothers, 1947.

1378. **Earl, L.** "Manitoba." *Western Business and Industry* 37 (July 1963), pp. 25-44. [A continuing feature.]

1379. **Gardiner, A.G.** "The Electrical Power Industry of Manitoba: An Economic Analysis." M.A. Thesis (University of Manitoba, 1963).

1379A. **Good, W.S., and Beckman, M.D.** "A Prairie Distribution System in Transition: The Case of Farm Machinery Parts in Manitoba." *Prairie Forum* 2 (1977), pp. 43-56.

1380. **Grose, R.E.** "Manufacturing in Manitoba—Growth and Trends." *Canadian Geographical Journal* 46 (1953), pp. 84-110.

1381. **Grose, R.E., ed.** *Industrial Resources of Manitoba.* Winnipeg: Department of Industry and Commerce, 1954.

1382. **Johnson, T.A.** "The Needle Trades in Winnipeg: A Study in Trade Unions." M.A. Thesis (University of Manitoba, 1948).

1383. **Little, A.D.** *Economic Survey of Northern Manitoba.* Winnipeg: Department of Industry and Commerce, 1958.
1384. **Lowe, P.** "All Western Dollars [Alloway & Champion]." H.S.S.M. *Transactions* Series III, 2 (1945-46), pp. 10-25.
1385. **MacDowell, G.F.** *The Brandon Packers Strike: A Tragedy of Errors.* Toronto: McClelland and Stewart, 1971.
1386. **McLeod, D.R.** "Industry and Industrial Legislation in Manitoba." M.A. Thesis (University of Manitoba, 1931).
1387. **McNaught, K., and Bercuson, David J.** *The Winnipeg Strike: 1919.* Toronto: Longman, 1974.
1388. **Mardon, H.L.** "Manitoba's Economic and Industrial Progress." *Western Business and Industry* 40 (August 1966), pp. 3-39.
1389. **Masters, D.C.** *The Winnipeg General Strike.* Toronto: University of Toronto Press, 1950.
1390. **Moore, George A.** "Manitoba's Railways. Part I: The First Forty Years." *Canadian Rail* 282 (1975), pp. 199-221.
1391. ———. "Manitoba's Railways: Part II." *Canadian Rail* 285 (1975), pp. 294-311.
1392. **Nelles, H.V.** "Public Ownership of Electrical Utilities in Manitoba and Ontario, 1906-1930." *C.H.R.* 58 (1976), pp. 461-484.
1392A. **Partridge, Richard S.** "The Economic Efficiency of Publicly Owned Hydro-Electric Utilities with Specific Reference to Manitoba Hydro." M.A. Thesis (University of Manitoba, 1969).
1393. **Penner, Norman, ed.** *Winnipeg 1919: The Strikers Own History of the Winnipeg General Strike.* 1973. 2nd. ed. Toronto: James Lorimer, 1975.
1394. **Phillips, P.A.** "Women in the Manitoba Labour Market: A Study of Their Changing Economic Role." In H.C. Klassen, ed. *The Canadian West* (Calgary, 1977), pp. 79-92.
1395. **Rea, J.E., ed.** *The Winnipeg General Strike.* Canadian History through the Press Series. Toronto: Holt, Rinehart, and Winston, 1973.
1396. **Regehr, T.D.** "The National Policy and Manitoba Railway Legislation, 1879-1888." M.A. Thesis (Carleton University, 1963).
1397. **Rogge, J.R.** "Some Recent Economic Developments in Northern Manitoba." *Geography* 58 (1972), pp. 207-216.
1398. **Ross, D.S.G.** "History of the Electrical Industry in Manitoba." H.S.S.M. *Transactions* Series III, 20 (1963-64), pp. 49-70.

1398A. **Saper, Arthur M.** "Formulating a Regional Economic Development Strategy: The Key Industry Approach for Manitoba." M.A. Thesis (University of Manitoba, 1973).

1399. **Siegfried, N.R.** "Industrial Growth in Southern Manitoba: A Hopeful Example for the Prairie Provinces?" In B.M. Barr, ed. *The Kootenay Collection of Research Studies in Geography* (Vancouver: B.C. Geographical Series, no. 18, 1974), pp. 21-34.

1400. **Short, R.B.** "The Wholesale Function in Winnipeg." M.A. Thesis (University of Manitoba, 1973).

1401. **Snidal, D.J.** "Financial History of Manitoba from 1950 to 1965." M.A. Thesis (University of Manitoba, 1967).

1402. **Spector, David.** "Winnipeg's First Labour Unions." *Manitoba Pageant* 21 (Summer 1976), pp. 13-14.

1403. **Sutcliffe, J.H.** "The Economic Background of the Winnipeg General Strike: Wages and Working Conditions." M.A. Thesis (University of Manitoba, 1972).

1403A. **Thomas, Lillian Jean.** "A Test of Social Conflict Theory: The Case of the Winnipeg General Strike." M.A. Thesis (University of Manitoba, 1977).

1404. **Wallace, R.C.** *The Resources of Manitoba and Their Development.* Winnipeg: The University, 1918.

1405. **Weir, T.R.,** ed. *Economic Atlas of Manitoba.* Winnipeg: Department of Industry and Commerce, 1960.

1406. **Winkler, H.W.** "Early Manitoba Railroads." H.S.S.M. *Transactions* Series III, 10 (1953-54), pp. 5-13.

1407. **Woods, H.D.** "Labour Relations in the Public Service, Manitoba." *Industrial Relations* 30 (April 1975), pp. 3-27.

f. Education and Social and Cultural Development

1408. **Allen, Richard.** "Children of Prophecy: Wesley College Students in an Age of Reform [1890-1918]." *Red River Valley Historian* (Summer 1974), pp. 15-20.

1409. **Ariano, A.A., and Lam, Y.-L.J.** "French Language Instruction: A Closer Look at Schools in Southwestern Manitoba." *Prairie Forum* 1 (1976), pp. 151-162.

1410. **Bedford, Allen Gerald.** *The University of Winnipeg.* Toronto and Buffalo: University of Toronto Press, 1975.

1411. **Bellan, R.C.** "Relief in Winnipeg: The Economic Background." M.A. Thesis (University of Toronto, 1941).

1412. **Belton, G.S.** "A History of the Origin and Growth of Schools in the City of St. Boniface." M.Ed. Thesis (University of Manitoba, 1959).

1413. **Benoit, D.P.** *L'Anglomanic au Canada: Résumé historique de la question des écoles du Manitoba.* Trois Rivières: Trifluvien, 1899.

1414. **Bilash, B.C.** "Bilingual Public Schools in Manitoba, 1897-1916." M.Ed. Thesis (University of Manitoba, 1960).

1414A. **Bjarnason, Carl.** "The Brandon School System: A Historical Survey and Ten Year Development Program." M.Ed. Thesis (University of Manitoba, 1962).

1415. **Bock, J.** "An Analysis of the Educational Effort of a Single Enterprise Community: Flin Flon, Manitoba." M.Ed. Thesis (University of Manitoba, 1970).

1416. **Booth, W.G.** "A Report of the Introduction, Organization and Development of the Dauphin-Ochre School Area Number One." M.Ed. Thesis (University of Manitoba, 1958).

1417. **Chaiko, R.M.** "An Analysis of the Educational Effort of a Single Enterprise Community: Pinawa, Manitoba." M.Ed. Thesis (University of Manitoba, 1970).

1418. **Choquette, Robert.** "Adélard Langevin et les questions scholaires du Manitoba et du nord-ouest, 1895-1915." *Revue de l'Université d'Ottawa* 46 (1976), pp. 324-344.

1419. **Clark, J.N.R.** "The Development of Education in the Swan River Valley." M.Ed. Thesis (University of Manitoba, 1949).

1420. **Clark, Lovell,** ed. *The Manitoba School Question: Majority Rule or Minority Rights?* Toronto: Copp Clark, 1968.

1421. **Coleman, P.E.** "The Distribution of Educational Services in Manitoba: An Analysis of the Effects of Provincial Policies, with Proposals for Change." D.Ed. Thesis (University of British Columbia, 1974).

1422. **Cooper, J.** "Red Lights of Winnipeg." H.S.S.M. *Transactions* Series III, 29 (1972-73), pp. 61-74.

1423. **Craig, J.E.** "Public Opinion in Manitoba and the Approach to War, 1931-1939." M.A. Thesis (University of Toronto, 1952).

1424. **Crunican, P.E.** "Father Lacombe's Strange Mission: The Lacombe-Langevin Correspondence on the Manitoba School Question, 1895-6." Canadian Catholic Historical Association. *Report 1959,* pp. 57-71.

1425. **Douglas, William.** *Freemasonry in Manitoba, 1864-1925.* Winnipeg: Winnipeg Research Committee of the Grand Lodge of Manitoba, A.F. & A.M., 1925.

1426. **Downie, D.A.** "A History of Physical Education in the Public High Schools of Manitoba." M.Ed. Thesis (University of Manitoba, 1961).

1427. **Ewart, John S.** *The Manitoba School Question.* Toronto: Copp Clark, 1894.

1428. **Francis, E.K.** "The Mennonite School Problem in Manitoba, 1874-1919." *Mennonite Quarterly Review* 27 (1953), pp. 204-236.

1429. **Fraser, W.J.** "A History of St. John's College, Winnipeg." M.A. Thesis (University of Manitoba, 1966).

1430. ———. *St. John's College, Winnipeg: 1866-1966.* Winnipeg: Wallingford Press, 1966.

1431. **Fromson, R.D.** "Acculturation or Assimilation: A Geographic Analysis of Residential Segregation of Selected Ethnic Groups, Metropolitan Winnipeg, 1951-1961." M.A. Thesis (University of Manitoba, 1965).

1431A. **Gonick, Fay M.** "Social Values in Public Education in Manitoba, 1910-1930." M.A. Thesis (University of Manitoba, 1974).

1432. **Gray, James H.** *The Boy from Winnipeg.* Toronto: Macmillan, 1970.

1433. **Hutchinson, R.** *A Century of Service: A History of the Winnipeg Police Force, 1874-1974.* Winnipeg: City of Winnipeg, 1974.

1434. **Kirkconnell, Watson.** *The Golden Jubilee of Wesley College, Winnipeg, 1888-1938: The Story of Fifty Years of Service in Preparing Young Men and Women for Life and Its Needs.* Winnipeg: Columbia Press, 1938.

1434A. **Klassen, Peter George.** "A History of Mennonite Education in Manitoba." M.Ed. Thesis (University of Manitoba, 1958).

1435. **Laing, G.A.** *A Community Organizes for War: The Story of the Greater Winnipeg Co-ordinating Board for War Services and Affiliated Organizations, 1939-1946.* Winnipeg: The Board, 1948.

1436. **Lawson, Elsie.** "Public Welfare in Manitoba." *Canadian Welfare Summary* 15 (September 1939), pp. 14-23.

1437. **Lindal, W.J.** "Manitoba College, Wesley College and United College." *Icelandic Canadian* 30 (Autumn 1971), pp. 11-19.

1438. **Lucow, W.H.** "The Origin and Growth of the Public School System in Winnipeg." M.Ed. Thesis (University of Manitoba, 1950).

1439. **McArton, D.** "75 Years in Winnipeg's Social History." *Canadian Welfare* 25 (October 1949), pp. 11-19.
1440. **Morrison, A.S.** "Literature in Manitoba, 1870-1930." H.S.S.M. *Transactions* Series III, 9 (1954), pp. 69-80.
1441. **Morton, W.L.** "The Manitoba Schools and Canadian Nationalism, 1890-1916." Canadian Historical Association. *Annual Report 1951*, pp. 51-59.
1442. ———. *One University: A History of the University of Manitoba, 1877-1952*. Toronto: McClelland and Stewart, 1957.
1443. **Paterson, A.E.** "The Development of Kindergarten in Manitoba." M.Ed. Thesis (University of Manitoba, 1966).
1444. **Rumball, W.G., and MacLennan, D.A.** *Manitoba College... Being an Account of Her Achievements Past and Present, and Her Contribution to the Growth and Development of Western Canada and to the Progress of Presbyterianism*. Winnipeg, 1921.
1445. **Ruth, R.N.** "A History of Education of Icelanders in Manitoba." M.Ed. Thesis (University of Manitoba, 1960).
1446. **Shaw, W.T.** "The Role of John S. Ewart in the Manitoba School Question." M.A. Thesis (University of Manitoba, 1959).
1447. **Simms, E.F.** "A History of Public Education in Manitoba, 1870-1890." M.Ed. Thesis (University of Manitoba, 1944).
1448. **Stewart, Alistair M.** *The Youth Problem of Manitoba*. Winnipeg: Economic Survey Board, Province of Manitoba, 1939.
1449. **Syrnick, John H.** "Community Builders—Early Ukrainian Teachers." H.S.S.M. *Transactions* Series III, 21 (1964-65), pp. 25-34.
1450. **Taillon, Louis-Olivier.** "A propos des écoles de Manitoba." *Revue canadienne* 26 (1890), pp. 286-293.
1451. **Thomas, Paul.** "The Manitoba Law Reform Commission: A Critical Evaluation." *Dalhousie Law Journal* 2 (1915), pp. 417-443.
1452. **Thompson, John H.** "The Prohibition Question in Manitoba, 1892-1928." M.A. Thesis (University of Manitoba, 1969).
1453. ———. "The Voice of Moderation: The Defeat of Prohibition in Manitoba." In S.M. Trofimenkoff, ed. *The Twenties in Western Canada* (Ottawa, 1972), pp. 170-190.
1454. **Vidal, H.V.** "The History of the Manitoba Teachers' Society." M.Ed. Thesis (University of Manitoba, 1958).
1455. **Weaver, Emily P.** *Sisters of St. Boniface*. Toronto: Ryerson, 1930.

1456. **Wilson, J.G.** "A History of Home Economics in Manitoba, 1826-1966." M.Ed. Thesis (University of Manitoba, 1966).
1457. **Woods, D.S.** *Education in Manitoba: A Preliminary Report.* 2 vols. Winnipeg: Economic Survey Board, Province of Manitoba, 1938.

g. Urban Development

i) General

1458. **Abra, Marion.** *A History of the Municipality of Birtle, the Town of Birtle, and the Villages of Foxwarren and Solsgirth, 1894-1974.* Birtle: History Committee of the Municipality of Birtle, 1974.
1459. **Bell, M.J.** "Portage la Prairie from Earliest Times to 1907." M.A. Thesis (University of Manitoba, 1926).
1460. **Bock, J.** "An Analysis of the Educational Effort of a Single Enterprise Community: Flin Flon, Manitoba." M.Ed. Thesis (University of Manitoba, 1970).
1461. **Campbell, A.C.** "Churchill, 'Northern Metropolis.'" *Canadian Unionist* 6 (1933), pp. 167-170.
1462. **Chaiko, R.M.** "An Analysis of the Educational Effort of a Single Enterprise Community: Pinawa, Manitoba." M.Ed. Thesis (University of Manitoba, 1970).
1463. **Clark, W.L.R.** "Politics in Brandon City, 1899-1946." Ph.D. Thesis (University of Alberta, 1976).
1464. **Coleman, M.** *The Face of Yesterday: The Story of Brandon, Manitoba.* Brandon: Jr. Chamber of Commerce, 1957.
1465. **Collier, Anne M.** *A History of Portage la Prairie and Surrounding District.* Portage la Prairie: City Council, 1969.
1466. **Elias, P.D.** *Metropolis and Hinterland in Northern Manitoba.* Winnipeg: Manitoba Museum of Man and Nature, 1975.
1467. **Ewart, A.C.** "Municipal History of Manitoba." In S.M. Wickett, ed. *Municipal Government in Canada* (Toronto, 1907), pp. 131-148.
1468. **Ferguson, M.M.** *A History of St. James.* Winnipeg: The Author, 1967.
1469. **Harrington, L.** "Thompson, Manitoba Suburbia in the Bush." *Canadian Geographical Journal* 81 (1970), pp. 154-163.
1470. **Hecht, A.** "An Investigation into Central Place Aspects of Portage la Prairie." M.Sc. Thesis (University of Manitoba, 1968).

1471. **Hutchings, C.J.** "Municipal Taxation in Manitoba." M.A. Thesis (University of Manitoba, 1927).
1472. **MacDonald, D.I.** "A Study of Financial Problems of an Urban Municipality in Manitoba: The City of Brandon." M.A. Thesis (University of Toronto, 1938).
1473. **Metcalfe, J.H.**, ed. *The Tread of the Pioneers [Portage la Prairie].* Toronto: Ryerson, 1932.
1474. **Metcalfe, William H.** "Portage la Prairie." *Canadian Geographical Journal* 76 (1968), pp. 64-71.
1475. **Monu, E.D.** "Rural Migrants in an Urban Community: A Study of Migrants from the Interlake Region of Manitoba in Winnipeg and Brandon." M.A. Thesis (University of Manitoba, 1969).
1475A. **Neufeld, W.** "The Growth of Steinbach, 1873-1970." B.A. Essay (University of Winnipeg, 1971).
1476. **Phillips, A.D.** "The Development of Municipal Institutions in Manitoba to 1886." M.A. Thesis (University of Manitoba, 1948).
1477. **Phillips, Gordon C.** *The Rise and Fall of a Prairie Town: A History of Lauder, Manitoba.* 2 vols. Ottawa: The Author, 1974.
1478. **Pritchard, F.B.** "A Development Plan for Churchill, Manitoba." M.C.P. Thesis (University of Manitoba, 1970).
1478A. **Richtik, James M.** "Manitoba Service Centres in the Early Settlement Period." *Journal of the Minnesota Academy of Science* 34 (1967), pp. 17-21.
1479. **Ridout, Denzil G.** "Port Churchill." *Canadian Geographical Journal* 3 (1931), pp. 105-128.
1480. **Robinson, M.E., and Robinson, A.C.** "The Pas—Crossroads of the New North." *Canadian Geographical Journal* 45 (1952), pp. 54-63.
1481. **Rose, W.J.** "Early Minnedosa: The Crossing, the Town, and the Railway." H.S.S.M. *Transactions* Series III, 15 (1960), pp. 69-79.
1482. **Rowe, K.** "Brandon: The Wheat City." *Canadian Geographical Journal* 78 (1969), pp. 156-163.
1483. **Shipley, Nan.** *Road to the Forks: A History of the Community of Fort Garry.* Winnipeg: The Author, 1970.
1484. **Sim, V.W.** "The Pas, Manitoba." *Geographical Bulletin* 8 (1956), pp. 1-21.
1485. **Sinclair, Gordon.** "Cities and Towns of Manitoba." *Canadian Geographical Journal* 81 (1970), pp. 54-63.

1486. **Stadel, C.** "Service Areas of a Non-Primate City in the Canadian Prairies: The Case of Brandon, Manitoba." In A.H. Paul and E.H. Dale, eds. *Southern Prairies Field Excursion: Background Papers* (Regina, 1972), pp. 77-104.

1487. **Steen & Boyce, comp.** *Brandon, Manitoba, Canada, and Her Industries.* Winnipeg: Steen & Boyce, 1882.

1488. ————. *Emerson, Manitoba, and Her Industries: The Gateway City to the Golden Northwest.* Winnipeg: Steen & Boyce, 1882.

1489. ————. *Portage la Prairie, Manitoba, and Her Industries.* Winnipeg: Steen & Boyce, 1882.

1490. **Turnbull, I.D.** "Local Autonomy and Municipal Re-organization: A Study of Ethnic Influence on the Local Politics of St. Boniface." M.A. Thesis (University of Manitoba, 1967).

1491. **Venables, Alex.** *Muskeg to Metropolis: Thompson, Manitoba, 1957-1970.* Thompson: Thompson Centennial Committee, 1970.

1492. **Waddell, J.M.** *Dominion City: Facts, Fiction and Hyperbole.* Dominion City: S.W. Friesen, 1970.

1492A. **Walker, D., ed.** *Urban Growth: Choices for Manitobans.* Winnipeg: Institute of Urban Studies, 1976.

1493. **Williams, M.Y.** "Churchill, Manitoba." *Canadian Geographical Journal* 39 (1949), pp. 122-133.

1494. **Wilton, Sidney.** *The Pas: A History.* The Pas: Chamber of Commerce, 1970.

1495. **Winkler, H.W.** "Early Environs of Morden." *Manitoba Pageant* 16 (Spring 1971), pp. 8-10.

ii) Winnipeg

1496. **Anderson, J.C.** "Winnipeg: Golden Boy of the West." *Canadian Business* 28 (September 1955), pp. 24-29.

1497. **Arnold, A.J.** "Earliest Jews in Winnipeg, 1874-1882." *The Beaver* Outfit 305 (1974), pp. 4-11.

1498. **Artibise, Alan F.J.** "Advertising Winnipeg: The Campaign for Immigrants and Industry, 1874-1914." H.S.S.M. *Transactions* Series III, 27 (1970-71), pp. 75-106.

1499. ————. "Researching Winnipeg." *Urban History Review* 2-72 (1972), pp. 14-18.

1500. ———. "An Urban Environment: The Process of Growth in Winnipeg, 1874-1914." Canadian Historical Association. *Historical Papers 1972*, pp. 109-134.

1501. ———. "Mayor Alexander Logan of Winnipeg." *The Beaver* Outfit 304 (1974), pp. 4-12.

1502. ———. "Winnipeg and the City Planning Movement, 1910-1915." In David J. Bercuson, ed. *Western Perspectives I* (Toronto, 1974), pp. 10-20.

1503. ———. "The Origins and Incorporation of Winnipeg." In A.R. McCormack and Ian MacPherson, eds. *Cities in the West* (Ottawa, 1975), pp. 5-25.

1504. ———. "Winnipeg: Rise of a Metropolis." *Urban History Review* 1 (1975), pp. 43-50.

1505. ———. *Winnipeg: A Social History of Urban Growth, 1874-1914*. Montreal: McGill-Queen's University Press, 1975.

1506. ———. "Patterns of Population Growth and Ethnic Relationships in Winnipeg, 1874-1974." *Histoire sociale/Social History* 9 (1976), pp. 297-335.

1507. ———. "An Urban Economy: Patterns of Economic Change in Winnipeg, 1873-1971." *Prairie Forum* 1 (1976), pp. 163-188.

1508. ———. "Divided City: The Immigrant in Winnipeg Society, 1874-1921." In Gilbert A. Stelter and Alan F.J. Artibise, eds. *The Canadian City: Essays in Urban History* (Toronto, 1977), pp. 300-336.

1509. ———. "Winnipeg's City Halls, 1876-1965." *Manitoba Pageant* 22 (Spring 1977), pp. 5-10.

1510. ———. *Winnipeg: An Illustrated History*. History of Canadian Cities Series, vol. 1. Toronto: James Lorimer and National Museum of Man, 1977.

1511. **Artibise, Alan F.J., and Dahl, E.H.** *Winnipeg In Maps/Winnipeg par les cartes, 1816-1972*. Ottawa: Public Archives of Canada, 1975.

1512. ———. "Maps in the Study of Winnipeg's Urban Development." In A.R. McCormack and Ian MacPherson, eds. *Cities in the West* (Ottawa, 1975), pp. 139-158.

1513. **Avery, Donald.** "The Radical Alien and the Winnipeg General Strike of 1919." In Carl Berger and Ramsay Cook, eds. *The West and the Nation* (Toronto, 1976), pp. 209-231.

1514. **Axworthy, L., ed.** *The Future City: A Selection of Views on Government in Greater Winnipeg.* Winnipeg: Institute of Urban Studies, 1971.
1515. ———. *The Citizen and Neighbourhood Renewal.* Winnipeg: Institute of Urban Studies, 1972.
1516. ———. "Winnipeg: An Experiment in Innovation." *Canadian Forum* (May 1972), pp. 32-35.
1517. **Axworthy, L., and Cassidy, J.** *Unicity: The Transition.* Winnipeg: Institute of Urban Studies, 1971.
1518. **Axworthy, T.** *The Future City: The Politics of Innovation.* Winnipeg: Institute of Urban Studies, 1972.
1519. **Barrow, G.T.** "A Factorial Ecology of Three Cities: Edmonton, Regina and Winnipeg, 1961." M.A. Thesis (University of Calgary, 1972).
1520. **Baxter, R.S.** "The Use of Diagnostic Variables in Urban Analysis with Particular Reference to Winnipeg." M.A. Thesis (University of Manitoba, 1968).
1521. **Beaulieu, Paul.** "Participation in Winnipeg Area Local Elections." In P.H. Wichern, ed. *Studies in Winnipeg Politics* (Winnipeg, 1976), pp. 36-52.
1522. **Begg, Alexander, and Nursey, W.R.** *Ten Years in Winnipeg.* Winnipeg: Times Publishing House, 1879.
1523. **Bellan, R.C.** "Relief in Winnipeg: The Economic Background." M.A. Thesis (University of Toronto, 1941).
1524. ———. "The Development of Winnipeg as a Metropolitan Center." Ph.D. Thesis (Columbia University, 1958).
1525. ———. "Winnipeg, 1873-1914." Manitoba Society of Regional Studies. *Regional Review* 6 (1963), pp. 14-21.
1526. ———. "Rails across the Red—Selkirk or Winnipeg." H.S.S.M. *Transactions* Series III, 17 (1964), pp. 69-77.
1527. **Benoit, M.** "Saint-Boniface." *Habitat* 10 (1967), pp. 104-107.
1528. **Bercuson, David J.** *Confrontation at Winnipeg: Labor, Industrial Relations, and the General Strike.* Montreal: McGill-Queen's University Press, 1974.
1529. **Bernard, A.; Léveillé, J.; and Lord, G.** *Profile: Winnipeg. The Political and Administrative Structures of the Metropolitan Region of Winnipeg.* Ottawa: Ministry of State for Urban Affairs, 1975.

1530. **Bickel, R.P.** "Lord Selkirk Park, Winnipeg, Manitoba; An Urban Renewal Project." M.C.P. Thesis (University of Manitoba, 1966).
1531. **Blake, H.W.** *The Era of Streetcars in Winnipeg, 1881-1955.* Winnipeg: The Author, 1971.
1532. ———. *The Era of Interurbans in Winnipeg, 1902-1939.* Winnipeg: The Author, 1971.
1533. **Bock, J.K., and Bock, W.G.** "The People of Indian Ancestry in Greater Winnipeg." In J.H. Lagassé, ed. *A Study of the Population of Indian Ancestry Living in Manitoba.* Appendix 1. Vol. II (Winnipeg: Department of Agriculture and Immigration, 1959), pp. 1-132.
1534. **Bonnycastle, R.H.G.** "Metro Comes to Winnipeg." *Habitat* 4 (1961), pp. 2-7.
1535. **Bossen M.** "Rental Property Management in an Older Winnipeg Neighbourhood." *Urban Forum* 2 (Summer 1976), pp. 34-39.
1536. **Bradley, W.E.** "History of Transportation in Winnipeg." H.S.S.M. *Transactions* Series III, 15 (1960), pp. 7-38.
1537. **Bryce, George.** "The Five Forts of Winnipeg." Royal Society of Canada. *Proceedings and Transactions* 3 (1885), pp. 134-145.
1538. **Bryce, M.S.** *Historical Sketch of the Charitable Institutions of Winnipeg.* Winnipeg: *Manitoba Free Press*, 1899.
1539. **Cannell, S.** "Forty Years Ago: Reminiscences of Winnipeg." *Canadian Banker* 51 (1955), pp. 122-141.
1540. **Careless, J.M.S.** "The Development of the Winnipeg Business Community." Royal Society of Canada. *Proceedings and Transactions* 4th. ser. 8 (1970), pp. 239-254.
1541. **Chapman, G.F.** "Winnipeg: The Melting Pot." *Canadian Magazine* 33 (1909), pp. 409-416.
1542. ———. "Winnipeg: The Refining Process." *Canadian Magazine* 33 (1909), pp. 548-554.
1543. **Chisick, E.** "The Development of Winnipeg's Socialist Movement, 1900 to 1915." M.A. Thesis (University of Manitoba, 1972).
1544. **Clark, R., et al.** "Reform Politics in Winnipeg: Opening Things Up." *City Magazine* 1 (February-March 1975), pp. 29-36.
1545. **Cook, Gail C.A., and Feldman, Lionel E.** "Approaches to Local Government Reform in Canada: The Case of Winnipeg." *Canadian Tax Journal* 19 (1971), pp. 216-225.
1546. **Cowan, Anna M.** "Memories of Upper Fort Garry." *The Beaver* Outfit 266 (1935), pp. 25-30.

1547. **Dafoe, C.** "Winnipeg." *Habitat* 10 (1967), pp. 108-113.
1548. **Dafoe, John W.** "Early Winnipeg Newspapers." H.S.S.M. *Transactions* Series III, 3 (1946-47), pp. 14-24.
1549. **Dawson, Colleen.** *St. Vital: Past, Present and Future.* St. Vital: Gleenwood School, 1973.
1550. **Dickinson, Janet.** "The Public Campaign for Unicity: Case Study and Analysis." In P.H. Wichern, ed. *Studies in Winnipeg Politics* (Winnipeg, 1976), pp. 96-120.
1551. **Dingwall, C.W.** "Winnipeg and the Needle Trades." *Western Business and Industry* 20 (January 1946), pp. 18-21.
1552. **Douglas, William.** "The Forks Become a City." H.S.S.M. *Transactions* Series III, 1 (1944-45), pp. 51-80.
1553. ———. "Winnipeg Parks." H.S.S.M. *Transactions* Series III, 14 (1959), pp. 61-65.
1554. **Earl, L.** "Winnipeg Moves Ahead." *Western Business and Industry* 35 (November 1961), pp. 28-40.
1555. **Elliot, G.B.** *Winnipeg as It Is in 1874; And as It Was in 1860.* Ottawa: *Free Press* Office, 1875.
1556. **Ferguson, M.M.** *A History of St. James.* Winnipeg: The Author, 1967.
1557. **Fraser, W.J.** *St. John's College, Winnipeg: 1866-1966.* Winnipeg: Wallingford Press, 1966.
1558. **Fromson, R.D.** "Acculturation or Assimilation: A Geographic Analysis of Residential Segregation of Selected Ethnic Groups, Metropolitan Winnipeg, 1951-1961." M.A. Thesis (University of Manitoba, 1965).
1559. ———. "Planning in a Metropolitan Area: The Experiment in Greater Winnipeg." M.C.P. Thesis (University of Manitoba, 1970).
1560. **Fung, Y.H.** "Intra-urban Mobility in Winnipeg: A Study of Geographic Elements." M.A. Thesis (University of Manitoba, 1972).
1561. **Gerry, A.C.** "A Study of Urban Recreation with Particular Emphasis on Unicity Winnipeg." M.Arch. Thesis (University of Manitoba, 1972).
1562. **Goldenberg, H.C.** *Report of the Royal Commission on Municipal Finances and Administration of the City of Winnipeg.* Winnipeg: King's Printer, 1939.
1563. **Good, T.L.** "A Planning Analysis of Outdoor Recreation in the Winnipeg Region." M.C.P. Thesis (University of Manitoba, 1970).

1564. **Gordon, A.** "The Winnipeg Jewish Community: Patterns of Leadership in an Ethnic Subcommunity." M.A. Thesis (University of Manitoba, 1972).
1565. **Graham, J.W.** *Winnipeg Architecture, 1831-1960.* Winnipeg: University of Manitoba Press, 1960.
1566. **Gray, James H.** *The Boy from Winnipeg.* Toronto: Macmillan, 1970.
1567. **Hay, Elizabeth.** "The City of Winnipeg." *Empire Digest* 5 (1948), pp. 53-61.
1568. **Hayley, W.T.** "A Study of the Population of Greater Winnipeg." Manitoba Society of Regional Studies, *Regional Review* 2 (1964), pp. 1-14.
1569. **Healey, W.J.** *Winnipeg's Early Days: A Short Historical Sketch.* Winnipeg: Stovel Printing Co., 1927.
1570. ———. "Early Days in Winnipeg." *The Beaver* Outfit 280 (1949), pp. 22-25.
1571. **Henderson, A.M.** "From Fort Douglas to the Forks." H.S.S.M. *Transactions* Series III, 23 (1966-67), pp. 15-32.
1572. **Henderson, D.G.** "A Study of Housing and Environment Conditions in the City of Winnipeg." M.Arch. Thesis (University of Manitoba, 1952).
1573. **Herstein, Harvey H.** "The Growth of the Winnipeg Jewish Community and the Evolution of Its Educational Institutions." M.Ed. Thesis (University of Manitoba, 1964).
1574. ———. "The Growth of the Winnipeg Jewish Community and the Evolution of Its Educational Institutions." H.S.S.M. *Transactions* Series III, 22 (1966-69), pp. 27-66.
1575. **Hislop, Mary.** *The Streets of Winnipeg.* Winnipeg: T.W. Taylor, 1912.
1576. **Hood, M.L.** "Winnipeg—From Fort Garry to 1949." *Western Business and Industry* 23 (May 1949), pp. 42-44, 182-184.
1577. **Hossé, H.A.** "The Areal Growth and Functional Development of Winnipeg from 1870-1913." M.A. Thesis (University of Manitoba, 1956).
1578. **Hunter, A.A., and Latiff, A.H.** "Stability and Change in the Ecological Structure of Winnipeg: A Multi-Method Approach." *Canadian Review of Sociology and Anthropology* 10 (1973), pp. 308-334.

1579. **Hutchison, R.** *A Century of Service: A History of the Winnipeg Police Force, 1874-1974.* Winnipeg: City of Winnipeg, 1974.

1580. **Huzel, B.** "The Interurbans of Winnipeg." *Manitoba Pageant* 21 (Winter 1976), pp. 10-11.

1581. **Johnson, T.A.** "The Needle Trades in Winnipeg: A Study in Trade Unions." M.A. Thesis (University of Manitoba, 1948).

1582. **Kent, R.H.** "The Dissonant Decade: A Study of Conflict between the City of Winnipeg and the Metropolitan Corporation of Greater Winnipeg." M.B.A. Thesis (University of Manitoba, 1970).

1583. **Kerr, Donald.** "Wholesale Trade on the Canadian Plains in the Late Nineteenth Century: Winnipeg and Its Competition." In. H. Palmer, ed. *The Settlement of the West* (Calgary, 1977), pp. 130-152.

1584. **Kerri, James N.** "Indians in a Canadian City: Analysis of Social Adaptive Strategies." *Urban Anthropology* 5 (1976), pp. 143-156.

1585. **Kirkconnell, Watson.** *The Golden Jubilee of Wesley College, Winnipeg, 1888-1938: The Story of Fifty Years of Service in Preparing Young Men and Women for Life and Its Needs.* Winnipeg: Columbia Press, 1938.

1586. **Koch, E.** *Winnipeg: Gateway to the West.* Toronto: Holt, Rinehart and Winston, 1967.

1587. **Krawchak, P.** *The Ukrainians in Winnipeg's First Century.* Toronto: Kobzar Publishing Company, 1974.

1588. **Kuz, T.J., ed.** *Winnipeg, 1874-1974: Progress and Prospects.* Winnipeg: Manitoba Department of Industry and Commerce, 1974.

1589. **Laing, G.A.** *A Community Organizes for War: The Story of the Greater Winnipeg Co-ordinating Board for War Services and Affiliated Organizations, 1939-1946.* Winnipeg: The Board, 1948.

1590. **Lowe, P.** "All Western Dollars [Alloway & Champion]." H.S.S.M. *Transactions* Series III, 2 (1945-46), pp. 10-25.

1591. **Lucas, Fred G.** *An Historical Souvenir Diary of the City of Winnipeg.* Winnipeg: Cartwright and Lucas, 1923.

1592. **Lucow, W.H.** "The Origin and Growth of the Public School System in Winnipeg." M.Ed. Thesis (University of Manitoba, 1959).

1593. **Lunty, A.J., and Hurley, K.C.** *Armstrong's Point: An Historical Survey.* Winnipeg: Provincial Archives of Manitoba, 1969.

1594. **McArton, D.** "75 Years in Winnipeg's Social History." *Canadian Welfare* 25 (October 1949), pp. 11-19.

Plate 9. Winnipeg City Hall

1595. **McCormack, A.R.** "Radical Politics in Winnipeg: 1899-1915." H.S.S.M. *Transactions* Series III, 29 (1972-72), pp. 81-97.

1596. **McCracken, Melinda.** *Memories Are Made of This: What It Was Like to Grow Up in the Fifties [in Winnipeg].* Toronto: James Lorimer, 1975.

1597. **MacFarlane, R.O.** "Winnipeg in the Seventies—As Seen through the Local Press." *Manitoba Arts Review* 2 (Spring 1940), pp. 5-14.

1598. **McKillop, A.B.** "Citizen and Socialist: The Ethos of Political Winnipeg, 1919-1935." M.A. Thesis (University of Manitoba, 1970).

1598A. ———. "The Socialist as Citizen: John Queen and the Mayoralty of Winnipeg, 1935." H.S.S.M. *Transactions* Series III, 30 (1973-74), pp. 61-80.

1599. ———. "The Communist as Conscience: Jacob Penner and Winnipeg City Politics, 1934-35." In A.R. McCormack and Ian MacPherson, eds. *Cities in the West* (Ottawa, 1975), pp. 181-210.

1600. MacLeod, M.A. "The Company in Winnipeg." *The Beaver* Outfit 271 (1940), pp. 6-11.

1601. ———. "Winnipeg and the H.B.C." *The Beaver* Outfit 280 (1949), pp. 3-7.

1602. ———. "The City That Never Was." *The Beaver* Outfit 281 (1950), pp. 12-15.

1603. McNaught, K., and Bercuson, David J. *The Winnipeg Strike: 1919.* Toronto: Longman, 1974.

1604. MacPherson, L.G. "Report of the Royal Commission on the Municipal Finances and Administration of the City of Winnipeg, 1939." *C.J.E.P.S.* 6 (1940), pp. 68-72.

1605. Manitoba, Government of. *Proposals for Urban Reorganization in the Greater Winnipeg Area.* Winnipeg, 1970.

1606. Marlyn, J. *Under the Ribs of Death.* Toronto: McClelland and Stewart, 1957.

1607. Masters, D.C. "The English Communities in Winnipeg and in the Eastern Townships of Quebec." In M. Wade, ed. *Regionalism in the Canadian Community, 1867-1967* (Toronto, 1969), pp. 130-159.

1608. Mitchell, George, and Benham, M.L. *Winnipeg.* Winnipeg: City of Winnipeg, 1974.

1609. Mitchell, R. "How Winnipeg Waged War on Typhoid." *Manitoba Medical Review* 49 (1969), pp. 166-167.

1610. Morton, W.L. "Winnipeg and Manitoba, 1874-1922." *Manitoba Arts Review* 1 (Winter 1939), pp. 29-41.

1611. Mott, M.K. "The 'Foreign Peril': Nativism in Winnipeg, 1916-1923." M.A. Thesis (University of Manitoba, 1970).

1612. Micholson, T.G., and Yeates, M.H. "The Ecological and Spatial Structure of the Socio-Economic Characteristics of Winnipeg, 1961." *Canadian Review of Sociology and Anthropology* 6 (1969), pp. 162-170.

1613. O'Malley, M. "How Ontario Supplies Winnipeg's Water." *Canadian Geographical Journal* 91 (1975), pp. 28-31.

1614. **Page, J.E.** "Catholic Parish Ecology and Urban Development in the Greater Winnipeg Region." M.A. Thesis (University of Manitoba, 1958).
1615. **Painchaud, Robert.** "Les Francophones dans le monde des affaires de Winnipeg, 1870-1920." Saint-Boniface: La Société historique de Saint-Boniface, 1974.
1616. **Parr, J., ed.** *Speaking of Winnipeg.* Winnipeg: Queenston House, 1974.
1617. **Percira, C.P.** "East Indians in Winnipeg: A Study of the Consequences of Immigration for An Ethnic Group in Canada." M.A. Thesis (University of Manitoba, 1971).
1618. **Phillips, P.A.** "Power Politics: Municipal Affairs and Seymour James Farmer, 1909-1924." In A.R. McCormack and Ian MacPherson, eds. *Cities in the West* (Ottawa, 1975), pp. 159-180.
1619. **Plunkett, T.J.** *Unicity: A New Form of Unified Municipal Government in Greater Winnipeg.* Winnipeg: City of Winnipeg, 1972.
1620. **Pratt, D.F.** "Williams Ivens and the Winnipeg Labor Church." B.D. Thesis (St. Andrew's College, Saskatoon, 1962).
1621. **Ramsay, Alan.** "Winnipeg! City of Contrast and Beauty." *Canadian Geographical Journal* 26 (1943), pp. 44-47.
1622. **Ransom, E.J.** *Winnipeg, 1905: A Metropolis in the Making.* Winnipeg: Bulman Brothers, 1905.
1623. **Rea, J.E.** "The Politics of Conscience: Winnipeg after the Strike." Canadian Historical Association. *Historical Papers 1971,* pp. 276-288.
1624. ———. "How Winnipeg Had Nearly Won." In A.R. McCormack and Ian MacPherson, eds. *Cities in the West* (Ottawa, 1975), pp. 74-87.
1625. ———. "The Politics of Class: Winnipeg City Council, 1919-1945." In Carl Berger and Ramsay Cook, eds. *The West and the Nation* (Toronto, 1976), pp. 232-249.
1626. ———. "Parties and Power: An Analysis of Winnipeg City Council, 1919-1975." Appendix IV. *Report and Recommendations.* Committee of Review, City of Winnipeg Act. Winnipeg: Department of Urban Affairs, 1976.
1627. **Reynolds, G.F.** "The Man Who Created the Corner of Portage and Main." H.S.S.M. *Transactions* Series III, 26 (1969-70), pp. 5-40.
1628. **Rich, S. George.** "Planning in Metropolitan Winnipeg." *Community Planning Review* 12, no. 12 (1962), pp. 21-28.

1629. ———. "Floodway Prevents 1974 Winnipeg Flood." *Canadian Geographical Journal* 88 (1974), pp. 20-29.

1630. ———. "Metropolitan Winnipeg, 1943-1961." In A.R. McCormack and Ian MacPherson, eds. *Cities in the West* (Ottawa, 1975), pp. 237-268.

1631. **Richtik, James M., and Selwood, H.J.** "Metropolitan Winnipeg: An Introduction." In A.H. Paul and E.H. Dale, eds. *Southern Prairies Field Excursion: Background Papers* (Regina, 1972), pp. 3-20.

1632. **Robertson, Thomas B.** "Winnipeg—The Prairie Capital." *Canadian Geographical Journal* 7 (1933), pp. 133-142.

1633. **Robinson, B.W.** "Leisure: A Suburban Winnipeg Study." M.A. Thesis (University of Manitoba, 1968).

1633A. **Romanowski, E.T.** "Stability and Change in the Ecological Structure and Pattern of Winnipeg, 1951-1971." B.A. Essay (University of Winnipeg, 1975).

1634. **Rosenberg, L.** *The Jewish Community in Winnipeg.* Montreal: Canadian Jewish Congress, 1946.

1635. **Rostecki, R.R.** *The Historic Architecture of Winnipeg, 1880-1920.* Winnipeg: University of Winnipeg, 1972.

1636. ———. "Some Old Winnipeg Buildings." H.S.S.M. *Transactions* Series III, 29 (1972-73), pp. 5-22.

1637. ———. "The Decline and Rise of the Warehouse District of Winnipeg." *Heritage Canada* 2 (Summer 1976), pp. 28-31.

1638. ———. "The Early History of the Cauchon Block, Later the Empire Hotel." *Manitoba Pageant* 21 (Spring 1976), pp. 10-17.

1639. **Rowe, P.A.** "The Needle Trades in Winnipeg." *Western Business and Industry* 23 (November 1949), pp. 52-71.

1640. ———. "Winnipeg's Fur Trade." *Western Business and Industry* 24 (May 1950), pp. 64-69.

1641. **Rudnyckyj, J.B.** *Mosaic of Winnipeg Street Names.* Winnipeg: University of Manitoba, 1974.

1642. **Russenholt, E.S.** "The Power of a City." Unpublished manuscript (City of Winnipeg Hydro Office).

1643. **Selwood, H.J.** *The Winnipeg Townscape: A Survey Guide.* Winnipeg: Manitoba Environmental Council, Study No 7, 1976.

1643A. ———. "Urban Development and the Streetcar: The Case of Winnipeg, 1881-1913." *Urban History Review* 3-77 (1978), pp. 34-41.

1644. **Sheikh, Z.A.** "Housing Environment for Downtown Winnipeg." M. Arch. Thesis (University of Manitoba, 1968).

1645. **Shipley, Nan.** *Road to the Forks: A History of the Community of Fort Garry.* Winnipeg: The Author, 1970.

1646. **Short, R.B.** "The Wholesale Function in Winnipeg." M.A. Thesis (University of Manitoba, 1973).

1647. **Siamandas, G.** "Public Policy for Downtown Redevelopment in Winnipeg." M.A. Thesis (University of Manitoba, 1971).

1648. **Sisler, W.J.** *Peaceful Invasion.* Winnipeg: Ketchum Printing Co., 1944.

1649. **Sloane, D.L.; Rosender, J.M.; and Hernandez, M.J., eds.** *Winnipeg: A Centennial Bibliography.* Winnipeg: Manitoba Library Association, 1974.

1650. **Spector, David.** "Winnipeg's First Labour Unions." *Manitoba Pageant* 21 (Summer 1976), pp. 13-14.

1651. **Steen, J.E.** *Winnipeg: A Historical Sketch of Its Wonderful Growth, Progress & Prosperity.* Winnipeg: W.A. Martel, 1903.

1652. **Steen & Boyce, comp.** *Winnipeg, Manitoba, and Her Industries.* Chicago: Steen & Boyce, 1881.

1653. **Stinson, L.** *Political Warriors: Recollections of a Social Democrat.* Winnipeg: Queenston House, 1975.

1654. **Talbot, L.D.** "A Study of the Development of Winnipeg's Planned Shopping Centres and an Analysis of Selected Planned Shopping Centre Characteristics." M.A. Thesis (University of Manitoba, 1974).

1655. **Theron, J.D.** "The Redevelopment of the City Core of Winnipeg." M.C.P. Thesis (University of Manitoba, 1968).

1656. **Thompson, John H.** "The Political Career of Ralph H. Webb." *Red River Valley Historian* (Summer 1976), pp. 1-7.

1657. **Thompson, W.T., ed.** *The City of Winnipeg; the Capital of Manitoba and the Commercial, Railway, and Financial Metropolis of the Northwest: Past and Present Development and Future Prospects.* Winnipeg: The Commercial, 1886.

1658. **Thorarinson, S.A.** "Early Icelandic Builders in Winnipeg." *Icelandic Canadian* 25 (Spring 1967), pp. 24-30.

1659. **Turnbull, I.D.** "Local Autonomy and Municipal Reorganization: A Study of Ethnic Influence on the Local Politics of St. Boniface." M.A. Thesis (University of Manitoba, 1967).

1660. **Tuttle, C.R.** *The Civic Situation, Including a Brief History of the Corporation of Winnipeg from 1874 to the Present Time.* Winnipeg, 1883.

1661. **Vincent, D.B.** *The Indian-Métis Urban Probe.* Winnipeg: Institute of Urban Studies, 1971.

1662. **Waddell, Douglas.** "The Origins and Development of Metro Winnipeg." In P.H. Wichern, ed. *The Development of Urban Government in the Winnipeg Area* (Winnipeg, 1975), pp. 23-39.

1663. **Walker, D.** "Winnipeg and Trizec: Giving It All Away." *City Magazine* 2 (Summer 1976), pp. 24-32.

1664. **Watts, C.** "Ethnicity and Voting Patterns in City of Winnipeg Elections." In P.H. Wichern, ed. *Studies in Winnipeg Politics* (Winnipeg, 1976), pp. 53-69.

1665. **Weir, T.R.** "Land Use and Population Characteristics of Central Winnipeg." *Geographical Bulletin* 9 (1956), pp. 5-21.

1666. ———. "A Survey of the Daytime Population of Winnipeg." *Queen's Quarterly* 67 (1961), pp. 654-662.

1667. ———. "Winnipeg: A City in the Making." In David J. Bercuson, ed. *Western Perspectives I* (Toronto, 1974), pp. 21-32.

1668. **West, George E.** "The Relevance of Structural Reform of Local Government to the Solution of Metropolitan Problems: A Case Study of Greater Winnipeg." M.A. Thesis (University of Waterloo, 1974).

1669. **Wichern, P.H.** *Winnipeg's Unicity after Two Years: Evaluation of an Experiment in Urban Government.* Winnipeg: Department of Political Studies, University of Manitoba, 1974.

1670. ———. "Toward a History of Local Politics and Public Services in the Winnipeg Area: Research Notes and Sources." In P.H. Wichern, ed. *Studies in Winnipeg Politics* (Winnipeg, 1976), pp. 1-35.

1671. **Wichern, P.H., ed.** *The Development of Urban Government in the Winnipeg Area.* Background Papers on Winnipeg Government and Politics. Vol. I. Winnipeg: Department of Urban Affairs, Province of Manitoba, 1975.

1672. ———. *Studies in Winnipeg Politics.* Background Papers on Winnipeg Government and Politics. Vol. II. Winnipeg: Department of Urban Affairs, Province of Manitoba, 1976.

1673. **Wilmot, Fred.** *"Call 320": A Documentary Record of the 1950 Manitoba Flood and Red Cross Activities in the Disaster.* Winnipeg: Canadian Red Cross Society, c. 1950.

1674. "Winnipeg—The Gateway of the Canadian West." *Canadian Annual Review* (1912). "Special Supplement."
1675. **Winnipeg Parks and Recreation Department.** *The History and Development of Assiniboine Park and Zoo in Winnipeg, Manitoba, Canada.* Winnipeg, 1972.
1676. ———. *Kildonan Park: History and Development.* Winnipeg, 1972.
1677. ———. *St. Vital Park: History and Development.* Winnipeg, 1973.
1678. **Wiseman, N., and Taylor, K.W.** "Ethnic vs. Class Voting: The Case of Winnipeg, 1945." *Canadian Journal of Political Science* 7 (1974), pp. 314-328.
1679. **Yauk, T.B.** "Residential and Business Relocation from Urban Renewal Areas: A Case Study of the Lord Selkirk Park Experience." M.C.P. Thesis (University of Manitoba, 1973).

h. Bibliographical

1680. **Francis, E.K.** "A Bibliography on the Mennonites in Manitoba." *Mennonite Quarterly Review* 27 (1953), pp. 237-247.
1681. **Historical and Scientific Society of Manitoba.** *Local History in Manitoba: A Key to Places, Districts, Schools and Transport Routes.* Winnipeg, 1976.
1682. **Morley, Marjorie.** *A Bibliography of Manitoba from Holdings in the Legislative Library of Manitoba.* 1953. Revised. Winnipeg: Manitoba Legislative Library, 1970.
1683. **Province of Manitoba.** *Resource Materials: Native Peoples of Manitoba.* Winnipeg: Native Education Branch, Department of Education, 1976.
1684. **Scott, M.M.** *A Bibliography of Western Canadian Studies Relating to Manitoba.* Winnipeg: Western Canada Research Council, 1967.
1685. **Sloane, D.L.; Rosender, J.M.; and Hernandez, M.J., eds.** *Winnipeg: A Centennial Bibliography.* Winnipeg: Manitoba Library Association, 1974.

5

Saskatchewan

a. General

1686. **Alty, Stella W.** "The Influence of Climatic and Other Geographic Factors upon the Growth and Distribution of Population in Saskatchewan." *Geography* 24 (1939), pp. 10-23.
1687. **Atcheson, J.W.** "Community-Centered Regions in Northern Saskatchewan." M.A. Thesis (University of Saskatchewan, Regina, 1972).
1688. **Baker, W.B.** "Changing Community Patterns in Saskatchewan." *Canadian Geographical Journal* 56 (1958), pp. 44-56.
1689. **Black, N.F.** *History of Saskatchewan and the North-West Territories.* 2 vols. Regina: Saskatchewan Historical Company, 1913.
1690. **Bohi, C.W., and Grant, H.R.** "The Standardized Railroad Station in Saskatchewan: The Case of the Canadian National System." *Sask. Hist.* 29 (Autumn 1976), pp. 81-102.
1691. **Britnell, G.E.** "Saskatchewan, 1930-1935." *C.J.E.P.S.* 2 (1936), pp. 143-166.
1692. **Cameron, Alex R.** "Place Names." *Sask. Hist.* 1 (Spring 1948), pp. 23-24.
1693. ———. "The Legacy of the Fur Trade." *Sask. Hist.* 1 (Autumn 1948), pp. 21-22.
1694. **Campbell, M.W.** *The Saskatchewan.* Toronto: Clarke, Irwin, 1950.
1695. **Clements, M.** *By Their Bootstraps: A History of the Credit Union Movement in Saskatchewan.* Toronto: Clarke, Irwin, 1964.
1696. **Eager, Evelyn E.** "The Constitution of Saskatchewan." *Sask. Hist.* 15 (Spring 1962), pp. 41-57.
1697. **Edmonds, W.E.** "Steamboat Days on the Saskatchewan." *Queen's Quarterly* 56 (1949), pp. 231-239.

1698. **Fitzgerald, Denis Patrick.** "Pioneer Settlement in Northern Saskatchewan." Ph.D. Thesis (University of Minnesota, 1966).
1699. **Hanson, S.D.** "Policing the International Boundary Area in Saskatchewan, 1890-1910." *Sask. Hist.* 19 (Spring 1966), pp. 61-73.
1700. **Hawkes, John.** *The Story of Saskatchewan and Its People.* 3 vols. Chicago: S.J. Clarke Publishing Co., 1924.
1701. **Johnson, Gilbert.** "Place Names in Spy Hill Municipality." *Sask. Hist.* 9 (Winter 1956), pp. 19-20.
1702. **Kitto, F.H.** *The Province of Saskatchewan.* 1919. Rev. ed. Ottawa: Department of the Interior, 1923.
1703. **Kovach, J.J.** "Regional Development Planning for Saskatchewan." M.C.P. Thesis (University of Manitoba, 1970).
1704. **Kreutzweiser, Erwin E.** "Before the Railways." *Sask. Hist.* 1 (Winter 1948), pp. 8-10.
1705. **McCourt, E.A.** *Saskatchewan.* Toronto: Macmillan, 1968.
1706. **Moon, Robert.** *This Is Saskatchewan.* Toronto: Ryerson, 1953.
1707. **Oliver, E.H.** "The Settlement of Saskatchewan to 1914." Royal Society of Canada. *Proceedings and Transactions* 3d. ser. 20 (1926), sec. 2, pp. 63-87.
1708. **Peel, Bruce.** "On the Old Saskatchewan Trail." *Sask. Hist.* 1 (Spring 1948), pp. 1-9.
1709. ————. "Place Names." *Sask. Hist.* 2 (Spring 1949), p. 29.
1710. **Pohorecky, Z.S.** "Archaeology and Prehistory: The Saskatchewan Case." In Richard Allen, ed. *A Region of the Mind* (Regina, 1973), pp. 47-72.
1711. **Powell, T.J.D.** "Northern Settlement, 1929-1935." *Sask. Hist.* 30 (Autumn 1977), pp. 81-98.
1712. **Richards, J.H.** "Gross Aspects of Planning and Outdoor Recreation with Particular Reference to Saskatchewan." *Canadian Geographer* 11 (1967), pp. 117-123.
1713. ————. *Saskatchewan Geography: Physical Environment and Its Relationship with Population and Economic Base.* 1967. Rev. ed. Saskatoon: University of Saskatchewan, 1974.
1714. ————. "The Status of Saskatchewan vis-à-vis the Western Interior." In H.C. Klassen, ed. *The Canadian West* (Calgary, 1977), pp. 127-146.
1715. **Richards, J.H., and Fung, K.I., eds.** *Atlas of Saskatchewan.* Saskatoon: University of Saskatchewan, 1969.

1716. **Rolph, William K.** "Turner's Weekly: An Episode in Prairie Journalism." *Sask. Hist.* 4 (Autumn 1951), pp. 81-92.

1717. **Russell, E.T.P.**, ed. *What's in a Name: Travelling through Saskatchewan with the Story behind 1600 Place Names.* Saskatoon: Western Producer, 1973.

1718. **Saskatchewan, Province of.** *A Submission by the Government of Saskatchewan to the Royal Commission on Dominion-Provincial Relations.* Regina: King's Printer, 1937.

1719. **Schwartz, C.** *Contemporary Saskatchewan I: The Search for Stability.* Toronto: McClelland and Stewart, 1959.

1720. **Simpson, George W.** "Dust Gets in Your Eyes." *Sask. Hist.* 1 (Winter 1948), pp. 2-3.

1721. ———. "Saskatchewan at Mid Century." *Canadian Geographical Journal* 49 (1954), pp. 174-191.

1722. **Turner, Allan R.** "Saskatchewan Place Names." *Sask. Hist.* 18 (Autumn 1965), pp. 81-88.

1723. **Wahn, J.D.** "Appraisal of Settlement in Southwestern Saskatchewan." M.A. Thesis (University of Saskatchewan, 1947).

1724. **Wright, J.F.C.** "Saskatchewan." *Canadian Geographical Journal* 34 (1947), pp. 108-135.

1725. ———. "Saskatchewan's North." *Canadian Geographical Journal* 45 (1952), pp. 14-33.

1726. ———. *Saskatchewan: The History of a Province.* Toronto: McClelland and Stewart, 1955.

1727. ———. *Prairie Progress: Consumer Co-operation in Saskatchewan.* Saskatoon: Modern Press, 1956.

b. The People

1728. **Anderson, Alan B.** "Assimilation in the Bloc Settlement of North-Central Saskatchewan." Ph.D. Thesis (University of Saskatchewan, 1972).

1729. ———. "Ethnic Identity in Saskatchewan Block Settlements: A Sociological Appraisal." In H. Palmer, ed. *The Settlement of the West* (Calgary, 1977), pp. 186-225.

1730. **Andrews, Isabel A.** "The Crooked Lakes Reserves: A Study of Indian Policy in Practice from the Qu'Appelle Treaty to 1900." M.A. Thesis (University of Saskatchewan, Regina, 1972).

1731. **Baily, R.W.** "Housing for Indians and Métis in Northern Saskatchewan." *Habitat* 2 (1968), pp. 18-23.
1732. **Baker, H.R.** *Population Trends in Saskatchewan: Incorporated and Unincorporated Centers by Selected Years.* Saskatoon: University of Saskatchewan, Centre for Community Studies, 1961.
1733. **Barnhart, G.L.** "E.H. Oliver: A Study of Protestant Progressivism in Saskatchewan, 1909-1935." M.A. Thesis (University of Regina, 1977).
1734. **Betke, Carl.** "The Mounted Police and the Doukhobors in Saskatchewan, 1899-1909." *Sask. Hist.* 27 (Winter 1974), pp. 1-14.
1735. **Brass, Eleanor.** "The File Hills Ex-Pupil Colony." *Sask. Hist.* 6 (Spring 1953), pp. 66-69.
1736. **Buckley, Helen.** *The Indians and Métis of Northern Saskatchewan.* Saskatoon: University of Saskatchewan, Centre for Community Studies, 1963.
1737. **Davis, A.K.** "Edging into Mainstream: Urban Indians in Saskatchewan." In A.K. Davis, et al., eds. *A Northern Dilemma: Reference Papers* (Bellingham, Washington, 1965), pp. 338-585.
1738. **Dobbin, L.L.** "Prairie People: Mrs. Catherine Gillespie Motherwell." *Sask. Hist.* 14 (Winter 1961), pp. 17-26.
1739. **Fast, G.A., and Fast, J.** *To Find the Daily Bread [Mennonites in Saskatchewan].* Saskatoon: Western Producer, 1954.
1740. **Field, A.J.** "The Saskatoon Jewish Community, 1905-1962." Saskatoon: University Library, Shortt Collection, 1963.
1741. **Friesen, R.J.** "Old Colony Mennonite Settlements in Saskatchewan: A Study in Settlement Change." M.A. Thesis (University of Alberta, 1975).
1741A. **Friesen, R.J.** "Saskatchewan Mennonite Settlements: The Modification of an Old World Settlement Pattern." *Canadian Ethnic Studies* 9 (1977), pp. 72-90.
1742. **Ganzevoort, Herman, ed.** *A Dutch Homesteader on the Prairies: The Letters of Willem de Gelder, 1910-13.* Social History of Canada, vol. 16. Toronto: University of Toronto Press, 1973.
1743. **Huel, R.J.A.** "L'Association catholique franco-canadienne de la Saskatchewan: A Response to Cultural Assimilation." M.A. Thesis (University of Saskatchewan, Regina, 1969).
1744. ―――. "Msgr. Olivier-Elzéar: Guardian of French Catholic Interests in Saskatchewan." *Revue de l'Université d'Ottawa* 42 (1972), pp. 384-407.

1745. **Jackman, S.W.** "The Rowbottom Diaries [1906-1907]." *Sask. Hist.* 21 (Spring 1968), pp. 56-66.

1746. **Jackson, M.** "Une Minorité ignorée: Les Franco-Canadiens de la Saskatchewan." *Journal of Canadian Studies* 7, no. 3 (1972), pp. 1-20.

1747. **Johnson, Gilbert.** "James Moffat Douglas." *Sask. Hist.* 7 (Spring 1954), pp. 47-50.

1748. **Kennedy, J.J.** "Qu'Appelle Industrial School: White 'Rites' for the Indians of the Old North-West." M.A. Thesis (Carleton University, 1970).

1749. **Kirkwood, F.B.** "The Sudetan Settlement at St. Walburg, Saskatchewan." *Canadian Society of Technical Agriculture Review* 37 (1943), pp. 9-16.

1750. **Koester, Charles B.** "Nicholas Flood Davin: A Biography." Ph.D. Thesis (University of Alberta, 1971).

1751. **Keonoff, C.E.** *Wapella Farm Settlement (The First Successful Jewish Farm Settlement in Canada): A Pictorial History.* Winnipeg: Historical and Scientific Society of Manitoba and Jewish Historical Society of Western Canada, 1972.

1752. **Lindal, W.J.** *The Saskatchewan Icelanders: A Strand of the Canadian Fabric.* Winnipeg: Columbia Press, 1955.

1753. **Luk, L.W.C.** "The Assimilation of the Chinese in Saskatoon." M.A. Thesis (University of Saskatchewan, 1971).

1754. **Lyle, G.R.** *British Emigration into the Saskatchewan Valley, the Barr Colony, 1903: Its Bibliographical Foundation.* Decatur, Georgia: The Author, 1975.

1754A. **Merrill, L.I.** "Population Distribution in the Riding Mountains and Adjacent Plains of Manitoba and Saskatchewan, 1879-1946." M.A. Thesis (McGill University, 1953).

1755. **Naipaul, B.M.** "An Analysis in Historical Perspective of the Factors Which Contribute to the Retention of Ethnicity in the Community of Edenwald." In *Development of Agriculture on the Canadian Prairies: Proceedings of Seminar* (Regina, 1975), pp. 216-242.

1756. **Pick, Harry.** *Next Year [the Barr Colonists].* Toronto: Ryerson, 1928.

1757. **Poolner, Irene A.** "Unprincipled Women: The Saskatchewan Case." *Atlantis* 1 (1975), pp. 113-118.

1758. **Pohorecky, Z.S.** *Saskatchewan Indian Heritage: The First Two Hundred Centuries.* Saskatoon: University of Saskatchewan, 1970.

1759. **Raby, S.** "Indian Land Surrenders in Southern Saskatchewan." *Canadian Geographer* 18 (1973), pp. 36-52.
1760. **Seaborne, Adrian A.** "A Population Geography of Northern Saskatchewan." *Musk-Ox* 12 (1973), pp. 49-57.
1761. **Sinton, Robert.** *Looking Backward from the Eightieth Milestone, 1935 to 1854.* Regina: Paragon Business College, 1935.
1762. ———. "Looking Backward." *Sask. Hist.* 1 (Spring 1948), pp. 20-22.
1763. **Smeltzer, M.F.** "Saskatchewan Opinion on Immigration from 1925-1939." M.A. Thesis (University of Saskatchewan, 1950).
1764. **Steininger, F.** "George H. Williams: Agrarian Socialist." M.A. Thesis (University of Regina, 1976).
1765. **Thomas, Lewis H.** "Welsh Settlement in Saskatchewan, 1902-1914." *Western Historical Quarterly* 4 (1973), pp. 435-449.
1766. **Tracie, C.J.** "Ethnicity and Settlement in Western Canada: Doukhobor Village Settlement in Saskatchewan." In B.M. Barr, ed. *Western Canadian Research in Geography: The Lethbridge Papers* (Vancouver: B.C. Geographical Series, no. 21, 1975), pp. 67-76.
1767. **Tyre, Robert.** *Douglas in Saskatchewan: The Story of a Socialist Experiment.* Vancouver: Mitchell Press, 1962.
1768. **Valentine, V.F.** "Some Problems of the Métis of Northern Saskatchewan." *C.J.E.P.S.* 20 (1954), pp. 89-95.
1769. **Wagner, J.F.** "Heim Ins Reich: The Story of Loon River's Nazis." *Sask. Hist.* 29 (Spring 1976), pp. 41-50.
1770. **Wasylow, W.J.** "History of the Battleford Industrial School for Indians." M.Ed. Thesis (University of Saskatchewan, 1972).
1771. **Watson, Mrs. Edward.** "Reminiscences of Mrs. Edward Watson." *Sask. Hist.* 5 (Spring 1952), pp. 66-67.
1772. **Wetton, C.** *The Promised Land: The Story of the Barr Colonists.* Lloydminster *Times*, n.d.
1772A. **Young, Walter D.** "M.J. Coldwell: The Making of a Social Democrat." *Journal of Canadian Studies* 9, no. 3 (1974), pp. 51-60.

c. *Government and Politics*

1773. **Anderson, F.W.** "Some Political Aspects of the Grain Growers' Movement, 1915-1935, with Particular Reference to Saskatchewan." M.A. Thesis (University of Saskatchewan, 1940).

1774. **Appleblatt, Anthony.** "The School Question in the 1929 Saskatchewan Election." Canadian Catholic Historical Association. *Study Sessions* 43 (1976), pp. 75-90.
1775. **Badgley, R.F., and Wolfe, S.** *Doctor's Strike: Medical Care and Conflict in Saskatchewan.* Toronto: Macmillan, 1967.
1776. **Bocking, D.H.** "Premier Walter Scott: A Study of His Rise to Political Power." M.A. Thesis (University of Saskatchewan, 1959).
1777. ———. "Premier Walter Scott: His Early Career." *Sask. Hist.* 13 (Autumn 1960), pp. 81-99.
1778. ———. "Saskatchewan's First Provincial Election." *Sask. Hist.* 17 (Spring 1964), pp. 41-54.
1779. **Brennan, J.W.G.** "The Public Career of C.A. Dunning in Saskatchewan." M.A. Thesis (University of Saskatchewan, Regina, 1968).
1780. ———. "C.A. Dunning and the Challenge of the Progressives, 1922-1925." *Sask. Hist.* 22 (Winter 1969), pp. 1-12.
1781. ———. "Press and Party in Saskatchewan, 1914-1929." *Sask. Hist.* 27 (Autumn 1974), pp. 81-94.
1782. ———. "A Political History of Saskatchewan, 1905-1929." Ph.D. Thesis (University of Alberta, 1976).
1783. **Britnell, G.E.** "The Saskatchewan Debt Adjustment Program." *C.J.E.P.S.* 3 (1937), pp. 370-375.
1784. **Bronson, H.E.** "Saskatchewan Returns to 'Agrarian Socialism.'" *Lakehead Review* 5 (1972), pp. 17-28.
1785. **Brown, L.A.** "Progressivism and the Press in Saskatchewan, 1916-1926." M.A. Thesis (University of Saskatchewan, 1966).
1786. ———. "The Progressive Tradition in Saskatchewan." *Our Generation* 6 (1969), pp. 21-46.
1787. **Calderwood, W.** "The Decline of the Progressive Party in Saskatchewan, 1925-1930." *Sask. Hist.* 21 (Autumn 1968), pp. 81-99.
1788. ———. "Pulpit, Press and Political Reactions to the Ku Klux Klan in Saskatchewan." In S.M. Trofimenkoff, ed. *The Twenties in Western Canada* (Ottawa, 1972), pp. 191-229.
1789. **Chambers, Elizabeth.** "The Referendum and the Plebiscite." In Norman Ward and D.S. Spafford, eds. *Politics in Saskatchewan* (Don Mills, 1968), pp. 59-77.
1790. **Climenhaga, D.B.** "Public Finance in Saskatchewan during the Settlement Process, 1905-1929." M.A. Thesis (University of Saskatchewan, 1949).

1791. **Courtney, John C.** "Mackenzie King and the Prince Albert Constituency: The 1933 Redistribution." *Sask. Hist.* 29 (Winter 1976), pp. 1-13.
1792. **Courtney, John C., and Smith, David E.** "Voting in a Provincial General Election and a Federal By-Election: A Constituency Study of Saskatoon City." *C.J.E.P.S.* 32 (1966), pp. 338-353.
1793. ———. "A Constituency Study of Saskatoon City." In Norman Ward and D.S. Spafford, eds. *Politics in Saskatchewan* (Don Mills, 1968), pp. 221-237.
1794. ———. "Saskatchewan: Parties in a Politically Competitive Province." In M. Robin, ed. *Canadian Provincial Politics* (Scarborough, 1972), pp. 290-318.
1795. **Courville, L.D.E.** "The Saskatchewan Progressives." M.A. Thesis (University of Saskatchewan, Regina, 1971).
1796. ———. "The Conservatism of the Saskatchewan Progressives." Canadian Historical Association. *Historical Papers 1974*, pp. 157-182.
1797. **Douglas, Thomas D.** *Canadians Find Security with Freedom: C.C.F. in Saskatchewan Builds toward Cooperative Order.* New York: League for Industrial Democracy, 1949.
1798. **Eager, Evelyn L.** "The Government of Saskatchewan." Ph.D. Thesis (University of Toronto, 1957).
1799. ———. "The Paradox of Power in the Saskatchewan C.C.F., 1944-1961." In J.H. Aitchison, ed. *The Political Process in Canada: Essays in Honour of R. MacGregor Dawson* (Toronto, 1963), pp. 118-135.
1800. ———. "The Conservatism of the Saskatchewan Electorate." In Norman Ward and D.S. Spafford, eds. *Politics in Saskatchewan* (Don Mills, 1968), pp. 1-19.
1801. ———. "Wheat, Medicare and Gerrymander in the Saskatchewan Election of 1971." *Lakehead Review* 5 (1972), pp. 3-16.
1802. **Ferguson, George V.** "Charles Avery Dunning." *Queen's Quarterly* 65 (1958-59), pp. 570-577.
1803. **Franks, C.E.S.** "The Legislature and Responsible Government." In Norman Ward and D. Spafford, eds. *Politics in Saskatchewan* (Don Mills, 1968), pp. 20-43.
1804. **Hall, D.J.** "T.O. Davis and Federal Politics in Saskatchewan, 1896." *Sask. Hist.* 30 (Spring 1977), pp. 56-62.

1805. **Hamilton, Z.M.** "Prairie People: The Honourable G.W. Brown, 1860-1919." *Sask. Hist.* 18 (Winter 1965), pp. 32-37.

1806. **Hawkes, D.C.** "Democracy, Ideology and Interest Groups: A Case Study of Saskatchewan Credit Unions as a Political Interest Group." M.A. Thesis (Queen's University, 1972).

1807. **Higginbotham, C.H.** *Off the Record: The C.C.F. in Saskatchewan.* Toronto: McClelland and Stewart, 1968.

1808. **Hoffman, George J.** "The Saskatchewan Provincial Election of 1934: Its Political, Economic and Social Background." M.A. Thesis (University of Saskatchewan, Regina, 1973).

1809. ———. "Saskatchewan Catholics and the Coming of a New Politics, 1930-1934." In R. Allen, ed. *Religion and Society in the Prairie West* (Regina, 1974), pp. 65-88.

1810. ———. "The Saskatchewan Farmer-Labor Party, 1932-1934: How Radical Was It at Its Origin?" *Sask. Hist.* 28 (Spring 1975), pp. 52-64.

Plate 10. T.C. Douglas and the Banner of the C.C.F., Weyburn

1811. ———. "The Entry of the United Farmers of Canada, Saskatchewan Section into Politics: A Reassessment." *Sask. Hist.* 30 (Autumn 1977), pp. 99-109.

1812. **Koester, Charles B.**, ed. *The Measure of the Man: Selected Speeches of Woodrow Lloyd.* Saskatoon: Western Producer, 1976.

1812A. **Knuttila, K.M.** "The Saskatchewan Agrarian Movement, 1916-1926: A Case Study of Populism." M.A. Thesis (University of Regina, 1975).

1813. **Kyba, J.P.** "The Saskatchewan General Election of 1929." M.A. Thesis (University of Saskatchewan, 1964).

1814. ———. "Ballots and Burning Crosses." In Norman Ward and D.S. Spafford, eds. *Politics in Saskatchewan* (Don Mills, 1968), pp. 105-123.

1815. **Lipset, S.M.** *Agrarian Socialism: The Co-operative Commonwealth Federation in Saskatchewan. A Study in Political Sociology.* Berkeley and Los Angeles: University of California Press [Toronto: Oxford University Press], 1950.

1816. ———. "The C.C.F. in Saskatchewan." In H.G. Thorburn, ed. *Party Politics in Canada* (Scarborough, 1967), pp. 159-167.

1816A. **McCrea, R.L.** "Provincial and Municipal Taxation in Saskatchewan." M.A. Thesis (University of Manitoba, 1919).

1817. **MacDonald, C.** "How Saskatchewan Women Got the Vote." *Sask. Hist.* 1 (Autumn 1948), pp. 1-8.

1818. **McLeod, Keith A.** "Politics, Schools and the French Language, 1881-1931." In Norman Ward and D.S. Spafford, eds. *Politics in Saskatchewan* (Don Mills, 1968), pp. 124-150.

1819. **Menzies, June.** "Votes for Saskatchewan Women." In Norman Ward and D.S. Spafford, eds. *Politics in Saskatchewan* (Don Mills, 1968), pp. 78-92.

1820. **Milnor, A.J.** "Agrarian Protest in Saskatchewan, 1929-1948: A Study in Ethnic Politics." Ph.D. Thesis (Duke University, 1962).

1821. ———. "The New Politics and Ethnic Revolt, 1929-1938." In Norman Ward and D.S. Spafford, eds. *Politics in Saskatchewan* (Don Mills, 1968), pp. 151-177.

1822. **Mohamed, A.M.** "Keep Our Doctors Committees in the Saskatchewan Medicare Controversy." M.A. Thesis (University of Saskatchewan, 1964).

1823. **Morissette, Pierre.** "La Carrière politique de W.F.A. Turgeon, 1907-1921." M.A. Thesis (University of Regina, 1975).

1824. **Reid, Escott M.** "The Saskatchewan Liberal Machine before 1929." *C.J.E.P.S.* 2 (1936), pp. 27-40.

1825. ———. "The Saskatchewan Liberal Machine before 1929." In Norman Ward and D.S. Spafford, eds. *Politics in Saskatchewan* (Don Mills, 1968), pp. 93-104.

1826. **Rubin, M.W.** "The Response of the Bennett Government to the Depression in Saskatchewan, 1930-1935: A Study in Dominion-Provincial Relations." M.A. Thesis (University of Regina, 1975).

1827. **Russell, P.A.** "The Co-operative Government in Saskatchewan, 1929-1934." M.A. Thesis (University of Saskatchewan, 1970).

1828. ———. "The Cooperative Government's Response to the Depression, 1930-1934." *Sask. Hist.* 24 (Autumn 1971), pp. 81-100.

1829. **Saskatchewan Archives Board.** *Directory of Members of Parliament and Federal Elections for the North-West Territories and Saskatchewan, 1887-1966.* Regina and Saskatoon, 1967.

1830. ———. *Saskatchewan Executive and Legislative Directory, 1905-1970.* Regina and Saskatoon, 1971.

1831. **Saskatchewan Bureau of Publications.** *Progress Report from Your Government: A Survey of Saskatchewan Government Activity, 1944-1947.* Regina: The Bureau, 1947.

1832. **Saskatchewan, Province of.** *A Submission by the Government of Saskatchewan to the Royal Commission on Dominion-Provincial Relations.* Regina: King's Printer, 1937.

1833. **Sheps, M.C.** "Saskatchewan Plans Health Services." *Canadian Journal of Public Health* 36 (1945), pp. 175-180.

1834. **Sherdahl, R.M.** "The Saskatchewan General Election of 1944." M.A. Thesis (University of Saskatchewan, 1966).

1835. **Sinclair, Peter R.** "Populism in Alberta and Saskatchewan." Ph.D. Thesis (University of Edinburgh, 1972).

1836. ———. "The Saskatchewan C.C.F. and the Communist Party in the 1930s." *Sask. Hist.* 26 (Winter 1973), pp. 1-10.

1837. ———. "The Saskatchewan C.C.F.: Ascent to Power and the Decline of Socialism." *C.H.R.* 54 (1973), pp. 419-433.

1838. **Smiley, Donald V.** "Local Autonomy and Central Administrative Control in Saskatchewan." *C.J.E.P.S.* 26 (1960), pp. 299-315.

1839. **Smith, David E.** "The Membership of the Saskatchewan Legislative Assembly, 1905-1966." *Sask. Hist.* 20 (Spring 1967), pp. 41-63.

1840. ——. "The Membership of the Saskatchewan Legislative Assembly, 1905-1966." In Norman Ward and D.S. Spafford, eds. *Politics in Saskatchewan* (Don Mills, 1968), pp. 178-206.
1841. ——. "A Comparison of Prairie Political Development in Saskatchewan and Alberta." *Journal of Canadian Studies* 4, no. 1 (1969), pp. 17-25.
1842. ——. "Liberalism in Saskatchewan: The Evolution of a Provincial Party." In David J. Bercuson, ed. *Western Perspectives I* (Toronto, 1974), pp. 101-109.
1843. ——. *Prairie Liberalism: The Liberal Party in Saskatchewan, 1905-71*. Toronto: University of Toronto Press, 1975.
1844. Spafford, D.S. "The Elevator Issue, the Organized Farmer and the Government, 1908-1911." *Sask. Hist.* 15 (Autumn 1962), pp. 81-92.
1845. ——. "'Independent' Politics in Saskatchewan before the Nonpartisan League." *Sask. Hist.* 18 (Winter 1965), pp. 1-9.
1846. ——. "The Origin of the Farmers' Union of Canada." *Sask. Hist.* 18 (Autumn 1965), pp. 89-98.
1847. ——. "The 'Left Wing' 1921-1931." In Norman Ward and D.S. Spafford, eds. *Politics in Saskatchewan* (Don Mills, 1968), pp. 44-58.
1848. Stevenson, J.A. "Topics of the Day: The Saskatchewan Election." *Dalhousie Review* 24 (1944), pp. 219-224.
1849. Stewart, W.W. "The Single Tax in Saskatchewan." M.A. Thesis (University of Saskatchewan, 1948).
1850. Taylor, M.G. "The Organization and Administration of the Hospital Services Plan." Ph.D. Thesis (University of California, Berkeley, 1948).
1851. Thomas, Lewis H. "The Political and Private Life of F.W.G. Haultain." *Sask. Hist.* 23 (Spring 1970), pp. 50-58.
1852. Thomas, Lewis H., ed. "The Diary of Robert Martin: Part I." *Sask. Hist.* 6 (Spring 1953), pp. 53-65.
1853. ——. "The Diary of Robert Martin: Part II." *Sask. Hist.* 6 (Autumn 1953), pp. 102-114.
1854. Tollefson, Edwin A. *Bitter Medicine: The Saskatchewan Medicare Feud*. Saskatoon: Modern Press, 1964.
1855. ——. "The Aftermath of the Medicare Dispute in Saskatchewan." *Queen's Quarterly* 72 (1965), pp. 452-465.
1856. ——. "The Medicare Dispute." In Norman Ward and D.S. Spafford, eds. *Politics in Saskatchewan* (Don Mills, 1968), pp. 238-279.

1857. **Turner, Allan R.** "W.R. Motherwell: The Emergence of a Farm Leader." *Sask. Hist.* 11 (Autumn 1958), pp. 94-103.
1858. **Turner, Allan R., ed.** "Reminiscences of Hon. J.A. Calder." *Sask. Hist.* 25 (Spring 1972), pp. 55-75.
1859. **Tyre, Robert.** *Douglas in Saskatchewan: The Story of a Socialist Experiment.* Vancouver: Mitchell Press, 1962.
1860. **Unger, Gordon.** "James G. Gardiner, the Premier as Pragmatic Politician, 1926-1929." M.A. Thesis (University of Saskatchewan, 1967).
1861. ———. "James G. Gardiner and the Constitutional Crisis of 1929." *Sask. Hist.* 23 (Spring 1967), pp. 41-49.
1862. **Waggoner, M.A.** "The Co-operative Commonwealth Federation in Saskatchewan, A Socialist Movement." Ph.D. Thesis (University of Missouri, 1946).
1863. **Ward, Norman.** "The Contemporary Scene." In Norman Ward and D.S. Spafford, eds. *Politics in Saskatchewan* (Don Mills, 1968), pp. 280-303.
1864. ———. "The Changing of Spots in Saskatchewan." *Lakehead Review* 5 (1972), pp. 29-37.
1865. ———. "Rt. Hon. J.G. Gardiner and 1905." *Sask. Hist.* 28 (Autumn 1975), pp. 111-117.
1866. **Ward, Norman, and Spafford, D.S., eds.** *Politics in Saskatchewan.* Don Mills: Longmans, 1968.

d. Agriculture and Rural Development

1867. **Abramson, J.A.** *Rural to Urban Adjustment [in Saskatchewan].* Ottawa: Queen's Printer, 1968.
1868. **Anderson, W.J.** "The Place of the Small Farm in the Agricultural Economy of Saskatchewan." M.Sc. Thesis (University of Saskatchewan, 1944).
1869. **Archer, John H.** "The Saskatchewan Stock Growers' Association." *Sask. Hist.* 12 (Spring 1959), pp. 41-60.
1870. **Auld, F.H.** "The Saskatchewan Agricultural Societies' Association," *Sask. Hist.* 14 (Winter 1961), pp. 1-16.
1871. **Bocking, D.H., ed.** "Documents of Western History—The Saskatchewan Grain Growers' Association: White Bear Branch Minutes, 1915." *Sask. Hist.* 14 (Spring 1961), pp. 71-75.

1872. **Britnell, G.E.** "The Depression in Rural Saskatchewan." In Harold A. Innis and A.F.W. Plumptre, eds. *The Canadian Economy and Its Problems* (Toronto, 1934), pp. 97-109.

1873. **Campbell, J.B.** *The Swift Current Research Station, 1920-1970.* Ottawa: Department of Agriculture, 1971.

1874. **Carmeron, Bill, and Robertson, Terry.** *Saskatchewan Wheat Pool, 1924-1974.* Regina: Saskatchewan Wheat Pool, 1974.

1875. **Clark, S.D.** "Settlement in Saskatchewan with Special Reference to the Influence of Dry Farming." M.A. Thesis (University of Saskatchewan, 1931).

1876. **Eager, Evelyn, E.**, "Documents of Western History: The Saskatchewan Grain Growers' Association: Hillview Branch Minutes, 1910-1912." *Sask. Hist.* 13 (Spring 1960), pp. 63-72.

1877. **Eaton, Grace Elvira, and Vallée, Lloyd L.** *Green Hill: The Story of a Prairie Community and Its Pioneers.* Carlyle: The Authors, 1955.

1878. **Edwards, George F.** "The S.G.G.A. Convention of 1910." *Sask. Hist.* 3 (Spring 1950), pp. 66-67.

1879. **Fast, H.R.** "Changing Communities in Rural Saskatchewan." *Canadian Farm Economics* 7 (June 1972), pp. 8-20.

1880. **Frost, David B.** "The Climate of Southern Saskatchewan." In A.H. Paul and E.H. Dale, eds. *Southern Prairies Field Excursion: Background Papers* (Regina, 1972), pp. 213-242.

1881. **Green, S.J.** "The Origins and Operations of the Saskatchewan Farm Loan Board, 1917-1951." M.A. Thesis (University of Saskatchewan, 1951).

1882. **Grest, E.G.** "A Study of Horse and Tractor Power Used on Farms in Saskatchewan and Alberta." M.Sc. Thesis (University of Saskatchewan, 1932).

1883. **Groome, A.J.** "Homesteading on the Prairies (the Town of Fleming)." In *Development of Agriculture on the Prairies: Proceedings of Seminar* (Regina, 1975), pp. 23-29.

1884. **Knowles, Janet.** "Irrigation Development on the South Saskatchewan." In *Development of Agriculture on the Prairies: Proceedings of Seminar* (Regina, 1975), pp. 149-174.

1884A. **Laut, P.** "The Development of Community Pastures in Saskatchewan: A Case Study in the Development of Land Policy." In B.M. Barr, ed. *New Themes in Western Canadian Geography: The Langara Papers* (Vancouver: B.C. Geographical Series, no. 22, 1976), pp. 119-142.

1885. **Leitch, Adelaide.** "Pattern of Progress at Lac La Ronge." *Canadian Geographical Journal* 62 (1961), pp. 88-93.
1886. **McCourt, E.A.** *Home Is the Stranger.* Toronto: Macmillan, 1950.
1887. **McCrorie, James Napier.** *In Union Is Strength: The Saskatchewan Farmers Union.* Saskatoon: University of Saskatchewan, Centre for Community Studies, 1964.
1888. ———. "The Saskatchewan Farmers' Movement: A Case Study." Ph.D. Thesis (University of Illinois at Urbana-Champaign, 1972).
1889. **Munsterhjelm, Erik.** *The Wind and the Caribou.* Toronto and New York: Macmillan, 1953.
1890. **Niebel, M.R.** "Rev. Thomas Johnson and the Insinger Experiment." *Sask. Hist.* 11 (Winter 1958), pp. 1-17.
1891. **Oliver, E.H.** "The Beginnings of Agriculture in Saskatchewan." Royal Society of Canada. *Proceedings and Transactions* 3d. ser. 39 (1935), pp. 1-32.
1892. **Paul, A.H.** "Water Resources in Southern Saskatchewan." In A.H. Paul and E.H. Dale, eds. *Southern Prairies Field Excursion: Background Papers* (Regina, 1972), pp. 129-150.
1893. ———. "[Rural] Depopulation and Spatial Change in Southern Saskatchewan." In J.E. Spencer, ed. *Saskatchewan Rural Themes* (Regina, 1977), pp. 65-68.
1894. **Powrie, T.L.** "Labour and Population in Saskatchewan: A Study of Changes in Farm Labour Utilization and of Farm Population Growth in Saskatchewan, 1896-1951." M.A. Thesis (University of Saskatchewan, 1955).
1895. **Putnam, Ben, et al., eds.** *Fifty Years of Progress: Chiefly the Story of the Pioneers of the Watson District from 1900-1910.* Watson: Watson Board of Trade, 1951.
1896. **Rees, Ronald.** "Deserted Landscapes of Rural Saskatchewan." *Canadian Geographical Journal* 88 (1974), pp. 10-19.
1897. **Rodwell, L.** "Saskatchewan Homestead Records." *Sask. Hist.* 18 (Winter 1965), pp. 10-29.
1898. **Rondeau, Abbé Clairs.** *La Montagne de bois (Willow-Bunch, Sask.): Histoire de la Saskatchewan méridionale.* Québec: L'Action sociale, 1923.
1899. **Rorem, C.R.** *The Municipal Doctor System in Rural Saskatchewan.* Committee on the Costs of Medical Care, publication no. 11. Chicago: University of Chicago Press, 1931.

1900. **Royal Commission on Agriculture and Rural Life.** *History of Rural Local Government in Saskatchewan.* Regina: Queen's Printer, 1955.
1901. **Sahir, A.H.** "Some Aspects of Agriculture in Saskatchewan." In A.H. Paul and E.H. Dale, eds. *Southern Prairies Field Excursion: Background Papers* (Regina, 1972), pp. 107-128.
1902. ———. "Residential Pattern of Wheat Farmers in Southern Saskatchewan." Ph.D. Thesis (University of Minnesota, 1973).
1903. ———. "The Pattern of Residence of Wheat Farmers: An Investigation in Southern Saskatchewan." In J.E. Spencer, ed. *Saskatchewan Rural Themes* (Regina, 1977), pp. 25-63.
1904. **St. John, S.T.** "Homesteading at Wilcox." *Sask. Hist.* 2 (Winter 1949), pp. 23-27.
1905. **Schlichtmann, H.** "The Rural Settlements of Southern Saskatchewan." In A.H. Paul and E.H. Dale, eds. *Southern Prairies Field Excursion: Background Papers* (Regina, 1912), pp. 311-350.
1906. ———. "Land Disposal and Patterns of Farmstead Distribution in Southern Saskatchewan." In J.E. Spencer, ed. *Saskatchewan Rural Themes* (Regina, 1977), pp. 1-23.
1907. **Sherriff, A.B.** "Agricultural Co-operation in Saskatchewan." M.A. Thesis (University of Saskatchewan, 1923).
1908. **Spencer, J.E., ed.** *Saskatchewan Rural Themes.* Regina Geographical Studies No. 1. Regina: Department of Geography, University of Regina, 1977.
1909. **Stutt, R.A.** "Changes in Land Use and Farm Organization in the Prairie Area of Saskatchewan, 1951 to 1966." *Canadian Farm Economics* 5 (1971), pp. 11-19.
1910. **Thomas, Lewis H.** "The Search for Water on the Canadian Plains." *Sask. Hist.* 1 (Winter 1948), pp. 4-7.
1911. **Turner, Allan R.** "Pioneer Farming Experiences." *Sask. Hist.* 8 (Spring 1955), pp. 41-55.
1912. ———. "W.R. Motherwell and Agricultural Development in Saskatchewan, 1905-1918." M.A. Thesis (University of Saskatchewan, 1958).
1913. **Willmott, Donald E.** "The Formal Organizations of the Saskatchewan Farmers, 1900-1965." In A.W. Rasporich, ed. *Western Canada: Past and Present* (Calgary, 1975), pp. 28-41.
1914. **Wilson, J.** "An Economic Evaluation of Extending Agriculture in Northeastern Saskatchewan." M.A. Thesis (University of Alberta, 1973).

Plate 11. Grain Elevators on the C.P.R. Mainline, Lewvan, Saskatchewan

1915. **Yates, S.W.** *The Saskatchewan Wheat Pool: Its Origin, Organization and Progress, 1924-1935.* Saskatoon: United Farmers of Canada (Saskatchewan Section), 1947.

1916. **Yule, Annie I.** *Grit and Growth: The Story of Grenfell.* Regina: Monarch Press, 1967.

e. Economic Development and Labour

1917. **Archer, John H.** "The Saskatchewan Purchasing Company: An Early Co-operative." *Sask. Hist.* 5 (Spring 1952), pp. 55-65.

1918. **Arrowsmith, W.A.** "Northern Saskatchewan and the Fur Trade." M.A. Thesis (University of Saskatchewan, 1964).

1919. **Bronson, H.E.** "The Saskatchewan Meat Packing Industry." *Sask. Hist.* 26 (Winter 1973), pp. 24-37.

1920. **Cherwinski, Walter J.C.** "The Formative Years of the Trade Union Movement in Saskatchewan, 1905-1920." M.A. Thesis (University of Saskatchewan, 1966).

1921. ———. "Organized Labour in Saskatchewan: The T.L.C. Years, 1905-1945." Ph.D. Thesis (University of Alberta, 1971).

1922. **Dojcsak, G.V.** "The Mineral Resources of Southern Saskatchewan." In A.H. Paul and E.H. Dale, eds. *Southern Prairies Field Excursion: Background Papers* (Regina, 1972), pp. 243-266.
1923. **Ecroyd, L.G.** "Saskatchewan." *Western Business and Industry* 28 (December 1954), pp. 35-74. [A continuing feature.]
1924. **Fairbairn, D.A.** "The British-American Refinery Strike, Moose Jaw, Saskatchewan, 1965-1966." M.A. Thesis (University of Regina, 1975).
1925. **Hanson, S.D.** "The Estevan Strike and Riot, 1931." M.A. Thesis (University of Saskatchewan, Regina, 1972).
1926. ———. "Estevan, 1931." In Irving M. Abella, ed. *On Strike: Six Key Labour Struggles in Canada, 1919-1949* (Toronto, 1974), pp. 33-78.
1927. **Johnson, Gilbert.** "The Harmony Industrial Association: A Pioneer Cooperative." *Sask. Hist.* 4 (Winter 1951), pp. 11-20.
1928. ———. "The Germania Mutual Fire Insurance Company of Langenburg." *Sask. Hist.* 14 (Winter 1961), pp. 27-29.
1929. **Mackie, Victor J.** "Saskatchewan to Socialize Bus Lines." *Western Business and Industry* 19 (December 1945), pp. 84-92.
1930. ———. "Saskatchewan Industry and Jobs Curtailed." *Western Business and Industry* 20 (January 1946), pp. 80-85.
1931. **McLeod, J.T.** "Provincial Administration of Natural Resources in Saskatchewan, 1930-1955." M.A. Thesis (University of Saskatchewan, 1955).
1932. **Megill, William J.** "Potash: In Canada's Past and Saskatchewan's Present." *Canadian Geographical Journal* 68 (1964), pp. 178-187.
1933. **Oliver, E.H.** "Economic Conditions in Saskatchewan, 1870-1881." Royal Society of Canada. *Proceedings and Transactions* 3d ser. 27 (1933), sec. 2, pp. 15-40.
1934. **Reesor, B.W.** "The Origin and Development of the Saskatchewan Power Corporation." M.A. Thesis (University of Saskatchewan, 1955).
1935. **Rehmer, L.W.** "The Conservation of a Renewable Resource: The Timber Industry in Saskatchewan Prior to 1930." M.A. Thesis (University of Saskatchewan, 1964).
1936. **Tyre, Robert.** "Saskatchewan Turns to Industry." *Canadian Geographical Journal* 52 (1956), pp. 218-231.

1937. **White, C.O.** "Moose Jaw Opts for Private over Municipal or Provincial Ownership of Its Electrical Utility." In A.R. McCormack and Ian MacPherson, eds. *Cities in the West* (Ottawa, 1975), pp. 88-115.

1938. ———. "The Qu'Appelle Electrical Utility, 1906-1927." *Sask. Hist.* 28 (Winter 1975), pp. 1-8.

1939. ———. "The Humboldt Municipal Electrical Utility: A Grassroots Feature of the Saskatchewan Power Corporation." *Sask. Hist.* 29 (Autumn 1976), pp. 103-113.

1940. ———. *Power for a Province: A History of Saskatchewan Power.* Regina: Canadian Plains Research Center, 1976.

1941. **Wilmott, Donald E.** *Industry Comes to a Prairie Town.* Saskatoon: University of Saskatchewan, Centre for Community Studies, 1962.

f. Education and Social and Cultural Development

1942. **Bailey, A.W.** "Recollections and Reminiscences: The Year We Moved [The Impact of the Depression on a Farm Family]." *Sask. Hist.* 20 (Winter 1961), pp. 19-31.

1943. **Baker, W.B.** *Saskatchewan Approaches Community Development: Prerequisites for a Social Technology.* Saskatoon: University of Saskatchewan, Centre for Community Studies, 1961.

1944. **Bocking, D.H.** "The Saskatchewan Board of Film Censors, 1910-1935." *Sask. Hist.* 24 (Spring 1971), pp. 51-62.

1945. **Bocking, D.H.,** ed. "Experiences of a Depression Hobo." *Sask. Hist.* 22 (Spring 1969), pp. 60-65.

1946. **Brown, L.A.** "Unemployment Relief Camps in Saskatchewan, 1933-1936." *Sask. Hist.* 23 (Autumn 1970), pp. 81-104.

1947. **Buck, R.M.** "Little Pine: An Indian Day School." *Sask. Hist.* 18 (Spring 1965), pp. 55-62.

1948. **Cairns, V.B.** "A Study of Adult Education in Saskatchewan with Reference to the Canadian Scene." M.Ed. Thesis (University of Saskatchewan, 1950).

1949. **Calderwood, W.** "The Rise and Fall of the Ku Klux Klan in Saskatchewan." M.A. Thesis (University of Saskatchewan, Regina, 1968).

1950. ———. "Religious Reactions to the Ku Klux Klan in Saskatchewan." *Sask. Hist.* 26 (Autumn 1973), pp. 103-114.

1951. **Carter, D.J.** "The Archbishops' Western Canada Fund and the Railway Mission." *Sask. Hist.* 22 (Winter 1969), pp. 13-28.
1952. **Clements, M.** "'Listening In' on the Prairies." *Sask. Hist.* 9 (Winter 1956), pp. 16-18.
1953. **Crone, R.H.** "Aviation Pioneers in Saskatchewan." *Sask. Hist.* 28 (Winter 1975), pp. 9-28.
1954. **Goodwin, T.** "Recollections and Reminiscences of an English School Marm in Saskatchewan." *Sask. Hist.* 27 (Autumn 1974), pp. 103-107.
1955. **Greene, D.L.** "Reflections and Reminiscences: Early Pioneer Sports in Saskatchewan." *Sask. Hist.* 14 (Autumn 1961), pp. 110-113.
1956. **Grosman, Brian A.** "Law Reform: A Saskatchewan Viewpoint." *Dalhousie Law Journal* 2 (1925), pp. 455-472.
1957. **Heidt, Elizabeth.** "Folklore in Saskatchewan." *Sask. Hist.* 7 (Winter 1954), pp. 18-21.
1958. **Huel, R.J.A.** "The French Canadians and the Language Question, 1918." *Sask. Hist.* 23 (Winter 1970), pp. 1-15.
1959. ———. "The Teaching of French in Saskatchewan Public Schools." *Sask. Hist.* 24 (Winter 1971), pp. 13-24.
1960. ———. "French Language Education in Saskatchewan." In S.M. Trofimenkoff, ed. *The Twenties in Western Canada* (Ottawa, 1972), pp. 230-242.
1961. ———. "*La Survivance* in Saskatchewan: Schools, Politics and the Nativist Crusade for Cultural Conformity." Ph.D. Thesis (University of Alberta, 1975).
1962. **Hunter, A.T.** *Chronicle of Alcoholic Beverages in the North West Territories and Saskatchewan*. Regina: Commercial Printers, n.d.
1963. **Irwin, D.D.** "Behind the Footlights." *Sask. Hist.* 9 (Winter 1956), pp. 21-25.
1964. **Jameson, G.B.** "Vocational Education in the N.W.T. from 1870-1905, Saskatchewan from 1905-1950." M.Ed. Thesis (University of Saskatchewan, 1955).
1965. **King, Carlyle.** *The First Fifty: Teaching, Research and Public Service at the University of Saskatchewan, 1909-1959.* Toronto: McClelland and Stewart, 1959.
1966. ———. *Extending the Boundaries: Scholarship and Research at the University of Saskatchewan, 1909-1966.* Saskatoon: University of Saskatchewan, 1967.

1967. **Kirk, L.E.** "Early Years in the College of Agriculture." *Sask. Hist.* 12 (Winter 1959), pp. 23-30.

1968. **Kojder, A.M.** "The Saskatoon Women Teacher's Association: A Demand for Recognition." *Sask. Hist.* 30 (Spring 1977), pp. 56-62.

1969. **Lawton, A.** "Relief Administration in Saskatchewan during the Depression." *Sask. Hist.* 22 (Spring 1969), pp. 41-59.

1970. **Lyons, John E.** "A History of Doukhobor Schooling in Saskatchewan and British Columbia, 1899-1939." M.A. Thesis (University of Calgary, 1973).

1971. ———. "The (Almost) Quiet Evolution: Doukhobor Schooling in Saskatchewan." *Canadian Ethnic Studies* 8 (1976), pp. 23-27.

1972. **MacDonald, C.** "Pioneer Church Life in Saskatchewan." *Sask. Hist.* 13 (Winter 1960), pp. 1-18.

1973. **McDonald, R.J.** "The Presbyterian Church in Saskatchewan in the Nineteenth Century." *Sask. Hist.* 4 (Summer 1951), pp. 93-101.

1974. **McDougall, J.L.** "Recollections and Reminiscences: Cypress Hills Reminiscences." *Sask. Hist.* 23 (Winter 1970), pp. 27-30.

1975. **MacLean, Hugh.** "Recollections and Reminiscences: A Pioneer Prairie Doctor." *Sask. Hist.* 15 (Spring 1962), pp. 58-66.

1976. **McLeod, D.M.** "The History of Liquor Legislation in Saskatchewan, 1870-1947." M.A. Thesis (University of Saskachewan, 1948).

1976A. **McMenomy, Lorn E.** "A History of Secondary Education in Saskatchewan." M.Ed. Thesis (University of Manitoba, 1946).

1977. **Marshall, L.G.** "The Development of Education in Northern Saskatchewan." M.Ed. Thesis (University of Saskatchewan, 1966).

1978. **Morgan, E.C.** "Pioneer Recreation and Social Life." *Sask. Hist.* 18 (Spring 1965), pp. 41-55.

1979. **Morton, A.S.** *Saskatchewan: The Making of a University.* Toronto: University of Toronto Press, 1959.

1980. **Murray, Jean E.** "The Early History of Emmanuel College." *Sask. Hist.* 9 (Autumn 1956), pp. 81-101.

1981. ———. "The Contest for the University of Saskatchewan." *Sask. Hist.* 12 (Winter 1959), pp. 1-22.

1982. **Neatby, H. Blair.** "The Saskatchewan Relief Commission, 1931-34." *Sask. Hist.* 3 (Spring 1950), pp. 41-56.

1983. **Oliver, E.H.** *The Country School in Non-English Communities in Saskatchewan.* Saskatoon: Saturday Press and Prairie Farm, n.d.

1984. ———. "The Coming of the Barr Colonists." Canadian Historical Association. *Annual Report 1926,* pp. 65-86.
1985. **Oliver, E.H.** "The Presbyterian Church in Saskatchewan." Royal Society of Canada. *Proceedings and Transactions* 3d. Ser. 28 (1934), pp. 61-94.
1986. **O'Neill, P.B.** "Regina's Golden Age of Theatre: Her Playhouses and Players." *Sask. Hist.* 28 (Winter 1975), pp. 29-37.
1987. **Passmore, F.** "Methodist Memories of Saskatchewan." *Sask. Hist.* 8 (Winter 1955), pp. 11-16.
1988. **Payton, W.F.** *An Historical Sketch of the Diocese of Saskatchewan of the Anglican Church of Canada.* Prince Albert: Centennial Committee of the Diocese of Saskatchewan, 1974.
1989. **Pinno, Erhard.** "Temperance and Prohibition in Saskatchewan." M.A. Thesis (University of Saskatchewan, Regina, 1971).
1990. **Regina Local Council of Women.** *History of the Regina Local Council of Women, Commemorating Golden Jubilee, 1895-1945.* Regina: The Council, 1945.
1991. **Riddell, W.A.** *The First Decade, 1960-1970: A History of the University of Saskatchewan, Regina Campus.* Regina: University of Regina, 1974.
1992. **Rodwell, L.** "The Saskatchewan Association of Music Festivals." *Sask. Hist.* 16 (Winter 1963), pp. 1-21.
1993. **Roemer, M.I.** "Prepaid Medical Care and Changing Needs in Saskatchewan." *American Journal of Public Health* 46 (1956), pp. 1082-1088.
1994. ———. "Socialized Health Services in Saskatchewan." *Social Research* 25 (1958), pp. 87-101.
1995. **Simpson, George W.** "Father Delaire, Pioneer Missionary and Founder of Churches." *Sask. Hist.* 3 (Winter 1950), pp. 1-16.
1996. **Smith, Allison.** "J.D. Maveety and the Prince Albert *Times.*" *Sask. Hist.* 8 (Spring 1955), pp. 64-67.
1997. **Spinks, J.W.T.** *A Decade of Change: The University of Saskatchewan, 1959-1970.* Saskatoon: University of Saskatchewan, 1972.
1998. **Stone, G.M.** "The Regina Riot, 1935." M.A. Thesis (University of Saskatchewan, 1967).
1999. **Tagashira, K., and Lozowchuk, J.W.** "A Preliminary Report on Ethnicity and University Education in Saskatchewan, 1910-1962." In *Slavs in Canada.* Vol. 3 (Toronto, 1971), pp. 217-246.

2000. **Taylor, M.G.** "The Organization and Administration of the Saskatchewan Hospital Services Plan." Ph.D. Thesis (University of California, Berkeley, 1948).

2001. **Telford, Gertrude S.** "The First Child Welfare Conferences in Saskatchewan." *Sask. Hist.* 4 (Spring 1951), pp. 57-61.

2002. **Thomas, Lewis H.** "The Reports of the Board of Education." *Sask. Hist.* 2 (Autumn 1949), pp. 15-19.

2003. ———. *The University of Saskatchewan, 1909-1959.* Saskatoon: Modern Press, 1959.

2004. **Thompson, R.L.B.** *A Synoptic View of the Women's Christian Temperance Union, 1913-1973.* 3d. ed. Saskatoon: Early Mailing Service Ltd., 1975.

2005. **Thompson, W.P.** "A University in Trouble [University of Saskatchewan]." *Sask. Hist.* 17 (Autumn 1964), pp. 81-104.

2006. ———. *The University of Saskatchewan: A Personal History.* Toronto: University of Toronto Press, 1970.

2007. **Thomson, James S.** *Yesteryears at the University of Saskatchewan, 1937-1949.* Saskatoon: University of Saskatchewan, 1969.

2008. **Toombs, M.P.** "A Saskatchewan Experiment in Teacher Education, 1907-1917." *Sask. Hist.* 17 (Winter 1964), pp. 1-11.

2009. **Turner, Allan R.** "W.R. Motherwell and Agricultural Education, 1905-1918." *Sask. Hist.* 12 (Autumn 1959), pp. 81-96.

2010. **Tyre, Robert.** *Tales out of School.* Saskatoon: Saskatchewan Teachers' Federation, 1968.

2010A. **Waite, W.H.** "The History of Elementary and Secondary Education in Saskatchewan." M.Ed. Thesis (University of Manitoba, 1936).

g. Urban Development

i. General

2011. **Abrams, G.** *Prince Albert: The First Century, 1866-1966.* Saskatoon: Modern Press, 1966.

2012. **Abramson, J.A.** *Rural to Urban Adjustment [in Saskatchewan].* Ottawa: Queen's Printer, 1968.

2013. **Auclair, Elie J.** "Introduction générale à l'histoire de Gravelbourg." *Canada français* 19 (1931), pp. 249-257.

2014. **Belbeck, Dave, and Belbeck, Alice,** eds. *Golden Furrows: An Historical Chronicle of Swift Current.* Swift Current: The Local Council of Women, 1954.

2015. **Broadbridge, A.F.** "The History of Rosetown, 1904-1939." M.A. Thesis (University of Saskatchewan, 1949).

2016. **Carruthers, C.** "The Barr Colony." *A.H.R.* 1 (July 1953), pp. 16.

2017. **Dale, E.H.** "The Urban Centres of Southern Saskatchewan: Current Trends (1951-1971) and Prospects." In A.H. Paul and E.H. Dale, eds. *Southern Prairies Field Excursion: Background Papers* (Regina, 1972), pp. 267-310.

2018. **Dawson, G.F.** *The Municipal System of Saskatchewan.* 1947. Rev. ed. Regina: Department of Municipal Affairs, 1952.

2019. **Diefenbaker, John G.** "Prince Albert." *Habitat* 10 (1967), pp. 118-119.

2020. **Dykstra, T.L., and Ironside, R.G.** "The Effects of the Division of the City of Lloydminster by the Alberta-Saskatchewan Inter-Provincial Boundary." *Cahiers de géographie de Québec* 16 (1972), pp. 261-283.

2021. **Garrett, A.W.** *History of Milestone, 1893-1910.* Milestone: The Author, 1946.

2022. **Grant, Robert W.** *The Humboldt Story, 1903-1953.* Humboldt: Humboldt Board of Trade, 1954.

2023. **Greenblat, J.** *Those Were the Days in Swift Current.* Saskatoon: Modern Press, 1971.

2024. **Hébert, G.** *Les Débuts de Gravelbourg.* Gravelbourg: The Author, 1966.

2025. **King, A.** *Estevan: The Power Centre.* Saskatoon: Modern Press, 1967.

2026. **Kristjanson, L.F.** *Population Trends in the Incorporated Centers of Saskatchewan, 1921-1961.* Saskatoon: University of Saskatchewan, 1962.

2027. **Lawton, A.** "Urban Relief in Saskatchewan in the Depression." M.A. Thesis (University of Saskatchewan, 1970).

2028. **McCormick, James Hanna.** *Lloydminster, or Five Thousand Miles with the Barr Colonists.* London: Dranes, 1924.

2029. **McCracken, J.W.** "Yorkton during the Territorial Period, 1882-1905." M.A. Thesis (University of Saskatchewan, Regina, 1972).

2030. ———. "Yorkton during the Territorial Period, 1882-1905." *Sask. Hist.* 28 (Autumn 1975), pp. 95-110.

2031. **McCutcheon, M.K., and Young, R.C.** "The Development of Uranium City." *Canadian Geographer* 1 (1954), pp. 57-62.

2032. **Macdonald, R.H.** "Fort Battleford, Saskatchewan." *Canadian Geographical Journal* 67 (1963), pp. 54-61.

2033. **McGowan, D.C.** "A History of Swift Current and District to 1907." M.A. Thesis (University of Saskatchewan, Regina, 1972).

2034. ———. *Grassland Settlers: The Swift Current Region during the Era of the Ranching Frontier.* Regina: Canadian Plains Research Center, 1975.

2035. **McPherson, A.E.** "A History of the Battlefords to 1914." M.A. Thesis (University of Saskatchewan, 1966).

2036. ———. *The Battlefords: A History.* Saskatoon: Modern Press, 1968.

2037. **Matheson, M.H.** "Townsites and Urban Land Use in Southwestern Saskatchewan." *Canadian Geographer* 3 (1958), pp. 9-16.

2038. **Mellis, G.W.** "Mobility of Commercial Services and Their Impact on the Strength of Urban Communities in Saskatchewan: A Comparative Study Based on 1954 and 1967 Data." M.A. Thesis (University of Saskatchewan, Regina, 1971).

2039. **Moneo, G.W.** "The Major Trade Centre Communities of Saskatchewan, 1936-1966." M.A. Thesis (University of Calgary, 1970).

2040. **Murray, Jean E.** "The Provincial Capital Controversy in Saskatchewan." *Sask. Hist.* 5 (Autumn 1952), pp. 81-105.

2041. **Oliver, E.H.** "The Coming of the Barr Colonists." Canadian Historical Association. *Annual Report 1926,* pp. 65-87.

2042. **Pascoe, J.E.,** ed. *Moose Jaw, Saskatchewan: Golden Jubilee, 1903-1953.* Moose Jaw: Moose Jaw *Times Herald,* 1953.

2043. **Rendell, Alice.** "Letters from a Barr Colonist." *A.H.R.* 11 (Winter 1963), pp. 12-27.

2044. **Rodwell, L.** "Land Claims in the Prince Albert Settlement." *Sask. Hist.* 19 (Autumn 1966), pp. 1-23.

2045. ———. "Prince Albert River Lots." *Sask. Hist.* 19 (Autumn 1966), pp. 100-110.

2046. **Smith, Pamela J.** "The City of Moose Jaw Debenture Default, 1937-1945: A Case Study of Community Power." M.A. Thesis (University of Regina, 1974).

2047. **Tallant, Clive.** "The Break with Barr: An Episode in the History of the Barr Colony." *Sask. Hist.* 6 (Spring 1953), pp. 41-46.
2048. ———. "The North-West Mounted Police and the Barr Colony." *Sask. Hist.* 7 (Spring 1954), pp. 41-46.
2049. **White, C.O.** "Moose Jaw Opts for Private over Municipal or Provincial Ownership of Its Electrical Utility." In A.R. McCormack and Ian MacPherson, eds. *Cities in the West* (Ottawa, 1975), pp. 88-115.
2050. **Zides, Murray.** "Saskatchewan Community Planning." *Community Planning Review* 5 (1955), pp. 106-111.

  ii. Regina

2051. **Adams, D.L.** "Floods and Flood Management in the City of Regina, Saskatchewan, 1882-1974." M.A. Thesis (University of Calgary, 1974).
2052. **Anderson, F.W.** *Regina's Terrible Tornado.* Calgary: Frontiers Unlimited, 1964.
2053. **Barrow, G.T.** "A Factoral Ecology of Three Cities: Edmonton, Regina, and Winnipeg, 1961." M.A. Thesis (University of Calgary, 1972).
2054. **Begg, W.A.** "Town Planning in Regina." *Construction* 8 (1915), pp. 26-28.
2055. **Clements, M.** "Storm Clouds over Regina." *Sask. Hist.* 6 (Winter 1953), pp. 17-23.
2056. **Complin, Margaret.** "Floreat Regina." *Canadian Geographical Journal* 9 (1934), pp. 305-312.
2057. **Davis, E.N.** "Regina." *Habitat* 10 (1967), pp. 114-117.
2058. **Deane, R.B.** *Mounted Police Life in Canada: A Record of Thirty-One Years' Service.* London: Cassell, 1916.
2059. **Donkin, John G.** *Trooper and Redskin in the Far North-West: Recollections of Life in the North-West Mounted Police, Canada, 1884-1888.* London: Sampson, Low, Marston, Searle and Rivington, 1889.
2060. **Drake, Earl G.** "Regina 1882-1955." *Canadian Geographical Journal* 50 (1955), pp. 2-17.
2061. ———. "Regina in 1895: The Fair and the Fair Sex." *Sask. Hist.* 8 (Spring 1955), pp. 56-63.
2062. ———. *Regina: The Queen City.* Toronto: McClelland and Stewart, 1955.

2063. **Hammond, L.H.** "Regina." *Western Business and Industry* 30 (January 1956), pp. 58-59.

2064. **Hatcher, Colin K.** *Saskatchewan's Pioneer Streetcars: The Story of the Regina Municipal Railway.* Montreal: Railfare Enterprises, 1971.

2065. **Heimark, H.** "A Study of the City Centre for Regina, Saskatchewan." M.C.P. Thesis (University of Manitoba, 1968).

2066. **Hughes, M.** "The Functional Hierarchy of Business Centres in Regina." M.A. Thesis (University of Saskatchewan, Regina, 1972).

2067. **McAra, Peter.** *Sixty-Two Years on the Saskatchewan Prairies.* Regina, 1945.

2068. **Mahon, W.C.** *Real Estate Highlights, 1912-1972.* Regina: Regina Real Estate Board, 1972.

2069. **Martin, Mayor.** "Regina—Parks and Playgrounds." *Construction* 8 (1915), pp. 37-39.

2070. **Matravolgyi, T.A.** "Wascana Centre." *Canadian Geographical Journal* 82 (1971), pp. 60-65.

2071. **Mawson, T.H.** *Regina: A Preliminary Report on the Development of the City.* Regina: City of Regina, [1912?].

2072. **Murray, Jean E.** "The Provincial Capital Controversy in Saskatchewan." *Sask. Hist.* 5 (Autumn 1952), pp. 81-105.

2073. ———. "The Contest for the University of Saskatchewan." *Sask. Hist.* 12 (Winter 1959), pp. 1-30.

2074. **Neal, M.W.** *Regina, "Queen City of the Plains," 1903-1953.* Regina: Western Printers, 1953.

2075. **O'Neill, P.B.** "Regina's Golden Age of Theatre: Her Playhouse and Players." *Sask. Hist.* 28 (Winter 1975), pp. 29-37.

2076. **Powers, J.W.** *The History of Regina.* Regina: Leader Co., 1887.

2077. **Reese, N.A.** "Regina: Her Development." *Construction* 8 (1915), pp. 29-33.

2078. **Regina, Industrial Development Department.** *A Report on the Economic Development of the City of Regina.* Regina: City of Regina, 1960.

2079. **Reid, A.N.** "Informal Town Government in Regina, 1882-3." *Sask. Hist.* 6 (Autumn 1953), pp. 81-88.

2080. **Robinson, M.E.** *History of Wascana Creek.* Regina: Government of Saskatchewan, 1975.

2081. **Rosenberg, L.** "The History of the Regina Jewish Community." *Jewish Post* (1923). Copy in Provincial Archives of Saskatchewan, Regina.
2082. **Ross, M.** "Development in Regina." *Construction* 8 (1915), pp. 33-35.
2083. **Sinton, Robert.** *Looking Backward from the Eightieth Milestone, 1935 to 1854.* Regina: Paragon Business College, 1935.
2084. **Steele, S.B.** *Forty Years in Canada.* London: Herbert Jenkins, 1915.
2085. **Stone, G.M.** "The Regina Riot, 1935." M.A. Thesis (University of Saskatchewan, 1967).
2086. **Thomas, Lewis H.** "The Saskatchewan Legislative Building and Its Predecessors." Royal Architectural Institute of Canada. *Journal* 32 (1955), pp. 248-252.
2087. **Trotter, B.** *A Horseman and the West.* Toronto: Macmillan, 1925.
2088. **Turner, Allan R., ed.** "Documents of Western History: Wascana Creek and the 'Pile o' Bones.'" *Sask. Hist.* 19 (Autumn 1966), pp. 111-118.
2089. **Tyre, Robert.** "The Changing Face of Regina." *Western Business and Industry* 35 (April 1961), pp. 30-34.
2090. **Ukrainian Senior Citizens of Regina.** *From Dreams to Reality: A History of the Ukrainian Senior Citizens of Regina and District, 1896-1976.* Winnipeg: Trident Press, 1977.
2091. **Ward, Norman.** "Davin and the Founding of the *Leader.*" *Sask. Hist.* 6 (Winter 1953), pp. 13-16.
2092. **Weaver, Emily P.** "Regina: The Capital of Saskatchewan." *Canadian Magazine* 39 (1912), pp. 173-181.
2093. **Young, Walter D.** "M.J. Coldwell: The Making of a Social Democrat." *Journal of Canadian Studies* 9, no. 3 (1974), pp. 51-60.

iii. Saskatoon

2094. **Anderson, G.W., and Anderson, R.N., eds.** *Two White Oxen: A Perspective of Early Saskatoon, 1874-1905.* Saskatoon: G.W. Anderson, 1972.
2095. **Archer, John H.** "The History of Saskatoon." M.A. Thesis (University of Saskatchewan, 1948).
2096. ———. *Historic Saskatoon: A Concise Illustrated History of Saskatoon.* Saskatoon: Junior Chamber of Commerce, 1948.

2097. **Buckley, K.** *Growth and Housing Requirements: Report on Economic and Social Aspects of the Housing Problem in Saskatoon.* Saskatoon: University of Saskatchewan, 1958.

2098. **Buckwold, S.** "Land Policy in Saskatoon." *Habitat* 5 (1962), pp. 2-5.

2099. **Clubb, S.P.** *Saskatoon: The Serenity and the Surge.* Saskatoon: Midwest Litho Co., 1966.

2100. **Clubb, S.P., and Sarjeant, W.A.S.** *Saskatoon's Historic Buildings and Sites: A Survey and Proposals.* Saskatoon: Saskatoon Environmental Society, 1973.

2101. **Courtney, John C., and Smith, David E.** "Voting in a Provincial General Election and a Federal By-Election: A Constituency Study of Saskatoon City." *C.J.E.P.S.* 32 (1966), pp. 338-353.

2102. **Creighton, P.R.** "Taxation in Saskatoon: A Study in Municipal Finance." M.A. Thesis (University of Saskatchewan, 1925).

2103. **Delainey, W.P., and Sarjeant, W.A.S.** *Saskatoon, The Growth of a City. Part I: The Formative Years, 1882-1960.* Saskatoon: Saskatoon Environmental Society, 1974.

2104. **Field, A.J.** "The Saskatoon Jewish Community, 1905-1962." Saskatoon: University Library, Shortt Collection, 1963.

2105. **Gyuse, T.T.I.** "Service Centre Change in Metropolitan Hinterlands: A Case Study of Saskatoon and Calgary, 1951-1991." M.A. Thesis (University of Calgary, 1974).

2106. **Kerr, Don.** "Saskatoon: Boom and Bust on Third Avenue." *Next Year Country* 3 (1975), pp. 19-24.

2107. **Knowles, Eric.** "A 'Boomer' Settled in Saskatchewan and Built: When John East Came West." *Western Business and Industry* 20 (January 1946), pp. 60-64, 87.

2108. **Lawton, A.** "Relief Administration in Saskatoon during the Depression." *Sask. Hist.* 22 (Spring 1969), pp. 41-59.

2109. **Lim, H.S.** "Selected Characteristics of Population Distribution in the City of Saskatoon." M.A. Thesis (University of Saskatchewan, 1969).

2110. **Luk, L.W.C.** "The Assimilation of the Chinese in Saskatoon." M.A. Thesis (University of Saskatchewan, 1971).

2111. **Men of the City [Historical Association of Saskatoon].** *Narratives of Saskatoon, 1882-1912.* Saskatoon: The University Book-Store, 1927.

2112. **Murray, Jean E.** "The Provincial Capital Controversy in Saskatchewan." *Sask. Hist.* 5 (Autumn 1952), pp. 81-105.

2113. ———. "The Contest for the University of Saskatchewan." *Sask. Hist.* 12 (Winter 1959), pp. 1-22.

2114. **Nichol, John L.** *Through the Years with Knox.* Saskatoon: Knox Church, 1950.

2115. **Pattison, M.** *Cory in Recall.* Saskatoon: Rural Municipality of Cory, 1967.

2116. **Peel, Bruce, and Knowles, Eric.** *The Saskatoon Story, 1882-1952.* Saskatoon: Melville A. East, 1952.

2117. **Piper, J.** "Lots for Lots in Hub City: Land Development in Saskatoon." *Next Year Country* 2 (1974), pp. 18-22.

2118. ———. "Saskatoon Robs the Bank." *City Magazine* 1 (October 1974), pp. 16-20.

2119. **Ravis, D.** *Advanced Land Acquisition by Local Government: The Saskatoon Experience.* Saskatoon: City of Saskatoon, 1972.

2120. **Rees, Ronald.** "The 'Magic City on the Banks of the Saskatchewan': The Saskatoon Real Estate Boom of 1910-1913." *Sask. Hist.* 27 (Spring 1974), pp. 51-59.

2121. **Russell, E.T.P., ed.** *Streets and Roads of Saskatoon.* Saskatoon: Saskatoon Public Board of Education, 1973.

2122. **Siddigue, M.** "Patterns of Familial Decision-Making and Division of Labour: A Study of the Immigrant Indian-Pakistani Community of Saskatoon." M.A. Thesis (University of Saskatchewan, 1974).

2123. **Steck, W.F., and Sarjeant, W.A.S.** "The History and Achievements of the Saskatoon Environmental Society." *Urban History Review* 2-77 (1977), pp. 33-54.

2124. **Thomas, Lewis H.** "Saskatoon, 1883-1914." Unpublished Paper Read before Morton Historical Society, November 1944 (Saskatchewan Archives, Saskatoon).

2125. **Tiessen, Hugo.** "Saskatoon, Saskatchewan." *Canadian Geographical Journal* 86 (1973), pp. 54-61.

2126. **Tyre, Robert.** "The Changing Face of Saskatoon." *Western Business and Industry* 35 (April 1961), pp. 38-42.

2127. **Willmott, Donald E.** *Industry Comes to a Prairie Town.* Saskatoon: University of Saskatchewan, Centre for Community Studies, 1962.

h. Bibliographical

2127A. **Archer, John H.** "The Public Records in Saskatchewan." *Journal of the Society of Archivists* 2 (April 1960), pp. 16-25.

2128. **Dibb, Sandra, ed.** *Northern Saskatchewan Bibliography: Part I— Bibliography on Human Development in Northern Saskatchewan. Part II—Annotated Bibliography on Eco-Biology of Northern Saskatchewan.* Saskatoon: Institute for Northern Studies, University of Saskatchewan, 1975.

2129. **MacDonald, Mary Christine.** *Historical Directory of Saskatchewan Newspapers, 1878-1950.* Saskatoon: Saskatchewan Archives, 1951.

2130. ———. *Publications of the Government of the North-West Territories, 1876-1905, and of the Province of Saskatchewan, 1905-1952.* Regina: Legislative Library, 1952.

2131. **Paustian, Shirley I.** "Saskatchewan in Fiction." *Sask. Hist.* 1 (Autumn 1948), pp. 23-26.

2132. **Peel, Bruce.** "Saskatchewan Imprints before 1900." *Sask. Hist.* 6 (Autumn 1953), pp. 91-94.

2133. *Saskatchewan Homecoming '71: A Bibliography.* Regina: Bibliographic Services Division, Provincial Library, 1971. [Reprinted with supplement in 1972.]

2134. **Saskatchewan, Legislative Library.** *Catalogue of Newspapers on Microfilm in the Legislative Library (Archives Division) and Provincial Archives of Saskatoon.* Regina: Queen's Printer, 1958.

2134A. **Turner, Allan R.** "Archives and Local History Collections in Saskatchewan." *Canadian Library Journal* 29 (1972), pp. 205-208.

6

Alberta

a. General

2135. **Beale, A.M.** "Travels in Northern Alberta Sixty Years Ago." *Canadian Geographical Journal* 83 (1971), pp. 128-137.

2136. **Berry, Gerald L.** "Alberta-Montana Relationships." M.A. Thesis (University of Alberta, 1950).

2137. **Blue, John.** *Alberta, Past and Present, Historical and Biographical.* 3 vols. Chicago: Pioneer Historical Publishing Co., 1924.

2138. **Carpenter, David C.** "Alberta in Fiction: The Emergence of a Provincial Consciousness." *Journal of Canadian Studies* 10, no. 4 (1975), pp. 12-23.

2139. **Cantley, R.W.** "Jasper National Park." *Canadian Geographical Journal* 1 (1930), pp. 467-480.

2140. **Dawson, Carl A., and Murchie, R.W.** *The Settlement of the Peace River Country: A Study of a Pioneer Area.* Toronto: Macmillan, 1934.

2141. **Dempsey, Hugh A.** "Alberta through the Years." *Canadian Geographical Journal* 51 (1955), pp. 42-57.

2142. ———. "Writing-On-Stone and the Boundary Patrol." In Hugh A. Dempsey, ed. *Men in Scarlet* (Calgary, 1974), pp. 138-151.

2143. **Ellis, M.C.** "Local Migration in East Central Alberta." M.A. Thesis (University of Alberta, 1972).

2144. **Fidler, Vera.** "Cypress Hills: Plateau of the Prairie." *Canadian Geographical Journal* 87 (1973), pp. 28-35.

2145. **Fisher, C.L.** "Alberta, the Chinook Country." *Empire Digest* 3 (July 1946), pp. 72-78.

2146. **Forsey, Eugene A.** "Canada and Alberta: The Revival of Dominion Control over the Provinces." *Politics* 4 (1939), pp. 95-123.

2147. **Fryer, Harold.** *Ghost Towns of Alberta.* Langley: Stagecoach Publishing, 1976.

2148. **Getty, I.A.L.** "The Role of the Mounted Police Outposts in Southern Alberta." In Hugh A. Dempsey, ed. *Men in Scarlet* (Calgary, 1974), pp. 187-197.

2149. **Hardy, W.G., ed.** *The Alberta Golden Jubilee Anthology.* Toronto: McClelland and Stewart, 1955.

2150. ———. *Alberta, A Natural History.* Edmonton: Hurtig, 1967.

2150A. **Holmgren, Eric J.** *Alberta at the Turn of the Century: A Selection of Photographs from Ernest Brown, Harry Pollard and Other Photograph Collections in the Provincial Archives of Alberta.* Edmonton: Provincial Archives of Alberta, 1975.

2151. **Holmgren, Eric J., and Patricia M.** *2000 Place Names of Alberta.* Saskatoon: Modern Press, 1972.

2152. **Hooke, A.J.** "Alberta—Nature's Treasure House." *Canadian Geographical Journal* 35 (1947), pp. 154-177.

2153. **Horan, John W.** *"West, Nor' West": A History of Alberta.* Edmonton: Northgage Books, 1945.

2154. **Kroetsch, R.** *Alberta.* Toronto: Macmillan, 1968.

2155. **Liddell, K.E.** *This Is Alberta.* Toronto: Ryerson, 1952.

2156. ———. *Alberta Revisited.* Toronto: Ryerson, 1960.

2157. **Luxton, E.G.** *Banff: Canada's First National Park, A History and a Memory of Rocky Mountain Park.* Banff: Summer Thought, 1975.

2158. **McCaig, James.** *Alberta: A Survey of the Topography, Climate, Resources, Industries, Transportation and Communication, and Institutional Services of the Province of Alberta.* Edmonton: Department of Agriculture, 1919.

2159. **MacGregor, James G.** *A History of Alberta.* Edmonton: Hurtig, 1972.

2160. **MacInnes, C.M.** *In the Shadow of the Rockies.* London: Rivingtons, 1940.

2161. **MacRae, A.D.** *History of the Province of Alberta.* 2 vols. Calgary: Western Canadian History Co., 1912.

2162. **Magrath, C.A.** *The Galts, Father and Son: Pioneers in the Development of Southern Alberta.* Lethbridge: Lethbridge *Herald*, 1936.

Plate 12. Bow River Ranch near Cochrane, Alberta

2163. **Pearce, William.** "Establishment of National Parks in the Rockies." *A.H.R.* 10 (Summer 1962), pp. 8-17.

2164. **Pigeon, Louis Philippe.** "Impressions d'Alberta." *Canada français* (1933), pp. 921-925.

2165. **Poole, Colin.** "Identification of Mounted Police Outposts in Southern Alberta." In Hugh A. Dempsey, ed. *Men in Scarlet* (Calgary, 1974), pp. 198-211.

2166. **Stead, Robert J.C.** "The Yellowhead Pass." *Canadian Geographical Journal* 37 (1948), pp. 50-65.

2167. **Thirnbeck, A.R.** "An Analysis of a Group of Prairie Settlements North East of Calgary, Alberta." M.A. Thesis (University of Calgary, 1971).

2168. **Vanderhill, B.G.** "Trends in the Peace River Country." *Canadian Geographer* 7 (1963), pp. 33-41.

2169. **Villa-Arce, Jose.** "Alberta Provincial Police." *A.H.R.* 21 (Autumn 1973), pp. 16-19.

2170. **Wonders, William C., et al.** *Atlas of Alberta.* Edmonton: University of Alberta, 1969.

b. *The People*

2171. **Atwell, P.H.** "Kinship and Migration among Calgarian Residents of Indian Origin." M.A. Thesis (University of Calgary, 1969).
2172. **Bailey, Mary C.** "Reminiscences of a Pioneer." *A.H.R.* 15 (Autumn 1967), pp. 17-25.
2173. **Baldwin, Alice Sharples.** "The Sharples." *A.H.R.* 21 (Winter 1973), pp. 12-17.
2174. **Barclay, H.B.** "An Arab Community in the Canadian Northwest: A Preliminary Discussion of the Lebanese Community in Lac La Biche, Alberta." *Anthropologica* 10 (1968), pp. 143-156.
2175. ———. "The Holdeman Mennonites of Alberta: The Protestant Ethic versus the Spirit of Capitalism." In Richard Allen, ed. *Religion and Society in the Prairie West* (Regina, 1974), pp. 89-98.
2176. **Bargen, Peter F.** "Mennonite Settlements in Alberta." *A.H.R.* 2 (Winter 1954), pp. 13-22.
2177. **Barnes, J.A.** "Home on a Canadian Rockpile." *Canadian Geographical Journal* 67 (Winter 1964), pp. 18-21.
2178. **Bartlett, C.** "Early Mormon Settlement in Alberta." B.A. Honours Thesis (Lakehead University, 1973).
2179. **Baureiss, G.A.** "The Chinese Community of Calgary." *Canadian Ethnic Studies* 3 (1971), pp. 43-56.
2180. **Blackburn, John H.** *Land of Promise.* Toronto: Macmillan, 1970.
2181. **Boldt, E.D.** "Conformity and Deviance: The Hutterites of Alberta." M.A. Thesis (University of Alberta, 1966).
2182. **Brasser, Ted J.** "The Creative Visions of a Blackfoot Shaman." *Alberta History* 23 (Spring 1975), pp. 14-16.
2183. **Brick, A.L.** "Rev. J. Gough Brick and His Shaftesbury Mission Farm." *A.H.R.* 3 (Spring 1955), pp. 3-12.
2184. **Brunvand, Jan.** *Norwegian Settlers in Alberta.* Ottawa: National Museum of Man, 1974.
2185. **Burles, Gordon.** "Bill Peyto." *Alberta History* 24 (Winter 1976), pp. 5-11.
2186. **Byrne, T.C.** "The Ukrainian Community in North-Central Alberta." M.A. Thesis (University of Alberta, 1937).

2187. **Callihoo, Victoria.** "The Iroquois in Alberta." *A.H.R.* 7 (Spring 1959), pp. 17-18.
2188. **Card, B.Y.**, et al. *The Métis in Alberta Society.* Edmonton: University of Alberta, 1963.
2189. **Carter, D.J.** "The Rev'd. Samuel Trivett, Part 1." *A.H.R.* 21 (Spring 1973), pp. 13-19.
2190. **Cashman, Tony.** *Vice-Regal Cowboy [J.J. Bowlen].* Edmonton: Institute of Applied Art, 1957.
2191. **Chalmers, John W.** "John W. Niddrie." *A.H.R.* 19 (Winter 1971), pp. 26-29.
2192. **Comfort, D.J.** "Tom Draper, Oil Sands Pioneer." *Alberta History* 25 (Winter 1977), pp. 25-29.
2193. **Crawford, M.E.** "A Geographic Study of the Distribution of Population Change in Alberta, 1931-1961." M.A. Thesis (University of Alberta, 1962).
2194. **Daw, Ruth M.** "Sgt.-Major J.H.G. Bray, the Forgotten Horseman." In Hugh A. Dempsey, ed. *Men in Scarlet* (Calgary, 1974), pp. 152-162.
2195. **Dempsey, Hugh A.** "The Story of the Blood Reserve." *A.H.R.* 1 (Autumn 1953), pp. 27-36.
2196. ———. "The Indians of Alberta." *A.H.R.* 15 (Winter 1967), pp. 1-5.
2197. ———. "The Centennial of Treaty Seven." *Canadian Geographical Journal* 95 (1977), pp. 10-19.
2198. **Dempsey, Hugh A.**, ed. *The Best of Bob Edwards.* Edmonton: Hurtig, 1975.
2199. **Driben, Paul.** "We Are Métis: The Ethnography of a Halfbreed Community in Northern Alberta." Ph.D. Thesis (University of Minnesota, 1975).
2200. **Eggleston, Wilfrid.** "The People of Alberta." *Canadian Geographical Journal* 15 (1937), pp. 213-222.
2201. **Emanuel, L.** "Some Aspects of Ethnic Identity in an Edmonton Parish." *Canadian Ethnic Studies* 6 (1974), pp. 87-96.
2202. **Emery, George N.** "Methodist Missions among the Ukrainians." *A.H.R.* 19 (Spring 1971), pp. 8-19.
2203. **Evans, S.** "The Dispersal of Hutterite Colonies in Alberta, 1918-1971: The Spatial Expression of Cultural Identity." M.A. Thesis (University of Calgary, 1973).

2204. ———. "Spatial Bias in the Incidence of Nativism: Opposition to Hutterite Expansion in Alberta." *Canadian Ethnic Studies* 6 (1974), pp. 1-16.

2204A. ———. "The Spatial Expression of Cultural Identity: The Hutterites in Alberta." In B.M. Barr, ed. *The Kootenay Collection of Research Studies in Geography* (Vancouver: B.C. Geographical Series, No. 18, 1974), pp. 9-20.

2205. **Frémont, Donatien.** "Les Français dans l'Alberta." *Amérique française* 12 (1954), pp. 29-39.

2206. **Gershaw, F.W.** "Crowfoot, Famous Blackfoot Chief." *A.H.R.* 2 (Winter 1954), pp. 29-30.

2207. **Gerwin, E.** "A Survey of the German-Speaking Population in the Province of Alberta." M.A. Thesis (University of Alberta, 1938).

2208. **Griesbach, W.A.** "The Narrative of James Gibbons (Part 1)." *A.H.R.* 6 (Summer 1958), pp. 1-6.

2209. **Hanks, L.M., and Hanks, J.** *Tribe under Trust: A Study of the Blackfoot Reserve of Alberta.* Toronto: University of Toronto Press, 1950.

2210. **Hardisty, Richard.** "The Last Sun Dance." *Alberta Folklore Quarterly* 2 (1946), pp. 57-61.

2211. ———. "The Blackfoot Treaty." *A.H.R.* 5 (Summer 1957), pp. 20-22.

2212. **Hart, Edward J.** "The Emergence and Role of the Elite in the Franco-Albertan Community to 1914." In Lewis H. Thomas, ed. *Essays on Western History* (Edmonton, 1976), pp. 159-174.

2213. **Hatt, F.K.** "The Response to Directed Social Change on an Alberta Métis Colony." M.A. Thesis (University of Alberta, 1969).

2214. **Higginson, T.B.** "Moira O'Neill in Alberta." *A.H.R.* 5 (Spring 1957), pp. 22-25.

2214A. **Hull, V.L.** "A Geographic Study of the Impact of Two Ethnic Groups on the Rural Landscape in Central Alberta." M.A. Thesis (University of Alberta, 1965).

2215. **Iwaasa, David B.** "The Japanese in Southern Alberta, 1941-45." *Alberta History* 24 (Summer 1976), pp. 5-19.

2215A. **Jackson, W.** "Ethnicity and Areal Organization among French Canadians in the Peace River District, Alberta." M.A. Thesis (University of Alberta, 1970).

2216. **Jenness, Diamond.** *The Sarcee Indians of Alberta.* Ottawa: National Museum of Man, 1938.

2217. **Jennings, John.** "Policemen and Poachers—Indian Relations on the Ranching Frontier." In A.W. Rasporich and H.C. Klassen, eds. *Frontier Calgary* (Calgary, 1975), pp. 87-99.

2218. **Jordan, Mabel E.** "George Millward McDougall, Missionary and Nation-Builder." *A.H.R.* 3 (Winter 1955), pp. 24-33.

2219. ———. "Henry Bird Steinhauer and His Whitefish Lake Mission." *A.H.R.* 3 (Autumn 1955), pp. 11-12.

2220. **Knill, William D.** "The Hutterites: Cultural Transmission in a Closed Society." *A.H.R.* 16 (Summer 1968), pp. 1-10.

2220A. **Laatsch, W.G.** "Hutterite Colonization in Alberta." *Journal of Geography* 70 (1971), pp. 347-359.

2221. **Lee, Lawrence B.** "The Mormons Come to Canada, 1887-1902." *Pacific Northwest Quarterly* 59 (1968), pp. 11-22.

2221A. **Lehr, John C.** "Mormon Settlements in Southern Alberta." M.A. Thesis (University of Alberta, 1971).

2222. ———. "The Mormon Cultural Landscape in Alberta." In R. Leigh, ed. *Malaspina Papers: Studies in Human and Physical Geography* (Vancouver: B.C. Geographical Series, No. 17, 1973), pp. 25-34.

2223. ———. "Ukrainian Houses in Alberta." *A.H.R.* 21 (Autumn 1973), pp. 9-15.

2224. ———. "Changing Ukrainian House Styles." *Alberta History* 23 (Winter 1975), pp. 25-29.

2225. ———. *Ukrainian Vernacular Architecture in Alberta.* Occasional Paper No. 1. Edmonton: Historic Sites Service, 1976.

2225A. **Lester, G.A.** "The Distribution of Religious Groups in Alberta, 1961." M.A. Thesis (University of Alberta, 1966).

2226. **McAdam, Eben.** "Eben McAdam's Diary (Part 1)." *A.H.R.* 2 (Spring 1954), pp. 3-10.

2227. ———. "Eben McAdam's Diary (Part 2)." *A.H.R.* 2 (Summer 1954), pp. 34-41.

2228. **MacDonald, R.J.** "Hutterite Education in Alberta: A Test Case in Assimilation, 1920-1970." In A.W. Rasporich, ed. *Western Canada: Past and Present* (Calgary, 1975), pp. 133-149.

2229. **MacDonell, R.A.** "British Immigration Schemes in Alberta." *A.H.R.* 16 (Spring 1968), pp. 5-13.

2230. **MacEwan, Grant.** *Eye Opener Bob: The Story of Bob Edwards.* Edmonton: Institute of Applied Art, 1957.

2231. ———. *Fifty Mighty Men.* Saskatoon: Modern Press, 1958.

2232. ———. *John Ware's Cow Country.* Edmonton: Institute of Applied Art, 1960.

2233. **MacGregor, James G.** *Vilni Zemli (Free Lands): The Ukrainian Settlement of Alberta.* Toronto: McClelland and Stewart, 1969.

2234. ———. *Father Lacombe.* Edmonton: Hurtig, 1975.

2235. **McGusty, H.A.** "An Englishman in Alberta." *A.H.R.* 14 (Winter 1966), pp. 11-21.

2236. **McIntyre, M.L.** "Sarcee Demography, 1880-1925." M.A. Thesis (University of Calgary, 1975).

2237. **Mackie, M.** "Ethnic Stereotypes and Prejudice: Alberta Indians, Hutterites, and Ukrainians." *Canadian Ethnic Studies* 6 (1974), pp. 39-52.

2238. **Martin, John.** "Prairie Reminiscences." *A.H.R.* 10 (Spring 1962), pp. 5-19.

2239. **Niddrie, J.G.** "Sundre Settlers." *A.H.R.* 18 (Winter 1970), pp. 14-20.

2240. **Oka, Mike, and Mills, Harry.** "A Blood Indian's Story." *A.H.R.* 3 (Autumn 1955), pp. 13-16.

2241. **Palmer, H.** "Anti-Oriental Sentiment in Alberta, 1880-1920." *Canadian Ethnic Studies* 2 (1970), pp. 31-57.

2242. ———. "The Hutterite Land Expansion Controversy in Alberta." *Western Canadian Journal of Anthropology* 2 (1971), pp. 618-646.

2243. ———. *Land of Second Chance: A History of Ethnic Groups in Southern Alberta.* Lethbridge: Lethbridge *Herald*, 1972.

2244. ———. "Nativism and Ethnic Tolerance in Alberta, 1920-1972." Ph.D. Thesis (York University, 1973).

2245. ———. "Nativism in Alberta, 1925-1930." Canadian Historical Association. *Historical Papers 1974,* pp. 183-212.

2246. **Pierce, R.J.** "Rev. John Gough Brick." *A.H.R.* 4 (Spring 1956), pp. 17-21.

2247. **Pitt, E.L.** "The Hutterian Brethren in Alberta." M.A. Thesis (University of Alberta, 1949).

2248. **Potrebenko, Helen.** *This Is How We Worked: A History of Ukrainians in Alberta.* Toronto: N.C. Press, 1976.

2249. ———. *No Streets of Gold: A Social History of Ukrainians in Alberta.* Vancouver: New Star Books, 1977.
2250. **Ridge, Alan D.** "C.C. McCaul, Pioneer Lawyer." *A.H.R.* 21 (Winter 1973), pp. 21-25.
2251. **Roberts, L.E.**, ed. *Alberta Homestead: Chronicle of a Pioneer Family.* Austin: University of Texas Press, 1968.
2252. **Sawatzsky, A.A.** "The Mennonites of Alberta and Their Assimilation." M.A. Thesis (University of Alberta, 1964).
2253. **Shandro, P.A.** "The French Settlers at Trochu, 1903-1914." M.A. Thesis (McGill University, 1974).
2254. **Shaw, P.C.** "Dr. Frederick D. Shaw." *A.H.R.* 4 (Summer 1956), pp. 19-20.
2255. **Sproule, A.F.** "The Life and Influence on the Development of the Canadian West of Senator Patrick Burns." M.A. Thesis (University of Alberta, 1961).
2256. **Steele, C. Frank.** *Prairie Editor: The Life and Times of Buchanan of Lethbridge.* Toronto: Ryerson, 1961.
2256A. **Strong-Boag, Veronica.** "Canadian Feminism in the 1920s: The Case of Nellie L. McClung." *Journal of Canadian Studies* 12, no. 4 (1977), pp. 58-68.
2257. **Ukrainian Pioneers' Association of Alberta.** *Ukrainians in Alberta.* Edmonton: Ukrainian Archives, 1975.
2258. **Van Tighem, Frank.** "Father Leonard Van Tighem, O.M.I." *A.H.R.* 12 (Winter 1964), pp. 17-21.
2259. **Voisey, P.L.** "Two Chinese Communities in Alberta: An Historical Perspective." *Canadian Ethnic Studies* 2 (1970), pp. 15-30.
2260. **Walker, James.** "My Life in the North-West Mounted Police." *A.H.R.* 8 (Winter 1960), pp. 1-15.
2261. **Waywitka, Anne B.** "A Roumanian Pioneer." *A.H.R.* 21 (Autumn 1973), pp. 20-27.
2262. **Wilcox, A.G.** "Founding of the Mormon Community in Alberta." M.A. Thesis (University of Alberta, 1950).
2263. **Wilson, Thomas E.** *Trail Blazer of the Canadian Rockies.* Calgary: Glenbow-Alberta Institute, 1972.
2264. **Wonders, William C.** "Scandinavian Homesteaders." *Alberta History* 24 (Summer 1976), pp. 1-4.
2265. **Yackulic, G.A.** "Alberta's Blood Indians." *Western Business and Industry* 27 (October 1953), pp. 28-30, 56.

2266. **Young, T.C.** "Lewis James Swift, First White Man to Settle in Jasper National Park." *A.H.R.* 2 (Winter 1954), p. 31.

c. Government and Politics

2267. **Aberhart, W.** *Social Credit Manual.* Calgary: Western Printing and Litho Co., 1935.

2268. **Alberta, Province of.** *The Case for Alberta: Submissions to Royal Commission on Dominion-Provincial Relations.* Edmonton: King's Printer, 1938.

2269. **Anderson, O.** "The Alberta Social Credit Party: An Empirical Analysis of Membership, Characteristics, Participation, and Opinions." Ph.D. Thesis (University of Alberta, 1972).

2270. **Angus, H.F.** "The Portent of Social Credit in Alberta." *Pacific Affairs* 9 (1936), pp. 381-387.

2271. **Anton, Gordon A.** "The Liberal Party in Alberta: An Organizational Case Study." M.A. Thesis (University of Calgary, 1972).

2272. **Barr, John J.** *The Dynasty: The Rise and Fall of Social Credit in Alberta.* Toronto: McClelland and Stewart, 1974.

2273. **Betke, Carl.** "The United Farmers of Alberta, 1921-1935: The Relationship between the Agricultural Organization and the Government of Alberta." M.A. Thesis (University of Alberta, 1971).

2274. ———. "Farm Politics in an Urban Age: The Decline of the United Farmers of Alberta after 1921." In Lewis H. Thomas, ed. *Essays on Western History* (Edmonton, 1976), pp. 175-192.

2275. **Binns, Kenneth.** *Social Credit in Alberta: Report Prepared for the Government of Tasmania.* Hobart, Tasmania: Government Printer, 1947.

2276. **Boudreau, Joseph A.** *Alberta, Aberhart and Social Credit.* Toronto: Holt, Rinehart and Winston, 1975.

2277. **Britnell, G.E., and McGown, A.F.** "Alberta, Economic and Political." *C.J.E.P.S.* 2 (1936), pp. 512-549.

2278. **Douglas, C.H., et al.** *First Interim Report on the Possibilities of the Application of Social Credit Principles to the Province of Alberta.* Edmonton: King's Printer, 1935.

2279. ———. *The Alberta Experiment: An Interim Survey.* London: Eyre and Spottiswoode, 1937.

2280. **Elliott, David R.** "The Dispensational Theology and Political Ideology of William Aberhart." M.A. Thesis (University of Calgary, 1975).

2281. **Elton, D.K.** "Electoral Perception of Federalism: A Descriptive Analysis of the Alberta Electorate." Ph.D. Thesis (University of Alberta, 1973).

2282. **Embree, David Grant.** "The Rise of the United Farmers of Alberta." M.A. Thesis (University of Alberta, 1956).

2283. ———. "Rise of the United Farmers of Alberta." *A.H.R.* 5 (Autumn 1957), pp. 1-5.

2284. **Finlay, J.L.** *Social Credit: The English Origins.* Montreal: McGill-Queen's University Press, 1972.

2285. **Flanagan, Thomas E.** "Ethnic Voting in Alberta Provincial Elections, 1921-1971." *Canadian Ethnic Studies* 3 (1971), pp. 139-164.

2286. ———. "Social Credit in Alberta: A Canadian 'Cargo Cult'?" *Archives de sociologie des religions* 34 (1972), pp. 39-48.

2287. ———. "Political Geography and the United Farmers of Alberta." In S.M. Trofimenkoff, ed. *The Twenties in Western Canada* (Ottawa, 1972), pp. 138-169.

2288. ———. "Stability and Change in Alberta Provincial Elections." *A.H.R.* 21 (Autumn 1973), pp. 1-8.

2289. **Forsey, Eugene A.** "Canada and Alberta: The Revival of Dominion Control over the Provinces." *Politics* 4 (1939), pp. 95-123.

2290. **Friedmann, Karl A.** "Controlling Bureaucracy: Attitudes in the Alberta Public Service towards the Ombudsman." *Canadian Public Administration* 19 (1976), pp. 51-87.

2291. **Georgeson, M.R.** "A One-Party Dominant Party System: The Case of Alberta." M.A. Thesis (University of Calgary, 1974).

2292. **Giles, Mabel C.** *A Tribute to William Aberhart.* Calgary: Calgary Prophetic Bible Institute, 1943.

2293. **Gordon, S.B.** "R.B. Bennett, M.L.A., 1897-1905: The Years of Apprenticeship." M.A. Thesis (University of Calgary, 1975).

2294. **Grayson, J.P., and Grayson, L.M.** "The Social Base of Interwar Political Unrest in Urban Alberta." *Canadian Journal of Political Science* 7 (1974), pp. 289-313.

2295. **Groh, D.G.** "The Political Thought of Ernest Manning." M.A. Thesis (University of Calgary, 1970).

2296. **Hanson, E.J.** "Public Finance in Alberta Since 1935." *C.J.E.P.S.* 18 (1952), pp. 322-335.

2297. ———. "Provincial Arts in Alberta." *Canadian Tax Journal* 1 (1953), pp. 468-480.

2298. ———. *Local Government in Alberta*. Toronto: McClelland and Stewart, 1956.

2299. **Hiller, Harry H.** "A Critical Analysis of the Role of Religion in a Canadian Populist Movement: The Emergence and Dominance of the Social Credit Party in Alberta." Ph.D. Thesis (McMaster University, 1972).

2300. **Hostetler, John A.** "The Common Property Act of Alberta." *University of Toronto Law Journal* 14 (1961), pp. 125-128.

2301. **Hulmes, F.G.** "The Senior Executive and the Fifteenth Alberta Legislature: A Study in the Social and Political Background of Membership." M.A. Thesis (University of Alberta, 1970).

2302. **Irving, John A.** "Psychological Aspects of the Social Credit Movement in Alberta." *Canadian Journal of Psychology* 1 (1947), pp. 17-27, 75-86, 127-140.

2303. ———. "The Appeal of Social Credit." *Queen's Quarterly* 60 (1953), pp. 146-160.

2304. ———. *The Social Credit Movement in Alberta*. Toronto: University of Toronto Press, 1959.

2305. ———. "Interpretations of the Social Credit Movement." In H.G. Thorburn, ed. *Party Politics in Canada* (Scarborough, 1967), pp. 148-158.

2306. **Jameson, Sheilagh S.** "Give Your Other Vote to the Sister." *A.H.R.* 15 (Autumn 1967), pp. 10-16.

2307. **Johnson, L.P.V., and MacNutt, Ola.** *Aberhart of Alberta*. Edmonton: Institute of Applied Art, 1970.

2308. **Johnson, M.** "The Failure of the C.C.F in Alberta: An Accident of History?" M.A. Thesis (University of Alberta, 1974).

2309. **Kennedy, Orvis A.** *Principles and Policies of Social Credit*. Edmonton: Alberta Social Credit League, 1965.

2310. **Kenward, J.K.** "Political Manipulation and Rewards in the Crowsnest Pass, Southern Alberta." M.A. Thesis (Simon Fraser University, 1971).

2311. **Long, J.A.** "Maldistribution in Western Provincial Legislatures: The Case of Alberta." *Canadian Journal of Political Science* 2 (1969), pp. 345-355.

2312. **Long, J.A., and Quo, F.Q.** "Alberta: One Party Dominance." In M. Robin, ed. *Canadian Provincial Politics* (Scarborough, 1972), pp. 1-26.

2313. **MacEwan, Grant.** *Poking into Politics.* Edmonton: Institute of Applied Art, 1966.

2314. **McIntosh, W.A.** "The United Farmers of Alberta, 1909-1920." M.A. Thesis (University of Calgary, 1971).

2315. **McKinlay, F.M.** "The Honourable Irene Parlby." M.A. Thesis (University of Alberta, 1953).

2316. **MacLean, Una.** "The Honourable Irene Parlby." *A.H.R.* 7 (Spring 1959), pp. 1-6.

2317. **Macpherson, C.B.** *Democracy in Alberta: Social Credit and the Party System.* 1953. Rev. ed. Toronto: University of Toronto Press, 1962.

2318. **McQuarrie, A.H.** "The 1913 Provincial Election." *A.H.R.* 7 (Winter 1959), pp. 10-13.

2319. **Madsen, R.P.** "The Fiscal Development of Alberta." M.A. Thesis (University of Alberta, 1949).

2320. **Malliah, H.C.** "A Socio-Historical Study of the Legislators of Alberta, 1905-1967." Ph.D. Thesis (University of Alberta, 1970).

2321. **Mallory, J.R.** "Disallowance and the National Interest: The Alberta Social Credit Legislation of 1937." *C.J.E.P.S.* 14 (1948), pp. 342-357.

2322. ———. *Social Credit and the Federal Power in Canada.* Toronto: University of Toronto Press, 1954.

2323. **Manning, E.C.** *Political Realignment: A Challenge to Thoughtful Canadians.* Toronto: McClelland and Stewart, 1967.

2324. **Marton, E.G.** *Who's Who in Federal Politics from Alberta.* Lethbridge: University of Lethbridge, 1972.

2325. **Masson, J.K.** "The Demise of 'Alphabet Parties': The Rise of Responsible Party Politics in Cities." Occasional Paper No. 4. Edmonton: Department of Political Science, University of Alberta, 1976.

2326. **Miller, James A.** "The Alberta Press and the Conscription Issue in the First World War, 1914-1918." M.A. Thesis (University of Alberta, 1974).

2327. **Palmer, H., and Palmer, Tamara.** "The 1971 Election and the Fall of Social Credit in Alberta." *Prairie Forum* 1 (1976), pp. 123-134.

2328. **Pashak, L.B.** "The Populist Characteristics of the Early Social Credit Movement in Alberta." M.A. Thesis (University of Calgary, 1971).

2329. **Robert, G.R.** "Political Orientations of Calgary Children from Grades Four to Eight." M.Ed. Thesis (University of Calgary, 1969).

2330. **Rolph, William K.** *Henry Wise Wood of Alberta.* Toronto: University of Toronto Press, 1950.

2331. **Scawn, D.R.** "A History and Analysis of the 1971 Alberta General Election." M.A. Thesis (University of Calgary, 1973).

2332. **Schultz, Harold J.** "William Aberhart and the Social Credit Party: A Political Biography." Ph.D. Thesis (Duke University, 1959).

2333. ———. "Aberhart, the Organization Man." *A.H.R.* 7 (Spring 1959), pp. 19-26.

2334. ———. "The Social Credit Back-benchers Revolt, 1937." *C.H.R.* 41 (1960), pp. 1-18.

2335. ———. "A Second Term: 1940." *A.H.R.* 10 (Winter 1962), pp. 17-26.

2336. ———. "Portrait of a Premier: William Aberhart." *C.H.R.* 45 (1964), pp. 185-211.

2336A. **Schwartz, C.** "Social Credit Theory and Legislation in Alberta." M.A. Thesis (University of Manitoba, 1949).

2337. **Scratch, John R.** "The Editorial Reaction of the Alberta Press to the Bennett Government, 1930-1935." M.A. Thesis (University of Alberta, 1968).

2338. **Serfaty, Meir.** "The Unity Movement in Alberta." *A.H.R.* 21 (Spring 1973), pp. 1-9.

2339. **Sinclair, Peter R.** "Populism in Alberta and Saskatchewan." Ph.D. Thesis (University of Edinburgh, 1972).

2340. **Smith, David E.** "A Comparison of Prairie Political Development in Saskatchewan and Alberta." *Journal of Canadian Studies* 4, no. 1 (1969), pp. 17-25.

2341. **Smith, M.M.** "The Ideological Relationship between the United Farmers of Alberta and the Co-operative Commonwealth Federation." M.A. Thesis (McGill University, 1967).

2342. **Smith, P.D.** "The United Farmers of Alberta and the Ginger Group: Independent Political Action, 1919-1939." M.A. Thesis (University of Alberta, 1973).

2343. **Stanley, George F.G.** "From New Brunswick to Calgary—R.B. Bennett in Retrospect." In A.W. Rasporich and H.C. Klassen, eds. *Frontier Calgary* (Calgary, 1975), pp. 242-266.

2344. **Thomas, L.G.** "The Liberal Party in Alberta, 1905-1921." *C.H.R.* 28 (1947), pp. 411-427.

2345. ———. *The Liberal Party in Alberta: A History of Politics in the Province of Alberta, 1905-1921.* Toronto: University of Toronto Press, 1959.

2346. **Thomas, Lewis H.**, ed. *William Aberhart and Social Credit in Alberta.* Toronto: Copp Clark, 1977.

2347. **Voisey, P.L.** "The 'Votes for Women' Movement." *Alberta History* 23 (Summer 1975), pp. 10-23.

2348. **Waddell, W.S.** "Frank Oliver and the *Bulletin*." *A.H.R.* 5 (Summer 1957), pp. 7-12.

2349. **Ward, Norman.** "Hon. James Gardiner and the Liberal Party of Alberta, 1935-40." *C.H.R.* 56 (1975), pp. 303-322.

Plate 13. William Aberhart Broadcasting in the 1930's

2350. **Whalen, Hugh J.** "Distinctive Legislation of the Government of Alberta, 1935-1950." M.A. Thesis (University of Alberta, 1951).
2351. ———. "Social Credit Measures in Alberta." *C.J.E.P.S.* 18 (1952), pp. 500-517.
2352. **Willms, A.H.** "Public Utility Regulation in Alberta: A Case Study of the Natural Gas Distributing Industry." M.A. Thesis (University of Calgary, 1970).

d. Agriculture and Rural Development

2353. **Abell, A.S.** "Rural Municipal Government in Alberta: Taxation and Finance." M.A. Thesis (University of Toronto, 1940).
2354. ———. "Rural Municipal Difficulties in Alberta." *C.J.E.P.S.* 6 (1940), pp. 555-561.
2355. **Ahern, H.G.** "In Search of a Homestead." *A.H.R.* 13 (Spring 1965), pp. 16-18.
2356. **Albright, W.D.** "Past, Present and Future of the Peace." *Canadian Geographical Journal* 16 (1938), pp. 127-138.
2357. **Anderson, Raoul.** "Agricultural Development of the Alexis Stoney." *A.H.R.* 20 (Autumn 1972), pp. 16-20.
2358. **Ariza, J.H.** "Community Development Experiences in the Chipewyan Community of Cold Lake, Alberta." M.A. Thesis (University of Alberta, 1974).
2359. **Asante, E.O.** "The Incidence of Rural Property Taxation in Alberta." M.Sc. Thesis (University of Alberta, 1974).
2360. **Breen, D.H.** "The Cattle Compact: The Ranch Community in Southern Alberta, 1881-1896." M.A. Thesis (University of Calgary, 1969).
2361. ———. "The Mounted Police and the Ranching Frontier." In Hugh A. Dempsey, ed. *Men in Scarlet* (Calgary, 1974), pp. 115-139.
2362. **Brown, Donald Edward.** "A History of the Cochrane Area." M.A. Thesis (University of Alberta, 1951).
2363. ———. "The Cochrane Ranch." *A.H.R.* 4 (Autumn 1956), pp. 3-8.
2364. **Burnet, Jean.** *Next Year Country: A Study of Rural Social Organization in Alberta.* Toronto: University of Toronto Press, 1951.
2365. **Cameron D.; Nesbitt, L.D.; and Platt, A.W.** *Report of the Committee on Farm Organization.* Edmonton: Co-op Press, 1963.

2366. **Cantlon, Mrs. F.M.** "Breaking the Prairie Sod." *A.H.R.* 13 (Summer 1965), pp. 22-24.
2367. **Cochrane, H.G.** "Irrigation in Alberta." *A.H.R.* 16 (Spring 1968), pp. 14-18.
2368. **Cross, Alfred E.** "The Roundup of 1887." *A.H.R.* 13 (Spring 1965), pp. 23-27.
2369. **Dawson, Carl A.** *The Settlement of the Peace River Country: A Study of a Pioneer Area.* Toronto: Macmillan, 1934.
2370. **Dempsey, Hugh A.** "The Calgary-Edmonton Trail." *A.H.R.* 7 (Autumn 1959), pp. 16-21.
2371. **Den Otter, A.A.** "Irrigation and the Lethbridge *News.*" *A.H.R.* 18 (Autumn 1970), pp. 17-25.
2372. **Dreisziger, N.F.** "The Canadian-American Irrigation Frontier Revisited: The International Origins of Irrigation in Southern Alberta, 1885-1909." Canadian Historical Association. *Historical Papers 1975,* pp. 211-229.
2373. **Ellis, Frank H.** "Peace River's Second-Righters." *Canadian Geographical Journal* 53 (1956), pp. 94-101.
2374. **English, R.E.** "Agriculture in Alberta." *Canadian Geographical Journal* 56 (1958), pp. 98-113.
2375. **Ference, E.A.** "Literature Associated with Ranching in Southern Alberta." M.A. Thesis (University of Alberta, 1971).
2376. ———. "Alberta Ranching and Literature." In A.W. Rasporich and H.C. Klassen, eds. *Frontier Calgary* (Calgary, 1975), pp. 71-86.
2377. **Fowler, Roy L.** "Chronology of Farming in the Okotoks-High River Area, 1879-1930." *A.H.R.* 2 (Spring 1954), pp. 21-27.
2378. **Garrison, Daphne.** "Edison Settlement." *A.H.R.* 10 (Winter 1962), pp. 1-7.
2379. **George, Ernest S.** "Ranching in Southern Alberta." *A.H.R.* 3 (Spring 1955), p. 33.
2379A. **Glenn, J.E.** "The Role of Government Legislation, Policy, and Agency Activity in Irrigation Development: The Cypress Hills Area, 1888-1968." M.A. Thesis (University of Calgary, 1968).
2380. **Grest, E.G.** "A Study of Horse and Tractor Power Used on Farms in Saskatchewan and Alberta." M.Sc. Thesis (University of Saskatchewan, 1932).
2381. **Harvey, J.M.** "A Community Development Model Illustrated with Hinton, Alberta." M.A. Thesis (University of Alberta, 1972).

2382. **Hughes, Katherine.** "The Last Great Roundup." *A.H.R.* 11 (Spring 1963), pp. 1-7.
2383. **Imrie, John M.** "Valley of the Peace." *Canadian Geographical Journal* 2 (1931), pp. 463-476.
2384. **Istvanffy, D.I.** "The History of Turner Valley." *A.H.R.* 2 (Autumn 1954), pp. 28-39.
2385. **Jameson, Sheilagh S.** "The Story of Trochu." *A.H.R.* 9 (Autumn 1961), pp. 1-9.
2386. ———. "Era of the Big Ranches." *A.H.R.* 18 (Winter 1970), pp. 1-9.
2387. **Johnson, Arthur H.** "Coming to Alberta." *Alberta History* 24 (Winter 1976), pp. 23-27.
2388. **Kerr, John R.** "Alhambra." *A.H.R.* 16 (Spring 1968), pp. 19-24.
2389. **Klippenstein, D.H.** "Recreational Enterprises for Farmers in Alberta: The Distribution of Existing Facilities and Farmers' Attitudes." M.A. Thesis (University of Alberta, 1973).
2390. **Lawrence, V H.** "Haying." *A.H.R.* 21 (Winter 1973), pp. 18-20.
2391. **Leppard, H.M.** "The Settlement of the Peace River Country." *Geographical Review* 25 (1935), pp. 62-78.
2392. **Lupton, A.A.** "Cattle Ranching in Alberta, 1874-1910: Its Evolution and Migration." *Albertan Geographer* 3 (1967), pp. 48-58.
2393. **MacGibbon, D.A.** *Report of the Commissioner on Banking and Credit with Respect to the Industry of Agriculture in the Province of Alberta.* Edmonton: King's Printer, 1922.
2394. **McGinnis, D.** "Farm Labour in Transition: Occupational Structure and Economic Dependency in Alberta, 1921-1951." In H. Palmer, ed. *The Settlement of the West.* (Calgary, 1977), pp. 174-186.
2395. **MacGregor, James G.** *The Land of Twelve-Foot Davis: A History of the Peace River Country.* Edmonton: Applied Art Products Ltd., 1952.
2396. **Nesbitt, L.D.** *Tides in the West [The Alberta Wheat Pool].* Saskatoon: Modern Press, 1962.
2397. **Peters, B.F.** "Community Development in the Small Rural Community: The Role of the Public Library." M.A. Thesis (University of Alberta, 1973).
2398. **Pollard, W.C.** *Pioneering in the Prairie West: A Sketch of the Parry Sound Colonies That Settled Near Edmonton.* Toronto: Nelson, 1926.

2399. **Prevey, C.F.** "The Development of the Dairy Industry in Alberta." M.A. Thesis (University of Alberta, 1950).

2400. **Priestley, Norman F.** "Half an Hour's Drive from Edmonton,' Recollections of a Homesteader." *A.H.R.* 4 (Autumn 1956), pp. 9-18.

2401. **Priestley, Norman F., and Swindlehurst, E.B.** *Furrows, Faith, and Friendship: The History of the Farm Movement in Alberta, 1905-1966.* Edmonton: Co-op Press, 1967.

2402. **Proudfoot, B.** "Agricultural Settlement in Alberta North of Edmonton." In A.W. Rasporich and H.C. Klassen, eds. *Prairie Perspectives 2* (Toronto, 1973), pp. 142-153.

2403. **Raby, S.** "Irrigation Development in Alberta." *Canadian Geographer* 9 (1965), pp. 31-40.

2404. **Roberts, Sarah Ellen.** *Alberta Homestead: Chronicle of a Pioneer Family.* Austin: University of Texas Press, 1971.

2405. **Roe, F.G.** "The Alberta Wet Cycle of 1899-1903: A Climatic Interlude." *Agricultural History* 28 (1954), pp. 112-120.

2406. **Swindlehurst, E.B.** *Alberta Agriculture: A Short History.* Edmonton: Department of Agriculture, 1967.

2407. **Tetreault, Alexis.** "Historic St. Albert: Its Foundation, 1861-68 (Part 1)." *A.H.R.* 2 (Spring 1954), pp. 11-20.

2408. ———. "Historic St. Albert: Highlights in the Development of Big Lake Settlement, 1868-76 (Part 2)." *A.H.R.* 2 (Summer 1954), pp. 16-23.

2409. ———. "Historic St. Albert: Trials & Disappointments, 1883-89 (Part 3)." *A.H.R.* 3 (Autumn 1955), pp. 17-20.

2410. ———. "Historic St. Albert: Transformation and Highlights, 1890-1954 (Part 4)." *A.H.R.* 5 (Winter 1957), pp. 25-29.

2410A. **Thirnbeck, A.R.** "An Analysis of a Group of Settlements Northeast of Calgary, Alberta." M.A. Thesis (University of Calgary, 1971).

2411. **Thomas, L.G.** "The Ranching Period in Southern Alberta." M.A. Thesis (University of Alberta, 1935).

2412. **Thomson, Georgina H.** "Some Early History of Parkland, Alberta." *A.H.R.* 3 (Autumn 1955), pp. 5-10.

2413. ———. *Crocus and Meadowlark Country.* Edmonton: Institute of Applied Art, 1963.

2414. **Vogelesang, R.R.** "The Initial Agricultural Settlement of the Morinville-Westlock Area, Alberta." M.A. Thesis (University of Alberta, 1972).

2415. **Waywitka, Anne B.** "Waugh Homesteaders and Their School." *Alberta History* 23 (Winter 1975), pp. 13-17.
2416. ———. "Homesteader's Woman." *Alberta History* 24 (Spring 1976), pp. 20-24.
2417. **Weinard, Philip.** "Early High River and the Whisky Traders." *A.H.R.* 4 (Summer 1956), pp. 12-16.

e. Economic Development and Labour

2418. **Armstrong, Christopher, and Nelles, H.V.** "Competition vs. Convenience: Federal Administration of Bow River Waterpowers, 1906-13." In H.C. Klassen, ed. *The Canadian West* (Calgary, 1977), pp. 163-180.
2419. **Askin, W.R.** "Labor Unrest in Edmonton and District and Its Coverage by the Edmonton Press, 1918-1919." M.A. Thesis (University of Alberta, 1973).
2419A. **Barr, B.M., and Fairburn, K.J.** "Inter-industry Manufacturing Linkages within Alberta." In B.M. Barr, ed. *New Themes in Western Canadian Geography: The Langara Papers* (Vancouver: B.C. Geographical Series, No. 22, 1976), pp. 37-66.
2420. **Brese, W.G.** "An Analysis of the Sulphur Industry in Alberta." M.A. Thesis (University of Alberta, 1961).
2421. **Britnell, G.E., and McGown, A.F.** "Alberta, Economic and Political." *C.J.E.P.S.* 2 (1936), pp. 512-549.
2422. **Bronson, H.E.** "A Review of Legislation Pertaining to Petroleum Resources: Government of Alberta, 1930-1957." M.A. Thesis (University of Alberta, 1958).
2423. **Court, Thomas.** "A Search for Oil." *A.H.R.* 21 (Spring 1973), pp. 10-12.
2423A. **Curtis, P.J.** "Some Aspects of Industrial Linkages in Edmonton's Oil Industry." M.A. Thesis (University of Alberta, 1972).
2424. **Den Otter, A.A.** "Sir Alexander Tilloch Galt, the Canadian Government and Alberta's Coal." Canadian Historical Association. *Historical Papers 1973*, pp. 21-42.
2425. ———. "Railways and Alberta's Coal Problem, 1880-1960." In A.W. Rasporich, ed. *Western Canada: Past and Present* (Calgary, 1975), pp. 84-98.
2426. **Draper, H.L.** "Alberta Coal." M.A. Thesis (McGill University, 1929).

2427. ———. *The Alberta Coal Problem.* Orillia: *Packet-Times* Press, 1930.

2428. **English, R.E.** "An Economic History of Northern Alberta." M.S.A. Thesis (University of Toronto, 1933).

2429. **Gertler, L.O.** "Some Economic and Social Influences on Regional Planning in Alberta." *Plan Canada* 1 (1960), pp. 115-121.

2430. **Gould, Edwin.** *Oil.* Saanichton: Hancock House, 1976.

2431. **Gray, E.** *Impact of Oil.* Toronto: Ryerson, 1969.

2432. **Hanson, E.J.** "A Financial History of Alberta." Ph.D. Thesis (Clark University, 1952).

2433. ———. *Dynamic Decade: The Evolution and Effects of the Oil Industry in Alberta.* Toronto: McClelland and Stewart, 1958.

2434. **Ironside, R.G., and Hamilton, S.A.** "Historical Geography of Coal Mining in the Edmonton District." *A.H.R.* 20 (Summer 1972), pp. 6-16.

2435. **Istvanffy, D.I.** "Turner Valley: Its Relationship to the Development of Alberta's Oil Industry." M.A. Thesis (University of Alberta, 1950).

2436. **Judy, J.W.** "Early Railroading in Northern Alberta." *A.H.R.* 6 (Summer 1958), pp. 12-19.

2437. **Karas, K.P.** "Labour and Coal in the Crowsnest Pass, 1925-1935." M.A. Thesis (University of Calgary, 1972).

2438. **Lee, T.R.** "A Manufacturing Geography of Edmonton." M.A. Thesis (University of Alberta, 1963).

2439. **McDonald, Hugh.** "Alberta Makes Money on Oil." *Western Business and Industry* 23 (May 1949), pp. 112-115.

2440. **McMillan, C.J.** "Trade Unionism in District 18, 1900-1925: A Case Study." M.B.A. Thesis (University of Alberta, 1969).

2441. **Magrath, C.A.** *The Galts, Father and Son, Pioneers in the Development of Southern Alberta.* Lethbridge: Lethbridge *Herald,* 1936.

2442. **Parrott, Michael.** "Turner Valley." *Canadian Geographical Journal* 69 (1964), pp. 140-151.

2443. **Pearse, Chas. R.** "Athabasca Tar Sands." *Canadian Geographical Journal* 76 (1968), pp. 2-9.

2444. **Pratt, L.** *The Tar Sands.* Edmonton: Hurtig, 1976.

2445. **Seager, Allen.** "The Pass Strike of 1932." *Alberta History* 25 (Winter 1977), pp. 1-11.

Alberta 169

Plate 14. Leduc Oil Well, Number One

2446. **Stout, C.H.** "Saddle Notches, Candles and Oil: Early Days in Leduc." *A.H.R.* 6 (Autumn 1958), pp. 16-24.
2447. **Taraska, E.A.** "The Calgary Craft Union Movement, 1900-1920." M.A. Thesis (University of Calgary, 1975).
2448. **Telmer, F.H.** "An Analysis of the Iron and Steel Industry in Alberta." M.A. Thesis (University of Alberta, 1964).

2449. **Trace, H.D.** "An Examination of Some Factors Associated with the Decline of the Coal Industry in Alberta." M.A. Thesis (University of Alberta, 1958).

2450. **Warren, John.** "Alberta-Progress." *Western Business and Industry* 37 (September 1963), pp. 28-75. [A continuing feature.]

2451. **Waywitka, Anne B.** "Strike at Waterways." *A.H.R.* 20 (Autumn 1972), pp. 1-5.

2452. ———. "Drumheller Strike of 1919." *A.H.R.* 21 (Winter 1973), pp. 1-7.

2453. ———. "Recollections of a Union Man." *Alberta History* 23 (Autumn 1975), pp. 6-20.

2453A. **Wilson, L.A.** "Some Factors Relating to the Attraction of Manufacturing Industries to the Province of Alberta." M.A. Thesis (University of Alberta, 1971).

2454. **Wright, R.W., and Mansell, R.L.** "The Role of Migration in Alberta's Economic Development, 1975-1985." In H. Palmer, ed. *The Settlement of the West* (Calgary, 1977), pp. 226-236.

2455. **Yackulic, G.A.** "The Economics of Alberta's Coal." *Western Business and Industry* 23 (May 1949), pp. 57-62, 184.

f. Education and Social and Cultural Development

2456. **Alexander, William Hardy.** "In the Beginning [University of Alberta]." *A.H.R.* 8 (Spring 1960), pp. 15-20.

2457. **Barclay, H.B.** "The Holdeman Mennonites of Alberta: The Protestant Ethic versus the Spirit of Capitalism." In R. Allen, ed. *Religion and Society in the Prairie West* (Regina, 1974), pp. 89-98.

2458. **Bate, J.P.** "Prohibition and the U.F.A." *A.H.R.* 18 (Autumn 1970), pp. 1-6.

2459. **Bibby, R.W.** "The Secular and the Sacred: A Study of Evangelism as Reflected in Membership Additions to Calgary Evangelical Churches, 1966-70." M.A. Thesis (University of Calgary, 1971).

2460. **Breen, D.H.** "Plain Talk from Plain Western Men." *A.H.R.* 18 (Summer 1970), pp. 1-13.

2461. **Burnet, Jean.** *Next-Year Country: A Study of Rural Social Organization in Alberta.* Toronto: University of Toronto Press, 1951.

2462. **Cameron, Donald.** *Campus in The Clouds [Banff School of Fine Arts].* Toronto: McClelland and Stewart, 1956.

2463. **Campbell, G.** "History of the Alberta Community College System, 1957-1969." Ph.D. Thesis (University of Calgary, 1972).

2464. **Carter, Eva.** *Thirty Years of Progress: A History of the United Farm Women of Alberta.* Calgary: John D. McAra, 1944.

2465. **Cashman, Tony.** *Singing Wires: The Telephone in Alberta.* Edmonton: Alberta Government Telephones Commission, 1972.

2466. **Chalmers, John W.** *Schools of the Foothills Province: The Story of Public Education in Alberta.* Toronto: University of Toronto Press, 1967.

2467. ———. *Teachers of the Foothill Province.* Toronto: University of Toronto Press, 1968.

2468. **Chapman, T.L.** "Drug Use in Western Canada." *Alberta History* 24 (Autumn 1976), pp. 18-27.

2469. **Clarke, L.H.** "Public Provisions for the Mentally Ill in Alberta, 1907-1936." M.A. Thesis (University of Calgary, 1973).

2470. **Collins, P.V.** "The Public Health Policies of the United Farmers of Alberta Government, 1921-1935." M.A. Thesis (University of Western Ontario, 1969).

2471. **Cote, J.E.** "The Introduction of English Law in Alberta." *Alberta Law Review* 3 (1964), pp. 262-292.

2472. **Daniels, L.A.** "The History of Education in Calgary." M.A. Thesis (University of Washington, 1954).

2473. **Deiseach, D.** "Fiscal Equalization of School System Revenues under the Alberta School Foundation Program, 1961-1971." Ph.D. Thesis (University of Alberta, 1974).

2474. **Den Otter, A.A.** "Social Life of a Mining Community: The Coal Branch." *A.H.R.* 17 (Autumn 1969), pp. 1-11.

2475. **Drake, Beverly A.** "Edison School District." *A.H.R.* 19 (Autumn 1971), pp. 21-24.

2476. **Foran, M.L.** "Bob Edwards and Social Reform." *A.H.R.* 21 (Summer 1973), pp. 13-17.

2477. **Getty, I.A.L.** "The Church Missionary Society among the Blackfoot Indians of Southern Alberta, 1880-1895." M.A. Thesis (University of Calgary, 1971).

2478. **Glick, I.N.** "An Analysis of the Human Resources Development Authority in Alberta." M.A. Thesis (University of Alberta, 1972).

2479. **Gordon, R.K.** "University Beginnings in Alberta." *Queen's Quarterly* 58 (1951-52), pp. 487-496.

2480. **Goresky, Isidore.** "The Beginning and Growth of the Alberta School System." M.Ed. Thesis (University of Alberta, 1945).

2481. **Harrington, L.** "The Calgary Stampede." *Canadian Geographical Journal* 48 (1954), pp. 222-228.

2482. **Hodgson, E.D.** "The Nature and Purposes of the Public School in the Northwest Territories (1885-1905) and Alberta (1905-1963)." Ph.D. Thesis (University of Alberta, 1964).

2483. **Holmgren, Eric J.** "William Newton and the Anglican Church." *Alberta History* 23 (Spring 1975), pp. 17-25.

2484. **Hosie, Inez B.** "Little White School House." *A.H.R.* 15 (Autumn 1967), pp. 26-28.

2485. **Houghton, J.R.** "The Calgary Public School System, 1939-1969: A History of Growth and Development." M.Ed. Thesis (University of Calgary, 1971).

2486. **Inderwick, Mary E.** "A Lady and Her Ranch." *A.H.R.* 15 (Autumn 1967), pp. 1-9.

2487. **Jamieson, F.C.** "The 19th Alberta Dragoons in the First World War." *A.H.R.* 7 (Autumn 1959), pp. 22-28.

2488. **Johnson, Ronald C.** "Resort Development at Banff." *Alberta History* 23 (Winter 1975), pp. 18-24.

2489. **Lewis, Maurice H.** "The Anglican Church and Its Mission Schools Dispute." *A.H.R.* 14 (Autumn 1966), pp. 7-13.

2490. **Lysne, D.E.** "Welfare in Alberta, 1905-1936." M.A. Thesis (University of Alberta, 1966).

2491. **Macdonald, John.** *The History of the University of Alberta, 1908-1958.* Edmonton: University of Alberta, 1958.

2492. **Macdonald, Robert J.** "Hutterite Education in Alberta: A Test Case in Assimilation." *Canadian Ethnic Studies* 8 (1976), pp. 9-22.

2493. **McGugan, Angus C.** "The Drama of Medicine in Alberta." *A.H.R.* 4 (Summer 1956), pp. 3-7.

2494. ―――. *The First Fifty Years: A History of the University of Alberta Hospital.* Edmonton: University of Alberta, 1965.

2495. **McKenzie, Mrs. M.J.** "School Memories." *A.H.R.* 7 (Winter 1959), pp. 14-17.

2496. **McLean, R.** "A Most Effectual Remedy—Temperance and Prohibition in Alberta, 1875-1915." M.A. Thesis (University of Calgary, 1969).

2497. **MacLean, Una.** "The Famous Five." *A.H.R.* 10 (Spring 1962), pp. 1-4.

2498. **McLeod, N.L.** "Calgary College, 1912-1915: A Study of an Attempt to Establish a Privately Financed University in Alberta." M.A. Thesis (University of Calgary, 1970).

2499. **McNab, K.M.** "A History of the Alberta Teacher's Association." M.A. Thesis (University of Alberta, 1949).

2500. **Maerz, L.P.** "Religious Education in Alberta Public Schools." M.A. Thesis (University of Calgary, 1974).

2501. **Mann, William E.** *Sect, Cult and Church in Alberta.* 1955. Reprint. Toronto: University of Toronto Press, 1972.

2502. **Miller, James A.** "The Alberta Press and the Conscription Issue in the First World War, 1914-1918." M.A. Thesis (University of Alberta, 1974).

2503. **Molyneaux, Marianne M.** "Early Days in Alberta." *A.H.R.* 8 (Spring 1960), pp. 6-14.

2504. **Navalkouski, Anna.** "Shandro School." *A.H.R.* 18 (Autumn 1970), pp. 8-14.

2505. **Nearing, Peter A.** "Rev. John R. MacDonald, St. Joseph's College and the University of Alberta." Canadian Catholic Historical Association. *Study Sessions 1975,* pp. 71-90.

2506. **Patterson, R.S.** "The Establishment of Progressive Education in Alberta." Ph.D. Thesis (Michigan State University, 1968).

2507. **Philip, Catherine.** "The Fair Frail Flower of Western Womanhood." In A.W. Rasporich and H.C. Klassen, eds. *Frontier Calgary* (Calgary, 1975), pp. 114-123.

2508. **Peake, Frank A.** "The Beginnings of the Diocese of Edmonton, 1875-1918." M.A. Thesis (University of Alberta, 1952).

2509. **Rolland, Walpole.** "My Alberta Notebook." *A.H.R.* 18 (Winter 1970), pp. 21-23.

2510. **Schultz, Earl L.** "Education in the Bruderheim Area." *A.H.R.* 20 (Autumn 1972), pp. 21-27.

2511. **Simon, Frank.** "History of the Alberta Provincial Institute of Technology and Art." M.Ed. Thesis (University of Alberta, 1962).

2512. **Sparby, Harry T.** "A History of the Alberta School System to 1925." Ph.D. Thesis (Stanford University, 1958).

2513. **Stamp, R.M.** *School Days: A Century of Memories.* Calgary: Calgary Board of Education and McClelland and Stewart West, 1975.

2514. **Stanley, George Douglas.** "Medical Pioneering in Alberta." *A.H.R.* 1 (Winter 1953), pp. 6-15.

2515. **Thorner, T.** "The Not So Peaceable Kingdom: A Study of Crime in Southern Alberta, 1874-1905." M.A. Thesis (University of Calgary, 1976).

2516. **Tims, John W.** "Anglican Beginnings in Southern Alberta." *A.H.R.* 15 (Spring 1967), pp. 1-11.

2517. **Walker, Bernal E.** "Public Secondary Education in Alberta: Organization and Curriculum, 1889-1951." Ph.D. Thesis (Stanford University, 1955).

2518. **Weston, Phyllis E.** "The History of Education in Calgary." M.A. Thesis (University of Alberta, 1951).

2519. ———. "A University for Calgary." *A.H.R.* 11 (Summer 1963), pp. 1-11.

2520. **Williams, J. Earl.** "Origin and Development of Public Telephones in Alberta." *A.H.R.* 11 (Spring 1963), pp. 8-12.

2521. **Wilson, L.J.** "Educational Role of the United Farm Women of Alberta." *Alberta History* 25 (Spring 1977), pp. 28-36.

2522. **Wong, C.S.J.** "Assimilation and Education: A Study of Postwar Immigrants in Edmonton and Calgary." M.S.W. Thesis (University of Alberta, 1972).

g. *Urban Development*

i. General

2523. **Bagley, Roy.** "Lacombe in the Nineties." *A.H.R.* 10 (Summer 1962), pp. 18-27.

2524. **Baker, A.M.** "The Red Deer Region." M.A. Thesis (University of Alberta, 1962).

2525. **Bettison, D.G.; Kenward, J.K.; and Taylor, L.** *Urban Affairs in Alberta.* Edmonton: University of Alberta Press, 1975.

2526. **Bhajan, E.R.** "Community Development Programs in Alberta: Analysis of Development Efforts in Five Communities." M.A. Thesis (University of Alberta, 1972).

2526A. **Boothroyd, Peter.** "The Energy Crisis and Future Urban Form in Alberta." *Plan Canada* 16 (1976), pp. 137-146.

2527. **Burpee, Lawrence J.** "Where Rail and Airway Meet [Fort McMurray]." *Canadian Geographical Journal* 10 (1935), pp. 239-246.
2528. **Carpenter, J.H.** *The Badge and the Blotter: A History of the Lethbridge Police.* Lethbridge: Whoop-Up Country Chapter, Historical Society of Alberta, 1975.
2529. **Dawe, R.W.** "The Development of the Red Deer Community in Relation to the Development of Western Canada." M.A. Thesis (University of Alberta, 1954).
2530. **Den Otter, A.A.** "Coal Town in Wheat Country: Lethbridge, Alberta, 1885-1905." *Urban History Review* 1-76 (1976), pp. 3-5.
2531. ———. "Urban Pioneers of Lethbridge." *Alberta History* 25 (Winter 1977), pp. 15-24.
2532. **Donaldson, R.M.** "The Economic Base of Camrose." M.A. Thesis (University of Alberta, 1965).
2533. **Duggan, J.J.** *Cities of Alberta: Submission to Royal Commission on Dominion-Provincial Relations.* Edmonton, 1938.
2534. **Dykstra, T.L., and Ironside, R.G.** "The Effects of the Division of the City of Lloydminster by the Alberta-Saskatchewan Inter-Provincial Boundary." *Cahiers de géographie de Québec* 16 (1972), pp. 261-283.
2535. **Finlay, R.E.** "An Historical Sketch of Vegreville, 1901-02." *A.H.R.* 3 (Winter 1955), pp. 16-23.
2536. **Fryer, Harold.** *Ghost Towns of Alberta.* Langley: Stagecoach Publishing, 1976.
2537. **Gaetz, A.L.** *Park Country: A History of Red Deer and District.* Vancouver: Wrigley Publishing, 1948.
2538. **Gilpin, John.** "The City of Strathcona, 1891-1912." M.A. Thesis (University of Alberta, 1977).
2539. **Grayson, J.P., and Grayson, L.M.** "The Social Base of Interwar Political Unrest in Urban Alberta." *Canadian Journal of Political Science* 7 (1974), pp. 289-313.
2540. **Gregg, R.C.** "The Star of the West [Edson, Alberta]." *Community Planning Review* 13 (1963), pp. 2-10.
2541. **Harrington, L.** "Medicine Hat—'The Town that was Born Lucky.'" *Canadian Geographical Journal* 80 (1970), pp. 126-133.
2542. **Kerri, James N.** "Fort McMurray: One of Canada's Resource Frontier Towns." M.A. Thesis (University of Manitoba, 1970).

2543. **Kipling, Rudyard.** "The Town That Was Born Lucky [Medicine Hat]." *A.H.R.* 11 (Winter 1961), pp. 5-7.

2544. **McIntosh, R.G., and Housego, I.E., eds.** *Urbanization and Urban Life in Alberta.* Edmonton: Alberta Human Resources Council, 1970.

2545. **Masson, J.K.** "The Demise of 'Alphabet Parties': The Rise of Responsible Party Politics in Cities." Occasional Paper No. 4. Edmonton: Department of Political Science, University of Alberta, 1976.

2546. **Morrow, J.W.** *Early History of the Medicine Hat Country.* Medicine Hat: Medicine Hat *News*, 1923.

2547. **Mowers, Cleo W.** "Lethbridge, Alberta." *Canadian Geographical Journal* 84 (1972), pp. 140-151.

2548. **Pépin, C.L.** *Histoire de St.-Paul, Alberta, 1896-1951.* Trois Rivières: Le Bien Public, 1952.

2549. **Ream, P.T.** *The Fort on the Saskatchewan: A Resource Book on Fort Saskatchewan and District.* Edmonton: Metropolitan Printing, 1974.

2550. ———. *The Fort on the Saskatchewan.* Fort Saskatchewan: Fort Saskatchewan Historical Society, 1975.

2551. **Reynolds, A.** *"Siding 16": An Early History of Wetaskiwin to 1930.* Wetaskiwin: Wetaskiwin Alberta-R.C.M.P. Centennial Committee, 1975.

2552. **Snider, E.L., and Kupfer, G.** *Urbanization in Alberta: A Sociological Perspective.* Population Reprints No. 9. Edmonton: University of Alberta, 1974.

2553. **Stephenson, A.T.** "Red Deer's System of Government by Commission." *Western Municipal News* 6 (1911), pp. 15-16.

2554. **Torhjelm, Gary Douglas.** "The Urban Hierarchy in Alberta." M.A. Thesis (University of Calgary, 1972).

2555. **Watson, K.F.** "Landbanking in Red Deer." M.A. Thesis (University of British Columbia, 1974).

2556. **West, Karen.** "Cardston: The Temple City of Canada." *Canadian Geographical Journal* 71 (1965), pp. 162-169.

ii. Calgary

2557. **Atwell, P.H.** "Kinship and Migration among Calgarian Residents of Indian Origin." M.A. Thesis (University of Calgary, 1969).

2558. **Baine, R.P.** *Calgary: An Urban Study.* Toronto: Clarke, Irwin, 1973.

2559. **Barr, B.M.**, ed. *Calgary: Metropolitan Structure and Influence.* Western Geographical Series, Volume 11. Victoria: University of Victoria, 1975.

2560. **Baskett, H.R.** "Concepts of Neighbourhood: Perspectives of Planners and Downtown High-Rise Dwellers in the City of Calgary." M.A. Thesis (University of Calgary, 1970).

2561. **Baureiss, G.A.** "The City and the Sub-community: The Chinese of Calgary." M.A. Thesis (University of Calgary, 1971).

2562. ———. "The Chinese Community of Calgary." *Canadian Ethnic Studies* 3 (1971), pp. 43-56.

2563. ———. "The Chinese Community in Calgary." *A.H.R.* 22 (Spring 1974), pp. 1-8.

2564. **Bernard, A.; Léveillé, J.; and Lord, G.** *Profile: Calgary, The Political and Administrative Structures of the Metropolitan Region of Calgary.* Ottawa: Ministry of State for Urban Affairs, 1975.

2565. **Boal, F.W., and Johnson, D.B.** "The Functions of Retail and Service Establishments on Commercial Ribbons." *Canadian Geographer* 9 (1965), pp. 154-169.

2566. **Braden, Thomas B.** "When the *Herald* Came to Calgary." *A.H.R.* 9 (Summer 1961), pp. 1-4.

2567. **Breen, D.H.** "The Canadian West and the Ranching Frontier, 1875-1922." Ph.D. Thesis (University of Alberta, 1972).

2568. ———. "Calgary: The City and the Petroleum Industry Since World War Two." *Urban History Review* 2-77 (1977), pp. 55-71.

2569. **Bussard, Laurence H.** "Early History of Calgary." M.A. Thesis (University of Alberta, 1935).

2570. ———. "The Establishment of Fort Calgary." *A.H.R.* 3 (Winter 1955), pp. 34-41.

2571. **Bryne, M.B.V.** "The Early History of the Catholic Church in Calgary." In A.W. Rasporich and H.C. Klassen, eds. *Frontier Calgary* (Calgary, 1975), pp. 169-180.

2572. **Carter, D.J.** *Where the Wind Blows: A History of the Anglican Diocese of Calgary.* Calgary: Kyle Printers, 1968.

2573. ———. *Calgary's Anglican Cathedral.* Calgary: Kyle Printers, 1973.

2574. ———. "Calgary's Early Anglicans." In A.W. Rasporich and H.C. Klassen, eds. *Frontier Calgary* (Calgary, 1975), pp. 190-202.

2575. **Century Calgary Historical Series.** Calgary: Century Calgary Publications, 1975. Vol. 1: *Past and Present: People, Places and Events in Calgary.* Vol. 2: *Communities of Calgary: From Scattered Towns to a Major City.* Vol. 3: *Young People of All Ages: Sports, Schools and Youth Groups in Calgary.* Vol. 4: *The Search for Souls: Histories of Calgary Churches.* Vol. 5: *At Your Service, Part One: Calgary's Library, Parks Department, Military, Medical Services and Fire Department.* Vol. 6: *At Your Service, Part Two: Calgary's Police Force, Navy Base, Post Office, Transit System and Private Service Groups.* Photographic Collections. Vol. 1: *A Walk through Old Calgary: Early Buildings Extant in 1975.* Vol. 2: *Be It Ever So Humble: A Photoessay on Calgary's Old Homes.*

2576. **Christenson, R.A.** The Calgary and Edmonton Railway and the *Edmonton Bulletin.*" M.A. Thesis (University of Alberta, 1967).

2577. **Coats, Douglas.** "Calgary: The Private Schools, 1900-16." In A.W. Rasporich and H.C. Klassen, eds. *Frontier Calgary* (Calgary, 1975), pp. 141-152.

2578. **Coppock, K.** "Calgary and the Company." *The Beaver* Outfit 271 (1941), pp. 42-47.

2579. **Cunniffe, Richard.** *Calgary in Sandstone.* Calgary: Historical Society of Alberta, 1969.

2580. **Daniels, L.A.** "The History of Education in Calgary." M.A. Thesis (University of Washington, 1954).

2581. **Dawson, Brian J.** "The Chinese Experience in Frontier Calgary: 1885-1910." In A.W. Rasporich and H.C. Klassen, eds. *Frontier Calgary* (Calgary, 1975), pp. 124-140.

2582. **Dempsey, Hugh A.** "Calgary's First Stampede." *A.H.R.* 3 (Summer 1955), pp. 3-13.

2583. ———. "Calgary-Edmonton Trail." *A.H.R.* 7 (Autumn 1954), pp. 16-21.

2584. ———. "Brisebois: Calgary's Forgotten Founder." In A.W. Rasporich and H.C. Klassen, eds. *Frontier Calgary* (Calgary, 1975), pp. 28-40.

2585. **Dempsey, Hugh A.,** ed. *The Best of Bob Edwards.* Edmonton: Hurtig, 1975.

2586. **Diemer, H.L.** "Annexation and Amalgamation in the Territorial Expansion of Edmonton and Calgary." M.A. Thesis (University of Alberta, 1975).

2587. **Ecroyd, L.G.,** et al. "Calgary, 1961." *Western Business and Industry* 35 (September 1961), pp. 44-56.

2588. **Elliott, G.B.** *Calgary, Alberta, Canada, Her Industries and Resources.* Calgary: Burns and Elliott, 1885.

2589. **Evans, S.** "Spatial Aspects of the Cattle Kingdom: The First Decade, 1882-92." In A.W. Rasporich and H.C. Klassen, eds. *Frontier Calgary* (Calgary, 1975), pp. 41-56.

2590. **Foran, M.L.** "The Calgary Town Council, 1884-1895: A Study of Local Government in a Frontier Environment." M.A. Thesis (University of Calgary, 1970).

2591. ———. "The Travis Affair and the Town of Calgary, 1885-1886." *A.H.R.* 19 (Autumn 1971), pp. 1-7.

2592. ———. "Urban Calgary, 1884-1895." *Histoire sociale/Social History* 5 (April 1973), pp. 61-76.

2593. ———. "Bob Edwards and Social Reform." *A.H.R.* 21 (Summer 1973), pp. 13-17.

2594. ———. "Early Calgary, 1875-1895: The Controversy Surrounding the Townsite Location and the Direction of Town Expansion." In A.R. McCormack and Ian MacPherson, eds. *Cities in the West* (Ottawa, 1975), pp. 26-47.

2595. ———. "Land Speculation and Urban Development in Calgary, 1884-1912." In A.W. Rasporich and H.C. Klassen, eds. *Frontier Calgary* (Calgary, 1975), pp. 203-220.

2596. **Fraser, W.B.** *Calgary.* Toronto: Holt, Rinehart and Winston, 1967.

2597. **Gibson, J.S.** "The Impact of the Railroad on Urban Patterns: An Alberta Example." *Albertan Geographer* 1 (1964-65), pp. 41-46.

2598. ———. "An Evaluation of the Role of Physical Factors in the Evolution of Land Use in the Bow River Valley in Calgary." M.A. Thesis (University of Alberta, 1965).

2599. **Gray, James H.** "Calgary Celebrates." *The Beaver* Outfit 281 (1950), pp. 6-11.

2600. **Gyuse, T.T.I.** "Service Centre Change in Metropolitan Hinterlands: A Case Study of Saskatoon and Calgary, 1951-1971." M.A. Thesis (University of Calgary, 1974).

2601. **Harasym, D.G.** "The Planning of New Residential Areas in Calgary, 1944-1973." M.A. Thesis (University of Alberta, 1975).

2602. **Harrington, L.** "The Calgary Stampede." *Canadian Geographical Journal* 48 (1954), pp. 222-228.

2603. **Hatcher, Colin K.** *Stampede City Streetcars: The Story of the Calgary Municipal Railway.* Montreal: Railfare Enterprises Ltd., 1975.

2604. **Houghton, J.R.** "The Calgary Public School System, 1939-1969: A History of Growth and Development." M.Ed. Thesis (University of Calgary, 1971).

2605. **Jameson, Sheilagh S.** "A Visit to Calgary's New Museum." *A.H.R.* 13 (Spring 1965), pp. 19-22.

2606. ———. "The Era of the Big Ranches." *A.H.R.* 18 (Winter 1970), pp. 1-9.

2607. ———. "The Social Elite of the Ranch Community and Calgary." In A.W. Rasporich and H.C. Klassen, eds. *Frontier Calgary* (Calgary, 1975), pp. 57-70.

2607A. ———. "The Archives of the Glenbow-Alberta Institute (Calgary)." *Urban History Review* 3-77 (1978), pp. 69-79.

2608. **Johnston, P.A., and Nodwell, L.M.** *Metropolitan Calgary Population: Historical Review, 1946-1970.* Calgary: City of Calgary, 1970.

2609. **Kennedy, N.J.** "The Growth and Development of Music in Calgary, 1875-1920." M.A. Thesis (University of Alberta, 1952).

2610. **Klassen, H.C.** "Social Trouble in Calgary in the Mid-1890's." *Urban History Review* 3-74 (1975), pp. 8-16.

2611. ———. "Life in Frontier Calgary." In A.W. Rasporich, ed. *Western Canada: Past and Present* (Calgary, 1975), pp. 42-57.

2612. ———. "The Bond of Brotherhood and Calgary Workingmen." In A.W. Rasporich and H.C. Klassen, eds. *Frontier Calgary* (Calgary, 1975), pp. 266-272.

2613. ———. "Bicycles and Automobiles in Early Calgary." *Alberta History* 24 (Spring 1976), pp. 1-8.

2614. **Lawrence, M.C.** "U.S. Expatriates in Calgary and Their Problems." M.S.W. Thesis (University of Calgary, 1972).

2615. **Levin, A.** "A Soviet Jewish Family Comes to Calgary." *Canadian Ethnic Studies* 6 (1974), pp. 53-66.

2616. **MacEwan, Grant.** *Eye Opener Bob.* Edmonton: Hurtig, 1957.

2617. ———. *Poking into Politics.* Edmonton: Institute of Applied Art, 1966.

2618. ———. "Calgary." *Habitat* 10 (1967), pp. 120-123.

2619. ———. *Calgary Cavalcade: From Fort to Fortune.* Saskatoon: Western Producer Book Service, 1975.

2620. ———. "The Town-Country Background at Calgary." In A.W. Rasporich and H.C. Klassen, eds. *Frontier Calgary* (Calgary, 1975), pp. 1-5.

2621. **McGinnis, D.** "A City Faces an Epidemic." *Alberta History* 24 (Autumn 1976), pp. 1-11.

2622. ———. "Birth to Boom to Bust: Building in Calgary, 1875-1914." In A.W. Rasporich and H.C. Klassen, eds. *Frontier Calgary* (Calgary, 1975), pp. 6-19.

2623. **McLeod, N.L.** "Calgary College, 1912-1915: A Study of an Attempt to Establish a Privately Financed University in Alberta." Ph.D. Thesis (University of Calgary, 1970).

2624. **McNeill, Leishman.** *Tales of the Old Town: Calgary 1875-1950.* Calgary: The *Herald*, 1951.

2625. **Mawson, T.H.** *Calgary: A Preliminary Scheme for Controlling the Economic Growth of Calgary.* Calgary: City Planning Commission, 1914.

2626. **May, Mrs. Ernest G.** "A British Bride-to-Be Comes to Calgary." *A.H.R.* 6 (Winter 1958), pp. 19-24.

2627. **Mohan, E.M.** "Aspects of Intra-urban Mobility: Calgary 1963-68." M.A. Thesis (University of Calgary, 1971).

2628. **Morrison, E.C., and Morrison, P.N.R.**, eds. *The Story of Calgary.* Calgary: Calgary Publishing Co., 1950.

2629. **Newinger, Scott.** "The Street Cars of Calgary." *A.H.R.* 22 (Summer 1974), pp. 8-12.

2630. **Peach, John S.** "Calgary, The Foothills City." *Canadian Geographical Journal* 53 (1956), pp. 168-181.

2631. **Peddie, Richard.** "Urban Parks and Planning in Calgary." M.A. Thesis (University of Calgary, 1968).

2632. **Peitchinis, Stephen G.** "Why Should Anyone in Calgary Need Aid." *Canadian Welfare* 5 (1969), pp. 6-13.

2633. **Perry, Fraser J.** "Central Methodist Church before World War One." In A.W. Rasporich and H.C. Klassen, eds. *Frontier Calgary* (Calgary, 1975), pp. 181-189.

2634. **Philip, C.R.** "The Women of Calgary and District, 1875-1914." M.A. Thesis (University of Calgary, 1975).

2635. **Pratt, J.** "Calgary: A Study in Optimism." *Canadian Magazine* 35 (1910), pp. 483-490.

2636. **Rasporich, A.W., and Klassen, H.C.**, eds. *Frontier Calgary: Town City, and Region, 1875-1914.* Calgary: McClelland and Stewart West, 1975.

Plate 15. Downtown Calgary across the Bow River

2637. **Reeves, B.O.K.** "'Kootsisaw': Calgary before the Canadians." In A.W. Rasporich and H.C. Klassen, eds. *Frontier Calgary* (Calgary, 1975), pp. 20-27.

2638. **Saarinon, T.F.** "The Changing Office Functions in Calgary's Central Business District, 1948-1962." M.A. Thesis (University of Chicago, 1963).

2639. **Smith, Peter J.** "A Study of Calgary's Past and Probable Future Population Growth." Calgary: City Planning Department, 1959.

2640. ———. "Calgary: A Study in Urban Pattern." *Economic Geography* 38 (1962), pp. 315-329.

2641. ———. "Change in a Youthful City: The Case of Calgary, Alberta." *Geography* 56 (1971), pp. 1-14.

2642. ———. "Edmonton and Calgary: Growing Together." *Canadian Geographical Journal* 92 (1976), pp. 26-33.

2643. **Stamp, R.M.** *School Days: A Century of Memories.* Calgary: Calgary Board of Education and McClelland and Stewart West, 1975.

2644. ———. "The Response to Urban Growth: The Bureaucratization of Public Education in Calgary, 1884-1914." In Gilbert A. Stelter and Alan F.J. Artibise, eds. *The Canadian City: Essays in Urban History* (Toronto, 1977), pp. 282-299.

2645. **Stanley, George F.G.** "The Naming of Calgary." *Alberta History* 23 (Summer 1975), pp. 7-9.

2646. **Stead, Robert J.C.** "Calgary—City of the Foothills." *Canadian Geographical Journal* 36 (1948), pp. 154-171.

2647. **Stokes, E.B.** "The Development and Evaluation of an Urban Growth Model for Calgary." M.A. Thesis (University of Calgary, 1973).

2648. **Strom, T.** "With Eau Claire in Calgary." *A.H.R.* 12 (Summer 1964), pp. 1-11.

2649. **Takla, E.F.** "Changes in Land Use Patterns in Downtown Calgary, 1953-1969." M.A. Thesis (University of Calgary, 1971).

2650. **Taraska, E.A.** "The Calgary Craft Union Movement, 1900-1920." M.A. Thesis (University of Calgary, 1975).

2651. **Thomas, L.G.** "The Rancher and the City: Calgary and the Cattlemen, 1883-1914." Royal Society of Canada. *Proceedings and Transactions.* 4th ser. 6 (1968), pp. 203-215.

2652. **Thorner, T.** "The Not-So-Peaceful Kingdom—Crime and Criminal Justice in Frontier Calgary." In A.W. Rasporich and H.C. Klassen, eds. *Frontier Calgary* (Calgary, 1975), pp. 100-113.

2653. **Trouth, N.S.** "Land Development in Calgary." *Habitat* 5 (1962), pp. 14-23.

2654. **Voisey, P.L.** "In Search of Wealth and Status: An Economic and Social Study of Entrepeneurs in Early Calgary." In A.W. Rasporich and H.C. Klassen, eds. *Frontier Calgary* (Calgary 1975), pp. 221-241.

2655. **Ward, Tom.** *Cowtown: An Album of Early Calgary.* Calgary: McClelland and Stewart West, 1975.

2656. **Weadick, Guy.** "Origin of the Calgary Stampede." *A.H.R.* 14 (Autumn 1966), pp. 20-24.

2657. **Weston, Phyllis E.** "The History of Education in Calgary." M.A. Thesis (University of Alberta, 1931).

2658. ———. "A University for Calgary." *A.H.R.* 11 (Summer 1963), pp. 1-11.

2659. **Wong, C.S.J.** "Assimilation and Education: A Study of Post-War Immigrants in Edmonton and Calgary." M.S.W. Thesis (University of Alberta, 1972).
2660. **Zieber, G.H.** "Inter- and Intra-City Location Pattern of Oil Offices for Calgary and Edmonton, 1950-1970." Ph.D. Thesis (University of Alberta, 1971).
2661. ———. "The Dispersed City Hypothesis with Reference to Calgary and Edmonton." *Albertan Geographer* 9 (1973), pp. 4-13.

  iii. Edmonton

2662. **Anderson, James.** "Economic Base Measurement and Changes in the Base of Metropolitan Edmonton, 1951-1961." *Albertan Geographer* 4 (1968), pp. 4-9.
2663. **Askin, W.R.** "Labor Unrest in Edmonton and District and Its Coverage by the Edmonton Press, 1918-1919." M.A. Thesis (University of Alberta, 1973).
2664. **Banson, M.J.** "The Evolution of the Central Area of Edmonton, 1946-1967." M.A. Thesis (University of Alberta, 1967).
2665. **Barrow, G.T.** "A Factoral Ecology of Three Cities: Edmonton, Regina and Winnipeg, 1961." M.A. Thesis (University of Calgary, 1972).
2666. **Bedford, Elaine.** "An Historical Geography of Settlement in the North Saskatchewan River Valley, Edmonton." M.A. Thesis (University of Alberta, 1976).
2667. **Bernard, A.; Léveillé, J.; and Lord, G.** *Profile: Edmonton, The Political and Administrative Structures of the Metropolitan Region of Edmonton.* Ottawa: Ministry of State for Urban Affairs, 1974.
2668. **Betke, Carl.** "The Social Significance of Sport in the City: Edmonton in the 1920s." In A.R. McCormack and Ian MacPherson, eds. *Cities in the West* (Ottawa, 1975), pp. 211-236.
2669. **Betts, G.M.** "The Edmonton Aldermanic Election of 1962." M.A. Thesis (University of Alberta, 1963).
2670. **Burry, Shierlaw.** "Edmonton to the Klondike." *A.H.R.* 21 (Spring 1973), pp. 20-25.
2671. **Cameron, B.** "The City on the Saskatchewan." *Canadian Magazine* 15 (1900), pp. 99-107.
2672. **Cashman, Tony.** *The Edmonton Story.* Edmonton: Institute of Applied Art, 1956.

2673. ———. *The Best Edmonton Stories.* Edmonton: Hurtig, 1976.

2674. **Chan, W.M.W.** "The Impact of the Technical Planning Board on the Morphology of Edmonton." M.A. Thesis (University of Alberta, 1969).

2675. **Chives, B.** "Friendly Games: Edmonton's Olympic Alternative." *City Magazine* 1 (September 1975), pp. 48-54.

2676. **Christenson, R.A.** "The Calgary and Edmonton Railway and the *Edmonton Bulletin.*" M.A. Thesis (University of Alberta, 1967).

2677. **Corbett, E.A.** *McQueen of Edmonton.* Toronto: Ryerson, 1934.

2677A. **Curtis, P.J.** "Some Aspects of Industrial Linkages in Edmonton's Oil Industry." M.A. Thesis (University of Alberta, 1972).

2678. **Dale, E.H.** "The Role of Successive Town and City Councils in the Evolution of Edmonton, Alberta, 1892-1966." Ph.D. Thesis (University of Alberta, 1969).

2679. ———. "Edmonton's Civic Centre." *Community Planning Review* 20 (Summer 1970), pp. 2-9.

2680. ———. "Decision-Making in Edmonton: Planning without a Plan, 1913-1945." *Plan* 2 (1971), pp. 134-147.

2681. **Dant, N.** "Edmonton: Practical Results of Planning Measures Since 1950." *Community Planning Review* 4 (1954), pp. 31-40.

2681A. **Day, John P.** "Edmonton Civic Politics, 1891-1914." *Urban History Review* 3-77 (1978), pp. 42-68.

2682. **Diemer, H.L.** "Annexation and Amalgamation in the Territorial Expansion of Edmonton and Calgary." M.A. Thesis (University of Alberta, 1975).

2683. **Duggan, D.M.** *Review of Municipal Government Organization.* Edmonton: City of Edmonton, 1923.

2684. **Dunn, J.T.** "To Edmonton in 1892." *The Beaver* Outfit 281 (1950), pp. 3-5.

2685. **Ecroyd, L.G.** "Edmonton: City of Superlatives." *Western Business and Industry* 28 (January 1954), pp. 37-40.

2686. ———. "Edmonton Today." *Western Business and Industry* 35 (1961), pp. 20-24.

2687. **Edmonds, W.E.** *Edmonton Past and Present; A Brief History.* Edmonton: Douglas Printing Co., 1943.

2688. **Edmonton Journal.** "Roots: The Ethnic History of Edmonton." Edmonton, 1976. [Reprint of articles in *Journal.*]

2689. **Emanuel, L.** "Some Aspects of Ethnic Identity in an Edmonton Parish." *Canadian Ethnic Studies* 6 (1974), pp. 87-96.
2690. **Gillese, J.P.** "Big Boom Town." *Canadian Business* 26 (September 1953), pp. 22-24, 116-118.
2691. **Gilpin, John.** "The City of Strathcona, 1891-1912." M.A. Thesis (University of Alberta, 1977).
2692. **Hanson, E.J.** *An Economic Base Study of the Edmonton Metropolitan Area.* Edmonton: University of Alberta, 1957.
2693. **Hardy, W.G.** "Edmonton." *Habitat* 10 (1967), pp. 124-127.
2694. **Hassbrung, M.** "Land Use Diversity in the Rural-Urban Fringe Zone of Edmonton." *Albertan Geographer* 6 (1970), pp. 59-64.
2695. **Hodgson, M.C.** "The Fiscal Development of the City of Edmonton Since 1946." M.A. Thesis (University of Alberta, 1965).
2696. **Jamieson, F.C.** "Edmonton Courts and Lawyers in Territorial Times." *A.H.R.* 4 (Winter 1956), pp. 3-9.
2697. **Jones, O.D.** "The Historical Geography of Edmonton, Alberta." M.A. Thesis (University of Toronto, 1962).
2698. **Jordan, Mabel E.** "Edmonton Old and New." *Canadian Geographical Journal* 51 (1955), pp. 244-247.
2699. **King, Mona S.** "Some Aspects of Post-War Migration to Edmonton, Alberta." M.A. Thesis (University of Alberta, 1971).
2700. **Kupfer, G.** *Edmonton Study: Community Opportunity Assessment.* Edmonton: Government of Alberta, Department of Human Resources, 1967.
2701. **Lai, H.** "Evolution of the Railway Network of Edmonton and Its Land Use Effect." M.A. Thesis (University of Alberta, 1967).
2702. **La Rose, H.** "The City of Edmonton Archives." *Urban History Review* 3-74 (1975), pp. 2-7.
2703. **Lee, T.R.** "A Manufacturing Geography of Edmonton." M.A. Thesis (University of Alberta, 1963).
2704. **McCann, L.D.** *Neighbourhoods in Transition: Processes of Land Use and Physical Change in Edmonton's Residential Areas.* Studies in Geography, Occasional Paper 2. Edmonton: University of Alberta, 1975.
2705. **McConnell, R.S.** "Planning in Edmonton, Alberta." *Journal of the Town Planning Institute* 44 (1957-58), pp. 39-43.

2706. **McCracken, K.W.J.** "Patterns of Intra-Urban Migration in Edmonton and the Residential Relocation Process." Ph.D. Thesis (University of Alberta, 1973).
2707. **McDonald, Hugh.** "Edmonton Is Booming Cautiously." *Western Business and Industry* 23 (May 1949), pp. 106-110.
2708. **McGilloary, C.L.** "Mental Maps of a Canadian City: Edmonton, Alberta." *Albertan Geographer* 10 (1974), pp. 30-42.
2709. **MacGregor, James G.** *Edmonton Trader: The Story of John A. McDougall.* Toronto: McClelland and Stewart, 1963.
2710. ———. *The Klondike Rush through Edmonton, 1897-1898.* Toronto: McClelland and Stewart, 1970.
2711. ———. *Edmonton: A History.* 1967. 2d. ed. Edmonton: Hurtig, 1975.
2712. **Mailloux, I.D.** "Computerized Map: City of Edmonton." M.A. Thesis (University of Alberta, 1973).
2713. **Marlyn, F., and Lash, H.N.** "The Edmonton District: A City-Centred Multiple Resource Region." *Resources for Tomorrow: Conference Background Papers.* Vol. 1 (Ottawa, 1961), pp. 455-468.
2714. **Nicoll, Ian M.** "Urban Municipal Finance in a Period of Expansion: A Study of the City of Edmonton." M.A. Thesis (University of Alberta, 1950).
2715. **Niddrie, J.G.** "The Edmonton Boom of 1911-1912." *A.H.R.* 13 (Spring 1965), pp. 1-6.
2716. **Ockley, B.A.** "A History of Early Edmonton." M.A. Thesis (University of Alberta, 1932).
2717. **Oliver, Frank.** "The Founding of Edmonton." *Queen's Quarterly* 37 (1930), pp. 78-94.
2718. **Parnell, C.** "The Founding of Fort Edmonton." *The Beaver* Outfit 276 (1945), pp. 3-4.
2719. **Peake, Frank A.** "Anglican Beginnings in and about Edmonton." *A.H.R.* 3 (Spring 1955), pp. 15-32.
2719A. **Podmore, D.R.; McGlashan, S.; and Steen, P.** "Railway Relocation: The Edmonton Approach." *Contact: Journal of Urban and Environmental Affairs* 9, no. 1 (1977), pp. 133-144.
2720. **Rose, R.T.** "Edmonton: Boom Town Plus." *Canadian Business* 16 (July 1943), pp. 86-92.

2721. **Scott, W.G.** "Urban Growth Management: The Development of a Program for the Edmonton Area." M.Sc. Thesis (University of British Columbia, 1976).

2722. **Shute, A.J.** *Edmonton Access Catalogue, 1975-76.* Edmonton: Tree Frog Press, 1975.

2723. **Smith, Peter J.** "Fort Saskatchewan: An Industrial Satellite of Edmonton." In L.O. Gertler, ed. *Planning the Canadian Environment* (Montreal, 1968), pp. 250-265.

2724. ———. "Edmonton and Calgary: Growing Together." *Canadian Geographical Journal* 92 (1976), pp. 26-33.

2725. **Smith, Peter J., and Bannon, M.J.** "The Dimensions of Change in the Central Area of Edmonton." In W.R. Derrick Sewell and H.D. Foster, eds. *The Geographer and Society* (Victoria, 1970), pp. 184-199.

2726. **Snyder, H.M.** "Variables Affecting Immigrant Adjustments: A Study of Italians in Edmonton." M.A. Thesis (University of Alberta, 1966).

2727. **Suski, J.G.** *Edmonton: Short History.* Edmonton: City of Edmonton, 1965.

2728. **Thomas, L.G.** "Mission Church in Edmonton: An Anglican Experiment in the Canadian West." *Pacific Northwest Quarterly* 49 (1958), pp. 55-60.

2729. **Walchuk, W.** "Planning Edmonton's Future." *Community Planning Review* 18 (1968), pp. 4-9.

2730. **Watt, A.B.** "Edmonton." *Canadian Geographical Journal* 33 (1946), pp. 242-251.

2731. **Weaver, John C.** "Edmonton's Perilous Course, 1904-1929." *Urban History Review* 2-77 (1977), pp. 10-19.

2732. **Wonders, William C.** "Edmonton, Alberta: Some Current Aspects of Its Urban Geography." *Canadian Geographer* 2 (1957), pp. 7-20.

2733. ———. "River Valley City—Edmonton on the North Saskatchewan." *Canadian Geographer* 3 (1959), pp. 8-16.

2734. ———. "Repercussions of War and Oil on Edmonton, Alberta." *Cahiers de géographie de Québec* 3 (1959), pp. 343-351.

2735. **Wong, C.S.J.** "Assimilation and Education: A Study of Post-War Immigrants in Edmonton and Calgary." M.S.W. Thesis (University of Alberta, 1972).

2736. **Woychuk, J.K.** "Tax-Exempt Property: City of Edmonton, 1970." M.A. Thesis (University of Alberta, 1972).

2737. **Zieber, G.H.** "The Dispersed City Hypothesis with Reference to Calgary and Edmonton." *Alberta Geographer* 9 (1973), pp. 4-13.

h. Bibliographical

2738. **Cameron Library.** *The Alberta Folklore and Local History Collection.* Edmonton: University of Alberta, 1966.
2739. **Palmer, H.** "Ethnic Groups and Inter-Ethnic Relations in Alberta, 1972-1974: A Bibliography." *Canadian Ethnic Studies* 6 (1974), pp. 71-72.
2740. **Peel, Bruce.** "Alberta Imprints before 1900." *A.H.R.* 3 (Summer 1955), pp. 41.
2741. **Task Force on Urbanization.** *Index of Urban and Regional Studies, Province of Alberta.* 5 Vols. Edmonton: Alberta Municipal Affairs Department, 1973-1975.

7

British Columbia

a. General

2742. **Affleck, E.L.** *Sternwheelers, Sandbars and Switchbacks: A Chronicle of Steam Transportation in the British Columbia Waterways of the Columbia River System, 1865-1965.* Vancouver: Alexander Nicolls Press, 1973.

2743. **Akrigg, G.P.V., and Akrigg, H.B.** *1001 British Columbia Place Names.* 1969. 3d. ed. Vancouver: Discovery Press, 1973.

2744. **Atkins, B.R.; Affleck, E.L.; and Forde, G.B.** *Columbia River Chronicles: A History of the Kootenay District in the 19th Century.* Vancouver: Alexander Nicolls Press, 1976.

2745. **Bancroft, Hubert Howe.** *History of British Columbia, 1792-1887.* 1887. Reprint. New York: Arno Press, 1967.

2746. **Begg, Alexander.** *History of British Columbia from Its Earliest Discovery to the Present Time.* 1895. Reprint. Toronto: McGraw-Hill-Ryerson, 1973.

2747. **Black, E.R.** "British Columbia: The Politics of Exploitation." In R.A. Shearer, ed. *Exploiting Our Economic Potential* (Toronto, 1968), pp. 23-41.

2748. **Brack, David M.** "The Ocean Coasts of Canada." *Canadian Geographical Journal* 87 (1973), pp. 4-15.

2748A. **Burns, R.M.** "British Columbia: Perceptions of a Split Personality." In Richard Simeon, ed. *Must Canada Fail?* (Montreal: McGill-Queen's University Press, 1977), pp. 63-72.

2749. **Cail, Robert E.** *Land, Man and the Law: The Disposal of Crown Lands in British Columbia, 1871-1913.* Vancouver: University of British Columbia Press, 1974.

2750. **Carlson, Roy L., ed.** "Archaeology in British Columbia." *BC Studies* 6 and 7 (1970), pp. 1-152.
2751. **Cash, Gwen.** *A Million Miles from Ottawa.* Toronto: Macmillan, 1942.
2752. **Clark, Cecil.** *Tales of the British Columbia Provincial Police.* Sidney: Gray's Publishing, 1971.
2753. **Corrigall, M., and Arthurs, V.** *The History of Hornby Island.* Courtenay: Comox District *Free Press*, 1969.
2754. **Currie, W.H.** "Western Pilgrimage." *Canadian Geographical Journal* 20 (1940), pp. 269-285.
2755. **Dalzell, K.E.** *The Queen Charlotte Islands, 1774-1966.* Terrace: C.M. Adam, 1968.
2756. ———. *The Queen Charlotte Islands—Book 2: Of Places and Names.* Prince Rupert: Cove Press, 1973.
2757. **Day, David, ed.** "Rural History, Regional Studies and Literature in British Columbia." *Sound Heritage* 4 (1975), pp. 1-54.
2758. **De Volpi, Charles P.** *British Columbia, A Pictorial Record: Historical Prints and Illustrations of the Province of British Columbia, Canada, 1778-1891.* Don Mills: Longmans, 1973.
2759. **Ellis, Frank H.** "Pioneer Flying in British Columbia, 1910-1914." *B.C.H.Q.* 3 (1939), pp. 227-261.
2760. **Englebert, R.** *This Is Vancouver Island.* Victoria: Diggon-Hibben, 1948.
2761. **Fahey, John.** *Inland Empire: D.C. Corbin and Spokane.* Seattle: University of Washington Press, 1965.
2762. **Fairford, Ford.** *British Columbia.* London: Pitman & Sons, 1914.
2762A. **Forward, C.N., ed.** *Environment and Man in British Columbia and Washington.* Bellingham: Western Washington State College, 1974.
2763. **Friesen, Jean, and Ralston, Keith, eds.** *Historical Essays on British Columbia.* Toronto: McClelland and Stewart, 1976.
2764. **Galloway, C.F.J.** *The Call of the West: Letters from British Columbia.* London: T. Fisher Unwin, 1916.
2765. **Goodchild, F.H.** *British Columbia: Its History, People and Industries.* Vancouver: Allen and Unwin, 1951.
2766. **Gough, Barry M.** *The Royal Navy and the Northwest Coast of North America, 1810-1914: A Study of British Maritime Ascendancy.* Vancouver: University of British Columbia Press, 1971.

2767. ———. "The Character of the British Columbia Frontier." *BC Studies* 32 (1976-77), pp. 28-40.

2768. **Gough, John.** "British Columbia." *Canadian Geographical Journal* 35 (1947), pp. 2-35.

2769. **Gosnell, R.E.** *A History of British Columbia.* Victoria: Hill Binding, 1906.

2770. ———. "British Columbia and British International Relations." American Academy of Political and Social Science. *Annals* 45 (1913), pp. 1-13.

2771. **Griffin, Harold.** *British Columbia: The People's Early Story.* Vancouver: Tribune Publishing Company, 1958.

2771A. **Haig-Brown, Roderick.** *The Living Land: The Natural Resources of British Columbia.* Toronto: Macmillan, 1961.

2772. **Hague, Reece H.** "Where B.C. Ends and Alaska Begins." *Canadian Geographical Journal* 1 (1930), pp. 403-415.

2773. **Hamilton, J.H.** "The 'All-Red Route,' 1893-1953: A History of the Trans-Pacific Mail Service between British Columbia, Australia, and New Zealand." *B.C.H.Q.* 20 (1956), pp. 1-126.

2774. **Harrington, L.** "The Queen Charlotte Islands." *Canadian Geographical Journal* 39 (1949), pp. 44-59.

2775. **Hoagland, Edward.** *Notes from the Century Before: A Journal from B.C.* New York: Random House, 1969.

2776. **Howard, Irene.** *Bowen Island, 1872-1972.* Victoria: Morriss Printing, 1973.

2777. **Howay, F.W.** *British Columbia: The Making of a Province.* Toronto: Ryerson, 1928.

2778. ———. "The Settlement and Progress of British Columbia, 1871-1914." In Jean Friesen and Keith Ralston, eds. *Historical Essays on British Columbia* (Toronto, 1976), pp. 23-43.

2779. **Howay, F.W.; Sage, Walter N.; and Angus, H.F.** *British Columbia and the United States.* Toronto: Ryerson, 1942.

2780. **Howay, F.W., and Scholfield, E.O.S.** 4 vols. *British Columbia.* Winnipeg: S.J. Clarke, 1914.

2781. **Howell-Jones, G.I.** "A Century of Settlement Change: A Study of the Evolution of Settlement Patterns in the Lower Mainland of British Columbia." M.A. Thesis (University of British Columbia, 1966).

2782. **Hunter, Murray T.** "Coast Defence in British Columbia, 1939-1941: Attitudes and Realities." *BC Studies* 28 (1975-76), pp. 3-28.

2783. **Ireland, W.E.** "The Evolution of the Boundaries of British Columbia." *B.C.H.Q.* 3 (1939), pp. 263-282.
2784. ———. "British Columbia's American Heritage." Canadian Historical Association. *Annual Report 1948,* pp. 67-73.
2785. **Jackman, S.W.** *Vancouver Island.* Toronto: Griffin House, 1972.
2786. **Johannson, P.R.** "A Study in Regional Strategy: The Alaska-British Columbia-Yukon Conferences." *BC Studies* 28 (1975-76), pp. 29-52.
2787. **Johns, H.P.** "British Columbia's Campaign for Better Terms, 1871-1907." M.A. Thesis (University of British Columbia, 1935).
2788. **Jones, J. Michael.** "The Railroad Healed the Breach [The Esquimalt and Nanaimo Railway]." *Canadian Geographical Journal* 73 (1966), pp. 98-101.
2789. **Jordan, Mabel E.** "The British on San Juan Island." *Canadian Geographical Journal* 59 (1959), pp. 14-19.
2790. **Kerr, James.** "British Columbia Place Names." *Canadian Geographical Journal* 2 (1931), pp. 153-170.
2791. **Kiewiet, C.W., and Underhill, F.H., eds.** *Dufferin-Carnarvon Correspondence, 1874-1878.* Toronto: Champlain Society, 1955.
2792. **Laing, F.W.** "Hudson's Bay Company Lands and Colonial Farm Settlement on the Mainland of British Columbia." *Pacific Historical Review* 7 (1938), pp. 327-342.
2793. **Lamb, W. Kaye.** "Empress to the Orient: Part I." *B.C.H.Q.* 4 (1940), pp. 29-50.
2794. ———. "A Bent Twig in British Columbia History." Canadian Historical Association. *Annual Report 1948,* pp. 86-92.
2795. **Leeson, W. Roy.** "British Columbia: Better Terms and Provincial Rights, 1900-1941." *Kumtucks Review* (1975), pp. 47-62.
2796. **Liddell, K.F.** *This Is British Columbia.* Toronto: Ryerson, 1958.
2797. **Lower, J.A.** "The Construction of the Grand Trunk Pacific Railway in British Columbia." *B.C.H.Q.* 4 (1940), pp. 163-183.
2798. ———. *Canada on the Pacific Rim.* Toronto: McGraw-Hill Ryerson, 1975.
2799. **Lyndell, Honoree B.** "Isles of Strait of Georgia." *Canadian Geographical Journal* 4 (1932), pp. 19-36.
2800. **McCabe, James O.** *The San Juan Water Boundary Question.* Toronto: University of Toronto Press, 1965.
2801. **McKelvie, B.A.** *Early History of the Province of British Columbia.* Toronto: Dent, 1926.

2802. **MacKirdy, K.A.** "Conflict of Loyalties: The Problem of Assimilating the Far Wests into the Canadian and Australian Federations." *C.H.R.* 32 (1951), pp. 337-355.
2803. **MacNab, F.** *British Columbia for Settlers.* London: Chapman and Hall, 1898.
2804. **Maxwell, J.A.** "Lord Dufferin and the Difficulties with British Columbia, 1874-7." *C.H.R.* 12 (1931), pp. 364-389.
2805. **Métin, Albert.** *La Colombie Britannique.* Paris: Librairie Armond Colin, 1908.
2806. **Morice, A.G.** *History of the Northern Interior of British Columbia.* 1915. Reprint. Fairfield, Washington: Ye Galleon Press, 1971.
2807. **Netboy, Anthony,** ed. *The Pacific Northwest.* Toronto: Doubleday, 1963.
2808. **Oglesby, J.C.M.** "British Columbia and the Near East Crisis, 1922." *Pacific Northwest Quarterly* 50 (1959), pp. 108-114.
2809. **Ormsby, Margaret A.** "The Relations between British Columbia and the Dominion of Canada, 1871-1885." Ph.D. Thesis (Bryn Mawr College, 1937).
2810. ———. "Prime Minister Mackenzie, the Liberal Party and the Bargain with British Columbia." *C.H.R.* 26 (1945), pp. 148-173.
2811. ———. "Canada and the New British Columbia." Canadian Historical Association. *Annual Report 1948,* pp. 74-85.
2812. ———. *British Columbia: a History.* 1958. Rev. ed. Toronto: Macmillan, 1971.
2813. ———. "Neglected Aspects of British Columbia History." *British Columbia Library Quarterly* 23 (1960), pp. 9-16.
2814. ———. "A Horizontal View." Canadian Historical Association. *Annual Report 1968,* pp. 1-13.
2815. **Peake, Frank A.** *History of the Anglican Church in British Columbia.* Vancouver: Mitchell Press, 1959.
2816. **Pearson, D.F.** "An Historical Outline of Mapping in British Columbia." *Canadian Cartographer* 2 (1974), pp. 114-124.
2817. **Plaskett, J.S.** "Empress to the Orient: Part II." *B.C.H.Q.* 4 (1940), pp. 79-111.
2818. **Pogue, B.G.** "Some Aspects of Settlement, Land-Use and Vegetation Change in the Revelstoke Area, B.C., 1885-1962." M.A. Thesis (University of Calgary, 1970).

2819. **Ramsey, Bruce.** *Ghost Towns of British Columbia.* Vancouver: Mitchell Press, 1963.

2820. **Read, S.E.** "Toponyms and the Fabric of Provincial History: A Review Article." *BC Studies* 14 (1972), pp. 83-90.

2821. **Reimer, Derek, ed.** "The Gulf Islanders." *Sound Heritage* 5 (1977), pp. 1-78.

2822. **Rickard, T.A.** *Historic Backgrounds of British Columbia.* Victoria: The Author, 1948.

2823. **Robin, Martin.** *The Rush for Spoils: The Company Province, 1871-1933.* Toronto: McClelland and Stewart, 1972.

2824. ———. *Pillars of Profit: The Company Province, 1934-1972.* Toronto: McClelland and Stewart, 1973.

2825. **Robinson, J. Lewis, ed.** *British Columbia: Studies in Canadian Geography.* Toronto: University of Toronto Press, 1972.

2826. **Robinson, J. Lewis, and Hardwick, W.G.** *British Columbia: One Hundred Years of Geographical Change.* Vancouver: Talonbooks, 1973.

2827. **Rodney, W.** "Russian Revolutionaries in the Port of Vancouver, 1917." *BC Studies* 16 (1972-73), pp. 25-31.

2827A. **Roy, Patricia, E.** "The Changing Role of Railways in the Lower Fraser Valley, 1885-1965." In A.H. Siemens, ed. *Lower Fraser Valley: Evolution of a Cultural Landscape* (Vancouver: B.C. Geographical Series, No. 9, 1968), pp. 51-68.

2828. ———. "The Company Province and Its Centennials: A Review of Recent British Columbia Historiography." *Acadiensis* 4 (1974), pp. 148-159.

2929. **Roy, R.H.** "The Early Defence and Militia of British Columbia, 1871-1885." *B.C.H.Q.* 18 (1954), pp. 1-28.

2830. ———, "British Columbia: An Historical Sketch." *Engineering Journal* 41 (1958), pp. 47-51.

2831. ———. *Sinews of Steel: The History of the British Columbia Dragoons.* Kelowna: British Columbia Dragoons, 1965.

2832. ———. "The Early Defense and Militia of the Okanagan Valley, 1871-1914." *Pacific Northwest Quarterly* 57 (1966), pp. 28-35.

2833. ———. "The First Military Intelligence Report of the Interior of British Columbia." *BC Studies* 1 (1968-69), pp. 20-26.

2834. ———. *The Seaforth Highlanders of Canada, 1919-1965.* Vancouver: Evergreen Press, 1969.

2835. ———. "Canadians in the North Pacific, 1943: Major-General Pearkes and the Kiska Operation." *BC Studies* 14 (1972), pp. 3-16.

2836. ———. "Major-General G.R. Pearkes and the Conscription Crisis in British Columbia, 1944." *BC Studies* 28 (1975-76), pp. 53-72.

2837. ———. "The Defence of Prince Rupert: An Eyewitness Account." *BC Studies* 31 (1976), pp. 60-77.

2838. ———. "From the Darker Side of Canadian Military History— Meeting in the Mountains—The Terrace Incident." *Canadian Defence Quarterly* 6 (1976), pp. 42-55.

2839. Sage, Walter N. "Canada on the Pacific, 1866-1925." *Washington Historical Quarterly* 17 (1926), pp. 91-108.

2840. ———. "The Critical Period of British Columbia History, 1866-1871." *Pacific Historical Review* 1 (1932), pp. 424-443.

2841. ———. "British Columbia Becomes Canadian." *Queen's Quarterly* 51 (1945), pp. 168-183.

2842. ———. "The North-West Mounted Police and British Columbia." *Pacific Historical Review* 18 (1949), pp. 345-362.

2843. Senior, Norman. "British Columbia, 1858-1958." *Canadian Geographical Journal* 56 (1958), pp. 212-219.

2844. Shelton, W.G., ed. *British Columbia and Confederation.* Victoria: University of Victoria, 1967.

2844A. Siemens, A.H. "The Process of Settlement in the Lower Fraser Valley." In A.H. Siemens, ed. *Lower Fraser Valley: Evolution of a Cultural Landscape* (Vancouver: B.C. Geographical Series, No. 9, 1968), pp. 27-50.

2845. Silverman, P.G. "History of the Militia and Defences of British Columbia, 1871-1914." M.A. Thesis (University of British Columbia, 1956).

2846. Smith, Ian. *The Unknown Island.* Vancouver: J.J. Douglas, 1973.

2847. Specht, Allen, ed. "Skeena Country." *Sound Heritage* 5 (1976), pp. 3-51.

2848. Stainer, John. "Settlement Problems in British Columbia." *Queen's Quarterly* 55 (1948), pp. 20-26.

2849. Tatreau, Doug, and Tatreau, Bobbe. *The Parks of British Columbia.* Vancouver: Mitchell Press, 1973.

2850. Taylor, Griffith. "British Columbia: A Study in Topographic Control." *Geographical Review* 32 (1942), pp. 372-402.

2851. **Tippett, Maria, and Cole, Douglas.** *Desolation and Splendour: Changing Perceptions of the British Columbia Landscape.* Toronto and Vancouver: Clarke, Irwin, 1976.

2852. **Touchie, Rodger.** *Vancouver Island: Portrait of a Past.* Vancouver: J.J. Douglas, 1975.

2853. **Walbran, John T.** *British Columbia Coast Names, 1592-1906: Their Origin and History.* 1909. Reprint. Seattle: University of Washington Press, 1972.

2854. **Walter, M.** *Early Days among the Gulf Islands of British Columbia.* Victoria: Diggon-Hibbon, 1946.

2855. **Watters, Reginald Eyre, ed.** *British Columbia: A Centennial Anthology.* Toronto: McClelland and Stewart, 1958.

2856. **Watts, Alfred.** *Lex Liberorum Rex: History of the Law Society of British Columbia, 1869-1973.* Vancouver: The Society, 1973.

2857. **Weeks, Kathleen S.** "The Royal Engineers, Columbia Detachment— Their Work in Helping to Establish British Columbia." *Canadian Geographical Journal* 27 (1943), pp. 30-45.

2858. **Williams, Merton Yarwood.** "Canada's Western Province, British Columbia." *Canadian Geographical Journal* 13 (1936), pp. 479-485.

2859. **Williams, Merton Yarwood, and Pillsbury, Richard W.** "The Gulf Islands of British Columbia." *Canadian Geographical Journal* 56 (1958), pp. 184-201.

2860. **Wilson, Alan.** "Fleming and Tupper: The Fall of the Siamese Twins, 1880 [The C.P.R. in B.C.]." In J.S. Moir, ed. *Character and Circumstance: Essays in Honour of Donald Grant Creighton* (Toronto, 1970), pp. 99-127.

2861. **Woodcock, George.** "Far Western Outposts: Vancouver Island and British Columbia." *History Today* 21 (1971), pp. 658-668.

2862. **Woodward, Frances.** "The Influence of the Royal Engineers on the Development of British Columbia." *BC Studies* 24 (1974-75), pp. 3-51.

b. The People

2863. **Adachi, Ken.** *The Enemy That Never Was: A History of the Japanese Canadians.* Toronto: McClelland and Stewart, 1976.

2864. **Ames, M.M.** "A Note on the Contributions of Wilson Duff to Northwest Coast Ethnology and Art." *BC Studies* 31 (1976), pp. 3-11.

2865. **Ames, M.M., and Inglis, J.** "Conflict and Change in British Columbia Sikh Family Life." *BC Studies* 20 (1973-74), pp. 15-49.

2866. **Andrews, G.S.** *Sir Joseph William Trutch, K.C.M.G., L.S., F.R.G.S., 1892-1904: Surveyor, Engineer, Statesman.* Victoria: British Columbia Lands Service, 1972.

2867. **Angus, H.F.** "The Legal Status in British Columbia of Residents of Oriental Race and Their Descendants." *Canadian Bar Review* 9 (1931), pp. 1-12.

2868. **Antak, Ivan E.M.** "John Robson: British Columbian." M.A. Thesis (University of Victoria, 1972).

2869. **Appleton, Thomas E.** "Captain John T. Walbran, 1848-1913." *BC Studies* 5 (1970), pp. 24-35.

2870. **Audain, James.** *From Coalmine to Castle: The Story of the Dunsmuirs of Vancouver Island.* New York: Pageant Press, 1955.

2870A. **Avery, Donald, and Neary, Peter.** "Laurier, Borden and a White British Columbia." *Journal of Canadian Studies* 12, no. 4 (1977), pp. 24-34.

2871. **Barbeau, Marius.** "The North Pacific Coast—Its Human Mosaic." *Canadian Geographical Journal* 20 (1940), pp. 143-155.

2872. ———. *Totem Poles.* 2 vols. Ottawa: National Museum of Man, 1964.

2872A. **Bernard, Elaine.** "A University at War: Japanese Canadians at UBC during World War II." *BC Studies* 35 (1977), pp. 36-55.

2873. **Blake, T.M.** "Indian Reserve Allocation in British Columbia." *B.C. Perspectives* 3 (1973), pp. 21-31.

2874. **Boas, Franz.** *The Kwakiutl of Vancouver Island.* 1909. Reprint. New York: AMS Press, 1973.

2874A. **Bockemuehl, H.W.** "Doukhobor Impact on the British Columbia Landscape: An Historical-Geographical Study." M.A. Thesis (Western Washington State College, 1968).

2875. **Borden, Charles E.** "Wilson Duff (1925-1976): His Contributions to the Growth of Archaeology in British Columbia." *BC Studies* 13 (1977), pp. 3-12.

2876. **Brooks, G.W.S.** "Edgar Crow Baker: An Entrepreneur in Early British Columbia." M.A. Thesis (University of British Columbia, 1976).

2877. ———. "Edgar Crow Baker: An Entrepreneur in Early British Columbia." *BC Studies* 31 (1976), pp. 23-43.

2878. **Campbell, P.C.** *Chinese Coolie Immigration.* London: P.S. King, 1923.
2879. **Carr, Emily.** *Growing Pains: The Autobiography of Emily Carr.* Toronto: Oxford University Press, 1946.
2880. **Carter, S.M., ed.** *Who's Who in British Columbia, 1931.* Victoria: Victoria Printing and Publishing Company, 1930.
2881. **Cavelaars, A.A.C.** "Integration of a Group of Dutch Settlers in British Columbia." *International Migration* 5 (1967), pp. 38-54.
2882. **Cheng, Tien-Fang.** *Oriental Immigration in Canada.* Shanghai: Commercial Press, 1931.
2882A. **Cho, G., and Leigh, R.** "Patterns of Residence of Chinese in Vancouver." In J.V. Minghi, ed. *Peoples of the Living Land: Geography of Cultural Diversity in British Columbia* (Vancouver: B.C. Geographical Series, No. 15, 1972), pp. 67-84.
2883. **Clutesi, George.** *Potlatch.* Sidney: Gray's, 1969.
2883A. **Daniels, Roger.** "The Japanese Experience in North America: An Essay in Comparative Racism." *Canadian Ethnic Studies* 9 (1977), pp. 91-100.
2884. **Duff, Wilson.** *The Indian History of British Columbia. Vol. 1: The Impact of the White Man.* Victoria: Provincial Museum, 1969.
2885. **Eaton, L.K.** *The Architecture of Samuel Maclure.* Victoria: Art Gallery of Greater Victoria, 1971.
2885A. **Evenden, L.J., and Anderson, I.D.** "The Presence of a Past Community: [The Japanese in] Tashme, B.C." In J.V. Minghi, ed. *Peoples of the Living Land: Geography of Cultural Diversity in British Columbia* (Vancouver: B.C. Geographical Series, No. 15, 1972), pp. 41-66.
2886. **Fields, D.B., and Stanbury, W.T.** *The Economic Impact of the Public Sector upon the Indians of British Columbia.* Vancouver: University of British Columbia Press, 1974.
2887. **Fisher, Robin.** "Joseph Trutch and Indian Land Policy." *BC Studies* 12 (1971-72), pp. 3-33.
2888. ———. "An Exercise in Futility: The Joint Commission on Indian Land in British Columbia, 1875-1880." Canadian Historical Association. *Historical Papers 1975*, pp. 79-94.
2889. ———. *Contact and Conflict: Indian-European Relations in British Columbia, 1774-1890.* Vancouver: University of British Columbia Press, 1977.

2890. **Foner, Philip S.** "The Colored Inhabitants of Vancouver Island." *BC Studies* 8 (1970-71), pp. 29-33.
2891. **Forbes, Elizabeth.** *Wild Roses at Their Feet: Pioneer Women of Vancouver Island.* Vancouver: B.C. Centennial '71 Committee, 1971.
2891A. **Gibson, J.R.** "A Comparison of Anglo-Saxon, Mennonite, and Dutch Farms in the Lower Fraser Valley: A Methodological Study of Areal Differentiation and the Relative Influences of the Physical and Cultural Environments." M.A. Thesis (University of Oregon, Corvallis, 1959).
2891B. **Ginn, M.** "Rural Dutch Immigrants in the Lower Fraser Valley." M.A. Thesis (University of British Columbia, 1967).
2892. **Glynn-Ward, Hilda.** *The Writing on the Wall: Chinese and Japanese Immigration to B.C.* 1921. Reprint. Social History of Canada, vol. 20. Toronto: University of Toronto Press, 1974.
2893. **Gould, Jan.** *Women of British Columbia.* Saanichton: Hancock House, 1975.
2893A. **Habinski, A.A.** "Assimilation and Residential Location: The Jews in Vancouver." M.A. Thesis (Simon Fraser University, 1973).
2894. **Hallett, Mary E.** "A Governor-General's Views on Oriental Immigration to British Columbia, 1904-1911." *BC Studies* 14 (1972), pp. 51-72.
2895. **Hardwick, Francis C.,** ed. *From Far Beyond the Western Horizon: Canadians from the Indian Sub-Continent.* Vancouver: Tantalus Research, 1974.
2896. ———. *East Meets West: A Source Book for the Study of Chinese Immigrants and Their Descendants in Canada.* Vancouver: Tantalus Research, 1975.
2897. **Harker, D.E.** *The Woodwards: The Story of a Distinguished B.C. Family, 1850-1975.* Vancouver and Toronto: Mitchell Press, 1976.
2898. **Harvey, A.G.** "David Stuart: Okanagan Pathfinder and Founder of Kamloops." *B.C.H.Q.* 9 (1945), pp. 277-289.
2899. **Hawthorn, Audrey.** *Art of the Kwakiutl Indians and Other Northwest Coast Tribes.* Vancouver: University of British Columbia, 1967.
2900. **Hawthorn, H.B.,** ed. *The Doukhobors of British Columbia: Report of the Doukhobor Committee.* Vancouver: The University of British Columbia, 1952.
2901. ———. *The Doukhobors of British Columbia.* Vancouver: Dent, 1955.

2902. ———. "A Test of Simmel on the Secret Society: The Doukhobors of British Columbia." *American Journal of Sociology* 62 (1956), pp. 1-7.

2903. **Hawthorn, H.B.; Belshaw, C.S.; and Jamieson, Stuart Marshall.** *The Indians of British Columbia: A Study of Contemporary Social Adjustment.* Toronto: University of Toronto Press, 1960.

2904. **Haynes, John Carmichael.** "Pioneer of the Okanagan and Kootenay." *B.C.H.Q.* 4 (1943), pp. 183-201.

2905. **Hembroff-Schleicher, E.** *M.E.: A Portrayal of Emily Carr.* Toronto: Clarke, Irwin, 1969.

2906. **Hiebert, A.J.** "The Oriental As He Appears in Some of the Novels of British Columbia." *British Columbia Library Quarterly* 34 (1971), pp. 20-31.

2907. **Holt, S.** *Terror in the Name of God.* Toronto: McClelland and Stewart, 1964.

2908. **Hopwood, Victor G.** "William Fraser Tolmie: Natural Scientist and Patriot: Review Article." *BC Studies* 5 (1970), pp. 45-51.

2909. **Howard, Irene.** *Vancouver's Svenskar: A History of the Swedish Community.* Vancouver: Vancouver Historical Society, 1970.

2910. **Humphries, Charles W.** "War and Patriotism: The *Lusitania* Riot." *B.C. Historical News* 5 (1971), pp. 15-23.

2911. **Irwin, Jane, ed.** "Steveston: The Japanese-Canadian Experience." *Sound Heritage* 3 (1974), pp. 5-16.

2912. **Jenness, Diamond.** "Myths of the Carrier Indians of British Columbia." *Journal of American Folkculture* 29 (1916), pp. 368-391.

2913. ———. *The Sekani Indians of British Columbia.* Ottawa: National Museum of Man, 1947.

2914. **Johnson, F. Henry.** "The Doukhobors of British Columbia: The History of a Sectarian Problem in Education." *Queen's Quarterly* 70 (1963), pp. 528-541.

2915. ———. *John Jessop: Gold Seeker and Educator.* Vancouver: Mitchell Press, 1971.

2916. **Kerr, J.B.** *Biographical Dictionary of Well-Known British Columbians.* Vancouver: Kerr and Begg, 1890.

2917. **King, W.L.M.** *Report on Mission to England to Confer with the British Authorities on the Subject of Immigration to Canada from the Orient and Immigration from India in Particular.* Ottawa: King's Printer, 1908.

2918. **Knight, Rolf.** *A Very Ordinary Life.* Vancouver: New Star Books, 1974.

2919. **Knight, Rolf, and Koizumi, Maya.** *A Man of Our Times: The Life History of a Japanese-Canadian Fisherman.* Vancouver: New Star Books, 1977.

2920. **Kolehmainen, John Ilmari.** "Harmony Island: A Finnish Utopian Venture in British Columbia, 1901-1905." *B.C.H.Q.* 5 (1941), pp. 111-123.

2921. **Lai, Chuen-Yan.** "The Chinese Consolidated Benevolent Association in Victoria: Its Origins and Functions." *BC Studies* 15 (1972), pp. 53-67.

2922. ———. "Chinese Attempts to Discourage Emigration to Canada: Some Findings from Chinese Archives in Victoria." *BC Studies* 18 (1973), pp. 33-49.

2922A. ———. "Chinese Immigrants into British Columbia and Their Distribution, 1858-1970." *Pacific Viewpoint* 14 (1973), pp. 102-108.

2923. ———. "Home County and Clan Origins of Overseas Chinese in Canada in the Early 1880s." *BC Studies* 27 (1975), pp. 3-29.

2924. **Lambrou, Y.** "The Greek Community of Vancouver: Social Organization and Adaptation." M.A. Thesis (University of British Columbia, 1975).

2925. **La Violette, Forrest E.** "Two Years of Japanese Evacuation in Canada." *Far Eastern Survey* 13 (1944), pp. 93-100.

2926. ———. *The Canadian Japanese and World War II: A Sociological and Psychological Account.* Toronto: University of Toronto Press, 1948.

2927. ———. *The Struggle for Survival: Indian Cultures and the Protestant Ethic in British Columbia.* Toronto: University of Toronto Press, 1961.

2928. **Layton, Monique.** "Magico-Religious Elements in the Traditional Beliefs of Maillardville, B.C." *BC Studies* 27 (1975), pp. 50-61.

2929. **Lee, Carol F.** "The Road to Enfranchisement: Chinese and Japanese in British Columbia." *BC Studies* 30 (1976), pp. 44-76.

2930. **Lee, D.T.H., ed.** *The History of the Chinese in Canada.* Victoria: Victoria Chinese Benevolent Assn. and the Chinese Public School, 1960. [Printed in Chinese.]

2931. **Lewis, Claudia.** *Indian Families of the Northwest Coast.* Chicago: University of Chicago Press, 1970.

2932. **Lort, R.** "On Samuel Maclure, MRAIC." Royal Architectural Institute of Canada. *Journal* 35 (1958), pp. 114-115.

2933. **McEwen, Tom.** *He Wrote for Us: The Story of Bill Bennett, Pioneer Socialist Journalist.* Vancouver: Tribune, 1951.

2934. **McFeat, Tom, ed.** *Indians of the North Pacific Coast.* Toronto: McClelland and Stewart, 1966.

2935. **MacGill, E.G.** *My Mother the Judge: A Biography of Judge Helen Gregory MacGill.* Toronto: Ryerson, 1955.

2936. **MacInnis, Grace, and MacInnis, Angus.** *Oriental Canadians: Outcasts or Citizens?* Vancouver: Federationist Publishing, 1945.

2937. **MacInnes, Tom.** *Oriental Occupation of British Columbia.* Vancouver: Sun Publishing, 1927.

2938. **McKenzie, K.S.** *The Conflict of Values between Subcultural Groups: The Indian in Education.* Vancouver: University of British Columbia, 1969.

Plate 16. The Kwakiutl Village of Newitty in the Late 1870's

2939. **Maranda, E.K.** "B.C. Indian Myth and Education: A Review Article." *BC Studies* 25 (1975), pp. 125-134.

2940. **Marlatt, D.**, ed. *Steveston Recollected: A Japanese-Canadian History.* Victoria: Provincial Archives of British Columbia, 1975.

2941. **Minden, Robert,** ed. "'Strangers on the Earth': Meetings with Doukhobor Canadians in British Columbia." *Sound Heritage* 5 (1976), pp. 19-34.

2941A. **Minghi, J.V.**, ed. *Peoples of the Living Land: Geography of Cultural Diversity in British Columbia.* Vancouver: B.C. Geographical Series, No. 15, 1972.

2942. **Morris, Philip Alvin.** "Conditioning Factors Moulding Public Opinion in British Columbia Hostile to Japanese Immigration into Canada." M.A. Thesis (University of Oregon, 1963).

2943. **Morse, E.N.** "Some Aspects of the *Komagata Maru* Affair." Canadian Historical Association. *Annual Report 1936,* pp. 100-108.

2944. **Morton, James.** *In the Sea of Sterile Mountains: The Chinese in British Columbia.* Vancouver: J.J. Douglas, 1974.

2945. **Moser, Charles.** *Reminiscences of the West Coast of Vancouver Island.* Victoria: Acme Press, 1926.

2946. **Munday, J.G.** "East Indians in British Columbia: A Community in Transition." B.A. Essay (University of British Columbia, 1953).

2947. **Munro, J.A.** "British Columbia and the 'Chinese Evil': Canada's First Anti-Asiatic Immigration Law." *Journal of Canadian Studies* 6, no. 4 (1971), pp. 42-51.

2948. **Nakayama, T.M.** "Anglican Missions to the Japanese in Canada." Canadian Church Historical Society. *Journal* 8 (1966), pp. 26-47.

2949. **Newton, Norman.** *Fire in the Raven's Nest: The Haida of British Columbia.* Toronto: New Press, 1973.

2950. ———. "On Survivals of Ancient Astronomical Ideas among the Peoples of the Northwest Coast." *BC Studies* 26 (1975), pp. 16-38.

2951. **Norris, John.** *Strangers Entertained: A History of the Ethnic Groups of British Columbia.* Vancouver: B.C. Centennial '71 Committee, 1971.

2952. ———. "Margaret Ormsby." *BC Studies* 32 (1976-77), pp. 11-27.

2952A. **O'Brien, Robert W.** "Evacuation of Japanese from the Pacific Coast: Canadian and American Contrasts." State College of Washington. *Research Studies* 14 (1946), pp. 113-120.

2953. **Ormsby, Margaret, A.,** ed. *A Pioneer Gentlewoman in British Columbia: The Recollections of Susan Allison.* Vancouver: University of British Columbia Press, 1976.

2954. **Osterhout, S.S.** *Orientals in Canada: The Story of the Work of the United Church of Canada with Asiatics in Canada.* Toronto: United Church of Canada, 1929.

2955. **Peterson, Lester R.** "British Columbia's Depopulated Coast." *Raincoast Chronicles* 1 (1974), pp. 4-11.

2956. **Pethick, Derek.** *Men of British Columbia.* Saanichton: Hancock House, 1975.

2957. **Porteous, Neil.** "A Comparative Study of *Who's Who in British Columbia* for the Years 1931 and 1951." *B.C. Perspectives* 1 (1972), pp. 35-52.

2958. **Ralston, Keith.** "John Sullivan Deas: A Black Entrepreneur in British Columbia Salmon Canning." *BC Studies* 32 (1976-77), pp. 64-78.

2959. **Ramsey, A.B.** *A History of the German-Canadians in B.C.* Winnipeg: Natural Publishers, 1958.

2960. **Rankin, Harry.** *Rankin's Law: Recollections of a Radical.* Vancouver: November House, 1975.

2961. **Ravenhill, Alice.** *The Native Tribes of British Columbia.* Victoria: C.F. Banfield, 1938.

2961A. **Read, J.M.** "The Pre-War Japanese Canadians of Maple Ridge: Landownership and the Ken Tie." M.A. Thesis (University of British Columbia, 1975).

2962. **Reid, R.L.** "The Inside Story of the *Komagata Maru*." *B.C.H.Q.* 5 (1941), pp. 1-23.

2963. **Robinson, Leigh Burpee.** "To British Columbia's Totem Land: Expedition of Dr. Powell in 1873." *Canadian Geographical Journal* 24 (1942), pp. 80-93.

2963A. **Robinson, M.E.** "The Russian Doukhobors in West Kootenay, British Columbia." M.A. Thesis (Syracuse University, 1948).

2964. **Rohner, Ronald, and Rohner, Evelyn C.** *The Kwakiutl: Indians of British Columbia.* Toronto: Holt, Rinehart and Winston, 1970.

2965. **Rome, D.** "Early British Columbia Jewry: A Reconstructed Census." *Canadian Ethnic Studies* 3 (1971), pp. 57-62.

2966. **Roy, Patricia E.** "The Evacuation of the Japanese, 1942." In J.M. Bumsted, ed. *Documentary Problems in Canadian History* (Georgetown, 1969), pp. 215-240.

2967. ———. "The Oriental 'Menace' in British Columbia." In S.M. Trofimenkoff, ed. *The Twenties in Western Canada* (Ottawa, 1972), pp. 243-258.

2968. ———. "Educating the 'East': British Columbia and the Oriental Question in the Interwar Years." *BC Studies* 18 (1973), pp. 50-69.

2969. ———. "Protecting Their Pocketbooks and Preserving Their Race: White Merchants and Oriental Competition." In A.R. McCormack and Ian MacPherson, eds. *Cities in the West* (Ottawa, 1975), pp. 116-138.

2970. **Roy, R.H.** "A Berkhamsted Boy in the Foothills [George R. Pearkes]." *A.H.R.* 20 (Summer 1972), pp. 17-29.

2971. ———. *For Most Conspicuous Bravery: A Biography of Major-General George R. Pearkes, V.C., through Two World Wars.* Vancouver: University of British Columbia Press, 1977.

2972. **Sanders, D.** "The Nishga Case." *BC Studies* 19 (1973), pp. 3-20.

2972A. **Sandhu, K.S.** "Indian Immigration and Racial Prejudice in British Columbia: Some Preliminary Observations." In J.V. Minghi, ed. *Peoples of the Living Land: Geography of Cultural Diversity in British Columbia* (Vancouver: B.C. Geographical Series, No. 15, 1972), pp. 29-40.

2973. **Schieder, Rupert.** "Martin Allerdale Grainger." *Forest History* 2 (1967), pp. 6-13.

2974. **Schofield, Emily M.** *Charles Develier Schofield, Late Bishop of British Columbia.* Victoria: The Author, 1941.

2975. **Smith, Dorothy Blakey,** ed. *The Reminiscences of Doctor John Sebastian Helmcken.* Vancouver: University of British Columbia Press, 1975.

2976. **Smith, M.W.** *Indians of the Urban Northwest.* New York: AMS Press, 1969.

2977. **Stanbury, W.T.** "Indians in British Columbia: Level of Income, Welfare Dependency and the Poverty Rate." *BC Studies* 20 (1973-74), pp. 66-78.

2978. ———. "Reserve and Urban Indians in British Columbia." *BC Studies* 26 (1975), pp. 39-64.

2979. **Stanbury, W.T., and Siegal, Jay H.** *Success and Failure: Indians in Urban Society.* Vancouver: University of British Columbia Press, 1975.

2980. **Stewart, J.R.** "French Canadian Settlement in British Columbia." M.A. Thesis (University of British Columbia, 1956).

2981. **Straaton, K.V.** "The Political System of the Vancouver Chinese Community Associations and Leadership in the Early 1960s." M.A. Thesis (University of British Columbia, 1974).

2982. **Sugimoto, Howard H.** "Japanese Immigration, the Vancouver Riots, and Canadian Diplomacy." Seattle: University of Washington, 1966. [Unpublished manuscript.]

2983. ———. "The Vancouver Riots of 1907: A Canadian Episode." In H. Conroy and T.S. Miyakawa, eds. *East across the Pacific* (Santa Barbara, 1972), pp. 92-126.

2984. ———. "The Vancouver Riot and Its International Significance." *Pacific Northwest Quarterly* 64 (1973), pp. 163-174.

2985. **Sumida, R.** "The Japanese in British Columbia." M.A. Thesis (University of British Columbia, 1935).

2986. **Teit, James.** "Traditions of the Lillooet Indians of British Columbia." *Journal of American Folklore* 25 (1912), pp. 287-371.

2987. **Ujimoto, K.V.** "Contrasts in the Prewar and Postwar Japanese Community in British Columbia: Conflict and Change." *Canadian Review of Sociology and Anthropology* 13 (1976), pp. 80-89.

2988. **Usher, Jean.** "Duncan of Metlakatla: The Victorian Origins of a Model Indian Community." In W.L. Morton, ed. *The Shield of Achilles: Aspects of Canada in the Victorian Age* (Toronto, 1968), pp. 286-310.

2989. ———. *William Duncan of Metlakatla: A Victorian Missionary in British Columbia.* Ottawa: National Museum of Man, 1974.

2989A. **Villeneuve, P.Y.** "Changes over Time in the Residential and Occupational Structures of an Urban Ethnic Minority." In R. Leigh, ed. *Contemporary Geography: Western Viewpoints* (Vancouver: B.C. Geographical Series, No. 12, 1971), pp. 115-128.

2989B. ———. "Residential Location Problems in the French-Canadian Community of Maillardville." In J.V. Minghi, ed. *Peoples of the Living Land: Geography of Cultural Diversity in British Columbia* (Vancouver: B.C. Geographical Series, No. 15, 1972), pp. 85-106.

2989C. **Wagner, Philip L.** "The Persistence of Native Settlement in Coastal British Columbia." In J.V. Minghi, ed. *Peoples of the Living Land: Geography of Cultural Diversity in British Columbia* (Vancouver: B.C. Geographical Series, No. 15, 1972), pp. 15-28.

2990. **Ward, N. Lascelles.** *Oriental Missions in British Columbia.* Westminster: Society for the Propagation of the Gospel, 1925.

2991. **Ward, W. Peter.** "White Canada Forever: British Columbia's Response to Orientals, 1858-1914." Ph.D. Thesis (Queen's University, 1973).
2992. ———. "The Oriental Immigrant and Canada's Protestant Clergy, 1858-1925." *BC Studies* 22 (1974), pp. 40-55.
2993. ———. "British Columbia and the Japanese Evacuation." *C.H.R.* 57 (1976), pp. 289-308.
2994. **Weightman, Barbara A.** "Indian Social Space: A Case Study of the Musqueam Band of Vancouver, British Columbia." *Canadian Geographer* 20 (1976), pp. 171-186.
2995. **Weir, D.A.** "Some Characteristics of the Indian Population of British Columbia." B.A. Essay (University of Victoria 1965).
2995A. **Welsh, R.L.** "The Growth and Distribution of the Population of British Columbia, 1951-1961." M.A. Thesis (University of British Columbia, 1964).
2996. **White, Howard.** "Metlakatla: Bringing the Indians to Their Knees: The West Coast's First Christian Mission." *Raincoast Chronicles* 1 (1974), pp. 24-37.
2997. **Wild, Roland.** *Amor De Cosmos.* Toronto: Ryerson, 1958.
2998. **Williams, David R.** *The Man for a New Country: Sir Matthew Baillie Begbie.* Sidney: Gray's, 1977.
2999. **Willmott, W.E.** "Some Aspects of Chinese Communities in British Columbia." *BC Studies* 1 (1968-69), pp. 27-36.
3000. ———. "Approaches to the Study of the Chinese in British Columbia." *BC Studies* 4 (1970), pp. 38-52.
3001. **Wilson, J. Donald.** "Matti Kurikka: Finnish-Canadian Intellectual." *BC Studies* 20 (1973-74), pp. 50-65.
3002. **Woodcock, George, and Avakumovic, Ivan.** *The Doukhobors.* 1968. Reprint. Toronto: McClelland and Stewart, 1977.
3003. **Woodsworth, Charles J.** *Canada and the Orient: A Study in International Relations.* Toronto: Macmillan, 1941.
3004. **Wright, J.F.C.** "The Dukhobors." *Canadian Geographical Journal* 19 (1939), pp. 301-306.
3005. **Wynne, R.E.** "Reaction to the Chinese in the Pacific Northwest and British Columbia, 1850-1910." Ph.D. Thesis (University of Washington, 1964).
3006. ———. "American Labor and the Vancouver Anti-Oriental Riot." *Pacific Northwest Quarterly* 57 (1966), pp. 172-180.

3007. **Young, Charles H.; Reid, Helen R.Y.; and Carrothers, W.A.** *The Japanese-Canadians.* Toronto: University of Toronto Press, 1938.

c. *Government and Politics*

3008. **Alper, Donald.** "The Effects of Coalition Government on Party Structure: The Case of the Conservative Party in B.C." *BC Studies* 33 (1977), pp. 40-49.
3009. **Angus, H.F.** "The British Columbia Election, June, 1952." *C.J.E.P.S.* 18 (1952), pp. 518-525.
3010. **Artibise, Alan F.J.** "Electoral Reform in the City of Kamloops: A Background Paper." *Report on Local Government.* Kamloops: City of Kamloops, 1975.
3010A. **Avery, Donald, and Neary, Peter.** "Laurier, Borden and a White British Columbia." *Journal of Canadian Studies* 12, no. 4 (1977), pp. 24-34.
3011. **Black, E.R.** "The Progressive Conservative Party in British Columbia: Some Aspects of Organization." M.A. Thesis (University of British Columbia, 1960).
3012. **Blake, Donald.** "Another Look at Social Credit and the British Columbia Electorate." *BC Studies* 12 (1971-72), pp. 53-62.
3013. **British Columbia, Province of.** *British Columbia in the Canadian Confederation: A Submission Presented to the Royal Commission on Dominion-Provincial Relations by the Government of the Province of British Columbia.* Victoria: King's Printer, 1938.
3014. **Burns, R.M.** "British Columbia and the Canadian Federation." In R.M. Burns, ed. *One Country or Two?* (Montreal, 1971), pp. 253-273.
3015. **Carlsen, Alfred E.** "Major Developments in Public Finance in British Columbia, 1920-1960." Ph.D. Thesis (University of Toronto, 1961).
3016. ———. "Public Debt Operations in British Columbia Since 1952." *C.J.E.P.S.* 27 (1961), pp. 64-71.
3017. **Collier, Robert.** "The Evolution of Regional Districts in British Columbia." *BC Studies* 15 (1972), pp. 29-39.
3018. **Cramer, M.H.** "Women's Suffrage in British Columbia: A Victorian Viewpoint." M.A. Essay (University of Victoria, 1974).
3019. **Currie, A.W.** "Rate Control of Public Utilities in British Columbia." *C.J.E.P.S.* 10 (1944), pp. 381-390.

3020. **Dailyde, V.K.** "The Administration of W.J. Bowser, Premier of British Columbia, 1915-1916." M.A. Thesis (University of Victoria, 1976).

3021. **Dobie, Edith.** "Some Aspects of Party History in British Columbia, 1871-1903." *Pacific Historical Review* 1 (1932), pp. 235-251.

3022. ———. "Party History in British Columbia, 1903-1933." *Pacific Northwest Quarterly* 27 (1936), pp. 153-166.

3023. **Dwyer, M.J.** "Laurier and the British Columbia Liberal Party, 1896-1911: A Study in Federal-Provincial Relations." M.A. Thesis (University of British Columbia, 1961).

3024. **Easton, Robert, and Tennant, Paul.** "Vancouver Civic Party Leadership: Backgrounds, Attitudes, and Non-Civic Party Affiliations." *BC Studies* 2 (1969), pp. 19-29.

3025. **Elkins, David.** "Politics Makes Strange Bedfellows: The B.C. Party System in the 1952 and 1953 Provincial Elections." *BC Studies* 30 (1976), pp. 3-26.

3026. **Elliot, Gordon R.** "Henry P. Pellew Crease: Confederation or No Confederation." *BC Studies* 12 (1971-72), pp. 63-74.

3027. **Ellis, Walter E.W.** "Some Aspects of Religion in British Columbia Politics." M.A. Thesis (University of British Columbia, 1959).

3028. **England, Robert.** "Elections in British Columbia." *Public Affairs* 14 (1952), pp. 45-50.

3029. **Francis, R.A.** "Profile: BC's Bennett." *Western Business and Industry* 32 (July 1958), pp. 16-21.

3030. **Grantham, R.** "Some Aspects of the Socialist Movement in British Columbia, 1898-1933." M.A. Thesis (University of British Columbia, 1942).

3031. **Hermuses, Paul.** *Power without Glory: The Rise and Fall of the NDP Government in British Columbia.* Vancouver: Balsam Press Limited, 1976.

3032. **Hodgson, Maurice.** *The Squire of Kootenay West [A Biography of H.W. Herridge, M.P.].* Saanichton: Hancock House, 1975.

3033. **Horsfield, B.** "The Social Credit Movement in British Columbia." B.A. Essay (University of British Columbia, 1953).

3034. **Hunt, P.R.** "The Political Career of Sir Richard McBride." M.A. Thesis (University of British Columbia, 1953).

3035. **Ireland, W.E.** "Helmcken's Diary of the Confederation Negotiations, 1870." *B.C.H.Q.* 4 (1940), pp. 111-128.

3036. **Jackman, S.W.** *Portraits of the Premiers: An Informal History of British Columbia.* Sidney: Gray's, 1969.

3037. ———. *The Men at Cary Castle.* Victoria: Morriss Printing, 1972.

3038. ———. "The Diary of Simon Fraser Tolmie." *BC Studies* 5 (1970), pp. 36-44.

3039. **Johns, H.P.** "British Columbia's Campaign for Better Terms, 1871-1907." M.A. Thesis (University of British Columbia, 1935).

3040. ———. "British Columbia's Appeal to Sir Wilfrid Laurier for Better Terms." *C.H.R.* 17 (1936), pp. 423-430.

3041. **Johnson, P.R.** "British Columbia's Inter-Governmental Relations with the United States." Ph.D. Thesis (Johns Hopkins University, 1975).

3042. **Johnson, R.A.** "No Compromise—No Political Trading: The Marxian Socialist Tradition in British Columbia." Ph.D. Thesis (University of British Columbia, 1975).

3043. **Koenig, D.J.; Martin, G.R.; Goudy, H.G.; and Martin, M.** "The Year That British Columbia Went NDP: NDP Voter Support Pre- and Post-1972." *BC Studies* 24 (1974-75), pp. 65-86.

3044. **Koenig, D.J., and Proverbs, T.B.** "Class, Regional and Institutional Sources of Party Support within British Columbia." *BC Studies* 29 (1976), pp. 19-28.

3045. **Kopas, L.C.** "Political Action of the Indians of British Columbia." M.A. Thesis (University of British Columbia, 1972).

3046. **Kristianson, G.L.** "The Non-Partisan Approach to B.C. Politics: The Search for a Unity Party, 1972-1975." *BC Studies* 33 (1977), pp. 13-29.

3047. **Laponce, J.A.** *People vs. Politics: A Study of Opinions, Attitudes, and Perceptions in Vancouver Burrard, 1963-1965.* Toronto: University of Toronto Press, 1969.

3048. **Loosmore, T.R.** "The British Columbia Labour Movement and Political Action, 1879-1906." M.A. Thesis (University of British Columbia, 1954).

3049. **McCormack, A.R.** "The Emergence of the Socialist Movement in British Columbia." *BC Studies* 21 (1974), pp. 3-27.

3050. **MacDonald, K.J.** "Sources of Electoral Support for Provincial Political Parties in Urban British Columbia." *BC Studies* 15 (1972), pp. 40-52.

3051. **McGeer, Pat.** *Politics in Paradise.* Toronto: Peter Martin, 1972.

3052. **Mercer, E.B.** "Political Groups in British Columbia, 1871-1903." M.A. Thesis (University of British Columbia, 1937).
3053. **Miller, F.** "Vancouver Civic Political Parties: Developing a Model of Party-System Change and Stabilization." *BC Studies* 25 (1975), pp. 3-31.
3054. **Morley, Terence.** "The 1974 Federal General Election in British Columbia." *BC Studies* 23 (1974), pp. 34-46.
3055. ———. "Labour in British Columbia Politics." *Queen's Quarterly* 83 (1976), pp. 291-298.
3056. **Morton, James.** *Honest John Oliver.* London: Dent, 1933.
3057. **Munro, John M.** "Highways in British Columbia: Economics and Politics." *Canadian Journal of Economics* 8 (1975), pp. 192-204.
3058. **Oliver, Thelma.** "Political Socialization and Political Culture: A Case Study." M.A. Thesis (University of British Columbia, 1967).
3059. **Ormsby, Margaret A.** "Prime Minister Mackenzie, the Liberal Party, and the Bargain with British Columbia." *C.H.R.* 26 (1945), pp. 148-173.
3060. ———. "The United Farmers of British Columbia: An Abortive Third-Party Movement." *B.C.H.Q.* 17 (1953), pp. 53-73.
3061. ———. "T. Dufferin Pattullo and the Little New Deal." *C.H.R.* 43 (1962), pp. 277-297.
3062. **Parker, Ian D.** "Simon Fraser Tolmie and the British Columbia Conservative Party, 1916-1933." M.A. Thesis (University of Victoria, 1970).
3063. ———. "The Provincial Party." *BC Studies* 8 (1970-71), pp. 17-28.
3064. ———. "Simon Fraser Tolmie: The Last Conservative Premier of British Columbia." *BC Studies* 11 (1971), pp. 21-36.
3065. **Resnick, Philip.** "Social Democracy in Power: The Case of British Columbia." *BC Studies* 34 (1977), pp. 3-21.
3066. **Roberts, D.J.** "Doctrine and Disunity in the British Columbia Section of the C.C.F., 1932-1956." M.A. Thesis (University of Victoria, 1972).
3067. **Robin, Martin.** "The Social Basis of Party Politics in British Columbia." *Queen's Quarterly* 82 (1965-1966), pp. 675-690.
3068. ———. "British Columbia: The Politics of Class Conflict." In M. Robin, ed. *Canadian Provincial Politics* (Scarborough, 1972), pp. 27-68.

3069. **Ross, M.** "Amor De Cosmos: A British Columbia Reformer." M.A. Thesis (University of British Columbia, 1931).

3070. **Ruff, Norman J.** "Party Detachment and Voting Patterns in a Provincial Two-Member Constituency: Victoria 1972." *BC Studies* 23 (1974), pp. 3-24.

3071. **Rumley, Dennis.** "Stability and Change in Electoral Patterns: The Case of the 1972 British Columbia Provincial Election in Vancouver." Ph.D. Thesis (University of British Columbia, 1975).

3072. **Sage, Walter N.** "The Position of the Lieutenant-Governor in British Columbia in the Years following Confederation." In R. Flenley, ed. *Essays in Canadian History Presented to G.M. Wrong* (Toronto, 1939), pp. 178-203.

3073. ———. "Federal Parties and Provincial Groups in British Columbia, 1871-1903." *B.C.H.Q.* 12 (1948), pp. 151-169.

3074. ———. "British Columbia Becomes Canadian, 1871-1901." *Queen's Quarterly* 52 (1945), pp. 168-183.

3075. **Sanford, T.M.** "The Politics of Protest: The C.C.F. and the Social Credit League in British Columbia." Ph.D. Thesis (University of California, 1961).

3076. **Saywell, John T.** "The McInnes Incident in British Columbia." *B.C.H.Q.* 14 (1950), pp. 141-166.

3077. ———. "Labour and Socialism in British Columbia: A Survey of Historical Development before 1903." *B.C.H.Q.* 15 (1951), pp. 129-150.

3078. ———. "Sir Joseph Trutch: British Columbia's First Lieutenant Governor." *B.C.H.Q.* 19 (1955), pp. 71-92.

3079. **Shelton, W.G.**, ed. *British Columbia and Confederation.* Victoria: University of Victoria, 1967.

3080. **Sherman, Paddy.** *Bennett.* Toronto: McClelland and Stewart, 1966.

3081. **Smith, B.E.** "The British Columbia Land Commission Act, 1973." M.A. Thesis (University of British Columbia, 1975).

3082. **Smith, B.R.D.** "Sir Richard McBride—A Study in the Conservative Party of British Columbia, 1903-1916." M.A. Thesis (Queen's University, 1959).

3083. ———. "Sir Richard McBride." *Conservative Concepts* 1 (1959), pp. 19-28.

3084. **Sproule-Jones, Mark.** "Social Credit and the British Columbia Electorate." *BC Studies* 11 (1971), pp. 37-50.

3085. ———. "Social Credit and the British Columbia Electorate." *BC Studies* 12 (1971-72), pp. 34-45.

3086. **Stanley, George F.G.** "A 'Constitutional Crisis' in British Columbia." *C.J.E.P.S.* 21 (1955), pp. 281-292.

3087. **Steeves, Dorothy.** *The Compassionate Rebel: Ernest E. Winch and His Times.* 1960. Reprint. North Vancouver: J.J. Douglas, 1977.

3088. **Sutherland, N.** "T.D. Pattullo as a Party Leader." M.A. Thesis (University of British Columbia, 1960).

3089. **Tennant, Paul, and Zirnhelt, D.** "The Emergence of Metropolitan Government in Greater Vancouver." *BC Studies* 15 (1972), pp. 3-28.

3090. **Waites, K.A.** "Responsible Government and Confederation: The Popular Movement for Popular Government." *B.C.H.Q.* 6 (1942), pp. 97-124.

3091. **Walker, R.R.** *Politicians of a Pioneering Province.* Vancouver: Mitchell Press, 1969.

3092. **Warburton, T.R.** "Religious and Social Influences on Voting in Greater Victoria." *BC Studies* 10 (1971), pp. 3-25.

Plate 17. Parliament Buildings, Victoria, with One of the "Birdcages"

3093. **Webster, Daisy.** *Growth of the N.D.P. in B.C., 1900-1970: 81 Political Biographies.* Vancouver: B.C. New Democratic Party, 1970.
3094. **Weppler, D.M.** "Early Forms of Political Activity among White Women in British Columbia, 1880-1925." M.A. Thesis (Simon Fraser University, 1971).
3095. **Wilbur, Richard.** *H.H. Stevens (1878-1973).* Canadian Biographical Series, No. 6. Toronto: University of Toronto Press, 1977.
3096. **Worley, R.B.** *The Wonderful World of W.A.C. Bennett.* Toronto: McClelland and Stewart, 1971.
3097. **Young, Walter D.** "A Profile of Activists in the British Columbia NDP." *Journal of Canadian Studies* 6, no. 1 (1971), pp. 19-26.
3098. ———. "Ideology, Personality and the Origin of the CCF in British Columbia." *BC Studies* 32 (1976-77), pp. 139-162.

d. Agriculture and Rural Development

3099. **Affleck, E.L.** *Kootenay Pathfinders: Settlement in the Kootenay District, 1885-1920.* Vancouver: Alexander Nicolls Press, 1976.
3100. **Andrew, F.W.** *The Story of Summerland.* Penticton: Penticton Herald, 1945.
3101. **Atkins, B.R.; Affleck, E.L.; and Forde, G.B.** *Columbia River Chronicles: A History of the Kootenay District in the 19th Century.* Vancouver: Alexander Nicolls Press, 1976.
3102. **Bulman, T.A.** *Kamloops Cattlemen: One Hundred Years of Trail Dust.* Sidney: Gray's, 1972.
3103. **Caple, K.P.** "The British Columbia Apple Industry." M.S.A. Thesis (University of British Columbia, 1927).
3104. **Carroll, C.** *Three Bars: The Story of Douglas Lake [Cattle Company].* Vancouver: Mitchell Press, 1958.
3105. **Dalichow, Fritz.** *Agricultural Geography of B.C.* Vancouver: Versatile Publishing, 1972.
3106. **Davis, M.B., and Wheeler, R.Z.** "The Apple Industry of Canada." *Canadian Geographical Journal* 17 (1938), pp. 104-121.
3107. **Dendy, David R.B.** "One Huge Orchard: Okanagan Land and Development Companies before the Great War." B.A. Essay (University of Victoria, 1976).

3108. **Drummond, G.F.** "The Relation between Changes in the Rural Population and the Trend of Agricultural Production in British Columbia." *Scientific Agriculture* 20 (1939), pp. 87-103.
3109. **English, R.E.** "Problems of a Specialized Area: The Fraser Valley." In H.A. Innis, ed. *The Dairy Industry in Canada* (Toronto, 1937), pp. 213-245.
3110. **Francis, R.J.** "The Significance of American and Dutch Agricultural Settlement in Central British Columbia." Ph.D. Thesis (University of Minnesota, 1966).
3111. "Fruit Vegetables and Packing in the Okanagan." *Western Business and Industry* 23 (September 1949), pp. 73-107. [A continuing feature.]
3112. **Fumalle, M.J.** "Public Policy and the Preservation of Agricultural Land in the Southern Okanagan Valley." M.A. Thesis (University of Victoria, 1975).
3113. **Gellatly, D.H.** *A Bit of Okanagan History.* Westbank: Kelowna Printing, 1958.
3114. **Gibbard, J.E.** "Early History of the Fraser Valley, 1808-1885." M.A. Thesis (University of British Columbia, 1937).
3115. **Gray, Arthur W.** "The Story of Irrigation—Lifeblood of the Okanagan Valley's Economy." Okanagan Historical Society. *Report* (1968), pp. 69-80.
3115A. **Hatcher, Temple.** "A Study of the History and Regional Distribution of Wheat Production in British Columbia." M.Sc. Thesis (University of British Columbia, 1940).
3116. **Hoppenrath, I.** "Brocklehurst: Fragment of the Canadian Mosaic." *B.C. Perspectives* 3 (1973), pp. 3-14.
3117. **Johnson, Edward Philip.** "The Early Years of Ashcroft Manor." *BC Studies* 5 (1970), pp. 3-23.
3118. **Laing, F.W.** "Some Pioneers of the Cattle Industry." *B.C.H.Q.* 6 (1942), pp. 257-276.
3119. **Lee, Lawrence B.** "American Influences in the Development of Irrigation in British Columbia." In R.A. Preston, ed. *The Influences of the United States on Canadian Development* (Durham, 1972), pp. 144-163.
3120. **Leechman, Douglas.** "The First Farm on the Fraser." *Canadian Geographical Review* 64 (1962), pp. 168-173.
3121. **Leitch, Adelaide.** "The Okanagan Sagebrush Valley of Blossoms." *Canadian Geographical Journal* 53 (1956), pp. 12-21.

3122. **MacLachlan, Morag.** "The Success of the Fraser Valley Milk Producers' Association." *BC Studies* 24 (1974-75), pp. 52-64.
3123. **Marriott, H.** *Cariboo Cowboy.* Sidney: Gray's, 1966.
3124. **Menzie, E.L.** "The Economics of Beef Production in British Columbia." M.S.A. Thesis (University of British Columbia, 1955).
3125. **Neave, Roland.** "A History of Settlement in the Lac Du Bois Basin, 1840-1970: A Study in Sequent Occupancy." *B.C. Perspectives* 1 (1972), pp. 4-23.
3126. **Nelson, Denys.** *Fort Langley, 1827-1927: A Century of Settlement in the Valley of the Lower Fraser River.* Vancouver: Art Historical and Scientific Association, 1947.
3127. **Ormsby, Margaret A.** "A Study of the Okanagan Valley of British Columbia." M.A. Thesis (University of British Columbia, 1931).
3128. ———. "Fruit Marketing in the Okanagan Valley of British Columbia." *Agricultural History* 9 (1935), pp. 80-97.
3129. ———. "The History of Agriculture in British Columbia." *Scientific Agriculture* 20 (1939), pp. 61-72.
3130. ———. "Agricultural Development in British Columbia." *Agricultural History* 19 (1945), pp. 11-20.
3131. **Perry, G. Neil.** "The Significance of Agricultural Production and Trade in the Economic Development of British Columbia." *Scientific Agriculture* 20 (1939), pp. 73-86.
3132. **Reeves, C.M.** "The Establishment of the Kelowna Orcharding Area: A Study of Accommodation to Site and Situation." M.A. Thesis (University of British Columbia, 1974).
3133. **Richter, J.J.** "The Developing Pattern of B.C. Agriculture." *Transactions of the 15th B.C. Natural Resources Conference* (Victoria: Queen's Printer, 1964), pp. 151-164.
3134. **Riis, Nelson A.** "The Walhachin Myth: A Study of Settlement Abandonment." *BC Studies* 17 (1973), pp. 3-25.
3135. **Sampson, W.R.** "Kenneth McKenzie and the Origins of B.C. Agriculture." *B.C. Historical News* 6 (1973), pp. 16-26.
3136. **Siemens, A.H.,** ed. *Lower Fraser Valley: Evolution of a Cultural Landscape.* Vancouver: B.C. Geographical Series, no. 9, 1968.
3137. **Utley, James A.** "The Cloverdale Fair: A Historical and Contemporary Analysis." *B.C. Perspectives* 1 (1972), pp. 24-34.
3138. **Vanderhill, B.G.** "Pitt Polder: Dutch Enterprise on Canadian Soil." *Canadian Geographical Journal* 65 (1962), pp. 94-99.

3139. **Vrooman, C.W.** "A History of Ranching in British Columbia." *Economic Annalist* 11 (1941), pp. 20-25.

3139A. **Winter, George R.** "Agricultural Development in the Lower Fraser Valley." In A.H. Siemens, ed. *Lower Fraser Valley: Evolution of a Cultural Landscape* (Vancouver: B.C. Geographical Series, No. 9, 1968), pp. 101-116.

3140. **Woods, J.J.** *History and Development of the Agassiz-Harrison Valley.* Agassiz: Agassiz-Harrison *Advance*, 1941.

e. Economic Development and Labour

3141. **Abella, Irving M.** "Communism and Anti-Communism in the British Columbia Labour Movement: 1940-1948." In David J. Bercuson, ed. *Western Perspectives I* (Toronto, 1974), pp. 88-100.

3142. **Anderson, D.E.** "The Growth of Organized Labor in the Lumbering Industry of B.C." B.A. Essay (University of British Columbia, 1944).

3143. **Andrews, C.D.** "Cominco and the Manhattan Project." *BC Studies* 11 (1971), pp. 51-62.

3144. **Atherton, Jay.** "The British Columbia Origins of the Federal Department of Labour." *BC Studies* 32 (1976-77), pp. 93-105.

3145. **Baptie, Sue.** *First Growth: The Story of the British Columbia Forest Products.* Vancouver: J.J. Douglas, 1975.

3146. **Barker, Mary L.** *Natural Resources of B.C. and the Yukon Territory.* Vancouver: J.J. Douglas, 1977.

3147. **Barnes, H.D.** "The Nickel Plate Mine, 1898-1932." *B.C.H.Q.* 14 (1950), pp. 125-140.

3148. **Barr, B.M., and Fairburn, K.J.** "Growth Poles and Growth Centres: The Impact of the Kraft Pulp Industry on the Location of Growth in British Columbia." In R. Leigh, ed. *Malaspina Papers: Studies in Human and Physical Geography* (Vancouver: B.C. Geographical Series, No. 17, 1973), pp. 67-78.

3149. **Bennett, William.** *Builders of British Columbia.* Vancouver: Broadway Printers, 1937.

3150. **Bergren, M.** *Tough Timber: The Loggers of British Columbia.* Toronto: Progress, 1967.

3151. **Bescoby, I.M.** "Some Social Aspects of the American Mining Advance into the Cariboo and Kootenay." M.A. Thesis (University of British Columbia, 1935).

3152. **Bjonback, R.D.** "The Factors of Growth in Manufacturing Employment in Metropolitan Vancouver, 1949-1958." M.A. Thesis (Simon Fraser University, 1971).

3153. **Blain, L., et al.** "The Regional Impact of Economic Fluctuations during the Inter-War Period: The Case of British Columbia." *Canadian Journal of Economics* 8 (1974), pp. 355-380.

3154. **Carmichael, Herbert.** "Pioneer Days in Pulp and Paper." *B.C.H.Q.* 4 (1945), pp. 201-212.

3155. **Carrothers, A.W.R.** *A Study of the Operation of the Injunction in Labour-Management Disputes in British Columbia, 1946-1955.* Toronto: C.C.H. Canadian Limited, 1956.

3156. **Carrothers, W.A.** "The Barter Terms of Trade between British Columbia and Eastern Canada." *C.J.E.P.S.* 1 (1935), pp. 568-577.

3157. ———. "Forest Industries of British Columbia." In A.R.M. Lower, ed. *The North American Assault on the Canadian Forest* (Toronto, 1938), pp. 227-344.

3158. ———. *The British Columbia Fisheries.* Toronto: University of Toronto Press, 1941.

3159. **Carson, E.C.** "Mining in the Economy of B.C." *Western Business and Industry* 19 (December 1945), pp. 44-49.

3160. **Casaday, L.W.** "Labor Unrest and the Labor Movement in the Salmon Industry of the Pacific Coast." Ph.D. Thesis (University of California, Berkeley, 1938).

3161. **Caves, R.E., and Holton, R.H.** "An Outline of the Economic History of British Columbia, 1818-1951." In Jean Friesen and Keith Ralston, eds. *Historical Essays on British Columbia* (Toronto, 1976), pp. 152-166.

3162. **Chapman, J.D., et al.** *British Columbia Atlas of Resources.* Victoria: B.C. Natural Resources Conference, 1956.

3163. **Church, J.S.** "Mining Companies in the West Kootenay and Boundary Regions of British Columbia, 1890-1900: Capital Formation and Financial Operations." M.A. Thesis (University of British Columbia, 1961).

3164. **Clark, Paul.** "Kitimat—A Saga of Canada." *Canadian Geographical Journal* 49 (1954), pp. 152-173.

3165. **Clylsworth, J.A.** "Transport Development and Regional Economic Growth in Northwestern British Columbia." M.A. Thesis (University of British Columbia, 1974).

3166. **Cox, Thomas R.** *Mills and Markets: A History of the Pacific Coast Lumber Industry to 1900.* Seattle: University of Washington Press, 1974.

3167. **Currie, A.W.** "The Vancouver Coal Mining Company." *Queen's Quarterly* 70 (1963), pp. 50-63.

3168. **Dinwoodie, D.H.** "The Politics of International Pollution Control." *International Journal* 27 (1972), pp. 219-235.

3169. **Englebert, R.** *Men and Trees.* Vancouver: Vancouver Feature Publishers, 1974.

3170. **Flucke, A.F.** "A History of Mining in British Columbia." *B.C. Natural Resources Conference: Transactions of the Eighth Conference* (1955), pp. 6-26.

3171. **Forester, J.E., and Forester, A.D.** *Fishing: British Columbia's Commercial Fishing History.* Saanichton: Hancock House, 1975.

3172. **Fowler, S.S.** "Early Smelters in British Columbia." *B.C.H.Q.* 3 (1939), pp. 183-201.

3173. **Gladstone, P., and Jamieson, Stuart Marshall.** "Unionism in the Fishing Industry of British Columbia." *C.J.E.P.S.* 16 (1950), pp. 1-11.

3174. **Gould, Edwin.** *Logging: British Columbia's Logging History.* Saanichton: Hancock House, 1975.

3175. **Grainger, M. Allerdale.** *Woodsmen of the West.* 1908. Reprint. Toronto: McClelland and Stewart, 1954.

3176. **Griffin, Harold.** *British Columbia: The People's Early Story.* North Vancouver: Commonwealth Fund, 1958.

3177. **Hamilton, J.H.** *The Industries of British Columbia.* Vancouver: Progress Publishing, 1918.

3178. **Hardwick, W.G.** *Geography of the Forest Industry of Coastal British Columbia.* Vancouver: Department of Geography, University of British Columbia, 1963.

3179. ———. "The Forest Industry in Coastal British Columbia, 1870 to 1970." In R.M. Irving, ed. *Readings in Canadian Geography* (Toronto, 1972), pp. 318-323.

3180. ———. "Roll-on Roll-off Ferries: the Revolution in Marine Transportation in British Columbia." *Canadian Geographical Journal* 69 (1964), pp. 152-161.

3181. **Hill, A.V.** *Tides of Change.* Prince Rupert: Prince Rupert Fisherman's Co-Op, 1967.

3182. **Hodges, L.K.**, ed. *Mining in Southern British Columbia.* Seattle: Shorey Book Store, 1967.

3183. **Howard, Victor.** "The Vancouver Relief Camp Strike of 1935: A Narrative of the Great Depression." *Canada: An Historical Magazine* 1 (March 1973), pp. 9-16, 26-33.

3184. **I.L.W.U. Local 500 Pensioners.** *Man Along the Shore: The Story of the Vancouver Waterfront, 1860-1975.* Vancouver: College Printers, 1975.

3185. **Jamieson, Stuart Marshall.** *Heritage of Conflict.* Ithaca: Cornell University Press, 1950.

3186. ———. "Regional Factors in Industrial Conflict: The Case of British Columbia." *C.J.E.P.S.* 28 (1962), pp. 405-416.

3187. **Jordan, Mabel E.** "The Big Wheel on Perry Creek, British Columbia." *Canadian Geographical Journal* 47 (1953), pp. 21-23.

3188. **Kerfoot, Denis E.** *Port of British Columbia: Development and Trading Patterns.* Vancouver: Tantalus Research, 1966.

3189. **Knox, Paul.** "The Passage of Bill 39: Reform and Repression in British Columbia's Labour Policy." M.A. Thesis (University of British Columbia, 1974).

3190. **Knox, Paul, and Resnick, Philip**, eds. *Essays in B.C. Political Economy.* Vancouver: New Star Books, 1974.

3191. **Lamb, W. Kaye.** "Empress Odyssey: A History of the Canadian Pacific Service to the Orient, 1913-1945." *B.C.H.Q.* 12 (1948), pp. 1-78.

3192. **Lane, Marion.** "Unemployment during the Depression: The Problem of the Single Unemployed Transient in British Columbia, 1930-1938." B.A. Essay (University of British Columbia, 1966).

3193. **Lawrence, Joseph C.** "Markets and Capital: A History of the Lumber Industry of British Columbia, 1778-1952." M.A. Thesis (University of British Columbia, 1957).

3194. ———. "The Forest and the Trees: A Review Article." *BC Studies* 30 (1976), pp. 77-82.

3195. **Liversedge, Ronald.** *Recollections of the On to Ottawa Trek: With Documents Related to the Vancouver Strike and the On to Ottawa Trek.* Edited by Victor Hoar. Toronto: McClelland and Stewart, 1973.

3196. **Loosmore, T.R.** "The British Columbia Labour Movement and Political Action, 1879-1906." M.A. Thesis (University of British Columbia, 1954).

3197. **Lower, J.A.** "The Grand Trunk Pacific and British Columbia." M.A. Thesis (University of British Columbia, 1939).
3198. **Lyons, C.** *Salmon: Our Heritage.* Vancouver: Mitchell Press, 1969.
3199. **McCandless, Richard.** "Vancouver's 'Red Menace' of 1935: The Waterfront Situation." *BC Studies* 22 (1974), pp. 56-70.
3200. **McGovern, P.D.** "Industrial Development in the Vancouver Area." *Economic Geography* 37 (1961), pp. 189-206.
3201. **MacKay, D.R.** "A Survey of Labour Relations in the Metal Mining Industry of British Columbia." M.A. Thesis (University of British Columbia, 1949).
3202. **McKechnie, N.D.** "The Mineral Industry in British Columbia." *Canadian Geographical Journal* 78 (1969), pp. 76-89.
3203. **McKillop, W., and Mead, W.J.** *Timber Policy Issues in British Columbia.* Vancouver: University of British Columbia Press, 1976.
3204. **MacKinnon, T.J.** "The Forest Industry of British Columbia." *Geography* 56 (1971), pp. 231-236.
3205. **MacNeil, Grant, comp.** *The I.W.A. in British Columbia.* Vancouver: I.W.A., 1971.
3206. **Mitchell, Howard T.** "B.C. Electric and Industrial Power." *Western Business and Industry* 19 (November 1945), pp. 26-28, 155.
3207. **Morley, Terence.** "Public Affairs: Labour in British Columbia Politics." *Queen's Quarterly* 83 (1976), pp. 291-298.
3208. **Murray, Keith A.** "The Trail Smelter Case: International Air Pollution in the Columbia Valley." *BC Studies* 15 (1972), pp. 68-85.
3209. **Nelson, L.** "Range Resources in the Interior of British Columbia." *B.C. Perspectives* 5 (1974), pp. 19-40.
3210. **Nesbitt, J.G.** "Regional Differences in the Structure and Growth of Manufacturing in British Columbia." M.A. Thesis (University of British Columbia, 1973).
3211. **North, G., and Griffin, Harold.** *A Ripple, A Wave: The Story of Union Organization in the B.C. Fishing Industry.* Vancouver: Fisherman Publishing Society, 1974.
3212. **Orr, A.D.** "The Western Federation of Miners and the Royal Commission on Industrial Disputes in 1903 with Special Reference to the Vancouver Island Coal Miners' Strike." M.A. Thesis (University of British Columbia, 1968).
3213. "Pacific Coast Industrial Sites, Transportation and Shipping." *Western Business and Industry* 24 (February 1950), pp. 54-83.

Plate 18. Logging Truck, Nanaimo Lakes, B.C.

3214. **Paterson, D.G.** "European Financial Capital and British Columbia: An Essay on the Role of the Regional Entrepreneur." *BC Studies* 21 (1974), pp. 33-47.

3215. **Peters, J.E., and Shearer, Ronald A.** "The Structure of British Columbia's External Trade in 1939-1963." *BC Studies* 8 (1970-71), pp. 34-46.

3216. **Phillips, P.A.** *No Power Greater: A Century of Labour in British Columbia.* Vancouver: B.C. Federation of Labour, 1967.

3217. **Pitt, Dale L.** "What Mining Has Done for British Columbia." *Washington Historical Quarterly* 23 (1932), pp. 94-109.

3218. **Ralston, Keith.** "The 1900 Strike of the Fraser River Sockeye Salmon Fisherman." M.A. Thesis (University of British Columbia, 1965).

3219. ———. "Patterns of Trade and Investment on the Pacific Coast, 1867-1892: The Case of the British Columbia Salmon Canning Industry." *BC Studies* 1 (1968-69), pp. 37-45.

3220. **Ramsey, A.B.** *P.G.E., Railway to the North.* Vancouver: Mitchell Press, 1962.

3221. ———. *Mining in Focus: An Illustrated History of Mining in B.C.* Vancouver: Agency Press, 1968.

3222. **Reid, David J.** *The Development of the Fraser River Canning Industry, 1885-1913.* Vancouver: Pacific Region, Department of the Environment, 1973.

3223. ———. "Company Mergers in the Fraser River Salmon Canning Industry, 1885-1902." *C.H.R.* 56 (1975), pp. 282-302.

3224. **Rothery, Agnes.** *The Ports of British Columbia: The Story of Canada's Great Pacific Seaport Cities, Vancouver and Victoria.* Toronto: McClelland and Stewart, 1943.

3225. **Roy, Patricia E.** "The British Columbia Electric Railway Company, 1897-1928: A British Company in British Columbia." Ph.D. Thesis (University of British Columbia, 1970).

3226. ———. "Regulating the British Columbia Electric Railway: The First Public Utilities Commission in British Columbia." *BC Studies* 11 (1971), pp. 3-20.

3227. ———. "The Fine Arts of Lobbying and Persuading: The Case of the B.C. Electric Railway." In D.S. MacMillan, ed. *Canadian Business History: Selected Studies, 1497-1971* (Toronto, 1972), pp. 239-254.

3228. ———. "The B.C.E.R. and Its Street Railway Employees." *BC Studies* 16 (1972-73), pp. 3-24.

3229. ———. "Direct Management from Abroad: The Formative Years of the British Columbia Electric Railway." *Business History Review* 47 (1973), pp. 239-259.

3230. **Roy, R.H.** "'. . .in Aid of a Civil Power,' 1877 [Wellington Colliery Strike, Nanaimo]." *Canadian Defence Quarterly* 7 (1953), pp. 61-69.

3231. **Rumsey, F.** "The Metropolitan-Hinterland Relationship in British Columbia." B.A. Essay (University of British Columbia, 1973).

3232. **Saywell, John T.** "Labour and Socialism in British Columbia: A Survey of Historical Development before 1903." *B.C.H.Q.* 15 (1951-52), pp. 129-150.

3233. **Scott, A.D., ed.** "National Economic Issues: The View from the West Coast." *BC Studies* 13 (1972), pp. 3-136. [Special Issue.]

3234. **Scott, Jack.** *Sweat and Struggle: Working Class Struggles in Canada, 1789-1899.* Vancouver: New Star Books, 1974.

3235. ———. *Plunderbund and Proletariat: A History of the I.W.W. in B.C.* Vancouver: New Star Books, 1975.

3236. **Shearer, Ronald A.**, ed. *Exploiting Our Economic Potential.* Toronto: Holt, Rinehart and Winston, 1968.

3237. **Shearer, Ronald A.; Young, J.H.; and Munro, G.R.** *Trade Liberalization and a Regional Economy.* Toronto: University of Toronto Press, 1971.

3238. **Shortt, Adam.** *Report of Commission to Investigate the Economic Conditions and Operations of the B.C.E.R. Company and Subsidiary Companies.* Victoria: King's Printer, 1918.

3239. **Silverman, P.G.** "Aid of the Civil Power: The Nanaimo Coal Miners' Strike, 1912-1914." *Canadian Defence Quarterly* 4 (1974), pp. 46-52.

3240. **Sloan, W.A.** "The Crowsnest Pass during the Depression: A Socio-Economic History of Southeastern British Columbia, 1918-1939." M.A. Thesis (University of Victoria, 1968).

3241. **Stevens, Leah.** "The Grain Trade of the Port of Vancouver, British Columbia." *Economic Geography* 12 (1936), pp. 185-196.

3242. **Taylor, G.W.** *Timber: History of the Forestry Industry in British Columbia.* Vancouver: J.J. Douglas, 1975.

3243. **Tennant, Paul.** "Bylaws and Setbacks: The Oil Industry and Local Government in British Columbia." *BC Studies* 9 (1971), pp. 3-14.

3244. **Underhill, F.H.** "Labour Legislation in British Columbia." Ph.D. Thesis (University of California, Berkeley, 1936).

3245. **Walker, John F.** "Mining Development in British Columbia." *Canadian Geographical Journal* 45 (1952), pp. 114-133.

3246. **Wargo, A.J.** "The Great Coal Strike: The Vancouver Island Coal Miners' Strike, 1912-1914." M.A. Thesis (University of British Columbia, 1962).

3247. **Waterfield, D.** *Continental Waterboy: The Columbia River Controversy.* Toronto: Clarke, Irwin, 1970

3248. **Woodsworth, J.S.** *On the Waterfront: With the Workers on the Docks at Vancouver.* Ottawa: Mutual Press, 1928.

3249. **Wright, Paul, et al.** "BC Development." *Western Business and Industry* 34 (July 1960), pp. 21-66. [A continuing feature.]

3250. **Yerburgh, R.E.M.** "An Economic History of Forestry in British Columbia." M.A. Thesis (University of British Columbia, 1931).

f. Education and Social and Cultural Development

3251. **Allen, H.T.** "A View from the Manse: The Social Gospel and Social Crisis in British Columbia, 1929-1945." In Richard Allen, ed. *The Social Gospel in Canada* (Ottawa, 1975), pp. 154-184.

3252. **Bentley, Robert J.** "Attitudes in British Columbia towards Canadian Participation in the South African War." B.A. Essay (University of British Columbia, 1950).

3253. **Bernard, Elaine.** "A University at War: Japanese Canadians at UBC during World War II." *BC Studies* 35 (1977), pp. 36-55.

3254. **Bissley, Paul L.** *Early and Late Victorians: A History of the Union Club of British Columbia.* Sidney, B.C.: Review Printing, 1969.

3255. **Booth, Michael R.** "The Beginnings of Theatre in British Columbia." *Queen's Quarterly* 68 (1961), pp. 159-168.

3256. **Borden, Charles E.** "Culture History of the Fraser-Delta Region: An Outline." *BC Studies* 6 and 7 (1970), pp. 95-112.

3257. **Boyd, Denny.** *History of Hockey in B.C.* Vancouver: Canucks Publishing, 1970.

3258. **Brown, Maria J.** "Capilano College: A Study in the Development of a Regional or Community College." *BC Studies* 17 (1973), pp. 43-56.

3259. **Buchanan, Donald W.** "Emily Carr—Painter of the West Coast." *Canadian Geographical Journal* 33 (1946), pp. 186-187.

3260. **Burton, M.D.** "The Anglican Theological College of British Columbia, 1909-1927: Unity in Diversity." M.A. Thesis (University of Alberta, 1974).

3261. **Child, Alan H.** "A Little Tempest: Educational Control in British Columbia." *BC Studies* 16 (1972-73), pp. 57-70.

3262. **Conway, C.B.** "Pressure Points and Growing Pains in Beautiful British Columbia." *Journal of Education* 17 (1971), pp. 104-117.

3263. **Dahlie, Jorgen.** "Some Aspects of the Education of Minorities: The Japanese in B.C., Lost Opportunity?" *BC Studies* 8 (1970-71), pp. 3-16.

3264. ———. "The Japanese Challenge to Public Schools in Society in British Columbia." *Journal of Ethnic Studies* 3 (1974), pp. 10-24.

3265. **Down, Mary Margaret.** *A Century of Service: A History of the Sisters of Saint Ann and Their Contribution to Education in British Columbia, the Yukon and Alaska.* Victoria: Sisters of St. Ann, 1966.

3266. **Ellis, Walter E.W.** "Some Aspects of Religion in British Columbia Politics." M.A. Thesis (University of British Columbia, 1959).

3267. **Fisher, J.V.** "Financing Public Education in British Columbia." *Canadian Tax Journal* 3 (1955), pp. 410-419.

3268. **Foster, John K.** "Education and Work in a Changing Society: British Columbia, 1870-1930." M.A. Thesis (University of British Columbia, 1970).

3269. **Gibson, W.C.** *Wesbrook and His University.* Vancouver: The Library, University of British Columbia, 1973.

3270. **Government of Canada.** *A Century of Education in B.C.: Statistical Perspectives.* Ottawa: Statistics Canada, 1971.

3271. **Harris, R.C.** "Locating the University of British Columbia." *BC Studies* 32 (1976-77), pp. 106-125.

3272. **Harrison, Marilyn J.** "The Social Influence of the United Church of Canada in British Columbia, 1930-1948." M.A. Thesis (University of British Columbia, 1975).

3273. **Hiebert, A.J.** "Prohibition in British Columbia." M.A. Thesis (Simon Fraser University, 1969).

3274. ———. "Prohibition and Social Problems in British Columbia: The Example of the Okanagan." *B.C. Perspectives* 2 (1972), pp. 36-56.

3275. **Humphries, Charles W.** "The Banning of a Book in British Columbia." *BC Studies* 1 (1968-69), pp. 1-12.

3276. ———. "War and Patriotism: The *Lusitania* Riot." *B.C. Historical News* 5 (1971), pp. 15-23.

3277. **Hutchinson, H.K.** "Dimensions of Ethnic Education: The Japanese in British Columbia, 1880-1940." M.A. Thesis (University of British Columbia, 1972).

3278. **Johnson, F. Henry.** "1858-1958: A Century of Progress." *Journal of Education* 3 (1959), pp. 12-25.

3279. ———. "The Doukhobors of British Columbia: The History of a Sectarian Problem in Education." *Queen's Quarterly* 70 (1964), pp. 528-541.

3280. ———. *A History of Public Education in British Columbia.* Vancouver: University of British Columbia Publication Centre, 1964.

3281. ———. "The Ryersonian Influence on the Public School System of British Columbia." *BC Studies* 10 (1971), pp. 26-34.

3282. **Kelly, Nora.** *Quest for a Profession: The History of the Vancouver General Hospital School of Nursing.* Vancouver: Evergreen Press, 1973.

3283. **Logan, H.T.** *Tuum Est: A History of the University of British Columbia.* Vancouver: University of British Columbia, 1958.

3284. **Logan, H.T., and Roberts, A.F.** *The University Club of Vancouver: An Informal History.* Vancouver: University Club of Vancouver, 1973.

3285. **Lyons, John E.** "A History of Doukhobor Schooling in Saskatchewan and British Columbia, 1899-1939." M.A. Thesis (University of Calgary, 1973).

3286. **McNay, Diane.** "The Teachers of British Columbia and Superannuation." *BC Studies* 2 (1969), pp. 30-44.

3287. **Marchak, Patricia.** "Class, Regional, and Institutional Sources of Social Conflict in B.C." *BC Studies* 27 (1975), pp. 30-49.

3288. **Matters, D.L.** "A Report on Health Insurance: 1919." *BC Studies* 21 (1974), pp. 28-32.

3289. **Mosher, S.P.** "The Social Gospel in British Columbia: Social Reform as a Dimension of Religion, 1900-1920." M.A. Thesis (University of Victoria, 1974).

3290. **Oldham, Evelyn.** "Renaissance of Coast Indian Art." *Canadian Geographical Journal* 87 (1973), pp. 32-37.

3291. **Peake, Frank A.** *The Anglican Church in British Columbia.* Vancouver: Mitchell Press, 1959.

3292. **Reid, W., and Holm, B.** *Indian Art of the Northwest Coast: A Dialogue on Craftsmanship and Aesthetics.* Vancouver: J.J. Douglas, 1976.

3293. **Rodenhizer, John.** "The Student Campaign of 1922 to 'Build the University' of British Columbia." *BC Studies* 4 (1970), pp. 21-37.

3294. **Sandison, James, ed.** *Schools of Old Vancouver.* Vancouver: Vancouver Historical Society, 1971.

3294A. **Scott, William.** *The Story of St. Andrew's United Church, North Vancouver, 1865-1937.* Vancouver: North Shore Press, 1937.

3295. **Selman, Gordon R.** "Mechanics' Institutes in British Columbia." *Continuous Learning* 10 (1971), pp. 126-130.

3296. ———. "Adult Education in Barkerville, 1863-1875." *BC Studies* 9 (1971), pp. 38-54.

3297. ———. "A Chronology of Adult Education in B.C. before 1915." *Journal of Education* 18 (1971), pp. 115-122.

3298. **Simon Fraser University.** *A Report by the President on Its Early Years: 1965-1975.* Burnaby: S.F.U., 1973.

3299. **Sloan, W.A.** "The Crowsnest Pass during the Depression: A Socio-Economic History of Southeastern British Columbia, 1918-1939." M.A. Thesis (University of Victoria, 1968).

3300. **Stanbury, W.T.** "The Education Gap: Urban Indians in British Columbia." *BC Studies* 19 (1973), pp. 21-49.

3302. **Thornton, James E., ed.** "Adult Education in British Columbia." *Journal of Education* 18 (1972), pp. 1-129. [Special issue.]

3303. **Tippett, Maria.** "'A Paste Solitaire in a Steel Claw Setting': Emily Carr and Her Public." *BC Studies* 20 (1973-74), pp. 3-14.

3304. **Tippett, Maria, and Cole, Douglas L.** "Art In British Columbia—the Historical Sources." *BC Studies* 23 (1974), pp. 25-33.

3305. **Usher, Jean.** *William Duncan of Metlakatla: A Victorian Missionary in British Columbia.* Ottawa: National Museum of Man, 1974.

3306. **Varnals, D.** "The Doukhobors in the Kootenays: Signs of Stress." *B.C. Perspectives* 3 (1973), pp. 15-20.

3307. **Victoria College.** *Fiftieth Anniversary, Victoria College.* Victoria: Victoria College, 1952.

3308. **Waites, K.A., ed.** *The First Fifty Years: Vancouver High Schools, 1890-1940.* Vancouver, 1941.

3309. **Wright, A.J.** "A Study of the Social and Economic Development of the District of North Cowichan, 1850-1912." B.A. Essay (University of British Columbia, 1966).

3310. ———. "The Winter Years in Cowichan: A Study of the Depression in a Vancouver Island Community." M.A. Thesis (University of British Columbia, 1967).

g. *Urban Development*

i. General

3311. **Adams, John Q.** "Prince Rupert, British Columbia." *Economic Geography* 14 (1938), pp. 167-183.

3312. **Akrigg, H.B.** "History and Economic Development of the Shuswap Area." M.A. Thesis (University of British Columbia, 1964).

3313. **Ala, L.G.** "Ladner, British Columbia." M.A. Thesis (University of British Columbia, 1961).

3314. **Andrew, F.W.** *The Story of Summerland.* Penticton: Penticton Herald, 1945.

3315. **Andrews, Craig, comp.** *Bay Ave., Trail, 1897-1910.* Castlegar: Continneh Books, 1973.

3316. **Apps, M.J.** "From Isolation to Suburbia: The Urbanization of Bowen Island." B.A. Essay (University of British Columbia, 1973).

3317. **Artibise, Alan F.J.** "Electoral Reform in the City of Kamloops: A Background Paper." *Report on Local Government.* Kamloops: City of Kamloops, 1975.

3318. **Asante, Nadine.** *The History of Terrace.* Terrace: Terrace Public Library Association, 1973.

3319. **Atkinson, Reginald Noel.** *Historical Souvenir of Penticton, B.C., 1867-1967.* Penticton: Okanagan Historical Society, 1967.

3320. **Balf, M.** *Kamloops: A History of the District up to 1914.* Kamloops: Kamloops Museum Association, 1969.

3321. **Balf, R.** *Kamloops, 1914-1945.* Kamloops: Kamloops Museum Association, 1975.

3322. **Bilsland, W.W.** "Atlin, 1898-1910: The Story of a Gold Rush." *B.C.H.Q.* 16 (1952), pp. 121-179.

3323. ———. "The History of Revelstoke and the Big Bend." M.A. Thesis (University of British Columbia, 1955).

3324. **Black, J.A.** "Kamloops: A City in the Southern Inter-mountain Region of B.C." M.A. Thesis (Kent State University, Ohio, 1965).

3325. **Botting, P.J.** "The Village of Clinton." B.A. Essay (University of British Columbia, 1972).

3326. **Brougham, W.F.** "A Typical Mining Town—Nelson, B.C." *Canadian Magazine* 14 (1899), pp. 19-27.

3327. **Burnes, John R.** *North Vancouver: Saga of a Municipality in Its Formative Days, 1891-1907.* North Vancouver: Carson Graham School, 1972.

3328. **Carroll, H.** *History of Nanaimo Pioneers.* Nanaimo: Herald Presses, 1935.

3329. **Chambers, Edith D.** *History of Port Coquitlam.* Port Coquitlam: B.A. Thompson, 1973.

3330. **Cherrington, John.** *Mission on the Fraser: Patterns of a Small City's Progress.* Vancouver: Mitchell Press, 1974.

3331. **Clemson, Donovan.** "Kamloops: City in the Sage." *Canadian Geographical Journal* 74 (1967), pp. 18-27.

3332. **Collier, R.W.** "The Evolution of Regional Districts." *BC Studies* 15 (1972), pp. 29-39.

3333. **Crerar, A.D.** "Prince Rupert, B.C.—The Study of a Port and Its Hinterland." M.A. Thesis (University of British Columbia, 1951).

3334. **Cromwell, J.** "Social Space in the Rural-Urban Fringe: A Study of Fleetwood, B.C." M.A. Thesis (Simon Fraser University, 1970).

3334A. ———. "Perceptual Differences between Established and New Residents in the Urban-Rural Fringe: Surrey, B.C." In J.V. Minghi, ed. *Peoples of the Living Land: Geography of Cultural Diversity in British Columbia* (Vancouver: B.C. Geographical Series, No. 15, 1972), pp. 229-242.

3335. **Currie, Laurie.** *Princeton 100 Years.* Princeton: *Similkameen Spotlight* Publishing, 1967.

3336. **Dahl, Ervin.** *Gateway to the Interior: A Brief History of Hope.* Chilliwack: Chilliwack *Progress*, 1971.

3337. **Doe, Ernest.** *History of Salmon Arm, 1885-1912.* Salmon Arm: Salmon Arm *Observer*, 1947.

3338. **Forrester, E.A.M.** "The Urban Development of Central Vancouver Island." M.A. Thesis (University of British Columbia, 1966).

3339. **Gabriel, T.** *Vernon, B.C.: A Brief History.* Vernon: Vernon Centennial Committee, 1958.

3340. **Gibbard, J.E.** "Early History of the Fraser Valley, 1808-1885." M.A. Thesis (University of British Columbia, 1937).

3341. **Gray, Arthur W.** *Kelowna.* Kelowna: Kelowna Print, 1968.

3342. **Green, G.** *History of Burnaby and Vicinity.* North Vancouver: Shoemaker, McLean, and Veitch, 1947.

3343. **Hammond, T.** "Prince George." *Habitat* 10 (1967), pp. 158-161.

3344. **Hardwick, W.G.** "The Georgia Strait Urban Region." In J. Lewis Robinson, ed. *British Columbia* (Toronto, 1972), pp. 119-134.

3345. **Harrington, Robert F.** "Prince George: Western White Spruce Capital of the World." *Canadian Geographical Journal* 77 (1968), pp. 72-83.

3346. **Holdsworth, D.W., and Bailey, P.** *B.C. Urban History: Discovering the Past in the Present.* Vancouver: University of British Columbia, 1974.

3347. **Holmes, N.B.** "The Promotion of Early Growth in a Western City: A Case Study of Prince George, B.C., 1909-1915." B.A. Essay (University of British Columbia, 1974).

3348. **Hoppenrath, I.** "Brocklehurst: Fragment of the Canadian Mosaic." *B.C. Perspectives* 3 (1973), pp. 3-14.

3349. **Howard, Henry.** *Canada, the Western Cities: Their Borrowings and Assets.* London: Investor's Guardian, Ltd., 1914.

3350. **Howell-Jones, G.I.** "A Century of Settlement Change: A Study of the Evolution of Settlement Patterns in the Lower Mainland of British Columbia." M.A. Thesis (University of British Columbia, 1966).

3350A. ———. "The Urbanization of the Fraser Valley." In A.H. Siemens, ed. *Lower Fraser Valley: Evolution of a Cultural Landscape* (Vancouver: B.C. Geographical Series, No. 9, 1968), pp. 139-162.

3351. **Humphries, Charles W.** "The Writing of Local History: A Review Article." *BC Studies* 22 (1974), pp. 71-75.

3352. **Ireland, W.E.** *New Westminster: The Royal City: The First 100 Years.* New Westminster: *Columbian,* 1960.

3352A. **Ivanisko, H.I.** "Changing Patterns of Residential Land Use in the Municipality of Maple Ridge, 1930-1960." M.A. Thesis (University of British Columbia, 1964).

3353. **Johnson, Patricia M.** *A Short History of Nanaimo.* Nanaimo: Nanaimo B.C. Centennial Committee, 1958.

3354. **Jordan, Mabel E.** "The Century Old Bastion at Nanaimo." *Canadian Geographical Journal* 49 (1954), pp. 18-19.

3355. ———. "Esquimalt." *Canadian Geographical Journal* 50 (1955), pp. 124-132.

3356. **Kennedy, J.J.** "New Westminster, 1861-1869: A Disappointed Metropolis." *B.C. Historical News* 2 (1969), pp. 8-17.

3357. **Kennedy, J.H.** "The Differential Growth of Urban Centres in British Columbia, 1951-1961." M.A. Thesis (University of British Columbia, 1970).

3358. **Kidd, Thomas.** *History of Richmond Municipality.* Richmond: Kidd Book Sales, n.d.

3359. **Kilvert, Barbara.** "Vernon, Okanagan Valley." *The Beaver* Outfit 291 (1960), pp. 48-53.

3360. **Kopas, C.** *Bella Coola.* Vancouver: Mitchell Press, 1974.

3361. **Large, R.G.** *Prince Rupert: A Gateway to Alaska.* Vancouver: Mitchell Press, 1960.

3362. ———. "Prince Rupert." *Habitat* 10 (1967), pp. 154-157.

3363. **Ludditt, W.** *Barkerville.* Vancouver: Mitchell Press, 1974.

3364. **MacDonald, K.J.** "Sources of Electoral Support for Provincial Political Parties in Urban British Columbia." *BC Studies* 15 (1972), pp. 40-52.

Plate 19. Seiners with Their Nets Set in the Strait of Georgia

3365. **McDonald, M.L.** "New Westminster, 1859-1871." M.A. Thesis (University of British Columbia, 1947).

3366. **McGuire, B.J., and Wild, Roland.** "Kitimat—Tomorrow's City Today." *Canadian Geographical Journal* 59 (1959), pp. 142-161.

3367. **McKelvie, B.A.** "The Founding of Nanaimo." *B.C.H.Q.* 8 (1944), pp. 169-188.

3368. **MacKinnon, C.S.** "The Imperial Fortresses in Canada: Halifax and Esquimalt, 1871-1906." Ph.D. Thesis (University of Toronto, 1965).

3369. **McPhail, L.R.** "Local Government in British Columbia: A Case Study [of Kamloops]." In R. Leigh, ed. *Malaspina Papers: Studies in Human and Physical Geography* (Vancouver: B.C. Geographical Series, No. 17, 1973), pp. 51-56.

3370. **Mather, B.** *New Westminster; The Royal City.* Vancouver: Dent and the City of New Westminster, 1958.

3371. **Matheson, M.H.** "Some Effects of Coal Mining upon the Development of the Nanaimo Area." M.A. Thesis (University of British Columbia, 1950).

3372. **Miller, D.** "Residential Location and Expansion: Kamloops, B.C., 1950-1966." B.A. Essay (University of British Columbia, 1969).
3373. **Nelson, Denys.** *Fort Langley, 1827-1927: A Century of Settlement.* Vancouver: The Art, Historical, and Scientific Association, 1927.
3374. **Oak Bay Anniversary Committee.** *Golden Jubilee, 1906-1956: Fifty Years of Growth.* Oak Bay: Corporation of the District of Oak Bay, 1956.
3375. **Osing, Olga.** "Canada's Volcanic City: Rossland, B.C." *Canadian Geographical Journal* 73 (1966), pp. 166-171.
3376. **Paterson, T.W.** *Ghost Towns of Vancouver Island.* Langley: Stagecoach Publishing, 1975.
3377. **Patterson, F.J.** "A Financial History of the Corporation of the District of West Vancouver." M.A. Thesis (University of British Columbia, 1928).
3378. **Patterson, R.M.** "Kamloops." *Habitat* 10 (1967), pp. 134-137.
3379. **Pogue, B.G.** "Some Aspects of Settlement, Land-Use and Vegetation Change in the Revelstoke Area, B.C., 1885-1962." M.A. Thesis (University of Calgary, 1970).
3380. **Porteous, J.D.** "Gold River: An Instant Town in British Columbia." *Geography* 60 (1970), pp. 317-322.
3381. **Riis, Nelson A.** "The Walhachin Myth: A Study in Settlement Abandonment." *BC Studies* 17 (1973), pp. 3-25.
3382. **Rizui, A.A.B.** "Urbanization Trends in British Columbia, Canada." *Pakistan Geographical Review* 22 (1967), pp. 9-24.
3383. **Robinson, I.M.** "Planning for Small Communities in British Columbia." *Community Planning Review* 5 (1955), pp. 10-15.
3384. ———. "Urbanization in British Columbia." Vancouver: University of British Columbia, 1957. [Unpublished paper.]
3385. **Robinson, J. Lewis.** "Nanaimo, B.C." *Canadian Geographical Journal* 70 (1965), pp. 162-169.
3386. **Robinson, Leigh Burpee.** *Esquimalt: "Place of Shoaling Waters."* Esquimalt: The Author, 1947.
3387. **Rosenthal, H.M.** "Penticton Profile: A Case Study in Community Involvement." M.A. Thesis (Simon Fraser University, 1972).
3388. **Rumsey, F.** "The Metropolitan-Hinterland Relationship in British Columbia." B.A. Essay (University of British Columbia, 1973).
3389. **Runnalls, F.E.** "Boom Days in Prince George." *B.C.H.Q.* 8 (1944), pp. 281-306.

3390. ———. *A History of Prince George.* Vancouver: Wrigley Printing Co., 1946.

3391. **St. John, R.M.** "New Westminster on the Fraser." *Canadian Geographical Journal* 9 (1934), pp. 247-256.

3392. **Schurman, D.M.** "Esquimalt: Defence Problem, 1865-1887." *B.C.H.Q.* 19 (1955), pp. 57-70.

3393. **Scott, D., and Honic, E.** *Nelson: Queen City of the Kootenays: An Historical Profile.* Vancouver: Mitchell Press, 1972.

3394. **Serra, J.** *History of Armstrong, B.C.* Armstrong: J. Serra, 1967.

3395. **Sloan, W.A.** "The Crowsnest Pass during the Depression: A Socio-Economic History of Southeastern British Columbia, 1918-1939." M.A. Thesis (University of Victoria, 1968).

3396. **Smith, B.R.D.** "Some Aspects of the Social Development of Early Nanaimo." B.A. Essay (University of British Columbia, 1956).

3397. **Smith, D.B.** "The First Capital of British Columbia: Langley or New Westminster?" *B.C.H.Q.* 21 (1957-58), pp. 16-50.

3398. **Sproule-Jones, Mark, and Van Klaveren, Adrie.** "Local Referenda and Size of Municipality in British Columbia: A Note on Two of Their Interrelationships." *BC Studies* 8 (1970-71), pp. 47-50.

3399. **Stanbury, W.T.** "Reserve and Urban Indians in British Columbia." *BC Studies* 26 (1975), pp. 39-64.

3400. ———. *Success and Failure: Indians in Urban Society [in British Columbia].* Vancouver: University of British Columbia Press, 1975.

3401. **Stanbury, W.T.; Fields, D.B.; and Stevenson, D.** "B.C. Indians in an Urban Environment: Income, Poverty, Education and Vocational Training." *Manpower Review, Pacific Region* 5 (1972), pp. 11-33.

3402. **Stewart, J., and Monk, H.A.J.** *A History of Coquitlam and Fraser Mills, 1858-1958.* Coquitlam: District of Coquitlam, 1958.

3403. **Strongitharm, B.D.** "Local Government Re-Organization in Nanaimo, B.C." M.A. Thesis (University of British Columbia, 1975).

3404. **Taylor, Harry, comp.** *Powell River's First 50 Years.* Powell River: Powell River News, 1960.

3405. **Tennant, Paul.** "Bylaws and Setbacks: The Oil Industry and Local Government in British Columbia." *BC Studies* 9 (1971), pp. 3-14.

3406. **Trail Board of Trade.** *Trail, B.C., A Brief Story of the History and Development of the Most Important Industrial Center in Interior of British Columbia.* Trail: Board of Trade, 1931.

3407. **Trail Golden Jubilee Society.** *Trail, B.C.: A Half Century, 1901-1951.* Trail: Golden Jubilee Society, 1951.

3408. **Treleavan, G.F.** *The Surrey Story.* 3 Vols. Cloverdale: Surrey Museum and Historical Society, 1969-1972.

3408A. **Ulmer, A.** "A Comparison of Land Use Changes in Richmond, B.C.: A Study of Urban Expansion upon an Agricultural Area in a Rural-Urban Fringe." M.A. Thesis (University of British Columbia, 1964).

3408B. **Villeneuve, P.Y.** "Changes over Time in the Residential and Occupational Structures of an Urban Ethnic Minority." In R. Leigh, ed. *Contemporary Geography: Western Viewpoints* (Vancouver: B.C. Geographical Series, No. 12, 1971), pp. 115-128.

3409. **Wade, F.C.** *Experiments with the Single Tax in Western Canada.* Denver: National Tax Association, 1914.

3410. **Walden, P.S.** "A History of West Vancouver." M.A. Thesis (University of British Columbia, 1947).

3411. **Weir, J.R.** "New Westminster, B.C." *Canadian Geographical Journal* 36 (1948), pp. 22-38.

3412. **Wickett, S.M.** "Local Government in British Columbia." In Wickett, ed. *Municipal Government in Canada* (Toronto, 1907), pp. 213-220.

3413. **Willmott, W.E.** "Some Aspects of Chinese Communities in British Columbia Towns." *BC Studies* 1 (1968-69), pp. 27-36.

3414. **Woodland, Alan.** *New Westminster: The Early Years, 1858-1898.* New Westminster: Nunaga Publishing, 1973.

3415. **Woodward-Reynolds, K.M.** "A History of the City and District of North Vancouver." M.A. Thesis (University of British Columbia, 1943).

3416. **Wright, A.J.** "The Winter Years in Cowichan: A Study of the Depression in a Vancouver Island Community." M.A. Thesis (University of British Columbia, 1967).

3417. **Young, Cy.** "Prince George: Hub of British Columbia." *Western Business and Industry* 27 (August 1953), pp. 28-29, 65-68.

ii. Vancouver

3418. **Andrews, Margaret W.** "Epidemic and Public Health: Influenza in Vancouver, 1918-1919." *BC Studies* 34 (1977), pp. 21-44.

3419. **Ashlee, Ted.** *Gabby, Ernie and Me: A Vancouver Boyhood.* Vancouver: J.J. Douglas, 1976.

3420. **Ashworth, Mary.** "The Settlement of Immigrants in Greater Vancouver." *Canadian Welfare* 53 (1977), pp. 9-13.

3421. **Astles, A.R.** "The Role of Historical and Architectural Preservation in the Vancouver Townscape." In J.V. Minghi, ed. *Peoples of the Living Land: Geography of Cultural Diversity in British Columbia* (Vancouver: B.C. Geographical Series, No. 15, 1972), pp. 145-162.

3422. **Barford, J.C.** "Vancouver's Interurban Settlements." B.A. Essay (University of British Columbia, 1966).

3423. **Bartholomew, H., et al.** *A Plan for the City of Vancouver, B.C., Including Point Grey and South Vancouver and a General Plan of the Region.* Vancouver: Town Planning Commission, 1929.

3424. **Basi, R.S.** "The Vancouver Board of Trade: A Study of Its Organization and Role in the Community." M.A. Essay (University of British Columbia, 1953).

3425. **Bennett, M.L.** "Vancouver and the Company." *The Beaver* Outfit 270 (1940), pp. 32-37.

3426. **Bernard, A.; Léveillé, J.; and Lord, G.** *Profile: Vancouver. The Political and Administrative Structures of the Metropolitan Region of Vancouver.* Ottawa: Ministry of State for Urban Affairs, 1975.

3427. **Bissley, Paul L.** *The History of the Vancouver Club.* Vancouver: Vancouver Club, 1971.

3428. **Bland, John, and Spruce-Sales, Harold.** "Physical Planning in Vancouver's Government." *Community Planning Review* 2 (1952), pp. 18-26.

3429. **Boutilier, H.R.** "Vancouver's Earliest Days." *B.C.H.Q.* 10 (1946), pp. 151-170.

3430. **Bower, R.** *Stanley Park: An Island in the City.* Vancouver: November House, 1972.

3431. **Broadfoot, Barry, et al.** *The City of Vancouver.* Vancouver: J.J. Douglas, 1976.

3432. **Brooks, F.G.H.** "Vancouver's Origins." B.A. Essay (University of British Columbia, 1952).

3433. **Cain, Louis P.** "Water and Sanitation Services in Vancouver: An Historical Perspective." *BC Studies* 30 (1976), pp. 27-43.

3434. **Cavers, Anne S.** *Our School of Nursing, 1899-1949.* Vancouver: n.p., [1949].

3435. **Chao, M.** "Chinatown, Vancouver." M.V.P. Thesis (University of Oregon, 1971).
3436. **Cho, G.** "Residential Patterns of Chinese Households in Vancouver." M.A. Thesis (University of British Columbia, 1971).
3437. **Cho, G., and Leigh, R.** "Patterns of Residence of Chinese in Vancouver." In J.V. Minghi, ed. *Peoples of the Living Land: Geography of Cultural Diversity in British Columbia* (Vancouver: B.C. Geographical Series, No. 15, 1972), pp. 67-84.
3438. **Churchill, D.M.** "False Creek Development." M.A. Thesis (University of British Columbia, 1953).
3439. ———. *Local Government and Administration in the Lower Mainland Metropolitan Communities.* Vancouver: Metropolitan Joint Committee, 1959.
3440. **Collier, R.W., ed.** *The Port of Vancouver.* Vancouver: University of British Columbia Extension Department, 1966.
3441. **Collins, Barbara R.** "Indians in Vancouver." M.S.W. Thesis (University of British Columbia, 1966).
3442. **Cooper, M.G.S.** "Residential Segregation of Elite Groups in Vancouver." M.A. Thesis (University of British Columbia, 1971).
3443. **Corbett, D.C., and Toren, E.R.** *A Survey of Metropolitan Governments.* Vancouver: University of British Columbia, 1958.
3444. **Cornwall, I.H.B.** "A Geographical Study of the Port of Vancouver in Relation to Its Coastal Hinterland." M.A. Thesis (University of British Columbia, 1952).
3445. **Cran, G.A., and Hacking, N.** *Annals of the Royal Vancouver Yacht Club, 1903-1965.* Vancouver: R.V.Y.C., 1965.
3446. **Crerar, A.D.** "Planning in the Lower Mainland Region of British Columbia." *Canadian Geographer* 4 (1954), pp. 21-26.
3447. ———. "Population Density and Municipal Development—The Vancouver, B.C. Metropolitan Area." *Canadian Geographer* 9 (1957), pp. 1-6.
3448. **Cummings, D.E.** "Railway Entrances to Vancouver, 1887-1969." *Canadian Rail* 221 (1970), pp. 143-163.
3449. **Dalzell, A.G.** "Town Planning Problems in Vancouver." *Canadian Engineer* 52 (1927), pp. 616-618.
3450. **Daniels, C.H.** *A Narrative History of the Terminal City Club.* Vancouver: Terminal City Club, 1936.
3451. **Davis, C.** *Guide to Vancouver.* Vancouver: J.J. Douglas, 1973.

3452. ———. *The Vancouver Book.* Vancouver: J.J. Douglas, 1976.
3453. **Easton, Robert, and Tennant, Paul.** "Vancouver Civic Party Leadership: Background, Attitudes and Non-Civic Party Affiliations." *BC Studies* 2 (1969), pp. 19-29.
3454. **Ecroyd, L.G., et al.** "Greater Vancouver—Metropolis and Gateway." *Western Business and Industry* 35 (July 1961), pp. 38-53.
3455. **Forster, Victor Wadham.** *Vancouver through the Eyes of a Hobo.* Vancouver: McCormick Press, 1934.
3456. **Forward, C.N.** *Waterfront Land Use in Metropolitan Vancouver.* Ottawa: Queen's Printer, 1968.
3457. **Fountain, G.F.** "Zoning Administration in Vancouver." *Plan Canada* 2 (1961), pp. 115-124.
3458. **Francis, R.A.** "Victoria Vancouver: A Study in Contrasts on the West Coast." *Canadian Business* 30 (November 1957), pp. 30-33.
3459. **Freer, K.M.** *Vancouver: A Bibliography Compiled from Material in the Vancouver Public Library and the Special Collections of the University of British Columbia Library.* Vancouver: Vancouver Public Library, 1962.
3459A. **Gale, D.T.** "The Impact of Canadian Italians on Retail Functions and Facades in Vancouver, 1921-1961." In J.V. Minghi, ed. *Peoples of the Living Land: Geography of Cultural Diversity in British Columbia* (Vancouver: B.C. Geographical Series, No. 15, 1972), pp. 107-124.
3460. **Gayler, H.J.** "Private Residential Redevelopment in the Inner City: The West End of Vancouver, Canada." *Journal of the Town Planning Institute* 57 (1971), pp. 15-20.
3461. **Gibson, E.M.W.** "The Impact of Social Relief on Landscape Change: A Geographical Study of Vancouver." Ph.D. Thesis (University of British Columbia, 1972).
3462. ———. "Lotus Eaters, Loggers, and the Vancouver Landscape." In L.J. Evenden and F.F. Cunningham, eds. *Cultural Discord in the Modern World* (Vancouver: B.C. Geographical Series, No. 20, 1974), pp. 57-74.
3463. **Godemath, P.F.** "Advertising a City." *Westward Ho! Magazine* 5 (1909), pp. 555-558.
3464. **Gomery, D.** "A History of Early Vancouver." B.A. Essay (University of British Columbia, 1936).
3465. **Gordon, W.R.** "Industrial Vancouver." *B.C. Magazine* 7 (1911), pp. 626-629.

3466. **Grant, J.H.** "Burrard Inlet in Early Times." *B.C. Magazine* 7 (1911), pp. 487-497.

3466A. **Grant, K.F.** "Food Habits and Food Shopping Patterns of Greek Immigrants in Vancouver." In J.V. Minghi, ed. *Peoples of the Living Land: Geography of Cultural Diversity in British Columbia* (Vancouver: B.C. Geographical Series, No. 15, 1972), pp. 125-144.

3467. *Greater Vancouver Illustrated.* Vancouver: Dominion Illustrating, 1908.

3468. **Gunn, Angus M.** *Vancouver, B.C.: Profile of Canada's Pacific Metropolis.* Richmond: Smith Lithograph, 1968.

3469. **Gutstein, D.** "The Developers' TEAM: Vancouver's 'Reform' Party in Power." *City Magazine* 1 (1974-75), pp. 13-28.

3470. ———. *Vancouver, Ltd.* Toronto: James Lorimer, 1975.

3470A. **Habinski, A.A.** "Assimilation and Residential Location: The Jews in Vancouver." M.A. Thesis (Simon Fraser University, 1973).

3471. **Hardwick, W.G.** "Vancouver: The Emergence of a 'Core-Ring' Urban Pattern." In R.L. Gentilcore, ed. *Geographical Approaches to Canadian Problems* (Toronto, 1971), pp. 112-119.

3472. ———. *Vancouver.* Don Mills: Collier-Macmillan, 1974.

3473. **Hillman, W.A.** "The Magic of the Single Tax." *B.C. Magazine* 7 (1911), pp. 303-305.

3474. **Holdsworth, D.W.** "Vernacular Form in an Urban Context: A Preliminary Investigation of Facade Elements in Vancouver Housing." M.A. Thesis (University of British Columbia, 1971).

3475. ———. "House and Home in Vancouver: Images of West Coast Urbanism, 1886-1929." In Gilbert A. Stelter and Alan F.J. Artibise, eds. *The Canadian City: Essays in Urban History* (Toronto, 1977), pp. 186-211.

3476. **Howard, Irene.** *Vancouver's Svenskar: A History of the Swedish Community in Vancouver.* Vancouver: Vancouver Historical Society, 1970.

3477. **Howay, F.W.** "Early Settlement on Burrard Inlet." *B.C.H.Q.* 1 (1937), pp. 101-114.

3478. **Huel, R., et al.** *Vancouver's Past.* Vancouver: G. Soules Economic and Marketing Research, 1974.

3479. **Kalman, H.** *Exploring Vancouver: Ten Tours of the City and Its Buildings.* Vancouver: University of British Columbia Press, 1974.

3480. **Kennedy, W.** *Vancouver Tomorrow: A Search for Greatness.* Vancouver: Mitchell Press, 1975.

3481. **Kenvyn, R.** "Vancouver's Harbour and Shipping." *B.C. Magazine* 7 (1911), pp. 474-486.

3482. **Kerr, D.P.** "Vancouver: A Study in Urban Geography." M.A. Thesis (University of Toronto, 1943).

3483. **Klenke, M.** "Economic Revitalization of the Gastown Historic Site, 1966-1974." *Urban Reader* 3 (October 1975), pp. 20-23.

3484. **Kloppenborg, A., ed.** "Almost Vancouver: Plans and Proposals That Never Left the Drawing Board." *Urban Reader* 3 (November-December 1975), pp. 18-20.

3485. **Kloppenborg, A.; Niwinski, A.; Johnston, E.; and Gruetter, R., eds.** *Vancouver's First Century: A City Album, 1860-1960.* Vancouver: J.J. Douglas, 1977.

3486. **Kuthan, G., and Stainsby, D.** *Vancouver Sights and Insights.* Toronto: Macmillan, 1962.

3487. **Lamb, B.** "Origins of Vancouver Newspapers." M.A. Thesis (University of British Columbia, 1942).

3488. ———. "From 'Tickler' to 'Telegram': Notes on Early Vancouver Newspapers." *B.C.H.Q.* 12 (1948), pp. 175-199.

3489. **Lamb, W. Kaye.** "The Pioneer Days of the Trans-Pacific Service, 1887-1891." *B.C.H.Q.* 1 (1937), pp. 143-169.

3490. **Lambrou, Y.** "The Greek Community of Vancouver." M.A. Thesis (University of British Columbia, 1975).

3491. **Laponce, J.A.** *People vs. Politics: A Study of Opinions, Attitudes and Perceptions in Vancouver-Burrard, 1963-1965.* Toronto: University of Toronto Press, 1969.

3492. **Le Neveu, A.H.** "Vancouver as a Pacific Port." B.A. Essay (University of British Columbia, 1922).

3493. **Lewis, A.H.** *South Vancouver: Past and Present.* Vancouver: Western Publishing Bureau, 1920.

3494. **Lioy, M.** *Social Trends in Greater Vancouver: A Study of a North American Metropolis.* Vancouver: Gordon Soules Economic and Marketing Research, 1975.

3495. **Lopatin, I.A.** "Geography of Vancouver." M.A. Thesis (University of British Columbia, 1929).

3496. **McAfee, A.** "Evolving Inner-City Residential Environments: The Case of Vancouver's West End." In J.V. Minghi, ed. *Peoples of the Living Land: Geography of Cultural Diversity in British Columbia* (Vancouver: B.C. Geographical Series, No. 15, 1972), pp. 163-182.

3497. McCandless, Richard. "Vancouver's 'Red Menace' of 1935: The Waterfront Situation." *BC Studies* 22 (1974), pp. 56-70.

3498. McDonald, H.L. "Vancouver." *Habitat* 10 (1967), pp. 140-147.

3499. MacDonald, N. "Seattle, Vancouver and the Klondike." *C.H.R.* 49 (1968), pp. 234-246.

3500. ———. "Population Growth and Change in Seattle and Vancouver, 1880-1960." *Pacific Historical Review* 39 (1970), pp. 279-321.

3501. ———. "Vancouver in the Nineteenth Century." *Urban History Review* 1-75 (1975), pp. 51-54.

3502. ———. "A Critical Growth Cycle for Vancouver, 1900-1914." In Gilbert A. Stelter and Alan F.J. Artibise, eds. *The Canadian City: Essays in Urban History* (Toronto, 1977), pp. 142-159.

3503. ———. "The Canadian Pacific Railway and Vancouver's Development to 1900." *BC Studies* 35 (1977), pp. 3-35.

3504. McDonald, R.A.J. "Business Leaders in Early Vancouver, 1886-1914." Ph.D. Thesis (University of British Columbia, 1977).

3505. McDougall, R.J. "Vancouver Real Estate for Twenty-Five Years." *B.C. Magazine* 7 (1911), pp. 597-607.

3506. McGeer, Gerald G. "Vancouver's Golden Jubilee." *Canadian Geographical Journal* 13 (1936), pp. 11-24.

3507. McGill, A.S. "The Theory of Property Taxation and Its Application in the City of Vancouver." B.A. Essay (University of British Columbia, 1948).

3508. McGovern, P.D. "Industrial Development in the Vancouver Area." *Economic Geography* 37 (1961), pp. 189-206.

3509. McGregor, D. "The Marvel of Vancouver." *B.C. Magazine* 7 (1911), pp. 457-472.

3510. McGregor, D.A. "Adventures of Vancouver Newspapers, 1892-1926." *B.C.H.Q.* 10 (1946), pp. 89-142.

3511. MacInnes, Tom. "The Port of Vancouver." *Canadian Geographical Journal* 2 (1931), pp. 289-309.

3512. McKee, W.C. "The History of the Vancouver Park System, 1886-1929." M.A. Thesis (University of Victoria, 1976).

3513. ———. "The Resources of the Vancouver City Archives." *Urban History Review* 2-77 (1977), pp. 3-9.

3514. Makovski, L.W. "The Rise of the Merchant Princes." *B.C. Magazine* 7 (1911), pp. 542-550.

3515. ———. "The Rock on Which Vancouver Is Built: Financial Growth." *B.C. Magazine* 7 (1911), pp. 588-596.

3516. **Matters, Diane.** "The Development of Public Welfare Institutions in Vancouver, 1910-1920." B.A. Essay (University of Victoria, 1973).

3517. **Mawson, T.H.** "Vancouver: A City of Optimists." *Town Planning Review* 4 (1913), pp. 7-12.

3518. **Miller, F.** "Vancouver Civic Political Parties." Ph.D. Thesis (Yale University, New Haven, 1972).

3519. ———. "Vancouver Civic Political Parties: Developing a Model of Party-System Change and Stabilization." *BC Studies* 25 (1975), pp. 3-31.

3519A. **Minghi, J.V.; Rumley, Dennis; and Swain, H.** "The Vancouver Civic Election of 1970: A Preliminary Report." In R. Leigh, ed. *Contemporary Geography: Western Viewpoints* (Vancouver: B.C. Geographical Series, No. 12, 1971), pp. 97-114.

3520. **Minghi, J.V., and Rumley, Dennis.** "The Vancouver Civic Elections of 1970 and 1972: A Comparative Analysis." In B.M. Barr, ed. *The Kootenay Collection of Research Studies in Geography* (Vancouver: B.C. Geographical Series, No. 18, 1974), pp. 35-50.

3521. **Mitchell, N., and Forster, S.** *The Symphony Story.* Vancouver: Women's Committee, Vancouver Symphony Society, 1971.

3522. **Moogk, Peter N.** *Vancouver Defended: Guns and Gunners of the Lower Mainland, 1859-1949.* Surrey: Antonson, 1977.

3523. **Morley, A.** *Vancouver: From Milltown to Metropolis.* Vancouver: Mitchell Press, 1961.

3524. **Murphy, E.F.** *The Black Candle.* Toronto: Thomas Allen, 1922.

3525. **Namm, R.** "Relocation of Vancouver's Chinatown Residents under Urban Renewal." *Journal of Sociology and Social Welfare* 3 (1975), pp. 125-130.

3526. **Nicol, E.P.** *Vancouver.* Toronto: Doubleday, 1970.

3527. **Ogden, R.L.** "Vancouver City Archives: A New Resource." *Urban History Review* 1-74 (1974), pp. 20-23.

3528. **Okannesian, P.B.** "Deco Revisited: An Architect's Tour of Vancouver." *Western Living* 7 (1977), pp. 22-26.

3529. **Patillo, R.W.** *The West End of Vancouver: A Social Profile.* Vancouver: United Community Services, 1969.

3530. **Paton, J.A.** "The Inside Story of Point Grey." *B.C. Magazine* 7 (1911), pp. 735-737.

3531. **Patterson, F.J.** "The Financial History of the Corporation of the District of West Vancouver." M.A. Thesis (University of British Columbia, 1929).

3532. **Pendakur, V. Setty.** *Cities, Citizens and Freeways.* Vancouver: Transportation Development Agency, 1972.

3533. **Persons, Heather.** "Vancouver's Greek Community." *B.C. Motorist* 12 (November-December 1973), pp. 44-47.

3533A. **Peuker, T., and Rase, W.** "A Factoral Ecology of Greater Vancouver." In R. Leigh, ed. *Contemporary Geography: Western Viewpoints* (Vancouver: B.C. Geographical Series, No. 12, 1971), pp. 81-96.

3534. **Pethick, Derek.** *Vancouver Recalled: A Pictorial History to 1887.* Saanichton: Hancock House, 1974.

3535. **Playfair, W.** "Vancouver and the Railways." *B.C. Magazine* 7 (1911), pp. 498-504, 537-541.

3536. **Porter, Richard P.R.** "Vancouver: The Role of Ethnic Origin in Population Distribution." B.A. Essay (University of British Columbia, 1965).

3537. **Rankin, Harry.** *A Socialist Perspective for Vancouver.* Vancouver: Progress Books, 1974.

3538. ———. *Rankin's Law: Recollections of a Radical.* Vancouver: November House, 1975.

3539. **Robertson, A.E.** "The Pursuit of Power, Profit and Privacy: A Study of Vancouver's West End Elites, 1886-1914." M.A. Thesis (University of British Columbia, 1977).

3540. **Robinson, J. Lewis.** "How Vancouver Has Grown and Changed." *Canadian Geographical Journal* 89 (1974), pp. 40-48.

3541. **Rothery, Agnes.** *The Ports of British Columbia: The Story of Canada's Great Pacific Seaport Cities, Vancouver and Victoria.* Toronto: McClelland and Stewart, 1943.

3542. **Roy, Patricia E.** "Railways, Politicians and the Development of the City of Vancouver as a Metropolitan Centre, 1886-1929." M.A. Thesis (University of Toronto, 1963).

3543. ———. "The British Columbia Electric Railway Company, 1897-1928: A British Company in British Columbia." Ph.D. Thesis (University of British Columbia, 1970).

3544. ———. "Regulating the British Columbia Electric Railway: The First Public Utilities Commission in B.C." *BC Studies* 11 (1971), pp. 3-20.

3545. ———. "The Fine Art of Lobbying and Persuading: The Case of the B.C. Electric Railway." In D.S. Macmillan, ed. *Canadian Business History: Selected Studies, 1497-1971* (Toronto, 1972), pp. 125-143.

3546. ———. "The British Columbia Electric Railway and Its Street Railway Employees: Paternalism in Labour Relations." *BC Studies* 16 (1972-73), pp. 3-24.

3547. ———. "The Preservation of the Peace in Vancouver: The Aftermath of the Anti-Chinese Riot of 1887." *BC Studies* 31 (1976), pp. 44-59.

3548. **Sage, Walter N.** "Vancouver: The Rise of a City." *Dalhousie Review* 17 (1937), pp. 47-54.

3549. ———. "Vancouver: 60 Years of Progress." *Journal of Commerce Year Book 1947,* pp. 95-116.

3550. **Sandison, James.** *Schools of Old Vancouver.* Vancouver: Vancouver Historical Society, 1971.

3551. **Sinclair, Sylvia.** "Vancouver, B.C., and Sydney, Australia: A Comparison." *Canadian Geographical Journal* 68 (1964), pp. 28-37.

3552. **Soules, G.** *Vancouver at Your Feet.* Vancouver: Gordon Soules Economic and Marketing Research, 1971.

3553. **Steed, Guy F.P.** "Intrametropolitan Manufacturing: Spatial Distribution and Locational Dynamics in Greater Vancouver." *Canadian Geographer* 17 (1973), pp. 235-258.

3554. **Stevens, Leah.** "Rise of the Port of Vancouver, British Columbia." *Economic Geography* 12 (1936), pp. 61-70.

3555. ———. "The Grain Trade of the Port of Vancouver, British Columbia." *Economic Geography* 12 (1936), pp. 185-196.

3556. **Straaton, K.V.** "The Political System of the Vancouver Chinese Community Associations and Leadership in the Early 1960s." M.A. Thesis (University of British Columbia, 1974).

3557. **Stratton, P.R.V.** "Public Housing Experience in Vancouver." *Habitat* 3 (1960), pp. 20-23.

3558. **Tarasoff, K.** "Russians in the Greater Vancouver Area." In Inter-University Committee on Canadian Slavs. *Slavs in Canada* (Edmonton, 1966), pp. 138-147.

3559. **Taylor, L.D.** "What Single Tax Has Done for Vancouver." *B.C. Magazine* 6 (1910), pp. 411-415.

3560. **Tennant, Paul, and Zirnhelt, D.** "The Emergence of Metropolitan Government in Greater Vancouver." *BC Studies* 15 (1972), pp. 3-28.

3561. ———. "Metropolitan Government in Vancouver: The Strategy of Gentle Imposition." *Canadian Public Administration* 16 (1973), pp. 124-138.

3562. **Timms, P.T.** *Vancouver: The Golden Years, 1900-1910.* Vancouver: Vancouver Museums Association, 1971.

3563. **Waites, K.A., ed.** *The First Fifty Years: Vancouver High Schools, 1890-1940.* Vancouver: The Author, 1942.

3564. **Walhouse, F.** "The Influence of Minority Ethnic Groups on the Cultural Geography of Vancouver." M.A. Thesis (University of British Columbia, 1961).

3565. **Weston, G.** "Vancouver City Police." *B.C. Magazine* 7 (1911), pp. 558-561.

3566. **Whetter, D., et al.** *Forever Deceiving You: The Politics of Vancouver Development.* Vancouver: Urban Research Group, 1972.

3567. **Wilson, E.** "Young Vancouver." *Habitat* 10 (1967), pp. 138-139.

3568. **Woodsworth, J.S.** *On the Waterfront: With the Workers on the Docks at Vancouver.* Ottawa: Mutual Press, 1928.

3569. **Yarham, E.R.** "Vancouver's Romance: From Log Huts to 'Queen of the Pacific Shore.'" *United Empire* 27 (1936), pp. 180-183.

3570. **Young, E.M.** "The Hospitals and Charities of Vancouver City." *B.C. Magazine* 7 (1911), pp. 608-611.

3571. **Young, G.A.** "The Municipal Subdivision Approval Process in Metropolitan Vancouver." M.Sc. Thesis (University of British Columbia, 1974).

3572. **Young, R.E.** "Street of T'onak: Planning in Vancouver's Chinatown." M.A. Thesis (University of British Columbia, 1975).

iii. Victoria

3573. **Abraham, Dorothy.** *Romantic Vancouver Island: Victoria Yesterday and Today.* Victoria: Fleming Printing, 1969.

3574. **Armstrong, C.L.** "Victoria: The City of Certainties." *B.C. Magazine* 7 (1911), pp. 651-660.

3575. **Bentick, Brian Leslie.** "Saving, Investment, and the Land Market: Victoria, 1872-93." Ph.D. Thesis (Yale University, 1969).

3576. **Bissley, Paul L.** *Early and Late Victorians: A History of the Union Club of British Columbia.* Sidney: Review Printing, 1969.

3577. **Brooks, G.W.S.** "Edgar Crow Baker: An Entrepreneur in Early British Columbia." *BC Studies* 31 (1976), pp. 23-43.

3578. **Careless, J.M.S.** "The Business Community in the Early Development of Victoria, B.C." In D.S. Macmillan, ed. *Canadian Business History: Selected Studies, 1497-1971* (Toronto, 1972), pp. 104-123.

3579. **Cash, Gwen.** *A Million Miles from Ottawa.* Toronto: Macmillan, 1942.

3580. **Clack, Roderick D.** "Victoria's Downtown Improvement Plan." *Community Planning Review* 9 (1959), pp. 73-78.

3581. **Clark, C.** *The Best of Victoria, Yesterday and Today: A Nostalgic 115 Years' Pictorial History of Victoria.* Victoria: *Victoria Weekly*, 1973.

3582. **Cotton, P.** "Some Notes on the Transport of Architectural Ideas to Victoria, B.C." *British Columbia Library Quarterly* 31 (1967), pp. 23-28.

3583. **Diespecker, Richard Alan.** "The Jewel of Juan de Fuca [Victoria]." *Canadian Geographical Journal* 11 (1935), pp. 239-248.

3584. **England, Robert.** "A Victoria Real Estate Man: The Enigma of Sir Arthur Currie." *Queen's Quarterly* 65 (1958), pp. 210-221.

3585. **Farley, A.L.** "A Regional Study of Southeastern Vancouver Island." M.A. Thesis (University of British Columbia, 1949).

3586. **Fawcett, E.** *Some Reminiscences of Old Victoria.* Toronto: William Briggs, 1912.

3587. **Floyd, P.D.** "The Human Geography of Southeastern Vancouver Island, 1842-1891." M.A. Thesis (University of Victoria, 1970).

3588. **Forward, C.N.** *Land Use in the Victoria Area, B.C.* Ottawa: Queen's Printer, 1969.

3589. ———. "Parallelism of Halifax and Victoria." *Canadian Geographical Journal* 90 (1975), pp. 34-43.

3590. **Forward, C.N.**, ed. *Residential and Neighbourhood Studies in Victoria.* Western Geographical Series, Vol. 5. Victoria: University of Victoria, 1973.

3591. ———. *Victoria: Physical Environment and Development.* Western Geographical Series, Vol. 12. Victoria: University of Victoria, 1976.

3592. **Francis, R.A.** "Victoria-Vancouver: A Study in Contrasts on the West Coast." *Canadian Business* 30 (1957), pp. 30-33.

3593. **Gallacher, D.T.** "City in Depression: The Impact of the Years 1929-1939 on Greater Victoria, B.C." M.A. Thesis (University of Victoria, 1970).

3594. **Gregson, H.** *A History of Victoria, 1842-1970.* Victoria: Observer Publishing, 1970.

3595. **Hearne, G., and Wilkie, D.** *The Cordwood Ltd.: A History of the Victoria and Sydney Railway.* Victoria: B.C. Railway Association, 1971.

3596. **Holloway, G.F.** *The Empress of Victoria.* Victoria: Pacifica Productions, 1968.

3597. **Jupp, Ursula.** *From Cordwood to Campus in Gordon Head, 1852-1959.* Victoria: The Author, 1975.

3598. **Lai, Chuen-Yan.** "The Chinese Consolidated Benevolent Association in Victoria: Its Origins and Functions." *BC Studies* 15 (1972), pp. 53-67.

3599. **Lee, C.L.** "The Effect of Planning Controls on the Morphology of the City of Victoria." M.A. Thesis (University of Victoria, 1969).

3600. **Lines, K.** "A Bit of Old England: The Selling of Tourist Victoria." M.A. Thesis (University of Victoria, 1972).

3601. **Lort, J.C.** "Victoria Public Library." *British Columbia Library Quarterly* 31 (1967), pp. 3-22.

3602. **McCaffy, E.** "Victoria—The Beautiful." *Westward Ho! Magazine* 6 (1910), pp. 188-191.

3603. ———. "Victoria: A Metropolis in the Making." *Man to Man* 6 (1910), pp. 1060-1069.

3604. ———. "The Commercial Progress and Future of Victoria." *B.C. Magazine* 8 (1912), pp. 374-380.

3605. **McCann, L.D.** "The Structure and Pattern of Manufacturing in the Victoria Metropolitan Area." B.A. Essay (University of Victoria, 1966).

3606. **MacKinnon, C.S.** "The Imperial Fortresses in Canada: Halifax and Esquimalt, 1871-1906." Ph.D. Thesis (University of Toronto, 1965).

3607. **Myers, T.R.** *Ninety Years of Public Utility Service on Vancouver Island: A History of the B.C. Electric.* Victoria: B.C.E.R., 1954.

3608. **Nicol, E.P.** "Victoria." *Habitat* 10 (1967), pp. 148-153.

3609. **Oak Bay Anniversary Committee.** *Golden Jubilee, 1906-1956: Fifty Years of Growth.* Oak Bay: Corporation of the District of Oak Bay, 1956.

3610. **Pilton, J.W.** "Early Negro Settlement in Victoria." B.A. Essay (University of British Columbia, 1949).

3611. **Robinson, M.E.** "A Method for Investigating the Effects of Tourism on the Functional and Morphological Development of a City: As Applied to Greater Victoria, B.C." Ph.D. Thesis (Northwestern University, 1957).

3612. **Rothery, Agnes.** *The Ports of British Columbia: The Story of Canada's Great Pacific Seaport Cities, Vancouver and Victoria.* Toronto: McClelland and Stewart, 1943.

3613. **Roy, Patricia E.** "The Illumination of Victoria: Late Nineteenth-Century Technology and Municipal Enterprise." *BC Studies* 32 (1976-77), pp. 79-92.

3614. **Ruzicka, S.E.** "The Decline of Victoria as a Metropolitan Center, 1885-1901." M.A. Thesis (University of Victoria, 1973).

3615. **Shortt, Adam.** *Report of Dr. Adam Shortt Investigating the Financial Condition of the City of Victoria, B.C.* Victoria: Victoria Printing and Publishing Co., 1922.

3616. **Smyly, C.** "Heritage Lost: The Vanished Landmarks of Victoria." *Western Living* 6 (1976), pp. 22-26, 109.

3617. ———. "Heritage Saved [Victoria]." *Western Living* 6 (1976), pp. 40-48.

3618. **Sorby, T.C.** *The Harbour and City of Victoria.* Victoria: Inner Harbour Association of Victoria, 1917.

3619. **Victoria, Corporation of the City of.** *Victoria Illustrated.* Victoria: Ellis & Co., 1891.

3620. *Victoria in Your Pocket.* Victoria: I.Y.P. Publications Ltd., 1974.

3621. **Walden, F.E.** "The Social History of Victoria, B.C. 1858-1871." B.A. Essay (University of British Columbia, 1951).

3622. **Walker, M.** "Victoria: City of Many Facets." *Dalhousie Review* 24 (1945), pp. 399-401.

3623. **Warburton, T.R.** "Religious and Social Influences on Voting in Greater Victoria." *BC Studies* 10 (1971), pp. 3-25.

3624. **Wilson, J.W.** *Report on a Planning Program for the Capital Region of British Columbia.* New Westminster: Lower Mainland Regional Planning Board, 1952.

3625. **Woodcock, George, and Woodcock, I.** *Victoria.* Victoria: Morriss Printing, 1971.

3626. **Wright, J.M.** "The Settlement of the Victoria Region, British Columbia." M.A. Thesis (McGill University, 1956).

h. Bibliographical

3627. ———. "A Bibliography of the Arts and Crafts of Northwest Coast Indians." *BC Studies* 25 (1975), pp. 78-124.

3628. **Bradley, Ian L.** "Indian Music of the Pacific Northwest: An Annotated Bibliography of Research." *BC Studies* 31 (1976), pp. 12-22.

3629. **British Columbia Publishers Group.** *Books From British Columbia.* Vancouver, 1976. [Annual.]

3630. **Cairns, Alan C.** "The Study of the Provinces: A Review Article." *BC Studies* 14 (1972), pp. 73-82.

3631. **Careless, Virginia.** *Bibliography for the Study of British Columbia's Domestic Material History.* Ottawa: National Museum of Man, 1976.

3632. **Carter, Sue, comp.** "Books and Pamphlets about British Columbia." *PNLA Quarterly* 37 (1973), pp. 55-64.

3633. **Cole, Douglas L.** "Painting in British Columbia: A Review Article." *BC Studies* 23 (1974), pp. 50-53.

3634. **Cuddy, M.L., and Scott, J.J.** *British Columbia in Books: An Annotated Bibliography.* Vancouver: J.J. Douglas, 1974.

3635. **Day, David, ed.** "Aural History, Regional Studies and Literature in British Columbia." *Sound Heritage* 4 (1975), pp. 1-54.

3636. *Dictionary Catalogue of the Provincial Archives of British Columbia.* Boston: J.K. Hall, 1971.

3637. **Duff, Wilson, and Kew, M., comp.** "A Select Bibliography of Anthropology of British Columbia." *BC Studies* 19 (1973), pp. 73-121.

3638. **Edwards, M.H., and Lort, J.C.** *A Bibliography of British Columbia: Years of Growth, 1900-1950.* Victoria: University of Victoria, 1975.

3639. **Fladmark, K.R.** "Bibliography of the Archaeology of British Columbia." *BC Studies* 6 and 7 (1970), pp. 126-151.

3640. **Gilbert, S.R., ed.** "British Columbia Studies." *Communique: Canadian Studies* 1, no. 4 (1975), pp. 1-29.

3641. **Goard, Dean S., and Dickinson, Gary.** *A Bibliography of Social and Economic Research Pertaining to Rural British Columbia.* Ottawa: Department of Regional Economic Expansion, 1971.

3642. **Holmes, Marjorie C.** *Royal Commissions and Commissions of Inquiry in British Columbia, 1872-1942.* Victoria: King's Printer, 1945.

3643. ———. *Publications of the Government of British Columbia, 1871-1947*. Victoria: King's Printer, 1950.

3644. **Hoover, A.L., and Keddie, G.R.** *A Selected List of Publications on the Indians of British Columbia*. Victoria: B.C. Provincial Museum, 1976.

3645. **Horvath, Maria.** *A Doukhobor Bibliography Based on Material Available in the University of British Columbia Library*. 2 vols. and supplement. Vancouver: University of British Columbia Library, 1968-1970.

3646. **Jackson, John N.** "Geography and Planning in British Columbia: The Publications of the Lower Mainland Regional Planning Board." *Canadian Geographer* 8 (1964), pp. 92-96.

3647. **Lowther, Barbara J.** *A Bibliography of British Columbia: Laying the Foundations, 1849-1899*. Victoria: University of Victoria, 1968.

3648. **McIntyre, L., comp.** *Geography of British Columbia: Selected Bibliography, 1930-1965*. Vancouver: University of British Columbia Library, 1975.

3649. **Meyer, Ron H.** *A Selected Bibliography on Railways in British Columbia*. 2 vols. Vancouver: Pacific Coast Branch, Canadian Railroad Historical Association, 1973.

3650. **Napier, Nina.** "British Columbia: A Bibliography of Centennial Publications, 1957-1959." *B.C.H.Q.* 21 (1958), pp. 199-200.

3651. **Provincial Museum.** *A Selected List of Publications on the Indians of British Columbia*. Victoria: Department of Recreation and Conservation, 1970.

3652. **Ralston, Keith.** "Select Bibliography on the History of British Columbia." In Jean Friesen and Keith Ralston, eds. *Historical Essays on British Columbia* (Toronto, 1976), pp. 281-293.

3653. **Shibata, Y.** *Japanese-Canadians: An Annotated Bibliography*. Vancouver: Department of Anthropology, University of British Columbia, 1975.

3654. **Smart, John, ed.** *Materials Relevant to British Columbia Labour History in Record Group 27, Canada Department of Labour Records*. Ottawa: Public Archives of Canada, 1975.

3655. **Smith, Charles W.** *Pacific Northwest Americana: A Checklist of Books and Pamphlets Relating to the History of the Pacific Northwest*. New York: H.W. Wilson Company, 1921.

3656. **Smith, D.B.** *Ethnic Groups in British Columbia: A Selected Bibliography Based on a Check-List of Material in the Provincial Library and Archives.* Victoria: B.C. Centennial Committee, 1957.
3657. **Turnbull, Jean, comp.** *Periodical Articles, Pamphlets, Government Publications and Books Relating to the West Kootenay Region of British Columbia in the Selkirk College Library, Castlegar, B.C.* Castlegar: Selkirk College, 1968.
3658. **Wellwood, R.J., comp.** *Kootenaiana: A Listing of Books, Government Publications, Monographs, Journals, Pamphlets, etc., Relating to the Kootenay Area of the Province of British Columbia and Located in the Libraries of Notre Dame University of Nelson, B.C, and/or Selkirk College, up to 31 March 1976.* Castlegar: Selkirk College, 1976.
3659. **Woodcock, George.** "The Wilderness Observed: A Review Article." *BC Studies* 3 (1969), pp. 58-63.
3660. **Woodward, Frances.** "Bibliography of British Columbia." *BC Studies* 1 (1968-69). [A continuing feature.]
3661. ———. *Theses on British Columbia History and Related Subjects.* Vancouver: University of British Columbia Library, 1971. [Supplement, 1974.]
3662. ———. "Margaret Anchoretta Ormsby: Publications." *BC Studies* 32 (1976-77), pp. 163-169.

A Brief Guide to Western Canadian Studies

A. Newsletters and Journals

This list of scholarly periodicals contains only those devoted exclusively to Western Canada or to one of the Western provinces. For an indication of other journals that sometime contain material on Western Canada, the reader should consult the bibliography.

Prairie Forum (1976-).
Canadian Plains Research Center
University of Regina
Regina, Sask. S4S 0A2
A biannual, interdisciplinary journal containing articles and reviews on the Canadian Plains region.

Western Canadian Journal of Anthropology (1969-).
Department of Anthropology
University of Alberta
Edmonton, Alberta T6G 2H4
Successor to the *Alberta Anthropologist*, this quarterly journal publishes articles and reviews dealing with all branches of anthropology

Historical and Scientific Society of Manitoba *Transactions,* Third Series (1944-).
Manitoba Historical Society
Room M211
190 Rupert Avenue
Winnipeg, Man. R3B 0N2
An annual publication, the *Transactions* contain a selection of papers presented to the Manitoba Historical Society.

Manitoba Pageant (1952-).
Manitoba Historical Society
Room M211
190 Rupert Avenue
Winnipeg, Man. R3B 0N2
Issued quarterly, the *Pageant* carries short articles, usually illustrated.

Saskatchewan History (1948-).
Saskatchewan Archives Board
University of Saskatchewan
Saskatoon, Sask. S7N 0W0
Published three times per year, this journal carries articles, book reviews, notes and correspondence, documents, and recollections and reminiscences.

Alberta History (1975-).
Historical Society of Alberta
Box 4035, Station C
Calgary, Alberta T2K 2G7
A quarterly journal that succeeded the *Alberta Historical Review* published from 1953-1975, *Alberta History* carries illustrated articles on all aspects of the province's history and book reviews, documents, and notes.

Albertan Geographer (1964-).
Geography Students' Association
University of Alberta
Edmonton, Alberta T6G 2H4
An annual publication concentrating on the geography of Western Canada, theoretical and methodological problems in geography, and geographic education.

BC Studies (1968-).
University of British Columbia
2075 Wesbrook Mall
Vancouver, B.C. V6T 1W5
This quarterly journal helped fill the void created by the demise of the *British Columbia Historical Quarterly* in 1958. *BC Studies* carries articles from all the social sciences, as well as book reviews and an ongoing bibliography of B.C.

B.C. Historical News (1968-).
Department of History
University of Victoria
Victoria, B.C. V8W 2Y2
A quarterly publication that carries short articles, book reviews, and notes and comments.

Newest Review (1975-).
NeWest Press
13024-109 Ave.
Edmonton, Alberta T5B 3B5
Published ten times per year, this journal is devoted to politics, society, and culture in Western Canada.

Red River Valley Historian (1974-).
Red River Valley Historical Society
P.O. Box 85
Comstock, Minnesota 56525
A biannual journal carrying articles on both the American and the Canadian wests.

Western Canadiana Publications Project *Newsletter* (1977-).
English Department
Humanities Building
University of Alberta
Edmonton, Alberta T6G 2E5
Two issues per year contain notes on conferences, archives, research; a third issue is bibliographical.

Canadian Plains *Bulletin* (1973-).
Canadian Plains Research Center
University of Regina
Regina, Sask. S4S 0A2
A quarterly publication containing notes and comments on books, conferences, research projects.

B. Archives and Libraries

The detailed list that follows provides basic data on virtually all the major archives and libraries in Western Canada, with the exception of urban archives and museums. These are covered in:

Alan F.J. Artibise, "Canadian Urban Studies," *Communique: Canadian Studies* (April 1977).

Ann S. Cowan and Frank Corcoran, "Museums and Canadian Studies," *Communique: Canadian Studies* (May 1976).

There are several publications which should be consulted to supplement the following list. They are:

Directory of Canadian Records and Manuscript Repositories
(Ottawa: Association of Canadian Archivists, 1977). This guide is available

in libraries and archives or may be purchased for $3.00 from Valerie Cowan, 24 Edward Laurier Dr., Halifax, N.S. B3M 2C7. It contains data on most archival institutions in Canada.

Union List of Manuscripts in Canadian Repositories. 2 vols.
(Ottawa: Public Archives of Canada, 1975). This guide is also available in libraries and archives. The *Union List* includes 27,000 entries from 171 institutions. The entries represent units (collections) of papers varying in size from two to several hundred thousand pages. They are described under the names of individuals, corporate bodies, or government agencies which received, created, or accumulated the papers. Some personal data are given, such as the dates of birth and death, the principal occupation and the place of residence of persons under whose names the papers are listed. Details are also given regarding the type of papers, inclusive dates, linear extent, location, ownership of originals, and available finding aids, as well as a breakdown by categories and subjects, with reference to prominent persons, events and historical periods.

American Library Directory: A Classified List of Libraries in the United States and Canada. 29th Edition.
(New York and London: R.R. Bowker Co., 1974). Almost one hundred pages of this directory are devoted to Canadian libraries.

Finally, mention must be made of the Public Archives of Canada. Canada's major archival institution has a great deal of material relating to the four Western provinces. Inquiries should be directed to:

> Public Archives of Canada
> 395 Wellington Street
> Ottawa, Ontario
> K1A 0N3

The P.A.C. has a number of guides to its holdings and services. These are available on request.

Legislative Library of Manitoba
200 Vaughan Street
Winnipeg, Man. R3C 0P8
Established in 1870, the Provincial Library contains more than 80,000 books, one of the most comprehensive collections of government documents in Canada, and an excellent newspaper collection.

Provincial Archives of Manitoba
200 Vaughan Street
Winnipeg, Man. R3C 0P8
Contains significant collections of manuscripts, maps, pictures, and public records. Notable material includes Hudson's Bay Company records, papers and correspondence of Louis Riel, and papers of premiers and cabinet ministers.

Archives de l'Archidiocèse de Saint-Boniface
151 Avenue de la Cathédrale
Saint-Boniface, Man. R2H 0H6
Records dating from 1818.

Canadian Mennonite Brethren Archives
77 Henderson Highway
Winnipeg, Man. R2L 1L1
Material relating to Mennonite Brethren Church and to history of Mennonites.

Ukrainian Cultural and Educational Centre Archives
184 Alexander Ave. East
Winnipeg, Man. R2B 1C7
Material dealing with the history of Ukrainians in Canada and history of Ukrainian Nationalist Movement.

United Church Archives
Manitoba Conference
c/o Library
University of Winnipeg
515 Portage Avenue
Winnipeg, Man. R3B 2E9
Official records of the Manitoba Conference of the Methodist Church, of the United Church, and of the Presbyterian Synod of Manitoba.

University of Manitoba Archives
Elizabeth Dafoe Library
Winnipeg, Man. R3T 2N2
Notable holdings include papers of Frederick Philip Grove, Ralph Connor, and J.W. Dafoe.

Legislative Library of Saskatchewan
234 Legislative Building
Regina, Sask. S4S 0B3
Holdings include government documents, books and pamphlets, periodicals, and a good collection of Western Canadiana. It also maintains a Saskatchewan newspaper index.

Saskatchewan Archives
University of Regina
Regina, Sask. S4S 0A2
University of Saskatchewan
Saskatoon, Sask. S7N 0W0
Established in 1945, the archives offer a full range of services in both centres. Significant holdings include records of the government of the Northwest Territories, the Saskatchewan homestead records of the old federal department of the interior, and provincial government records. The Saskatchewan Archives have an excellent newspaper collection, and extensive manuscripts, photographs, and aural history tapes.

Lutheran Central Synod Archives
Lutheran Theological Seminary
Saskatoon, Sask. S7N 0X3
Manuscripts and photographs relating to Synod and its predecessors.

Lutheran Missouri Synod Archives
Manitoba-Saskatchewan District
1927 Grant Drive
Regina, Sask. S4S 4V6
Holdings include material on history of Synod, autobiographies of pioneers and pastors, and photographs.

Mohyla Institute Archives
1240 Temperance Street
Saskatoon, Sask. S7N 0P1
Records of the Institute, private papers, photographs, and collections of Ukrainian newspapers.

Royal Canadian Mounted Police Museum
P.O. Box 6500
Regina, Sask. S4P 3J7
Annual reports of the N.W.M.P., R.N.W.M.P., and R.C.M.P., as well as diaries, documents, papers, maps, photographs, and sound recordings relating to the force.

Saskatchewan Power Corporation Archives
Scarth and Victoria Streets
Regina, Sask. S4P 0S1
Records of S.P.C. and papers, maps, photographs, and sound recordings and film relating to the history and development of electricity and natural gas in Saskatchewan.

United Church Archives
Saskatchewan Conference
St. Andrew's College
University of Saskatchewan
Saskatoon, Sask. S7N 0W0
Records of the Presbyterian Synod of Saskatchewan, Saskatchewan Conference of Methodist and United Churches, and parish records.

University of Saskatchewan Archives
University Library
Saskatoon, Sask. S7N 0W0
University records and private papers of faculty, staff, and alumni.

Legislative Library of Alberta
216 Legislative Building
Edmonton, Alberta T5K 2B6
Holdings include books, government documents, pamphlets, periodicals, atlases, maps, and newspapers.

Provincial Archives of Alberta
12845-102nd Avenue
Edmonton, Alberta T5N 0M6
Established in 1963, its holdings include private manuscripts, government records, pamphlets, newspapers, maps, and photographs.

Glenbow-Alberta Institute Archives and Library Research Centre
Glenbow Centre
9th Avenue and 1st Street S.E.
Calgary, Alberta T2G 0P3
A major research centre for the history of Western Canada, the holdings of Glenbow Archives include: material on Indian history and culture; records of individuals, businesses, societies, and organizations; photographs, films, and tape recordings; C.P.R. records; and a comprehensive collection on ranching in southern Alberta. Glenbow's Library has an excellent collection of Western Canadiana. Guides to Glenbow's collections are published in the *Glenbow Archives Publication Series.*

Archives of the Canadian Rockies
Box 160
Banff, Alberta T0L 0C0
Records relating to Rocky Mountain region.

Medicine Hat Historical Foundation
1302 Bomford Crescent
Medicine Hat, Alberta T1A 5E6
Records relating to Medicine Hat area (including Cypress Hills), pioneer history, maps, photographs.

Oblate Archives of Alberta-Saskatchewan
9916-110th Street
Edmonton, Alberta T5K 1J3
Material relating to the Oblate Order, including records, maps, and photographs.

Red Deer and District Archives
4818-49th Street
Red Deer, Alberta T4N 1T8
Photographs, records, audio tapes, manuscripts, and biographies of pioneers of Red Deer and District.

Sir Alexander Galt Museum
Community Services Department
Lethbridge, Alberta T1J 0P6
Manuscripts and photographs pertaining to Southern Alberta.

Ukrainian Canadian Archives
9543-110th Avenue
Edmonton, Alberta T5H 1H3
Manuscripts, photographs, and publications pertaining to Ukrainian life, customs, traditions, and history in Canada, and especially in Alberta.

United Church Archives
Alberta Conference
St. Stephen's College
8830-112th Street
Edmonton, Alberta T0G 2J6
Records of United Church, and some predating church union.

University of Alberta—Special Collections
Cameron Library
University of Alberta
Edmonton, Alberta T6G 2J8
Literary manuscripts, private papers, and photographs relating to Alberta and other prairie provinces.

University of Alberta Archives
Rutherford Library
University of Alberta
Edmonton, Alberta T6G 2E1
Records of university and private papers, maps, and photographs.

University of Calgary—Special Collections
Library
University of Calgary
2920 - 24 Avenue N.W.
Calgary, Alberta T2N 1N4
Records of university, private papers, and records of architectural, local, political, and religious organizations.

Legislative Library of British Columbia
Parliament Buildings
Victoria, B.C. V8V 1X4
The collection of 600,000 items includes reference books, monographs, government documents, newspapers, and periodicals. A newspaper index is maintained.

Provincial Archives of British Columbia
655 Belleville Street
Victoria, B.C. V8V 1X4
The holdings of the Archives are found in five divisions: the library, the aural history division, map division, visual records division, and manuscript and government records division. Notable holdings include the Northwest Collection, one of the finest and most extensive collections of Northwest Americana on the continent, and over 90,000 photographs.

Anglican Church Archives
Synod of B.C. and the Yukon
6050 Chancellor Boulevard
Vancouver, B.C. V6T 1L4
Records of the Church and private papers, newspapers, photographs, books, and maps.

British Columbia Forest Products Limited Archives
1050 West Pender
Vancouver, B.C. V6E 2X3
Holdings include photographs, audio tapes, publications, pamphlets, and minutes and correspondence relating to the company.

British Columbia Telephone Company Archives
786 Seymour Street
Vancouver, B.C. V6B 3K9
Records and studies of B.C. Tel.

Fort Steele Regional History Library
Fort Steele Historic Park
Fort Steele, B.C. V0B 1N0
Records, publications, and photographs relating to East Kootenay region.

Kamloops Museum and Archives
207 Seymour Street
Kamloops, B.C. V2C 2E7
Holdings include H.B.C. journals and records (1840-1880), and records relating to Kamloops and region.

Maritime Museum of British Columbia
28-30 Bastion Square
Victoria, B.C. V8W 1H9
Books, periodicals, papers, charts, maps, and photographs.

Selkirk College Archives
Box 1200
Castlegar, B.C. V1N 3J1
Records, sound recordings, photographs, and films relating to West Kootenay region.

Simon Fraser University Archives
Burnaby, B.C. V5A 1S6
Records of university and municipal records of Burnaby and Port Coquitlam.

United Church Archives
B.C. Conference
Vancouver School of Theology
6000 Iona Drive
Vancouver, B.C. V6T 1L4
Records of United Church congregations, institutions, and clergy.

University of British Columbia —
Special Collections
2075 Wesbrook Mall
Vancouver, B.C. V6T 1W5
Records of university and manuscripts, papers, maps, photographs and audio-visual material relating to B.C.

University of Victoria — Special Collections
McPherson Library
University of Victoria
Victoria, B.C. V8W 2Y2
Records of university and private papers, military maps, photographs, and tapes of local cultural and historic interest.

Vancouver Maritime Museum
1905 Ogden Street
Vancouver, B.C. V6J 3J9
Holdings include a marine library, charts, logbooks, photographs, films, and sound recordings.

C. Organizations and Societies

Western History Group, Canadian Historical Association
Professor Alan F.J. Artibise, Chairman
Department of History
University of Victoria
Victoria, B.C. V8W 2Y2
Open to anyone interested in Western Canadian history, the group meets during the Western Canadian Studies Conference held in Calgary in February and during the Canadian Historical Association annual meeting held in June. The group organizes programmes for the C.H.A. annual meeting, assists in the organization of the Calgary conference, and generally serves as a forum for the discussion of problems faced by its membership.

Western Division, Canadian Association of Geographers
Professor L.J. Evendon, President
Department of Geography
Simon Fraser University
Burnaby, B.C. V5A 1S6
Created in 1959, this organization holds an annual meeting and several field trips each year. Membership is open to geographers from Alberta, British Columbia, and the American border states. The association deals with public issues and geography education and provides a forum for the presentation of research papers. The latter are published annually, and the association also maintains a biannual newsletter. For a guide to the publications see *Canadian Geographer* 20 (1976), pp. 330-331.

Prairie Division, Canadian Association of Geographers
Professor J.C. Everitt, Secretary-Treasurer
Department of Geography
Brandon University
Brandon, Man. R7A 6A9
Created in June 1977, this group is similar to the Western Division except that its focus is Manitoba and Saskatchewan. The new organization plans to establish and maintain contacts between prairie universities, encourage the participation of non-university people, and generally encourage geographic study. At the first annual meeting in October 1977, there were informal paper sessions, a business meeting and field trips.

Canadian Plains Research Center
University of Regina
Regina, Sask. S4S 0A2
Sponsors seminars, conferences, and meetings; helps agencies locate specialists for contract research; and is establishing an information system to record and correlate research data, documents, and other information relevant to the prairie provinces. The Center has an active publications programme that includes a journal (*Prairie Forum*), a newsletter (Canadian Plains Bulletin), occasional papers, proceedings of conferences, and the Canadian Plains Studies Series.

Glenbow-Alberta Institute
Glenbow Centre
9th Avenue and 1st Street S.E.
Calgary, Alberta T2G 0P3
The Institute was incorporated by act of the Alberta Legislature in 1966. It consists of an Archives, Museum, Library, and Art Gallery, and Departments of Education, History, Photography, and Ethnology. Glenbow has produced a large number of monographs, catalogues, guides, and other publications. A list is available on request.

The Jewish Historical Society of Western Canada
403 - 322 Donald Street
Winnipeg, Man. R3B 2H3
Founded in Winnipeg in 1968, the Society collects documents, photographs, memorabilia, and artifacts; records interviews with pioneers; sponsors meetings and exhibitions; and publishes papers and exhibits. The Society is an affiliate of the Canadian Jewish Congress and works in association with the following groups in Western Canada:

> History and Archives Committee
> Regina Jewish Community
> c/o Beth Jacob Synagogue
> 1640 Victoria Avenue
> Regina, Saskatchewan

History and Archives Committee
Jewish Community Centre
715 McKinnon Avenue
Saskatoon, Saskatchewan

History and Archives Committee
c/o Jewish Community Council
102 - 18th Avenue S.E.
Calgary, Alberta
T2G 1K8

History and Archives Committee
c/o Jewish Community Council
305 Mercantile Building
Edmonton, Alberta

Jewish Historical Society of B.C.
c/o Canadian Jewish Congress
950 West 41st Avenue
Vancouver, B.C.

Research Centre for Ethnic Studies
University of Calgary
2920 - 24th Avenue N.W.
Calgary, Alberta T2N 1N4
Created in 1969, the Centre promotes and co-ordinates research on all ethnic groups and acts as a resource and advisory institution for governments, universities, and individual scholars concerned with ethnic minorities.

Canada West Foundation
P.O. Box 1030
Calgary, Alberta T2P 1T4
An independent, non-profit organization incorporated in 1973. It initiates and conducts research and educational programmes and produces a wide variety of publications; a list of the latter is available on request.

Manitoba Historical Society
M211 - 190 Rupert Avenue
Winnipeg, Man. R3B 0N2
Incorporated in 1879, the objectives of the Society are to foster historical preservation, encourage research and publication, and promote public interest in Manitoba history. The Society regularly publishes two journals (H.S.S.M. *Transactions* and *Manitoba Pageant*) and documents (*Manitoba Record Society*), and has published a number of special volumes. There are throughout Manitoba a number of local chapters affiliated to the society.

Saskatchewan History and Folklore Society
448 - 29th Street East
Prince Alberta, Sask. S6V 1Y7
Formed in 1957, its aims are to gather and preserve the history and folklore of Saskatchewan; to mark and make accessible historic sites and trails; to prepare guide books; and to promote an increased knowledge of history. The Society publishes an occasional newsletter.

Alberta Historical Society
95 Holmwood Avenue N.W.
Calgary, Alberta T2K 2G7
Incorporated in 1907, the Society now has chapters in Edmonton, Calgary, and Lethbridge. It sponsors a journal (*Alberta History*) and a document series (*Alberta Record Society*), as well as regular meetings. Other activities include occasional publications and an on-going interest in the place of Alberta history in the provincial curriculum.

British Columbia Historical Association
3450 West 20th Avenue
Vancouver, B.C. V6S 1E4
Formed in 1922, the Association is a federation of member societies throughout B.C. Its aims are: to encourage historical research and stimulate public interest in B.C. history; to promote the preservation and marking of historical sites; and to publish historical sketches, studies, and documents. It publishes a regular newsletter, the B.C. Historical *News*.

Red River Valley Historical Society
P.O. Box 85
Comstock, Minn. 56525
An unique international society formed in 1964, it organizes the annual Northern Great Plains History Conference and publishes the *Red River Valley Historian*. It also promotes history education and historical preservation.

D. Specialized Series

In recent years, there has been a substantial increase in the number of specialized series devoted to all or part of Western Canada. As a result, the decision was made to include in this list only those series that have as their focus a broad area of Western Canada. Among the series not included here are the following: *Manitoba Record Society, Manitoba Geographical Series, Alberta Record Society,* and *University of Alberta Studies in Geography.*

Canadian Frontiers of Settlement
The drought and depression of the 1930's stimulated one of the best known and most valuable series of studies of the Canadian prairies. The series is the result of geographical, economic, historial, and sociological research into the settlement period of Western history. No student of the region can afford to ignore it, despite the generally pessimistic views of many of the authors regarding plains settlement and their preoccupations with the problems of their day. The volumes in the series have recently been reprinted by Kraus Reprint Company.

Vol. 1. William A. Mackintosh. *Prairie Settlement: The Geographical Setting* (1934).

Vol. 2. Arthur S. Morton. *History of Prairie Settlement.* Chester Martin. *"Dominion Lands" Policy* (1938).

Vol. 3. Not published.

Vol. 4. William A. Mackintosh, et al. *Economic Problems of the Prairie Provinces* (1935).

Vol. 5. R.W. Murchie, et al. *Agricultural Progress on the Prairie Frontier* (1936).

Vol. 6. Carl A. Dawson and R.W. Murchie. *The Settlement of the Peace River Country: A Study of a Pioneer Area* (1934).

Vol. 7. Carl A. Dawson. *Group Settlement: Ethnic Communities in Western Canada* (1936).

Vol. 8. Carl A. Dawson and Eva B. Younge. *Pioneering in the Prairie Provinces: The Social Side of the Settlement Process* (1940).

Vol. 9. Arthur R.M. Lower. *Settlement and the Forest Frontier in Eastern Canada.* Harold A. Innis. *Settlement and the Mining Frontier* (1936).

Social Credit in Alberta: Its Background and Development
The ten volumes in this series provide a major contribution to understanding not only Social Credit in Alberta, but the economic, political, and social development of Western Canada generally. With the exception of volume 5, all volumes in the series are still available from the University of Toronto Press.

Vol. 1. W.L. Morton. *The Progressive Party in Canada* (1950).

Vol. 2. D.C. Masters. *The Winnipeg General Strike* (1950).

Vol. 3. Jean Burnet. *Next-Year Country: A Study of Rural Organization in Alberta* (1951).

Vol. 4. C.B. Macpherson. *Democracy in Alberta: The Theory and Practice of a Quasi-Party System* (1953).

Vol. 5. J.R. Mallory. *Social Credit and the Federal Power in Canada* (1954).

Vol. 6. W.E. Mann. *Sect, Cult, and Church in Alberta* (1955).

Vol. 7. Vernon C. Fowke. *The National Policy and the Wheat Economy* (1957).

Vol. 8. L.G. Thomas. *The Liberal Party in Alberta: A History of Politics in the Province of Alberta, 1905-1921* (1959).

Vol. 9. S.D. Clark. *Movements of Political Protest in Canada, 1640-1840* (1959).

Vol. 10. John A. Irving. *The Social Credit Movement in Alberta* (1959).

Canadian Plains Studies
Volumes in this series are published periodically by the Canadian Plains Research Center in Regina and are available from there.

Vol. 1. Richard Allen, editor. *A Region of the Mind: Interpreting the Western Canadian Plains* (1973).

Vol. 2. Martin Louis Kovacs. *Esterhazy and Early Hungarian Immigration to Canada* (1974).

Vol. 3. Richard Allen, ed. *Religion and Society in the Prairie West* (1975).

Vol. 4. Don C. McGowan. *Grassland Settlers: The Swift Current Region during the Era of the Ranching Frontier* (1975).

Vol. 5. C.O. White. *Power for a Province: A History of Saskatchewan Power* (1976).

Vol. 6. Richard Allen, ed. *Man and Nature on the Prairies* (1976).

Vol. 7. *Western Canada 1909: Travel Letters by Wilhelm Cohnstaedt* (1976).

Western Canadian Studies Conference Proceedings.
Since 1969, the University of Calgary has sponsored an annual gathering of scholars interested in Western Canadian studies. A selection of the papers presented each year have been published. Those published to date are:

Vol. 1. David P. Gagan, ed. *Prairie Perspectives: Papers of the Western Canadian Studies Conference [1969].* Toronto: Holt, Rinehart and Winston, 1970.

Vol. 2. A.W. Rasporich and H.C. Klassen, eds. *Prairie Perspectives 2: Selected Papers of the Western Canadian Studies Conference, 1970, 1971.* Toronto: Holt, Rinehart and Winston, 1973.

Vol. 3. S.M. Trofimenkoff, ed. *The Twenties in Western Canada: Papers of the Western Canadian Studies Conference, March 1972.* Ottawa: History Division, National Museum of Man, 1972.

Vol. 4. David Jay Bercuson, ed. *Western Perspectives 1: Papers of the Western Canadian Studies Conference, 1973.* Toronto: Holt, Rinehart and Winston, 1974.

Vol. 5. A.W. Rasporich, ed. *Western Canada: Past and Present [Papers of the Western Canadian Studies Conference, 1974].* Calgary: McClelland and Stewart, West, 1975.

Vol. 6. Howard Palmer, ed. *The Settlement of the West [Papers of the Western Canadian Studies Conference, 1975].* Calgary: Comprint Publishing Company, 1977.

Vol. 7. Henry C. Klassen, ed. *The Canadian West: Social Change and Economic Development [Papers of the Western Canadian Studies Conference, 1976].* Calgary: Comprint Publishing Company, 1977.

Western Geographical Series
This series is published by the Geography Department of the University of Victoria. It emphasizes four areas: the teaching of geography, urban studies, Pacific studies, and resource management.

Vol. 1. W.R. Derrick Sewell and Harold D. Foster, eds. *The Geographer and Society* (1970).

Vol. 2. Harold D. Foster, ed. *Geographica* (1970).

Vol. 3. Harold D. Foster and W.R. Derrick Sewell, eds. *Resources, Recreation and Research* (1970).

Vol. 4. Timothy O'Riordan and Jonathan O'Riordan. *Okanagan Water Decisions* (1972).

Vol. 5. Charles N. Forward, ed. *Residential and Neighbourhood Studies in Victoria.* (1973).

Vol. 6. William M. Ross. *Oil Pollution as an International Problem: A Study of Puget Sound and the Strait of Georgia* (1973).

Vol. 7. C.J.B. Wood. *Handbook of Geographical Games* (1973).

Vol. 8. Francis M. Leversedge, ed. *Priorities in Water Management* (1974).

Vol. 9. W.R. Derrick Sewell, et al. *Modifying the Weather: A Social Assessment* (1974).

Vol. 10. M.C.R. Edgell and B.H. Farrell, eds. *Themes on Pacific Lands* (1974).

Vol. 11. Brenton M. Barr, ed. *Calgary: Metropolitan Structure and Influence* (1975).

Vol. 12. Harold D. Foster, ed. *Victoria: Physical Environment and Development* (1976).

Vol. 13. Derek V. Ellis, ed. *Pacific Salmon: Management for People* (1977).

B.C. Geographical Series

This series provides a wealth of source materials on a wide variety of topics. Most volumes are still in print and are available from the publisher, Tantalus Research Limited.

Vol. 1. W.G. Hardwick. *Geography of the Forestry Industry of British Columbia* (1964).

Vol. 2. Dennis Kerfoot. *Port of British Columbia* (1965).

Vol. 3. W.G. Hardwick and J.D. Chapman, eds. *Geographical Dialogues: University Viewpoints for Teachers* (1965).

Vol. 4. John Walforth. *Residential Location and Place of Work* (1966).

Vol. 5. H.V. Warren and E.F. Wilkes. *World Resource Production* (1965).

Vol. 6. Roger Leigh. *Specialty Retailing* (1966).

Vol. 7. J.V. Minghi, ed. *The Geographer and the Public Environment* (1967).

Vol. 8. G. Tomkins, ed. *Geographical Perspectives* (1968).

Vol. 9. A.H. Siemens, ed. *Lower Fraser Valley: Evolution of a Cultural Landscape* (1968).

Vol. 10. R.J. Claus and D. Rothwell. *Gasoline Retailing* (1970).

Vol. 11. R. Irving. *Amenity Agriculture: Agricultural Responding to City Growth* (1970).

Vol. 12. R. Leigh, ed. *Contemporary Geography: Western Viewpoints* (1971).

Vol. 13. J.V. Prescott. *The Evolution of Nigeria's Regional Boundaries, 1861-1971* (1971).

Vol. 14. O. Slaymaker and H.J. MacPherson. *Mountain Geomorphology* (1971).

Vol. 15. J.V. Minghi, ed. *Peoples of the Living Land: Cultural Diversity in B.C.* (1972).

Vol. 16. R. Leigh, ed. *Contemporary Geography: Research Trends* (1972).

Vol. 17. R. Leigh, ed. *Malaspina Papers: Studies in Human and Physical Geography* (1973).

Vol. 18. B.M. Barr, ed. *The Kootenay Collection of Research Papers in Geography* (1974).

Vol. 19. David Ley, ed. *Community Participation and the Spatial Order of the City* (1974).

Vol. 20. L.J. Evenden and F.F. Cunningham, eds. *Cultural Discord in the Modern World* (1974).

Vol. 21. B.M. Barr, ed. *Western Canadian Research in Geography: The Lethbridge Papers* (1975).

Vol. 22. B.M. Barr, ed. *New Themes in Western Canadian Geography: The Langara Papers* (1976).

Select Subject Index

Ethnic Groups

Americans, 88, 113, 138, 164, 180, 227, 310, 595, 1116, 2614, 2784, 3110, 3610
Anglo-Saxons, 95, 1202, 1359, 1754, 1756, 1772, 1984, 2016, 2028, 2041, 2043, 2048, 2229, 2626, 2789, 2891A. *See also* English, Scots.
Arabs, 2174

British. See Anglo-Saxons.

Chinese, 1753, 2110, 2179, 2259, 2561, 2562, 2563, 2581, 2870A, 2878, 2882A, 2896, 2921, 2922, 2922A, 2923, 2929, 2930, 2944, 2947, 2981, 2999, 3000, 3005, 3010A, 3413, 3435, 3436, 3437, 3547, 3556, 3572, 3598

Danes, 208, 272
Doukhobors, 226, 296, 297, 303, 724, 847, 1734, 1766, 1970, 1971, 2874A, 2900, 2901, 2902, 2907, 2914, 2963A, 3002, 3004, 3279, 3285, 3306, 3645
Dutch, 1742, 2881, 2891A, 2891B, 3110, 3138

East Indians, 1262, 1617, 2122, 2864, 2895, 2943, 2946, 2962, 2972A
English, 177, 194, 891, 1607, 1954, 2235

Finns, 2920, 3001
French, 170, 177, 195, 233, 241, 248, 293A, 294, 300, 735, 891, 925, 997, 1111, 1215, 1215A, 1227, 1274, 1286A, 1409, 1414, 1418, 1450, 1615, 1743, 1744, 1746, 1818, 1958, 1959, 1960, 1961, 2205, 2212, 2215A, 2253, 2980, 2989A, 2989B, 3408B

Germans, 197, 220, 260, 1230, 1769, 1928, 2207, 2959
Greeks, 2924, 3466A, 3490, 3533

Hungarians, 143
Hutterites, 198, 225, 235, 236, 244, 276, 277, 301, 848, 1241, 1263, 1264, 1270, 1271, 1355, 2181, 2203, 2204, 2204A, 2220, 2220A, 2228, 2237, 2242, 2247, 2492

Icelanders, 891, 1247, 1445, 1752
Indians, 192, 196, 199, 200, 203, 204, 206, 211, 212, 213, 223, 224, 238A, 243, 247, 249, 250, 251, 252, 258, 259, 263, 264, 265, 271, 275, 283, 286, 290, 293, 295, 299, 302, 308, 730, 732, 815, 826, 841, 865, 870, 879, 889, 890, 972, 979, 1018, 1047, 1056, 1074, 1249, 1250, 1533, 1584, 1661, 1683, 1730, 1731, 1736, 1737, 1748, 1758, 1759, 1770, 1947, 2171, 2182, 2187, 2195, 2196, 2198, 2206, 2209, 2210, 2211, 2216, 2217, 2236, 2237, 2240, 2265, 2477, 2557, 2873, 2874, 2883, 2884, 2886, 2887, 2888, 2889, 2899, 2903, 2912, 2913, 2927, 2931, 2934, 2938, 2939, 2949, 2961, 2964, 2976, 2977, 2978, 2979, 2986, 2988, 2989C, 2994, 2995, 2996, 3045, 3290, 3292, 3300, 3399, 3400, 3401, 3441, 3627, 3628, 3644, 3651
Italians, 3459A

Japanese, 307, 2215, 2863, 2872A, 2885A, 2892, 2911, 2919, 2925, 2926, 2929, 2940, 2942, 2948, 2952A, 2961A, 2966, 2982, 2985, 2987, 2993, 3007, 3253, 3263, 3264, 3277, 3653
Jews, 111, 193, 194, 207, 1214, 1220, 1221, 1237, 1239, 1240, 1258, 1268, 1497, 1564, 1573, 1574, 1634, 1740, 1751, 2081, 2104, 2615, 2893A, 2965, 3470A

Lebanese, 2174

Mennonites, 123, 142, 221, 222, 231, 232, 237, 261, 297, 501, 891, 1223, 1224,

266   Subject Index

1225, 1230A, 1233, 1234, 1235, 1245, 1277, 1279, 1280, 1282, 1333A, 1364, 1428, 1680, 1739, 1741, 1741A, 2175, 2176, 2252, 2457, 2891A
Métis, 202, 240, 242, 246, 268, 288, 289, 292, 298, 709, 904, 913, 914, 915, 925, 927, 929, 1017, 1054, 1219, 1236, 1248, 1260, 1272, 1276, 1284, 1661, 1683, 1736, 1768, 2188, 2199, 2213

Norwegians, 2184

Orientals, 118, 2241, 2867, 2882, 2894, 2906, 2917, 2936, 2937, 2954, 2967, 2968, 2969, 2990, 2991, 2992, 3003, 3006. *See also* Chinese, East Indians, Japanese.

Poles, 266, 279, 1242, 1278
Portuguese, 191

Roumanians, 254, 2261
Russians, 231, 1245, 2827, 2963A, 3558

Scandinavians, 114, 209, 716, 2184, 2264
Scots, 137, 282, 1117
Swedes, 2909, 3476
Syrians, 253

Ukrainians, 139, 143A, 255, 256, 267, 278, 287, 304, 305, 306, 737, 778, 854, 884, 891, 1069, 1244, 1246, 1257, 1285, 1449, 1587, 2090, 2186, 2202, 2223, 2224, 2225, 2233, 2237, 2248, 2249, 2257

Welsh, 178, 1765

Political Parties and Politicians

Aberhart, William, 2276, 2280, 2292, 2307, 2332, 2333, 2336, 2346

Bennett, R.B., 389, 1826, 2293, 2337, 2343
Bennett, W.A.C., 3029, 3080, 3096
Borden, Robert, 365, 415, 416, 2870A, 3010A
Bowser, W.J., 3020

Calder, J.A., 1858
Coldwell, M.J., 332, 1772A, 2093
Conservative Party. *See* Progressive Conservative Party.
Co-operative Commonwealth Federation, 318, 323, 328, 332, 346, 350, 394, 1331, 1797, 1799, 1807, 1815, 1816, 1831, 1834, 1836, 1837, 1862, 2308, 2341, 2342, 3066, 3075, 3087, 3098. *See also* New Democratic Party.
Crerar, T.A., 331, 1300

De Cosmos, Amor, 3069
Diefenbaker, John G., 320, 321, 322, 364

Douglas, T.C., 1767, 1859
Dunning, C.A., 1779, 1780, 1802

Gardiner, James G., 1860, 1861, 1865, 2349

Haultain, F.W.G., 1851

Irvine, William, 334

King, W.L.M., 1791

Laurier, Wilfrid, 317, 408, 1057, 2870A, 3010A, 3023, 3040
Liberal Party, 370, 379, 1330, 1824, 1825, 1842, 1843, 2271, 2344, 2345, 2349, 2810, 3023
Lloyd, Woodrow, 1812

McBride, Richard, 3034, 3082, 3083
McCarthy, D'Alton, 1318

Macdonald, John A., 21, 1064, 1292
Macdonald, Hugh John, 1301, 1316
Mackenzie, Alexander, 3059

Manning, Ernest, 2295, 2323
Meighen, Arthur, 329, 330
Motherwell, W.R., 1857, 1912, 2009

New Democratic Party, 318, 342, 392, 3031, 3043, 3065, 3093, 3097. See also Co-operative Commonwealth Federation.
Norquay, John, 1309

Oliver, Frank, 384
Oliver, John, 3056

Pattullo, T.D., 3061, 3088
Progressive Conservative Party, 320, 321, 322, 379, 1826, 3008, 3011, 3082
Progressive Party, 358, 359, 361, 380, 393, 1786, 1787, 1795, 1796, 3062, 3064
Puttee, Arthur, 1310

Roblin, Duff, 1312
Roblin, Rodmond P., 1305, 1327

Scott, Walter, 1777
Sifton, Clifford, 134, 172, 319, 333, 1057, 1287
Social Credit Party, 2267, 2269, 2270, 2272, 2275, 2276, 2278, 2284, 2286, 2299, 2302, 2303, 2304, 2305, 2309, 2317, 2321, 2322, 2327, 2328, 2332, 2334, 2335, 2336A, 2346, 2350, 2351, 3012, 3033, 3051, 3075, 3084, 3085
Socialist Party, 326, 643, 1288, 3030, 3049
Stevens, H.H., 3095
Stinson, Lloyd, 1328, 1653

Tolmie, S.F., 3062, 3064

United Farmers of Alberta, 2273, 2274, 2282, 2283, 2287, 2314, 2341, 2342, 2458
United Farmers of British Columbia, 3060
United Farmers of Canada, Saskatchewan Section, 1811
United Farmers of Manitoba, 1347, 1348

Wood, Henry Wise, 2330

Miscellaneous

North West Mounted Police. See Royal Canadian Mounted Police

Royal Canadian Mounted Police, 12, 22, 30, 44, 45, 49, 299, 348, 845, 852, 873, 984, 1019, 1034, 1040, 1049, 1052, 1062, 1064, 1065, 1065A, 1080, 1083, 1084, 1088, 1089, 1091, 1095, 1114, 1131, 1132, 1133, 1734, 2048, 2058, 2059, 2142, 2148, 2165, 2194, 2217, 2260, 2361, 2842

World War One, 703, 704, 785, 2326, 2487, 2502
World War Two, 488, 490, 641, 1423, 1435, 1589, 2568, 2835, 2836

Author Index

Abell, A.S., 2353, 2354
Abella, Irving M., 623, 624, 3141
Aberhart, W., 2267
Abler, T.S., 815
Abra, Marion, 1458
Abraham, Dorothy, 3573
Abrams, G., 2011
Abramson, J.A., 1867, 2012
Acheson, T.W., 622A
Adachi, Ken, 2863
Adams, D.L., 2051
Adams, John Q., 3311
Affleck, E.L., 2742, 2744, 3099
Ahenakeu, Edward, 958
Ahern, H.G., 2355
Akrigg, G.P.V., 2743
Akrigg, H.B., 2743, 3312
Ala, L.G., 3313
Albright, W.D., 2356
Alexander, Mary H.T., 1138
Alexander, William Hardy, 2456
Allan, D.D., 625
Allan, Iris, 959
Allen, H.T., 3251
Allen, Richard, 1, 2, 692, 693, 694, 695, 696, 697, 1408
Allen, William, 579
Alper, Donald, 3008
Alty, Stella W., 1686
Ambrose, Peter, 626
Ames, M.M., 2864, 2865
Anderson, Alan B., 1728, 1729
Anderson, C.H., 468
Anderson, D.E., 3142
Anderson, F.W., 894, 960, 961, 1773, 2052
Anderson, G.W., 2094
Anderson, Grace M., 191
Anderson, I.D., 2885A
Anderson, James, 2662
Anderson, J.A., 469
Anderson, J.C., 1496
Anderson, J.T.M., 698
Anderson, K., 627
Anderson, O., 3, 2269
Anderson, R.N., 2091
Anderson, Raoul, 2357
Anderson, W.J., 470, 614, 1868
Andrew, F.W., 3100, 3314
Andrews, C.D., 3143

Andrews, Craig, 3315
Andrews, G.S., 2866
Andrews, Isabel A., 192, 1018, 1730
Andrews, Margaret W., 815A, 3418
Angus, H.F., 2270, 2779, 2867, 3009
Antak, Ivan E.M., 2868
Anton, Gordon A., 2271
Appleblatt, Anthony, 1774
Appleton, John, 785
Appleton, Thomas E., 2869
Apps, M.J., 3316
Archer, John H., 2A, 816, 1869, 1917, 2095, 2096, 2127A
Archibald, E.S., 471
Ariano, A.A., 1409
Ariza, J.H., 2358
Armstrong, Christopher, 2418
Armstrong, C.L., 3574
Armstrong, P.C., 472, 606
Armstrong, R., 841
Armstrong, W.H.G., 699
Arnold, A.J., 193, 194, 1214, 1497
Arrowsmith, W.A., 1918
Arthurs, V., 2753
Artibise, Alan F.J., 804, 817, 881, 882, 1498, 1499, 1500, 1501, 1502, 1503, 1504, 1505, 1506, 1507, 1508, 1509, 1510, 1511, 1512, 3010, 3317
Asante, E.O., 2359
Asante, Nadine, 3318
Ashlee, Ted, 3419
Askin, W.R., 2419, 2663
Astles, A.R., 3420, 3421
Ashworth, Mary, 3421
Atcheson, J.W., 1687
Atherton, Jay, 3144
Atkin, Ronald, 1019
Atkins, B.R., 2744, 3101
Atkinson, Reginald Noel, 3319
Atwell, P.H., 2171, 2557
Auclair, Elie J., 2013
Audain, James, 2870
Audet, L.P., 782
Auld, F.H., 473, 1020, 1870
Avakumovic, Ivan, 303, 309, 3002
Avery, Donald, 110, 1366, 1513, 2870A, 3010A
Axworthy, L., 1514, 1515, 1516, 1517
Axworthy, T., 1518

Backeland, L.L., 1215, 1215A
Badgley, R.F., 1775
Badoux, Maurice, 195
Bagley, Roy, 2523
Bailey, A.W., 1942
Bailey, Mary C., 2172
Bailey, P., 3346
Bailey, R.W., 1731
Baine, R.P., 2558
Baines, S., 539
Baker, A.M., 2524
Baker, H.R., 1732
Baker, W.B., 1688, 1943
Baker, W.M., 310
Balawyder, T., 1367
Baldwin, Alice Sharples, 2173
Balf, M., 3320
Balf, R., 3321
Balian, O.S., 1368
Bancroft, Hubert Howe, 2745
Bandrowski, S., 474
Banson, M.J., 2664
Baptie, Sue, 3145
Barbeau, C., 196
Barbeau, Marius, 2871, 2872
Barclay, H.B., 2174, 2175, 2457
Barford, J.C., 3422
Bargen, Peter F., 2176
Barker, Mary L., 3146
Barnes, H.D., 3147
Barnes, J.A., 2177
Barnhart, G.L., 1733
Barr, B.M., 627A, 818, 818A, 2419A, 2559, 3148
Barr, John J., 3, 2272
Barrow, G.T., 786, 789, 1519, 2053, 2665
Bartholomew, H., 3423
Bartlett, C., 2178
Bartley, George, 962, 963
Barton, G.S.H., 475
Basi, R.S., 3424
Baskett, H.R., 2560
Bate, J.P., 2458
Baureiss, G.A., 2179, 2561, 2562, 2563
Baxter, R.S., 1520
Beale, A.M., 2135
Beaulieu, Paul, 1521
Beck, J. Murray, 311
Becker, A., 197
Beckman, M.D., 1379A
Beddone, H.C.J., 1332
Bedford, Allen Gerald, 1410
Bedford, Elaine, 2666
Begg, Alexander, 1022, 1023, 1139, 1522, 2746

Begg, W.A., 2054
Belbeck, Alice, 2014
Belbeck, Dave, 2014
Belkin, Simon, 111
Bell, M.J., 1459
Bellamy, D.J., 312
Bellan, R.C., 1411, 1523, 1524, 1525, 1526
Belshaw, C.S., 2903
Belton, G.S., 1412
Benham, M.L., 700, 1608
Bennett, J.W., 4, 112, 198, 476
Bennett, M.L., 3425
Bennett, William, 3149
Benoist, Charles, 1024
Benoit, D.P., 1216, 1413
Benoit, M., 1527
Bentick, Brian Leslie, 3575
Bentley, Robert J., 3252
Bercuson, David J., 5, 628, 629, 630, 819, 1369, 1370, 1371, 1372, 1387, 1528, 1603
Berger, Carl, 7, 820, 821
Bergrew, M., 3150
Bernard, A., 1529, 2564, 2667, 3426
Bernard, Elaine, 2872A, 3253
Berry, Gerald L., 1025, 2136
Berton, Pierre, 396, 397
Bescoby, I.M., 3151
Betke, Carl, 1734, 2273, 2274, 2668
Bettison, D.G., 2525
Betts, G.M., 2669
Bhajan, E.R., 2526
Bibby, R.W., 2459
Bicha, K., 113
Bickel, R.P., 1530
Bickersteth, J.B., 8
Biggar, E.B., 398
Bilash, B.N., 1217, 1414
Bilsland, W.W., 3322, 3323
Bingaman, S.E., 964, 965, 966
Binns, Kenneth, 2275
Binsfield, Edmund L., 821A
Birrell, Andrew J., 9
Bissley, Paul L., 3254, 3427, 3576
Bjarnason, Carl, 1414A
Bjonback, R.D., 3152
Bjork, K.O., 114
Black, E.R., 2747, 3011
Black, J.A., 3324
Black, N.F., 1689
Blackburn, John H., 2180
Bladen, M.L., 399, 400
Blain, L., 3153
Blake, Donald, 3012
Blake, H.W., 1531, 1532
Blake, T.M., 2873

Bland, John, 3428
Bland, Salem, 701
Bliss, Michael, 631
Blue, John, 2137
Boal, F.W., 2565
Boam, Henry J., 10
Boas, Franz, 2874
Bock, J., 1415, 1460
Bock, J.K., 1533
Bock, W.G., 1533
Bockemuehl, H.W., 2874A
Bocking, D.H., 401, 1026, 1027, 1028, 1029, 1030, 1031, 1776, 1777, 1778, 1871, 1944, 1945
Bohi, C.W., 1690
Boissonnault, C.M., 937
Boldt, E.D., 2181
Bone, P.T., 402
Bonenfant, J.C., 1140, 1218
Bonnycastle, R.H.G., 1534
Boon, T.C.B., 702
Booth, J.F., 477, 579
Booth, Michael R., 3255
Booth, W.G., 1416
Boothroyd, Peter, 2526A
Borden, Charles E., 2875, 3256
Bossen, M., 1535
Botting, P.J., 3325
Boudreau, Joseph A., 703, 704, 2276
Boulding, K.E., 478
Boulton, Charles A., 967
Boutilier, H.R., 3429
Bower, R., 3430
Bowes, R.P., 199
Bowles, R.S., 1286
Bowsfield, Hartwell, 822, 823, 895, 896, 897, 938
Boyd, C.F., 479
Boyd, Denny, 3257
Boyd, Hugh, 480
Brack, David M., 2748
Bracken, John, 481, 482
Braden, Thomas B., 2566
Bradley, Ian L., 3627, 3628
Bradley, W.E., 1536
Bradwin, E.W., 632
Brass, Eleanor, 1735
Brasser, Ted J., 2182
Bray, R.M., 1287
Breen, D.H., 11, 115, 483, 824, 825, 968, 2360, 2361, 2460, 2567, 2568
Brennan, J.W.G., 1779, 1780, 1781, 1782
Brese, W.G., 2420
Brick, A.L., 2183
Britnell, G.E., 313, 484, 485, 486, 487, 488, 489, 490, 1691, 1783, 1872, 2277, 2421
Broadbridge, A.F., 2015
Broadfoot, Barry, 116, 3431
Bronson, H.E., 1784, 1919, 2422
Brooks, F.G.H., 3432
Brooks, G.W.S., 2876, 2877, 3577
Brooks, I.R., 826
Brooks, J., 840
Brooks, W.H., 705, 1032
Brougham, W.F., 3326
Brown, Caroline, 12
Brown, D.H., 969
Brown, Donald Edward, 2362, 2363
Brown, L.A., 1785, 1786, 1946
Brown, Lorne, 12
Brown, Maria J., 3258
Brown, R. Craig, 13
Bruce, Jean, 14
Brunvand, Ian, 2184
Bryce, George, 1141, 1142
Bryce, M.S., 1538
Bryce, P.H., 200
Buchanan, Donald W., 201, 3259
Buck, R.M., 1947
Buckley, Helen, 1736
Buckley, K., 2097
Buckwold S., 2098
Buller, A.H.R., 491
Bulman, T.A., 3102
Burles, Gordon, 2185
Burmeister, K.H., 15
Burnes, John R., 3327
Burnet, Jean, 2364, 2461
Burns, R.M., 2748A, 3014
Burpee, Lawrence J., 403, 2527
Burry, Shierlaw, 2670
Burt, A.L., 16
Burton, F.W., 492
Burton, G.L., 493
Burton, M.D., 3260
Bussard, Lawrence H., 2569, 2570
Butler, W.F., 17
Butlin, J.A., 494
Byrne, M.B.V., 2571
Byrne, T.C., 2186

Cadden, P.G., 632A
Cahan, F.H., 138
Cail, Robert E., 2749
Cain, Louis P., 3433
Cairns, Alan O., 3630
Cairns, V.B., 1948
Calderwood, W., 1787, 1788, 1949, 1950
Callihoo, Victoria, 1033, 2187

Cameron, Alex R., 1692, 1693
Cameron B., 2671
Cameron, D., 2365
Cameron, Donald, 2462
Cameron, William Bleasdell, 970, 971
Campbell, A.C., 1461
Campbell, G., 2463
Campbell, J.B., 1873
Campbell, M.W., 18, 1694
Campbell, Maria, 202
Campbell, P.C., 2878
Camponi, L., 827
Cannell, S., 1539
Cantley, R.W., 2139
Cantlon, F.M., 2366
Caplan, Joseph, 495
Caple, K.P., 3103
Card, B.Y., 19, 706, 2188
Cardinal, Harold, 203, 204
Careless, J.M.S., 787, 829, 830, 1373, 1540, 3578
Careless, Virginia, 3631
Carlsen, Alfred E., 3015, 3016
Carlson, Roy L., 2750
Carlyle, W.J., 1144
Carmeron, Bill, 1874
Carmichael, Herbert, 3154
Carpenter, David C., 707, 2138
Carpenter, J.H., 2528
Carr, Emily, 2879
Carrigan, O., 314
Carrington, Philip, 708
Carroll, C., 3104
Carroll, H., 3328
Carrothers, A.W.R., 3155
Carrothers, W.A., 307, 3007, 3156, 3157, 3158
Carruthers, C., 2016
Carson, E.C., 3159
Carter, D.J., 117, 1951, 2189, 2572, 2573, 2574
Carter, Eva, 2464
Carter, S.M., 2880
Carter, Sue, 3632
Casaday, L.W., 3160
Cash, Gwen, 2751, 3579
Cashman, Tony, 20, 2190, 2465, 2672, 2673
Cassidy, J., 1517
Cavelaars, A.A.C., 2881
Cavers, Anne S., 3434
Cavert, W.L., 496
Caves, R.E., 634, 3161
Chaiko, R.M., 1417, 1462
Chakravarti, A.K., 497

Chalmers, John W., 205, 206, 709, 2191, 2466, 2467
Chambers, Edith D., 3329
Chambers, Elizabeth, 1789
Chambers, Ernest J., 1034
Chan, W.M.W., 2674
Chao, M., 3435
Chapman, G.F., 1541, 1542, 1543
Chapman, J.D., 3162
Chapman, T.L., 710, 2468
Charlebois, Peter, 898
Charles, J.L., 405
Cheng, Tien-Fang, 118, 2882
Cherrington, John, 3330
Cherwinski, Walter J.C., 1920, 1921
Chiel, Arthur A., 1220, 1221
Child, Alan H., 831, 3261
Chisick, E., 1288, 1543
Chives, B., 2675
Cho, G., 2882A, 3436, 3437
Chodos, Robert, 406
Chorney, Harold, 1145, 1373A
Choquette, Robert, 1035, 1418
Chown, S.D., 711
Christenson, R.A., 407, 2576, 2676
Church, G.C., 498, 499
Church, H.E., 1036
Church, J.S., 3163
Churchill, D.M., 3438, 3439
Clack, Roderick D., 3580
Clague, R.E., 1289
Clark, A.B., 315, 788
Clark, C., 3581
Clark, C.K., 899
Clark, Cecil, 2752
Clark, D., 900
Clark, J.N.R., 1419
Clark, Lovell, 1420
Clark, Paul, 3164
Clark, R., 1544
Clark, S.D., 712, 1875
Clark, W.L.R., 1290, 1463
Clarke, L.H., 2469
Clements, M., 1695, 1952, 2055
Clemson, Donovan, 3331
Cleverdon, Catherine L., 316
Climenhaga, D.B., 1790
Cline, John A., 1373B
Clinkskill, J., 1037, 1038
Clubb, S.P., 2099, 2100
Clutesi, George, 2883
Clylsworth, J.A., 3165
Coates, D., 850
Coates, Roy, 119, 120

Coats, Douglas, 2577
Cochrane, H.G., 2367
Cohen, Zir, 207
Cole, Douglas L., 1146, 2851, 3304, 3633
Coleman, G.P., 500
Coleman, M., 1464
Coleman, P.E., 1421
Collier, Anne M., 1465
Collier, R.W., 3332, 3440
Collier, Robert, 3017
Collins, Barbara R., 3441
Collins, P.V., 2470
Comfort, D.J., 2192
Complin, Margaret, 2056
Constantin-Weyer, M., 1147
Conway, C.B., 3262
Cook, G.L., 833
Cook, Gail C.A., 1545
Cook, Ramsay, 7, 317, 713, 714, 834, 1222
Cooke, E., 1291
Cooper, J., 1422
Cooper, M.G.S., 3442
Coppock, K., 2578
Corbett, D.C., 121, 122, 3443
Corbett, E.A., 2677
Corcoran, F., 835
Cornish, F.C., 972
Cornwall, I.H.B., 3444
Correll, Ernest, 123, 501, 1223, 1224, 1225
Corrigall, M., 2753
Cote, J.E., 2471
Cotton, P., 3582
Court, Thomas, 2423
Courtney, John C., 1791, 1792, 1793, 1794, 2101
Courville, L.D.F., 1795, 1796
Coutts, R.M., 408
Cowan, Ann S., 835
Cowan, Anna M., 1546
Cowan, J.G., 1374
Cox, Thomas R., 3166
Craig, J.E., 1423
Cramer, M.H., 3018
Cran, G.A., 3445
Crawford, M.E., 2193
Creighton, Donald G., 21, 1292
Creighton, P.R., 2102
Crerar, A.D., 3333, 3446, 3447
Cromwell, J., 3334, 3334A
Crone, R.H., 1953
Cross, Alfred E., 2368
Cross, Michael S., 318
Crunican, P.E., 1293, 1294, 1424
Cuddy, M.L., 3634

Culliton, John T., 124
Cummings, D.E., 3448
Cunniffe, Richard, 2579
Currie, A.W., 409, 410, 411, 412, 502, 3019, 3167
Currie, Laurie, 3335
Currie, W.H., 2754
Curtis, P.J., 2423A, 2677A

Dafoe, C., 1547
Dafoe, John W., 319, 1548
Dahl, E.H., 1511, 1512
Dahl, Ervin, 3336
Dahlie, Hallvard, 715
Dahlie, Jorgen, 208, 209, 716, 3263, 3264
Dailyde, V.K., 3020
Dale, E.H., 73, 503, 2017, 2678, 2679, 2680
Dalichow, Fritz, 3105
Daly, George Thomas, 717
Dalzell, A.G., 3449
Dalzell, K.E., 2755, 2756
Daniels, C.H., 3450
Daniels, L.A., 2472, 2580
Daniels, Roger, 2883A
Danielson, R.S., 504
Dant, N., 2681
Davidson, C.B., 1226, 1375
Davidson, J.W., 413
Davidson, W.M., 901, 902
Davies, W.K.D., 789
Davis, A.K., 1737
Davis, C., 3451, 3452
Davis, E.N., 2057
Davis, M.B., 3106
Davisson, Walter P., 505
Daw, Ruth M., 2194
Dawe, R.W., 2529
Dawson, Brian J., 2581
Dawson, Carl A., 210, 718, 2140, 2369
Dawson, Colleen, 1549
Dawson, G.F., 2018
Day, David, 2757, 3635
Day, John P., 2681A
Deane, R.B., 2058
Deiseach, D., 2473
Delainey, W.P., 2103
De Lisle, D., 1333A
De Mille, George, 636
Dempsey, Hugh A., 22, 211, 836, 973, 1040, 2141, 2142, 2195, 2196, 2197, 2198, 2370, 2582, 2583, 2584, 2585
Dendy, David R.B., 3107
Denison, Merrill, 506

Denney, C.D., 974
Denny, Cecil, 212, 213
Den Otter, A.A., 1041, 2371, 2424, 2425, 2474, 2530, 2531
DeVolpi, Charles P., 2758
Dhand, H., 903
Dibb, Sandra, 2128
Dickinson, Gary, 3641
Dickinson, Janet, 1550
Diefenbaker, John G., 320, 321, 322, 2019
Diemer, H.L., 2586, 2682
Diespecker, Richard Alan, 3583
Dillabough, J.V., 1376
Dingwall, C.W., 1551
Dinwoodie, D.H., 3168
Djwa, S.A., 719
Dobbin, L.L., 1738
Dobie, Edith, 3021, 3022
Doe, Ernest, 3337
Dojcsak, G.V., 1922
Donaldson, R.M., 2532
Donkin, John G., 2059
Donnelly, M.S., 1295, 1296
Dorge, L., 939, 1148, 1227
Dorin, Patrick C., 414
Doughty, H., 837
Douglas, C.H., 2278, 2279
Douglas, Thomas D., 1797
Douglas, William, 1377, 1425, 1552, 1553
Down, Mary Margaret, 3265
Downie, D.A., 1426
Dowse, Thomas, 1042, 1149
Drache, H.M., 1228, 1334
Drake, Beverly A., 2475
Drake, Earl G., 1043, 1044, 1045, 2060, 2061, 2062
Draper, H.L., 2426, 2427
Dreisziger, N.F., 2372
Driben, Paul, 2199
Drummond, G.F., 3108
Drummond, W.G., 507
Drummond, W.M., 508, 509
Duff, Wilson, 2884, 3637
Duggan, D.M., 2683
Duggan, J.J., 2533
Duke, Mary D., 838
Duncan, D.M., 1046, 1150
Dunlevy, Ursula, 904
Dunlop, Allan C., 976
Dunlop, J.S., 510
Dunn, J.T., 2684
Durkin, Douglas, 720
Dwyer, M.J., 3023
Dyck, B., 721
Dyck, N.E., 1047

Dyck, Ruth, 214
Dykstra, T.L., 2020, 2534

Eager, E., 1048
Eager, Evelyn L., 1696, 1798, 1799, 1800, 1801, 1876
Eagle, John A., 415, 416
Earl, L., 417, 1378, 1554
Easterbrook, W.T., 511, 512, 839
Easton, Robert, 3024, 3453
Eaton, Grace Elvira, 1877
Eaton, L.K., 2885
Ebbutt, Frank, 23
Ecroyd, L.G., 323, 1923, 2587, 2685, 2686, 3454
Edgar, J.H., 462
Edmonds, W.E., 1049, 1050, 1697, 2687
Edwards, E.E., 513
Edwards, George F., 1878
Edwards, M.H., 3638
Eggleston, Wilfrid, 24, 125, 2200
Ehlers, E., 126
Elias, P.D., 1151, 1466
Elkins, David, 3025
Elliot, Gordon R., 3026
Elliot, J.J., 215, 216
Elliott, David R., 2280
Elliott, G.B., 1555, 2588
Ellis, Frank H., 2373, 2759
Ellis, M.C., 2143
Ellis, Walter E.W., 3027, 3266
Elton, D.K., 25, 2281
Emanuel, L., 2201, 2689
Embree, David Grant, 2282, 2283
Emery, George N., 722, 723, 1229, 2202
England, Robert, 26, 127, 128, 129, 217, 218, 219, 3028, 3584
Englebert, R., 2760, 3169
English, R.E., 2374, 2428, 3109
Entz, W., 220, 1230
Epp, F.H., 221
Epp, George K., 222
Epp, O.J., 1230A
Essar, D., 1051
Evans, S., 2203, 2204, 2204A, 2589
Evenden, L.J., 2885A
Ewart, A.C., 1467
Ewart, John S., 1152, 1427
Eyler, Philip, 1297

Fahey, John, 2761
Fahrni, M., 1336
Fairbairn, D.A., 1924

Fairburn, K.J., 3148
Fairford, Ford, 2762
Falk, G.A., 223
Farley, A.L., 3585
Fast, G.A., 1739
Fast, H.R., 1879
Fast, J., 1739
Fawcett, E., 3586
Feldman, Lionel E., 1545
Fellows, C.M., 638
Ference, E.A., 2375, 2376
Ferguson, George V., 27, 28, 29, 1231, 1802
Ferguson, M.M., 1468, 1556
Fergusson, C.B., 977
Fetherstonhaugh, R.C., 30
Fidler, Vera, 2144
Field, A.J., 1740, 2104
Fields, D.B., 2886, 3399
Finlay, J.L., 2284
Finlay, R.E., 2535
Fisher, A.D., 224
Fisher, C.L., 2145
Fisher, J.V., 3267
Fisher, M., 1298
Fisher, Robin, 2887, 2888, 2889
Fisk, Larry J., 1299
Fitzgerald, Denis Patrick, 1698
Fitzpatrick, F.J.E., 1052
Fladmark, K.R., 3639
Flanagan, Thomas E., 905, 906, 907, 908, 909, 910, 2285, 2286, 2287, 2288
Fleming, H.A., 418
Flint, David, 225
Floyd, P.D., 3587
Flucke, A.F., 3170
Foner, Philip S., 2890
Foran, M.L., 2476, 2590, 2591, 2592, 2593, 2594, 2595
Forbes, Elizabeth, 2891
Forde, G.B., 2744
Fordham, R.C., 1337
Forester, A.D., 3171
Forester, J.E., 3171
Forin, John A., 978
Forrester, E.A.M., 3338
Forsey, Eugene A., 639, 640, 2146, 2289
Forster, S., 3521
Forster, Victor Wadham, 3455
Forward, C.N., 2762A, 3456, 3588, 3589, 3590, 3591
Foster, John K., 3268
Foster, W. Garland, 226
Fountain, G.F., 3457
Fournier, Leslie T., 419
Fowke, Donald, 324

Fowke, Edith, 227, 228, 229, 230, 325, 840, 1232
Fowke, V.C., 324, 490, 515, 516, 517, 518, 519, 520, 521, 641, 642
Fowler, Roy L., 2377
Fowler, S.S., 3172
Francis, E.K., 231, 232, 1233, 1234, 1235, 1428, 1680
Francis, R.A., 3029, 3458, 3592
Francis, R.J., 3110
Franks, C.E.S., 1803
Fraser, W.B., 979, 2596
Fraser, W.J., 1429, 1430, 1557
Freer, K.M., 3459
Frégault, Guy, 911
Frémont, Donatien, 233, 1153, 1154, 2205
Frideres, J.S., 234, 1215A
Friedmann, Karl A., 2290
Friedmann, Robert, 235, 236
Friesen, Gerald, 31, 31A, 326, 643
Friesen, I.I., 237
Friesen, Jean, 2763
Friesen, John, 1155, 1338
Friesen, R.J., 1741
Fromson, R.D., 1431, 1558, 1559
Frost, David B., 1880
Fryer, Harold, 2147, 2536
Fumalle, M.J., 3112
Fung, K.I., 1715
Fung, Y.H., 1560
Furniss, I.F., 522

Gabriel, T., 3339
Gaetz, A.L., 2537
Gagan, David P., 32
Galbraith, J.S., 130
Gale, D.T., 724, 3459A
Gallacher, D.T., 3593
Galloway, C.F.J., 2764
Ganzevoort, Herman, 1742
Gardiner, A.G., 1379
Garrett, A.W., 2021
Garrioch, A.C., 1339
Garrison, Daphne, 2378
Gayler, H.J., 3460
Gellatly, D.H., 3113
Gellner, John, 238
George, Ernest S., 2379
George, M.V., 131
Georgeson, M.R., 2291
Gereeke, K., 790
Gerry, A.C., 1561
Gershaw, F.W., 2206
Gertler, L.O., 2429

Gerwin, E., 2207
Getty, I.A.L., 1053, 2148, 2477
Gibbard, J.E., 3114, 3340
Gibbins, Roger, 238A, 327
Gibbon, J.M., 239, 420
Gibson, Dale, 1156
Gibson, E.M.W., 3461, 3462
Gibson, J.R., 2891A
Gibson, J.S., 2597, 2598
Gibson, Lee, 1156
Gibson, W.C., 3269
Gilbert, S.R., 3640
Giles, Mabel C., 2292
Gill, C.B., 1157
Gillese, J.P., 2690
Gillis, P., 841
Gilpin, John, 2538, 2691
Gilson, J.C., 1340
Ginn, M., 2891B
Giraud, Marcel, 240, 241, 242, 1054, 1236
Gislason, I., 33
Gladstone, P., 3173
Glaister, R.R., 53
Glazebrook, G.P. de T., 421
Glenn, J.E., 2379A
Glick, I.N., 2478
Glueck, A.C., 940
Glynn-Ward, Hilda, 2892
Goard, Dean S., 3641
Godemath, P.F., 3463
Godfrey, W.G., 328
Gold, N.L., 132
Goldenberg, H.C., 1562
Goldring, P., 1055
Gomery, D., 3464
Gonick, Fay M., 1431A
Good, T.L., 1563
Good, W.C., 523, 1379A
Goodchild, F.H., 2765
Goodwin, T., 1954
Gordon, A., 1237, 1564
Gordon, J.G., 1341
Gordon, R.K., 2479
Gordon, S.B., 2293
Gordon, W.R., 3465
Goresky, Isidore, 2480
Gosnell, R.E., 2769, 2770
Goudy, H.G., 3043
Gough, Barry M., 34, 2766, 2767
Gough, John, 2768
Gould, Edwin, 2430, 3174
Gould, Jan, 2893
Graham, J.W., 1565
Graham, Roger, 329, 330
Graham, W.R., 1056

Graham-Cumming, G., 243
Grainger, M. Allerdale, 3175
Granatstein, J.L., 842
Grant, George M., 35
Grant, H.C., 725, 1342
Grant, H.R., 1690
Grant, J.H., 3466
Grant, K.F., 3466A
Grant, Robert W., 2022
Grantham, R., 3030
Gray, Arthur W., 3115, 3341
Gray, E., 2431
Gray, James H., 524, 726, 727, 728, 729, 1432, 1566, 2599
Grayson, J.P., 2294, 2539
Grayson, L.M., 2294, 2539
Green, Alan G., 133, 645, 646, 647
Green, G., 3342
Green, S.J., 1881
Greenberg, Dolores, 422
Greenblat, J., 2023
Greene, D.L., 1955
Greenland, C., 912
Gregg, R.C., 2540
Gregson, H., 3594
Gresko, J., 730
Grest, E.G., 525, 1882, 2380
Griesbach, W.A., 2208
Griezic, F.J.K., 331, 1300
Griffin, H.L., 526, 527
Griffin, Harold, 2771, 3176, 3211
Grimes, W.E., 528
Grindley, T.W., 43, 529
Groh, D.G., 2295
Groome, A.J., 332, 1883
Grose, R.E., 1380, 1381
Grosman, Brian A., 1956
Gross, Paul S., 244
Groulx, Lionel, 941
Gruetter, R., 3485
Guertin, E.K., 1343
Guest, H.J., 1301
Gunn, Angus M., 731, 3468
Gunn, R.R., 530
Gutstein, D., 3469, 3470
Gyuse, T.T.I., 791, 2105, 2600

Habinski, A.A., 2893A, 3470A
Hacking, N., 3445
Hague, Reece H., 2772
Haig, Kennethe M., 1237A
Haig-Brown, Roderick, 2771A
Hall, D.J., 36, 134, 333, 913, 1057, 1804
Hall, Frank, 1158

Author Index 277

Hallett, Mary E., 2894
Hambley, G.H., 1344
Hamilton, J.H., 2773, 3177
Hamilton, L., 245
Hamilton, S.A., 2434
Hamilton, Z.M., 1805
Hammer, Josiah Austin, 135
Hammond, L.H., 2063
Hammond, T., 3343
Hanks, J., 2209
Hanks, L.M., 2209
Hann, R.G., 843
Hanson, E.J., 2296, 2297, 2298, 2432, 2433, 2692
Hanson, S.D., 1699, 1925, 1926
Harasym, D.G., 2601
Hardisty, Richard, 2210, 2211
Hardwick, Francis C., 2895, 2896
Hardwick, W.G., 2826, 3178, 3179, 3180, 3344, 3471, 3472
Hardy, E.A., 531
Hardy, John, 1058
Hardy, W.G., 2149, 2150, 2693
Hargreaves, M.W.M., 532
Harker, D.E., 2897
Harper, J.R., 732
Harrington, E.D., 1159
Harrington, L., 37, 980, 1469, 2481, 2541, 2602, 2774
Harrington, Robert F., 3345
Harris, Charles Edward, 1059
Harris, R.C., 844, 3271
Harris, T.H., 423, 648
Harrison, Marilyn J., 3272
Harrison, Richard, 733, 845
Hart, Edward J., 2212
Hart, J.E., 334
Hatcher, Colin K., 2064, 2603
Hatcher, Temple, 3115A
Hatt, F.K., 246, 2213
Harvey, A.G., 2898
Harvey, Horace, 1060, 1061
Harvey, J.M., 2381
Harvey, Robert, 1238
Hassbrung, M., 2694
Hawkes, D.C., 1806
Hawkes, John, 1700
Hawthorn, Audrey, 2899
Hawthorn, H.B., 2900, 2901, 2902, 2903
Hay, Elizabeth, 1567
Hay, James, 533
Haydon, A.L., 1062
Hayley, W.T., 1568
Haynes, John Carmichael, 2904
Haythorne, G.V., 534

Healey, W.J., 1569, 1570
Heaps, Leo, 335
Hearne, G., 3595
Hébert, G., 2024
Hecht, A., 1470
Hedges, J.B., 136, 424
Hedlin, Ralph, 336
Heggie, Grace F., 846
Heidt, Elizabeth, 1957
Heimark, H., 2065
Heintzman, Ralph, 38
Hembroff-Schleicher, E., 2905
Henderson, A.M., 1571
Henderson, C., 840
Henderson, D.G., 1572
Henderson, G.F., 425
Herbert, W.B., 535
Hermuses, Paul, 3031
Hernandez, M.J., 1649, 1685
Herstein, Harvey H., 1239, 1240, 1573, 1574
Hewetson, H.W., 426
Heydenkorn, B., 279
Hicks, D.C., 1302
Hicks, Joseph, 981
Hiebert, A.J., 2906, 3273, 3274
Hiemstra, Mary, 536
Higginbotham, C.H., 1807
Higginson, T.B., 2214
Higgs, David, 191
Higgs, R.L., 792
Higinbotham, John D., 39
Hill, A.V., 3181
Hill, Douglas, 40, 137, 1063
Hill, Robert B., 1160
Hiller, Harry H., 2299
Hillman, W.A., 3473
Hind, E. Cora, 537
Hislop, Mary, 1575
Hitsman, J.M., 982
Hoagland, Edward, 2775
Hodge, G.F., 427
Hodges, L.K., 3182
Hodgson, E.D., 2482
Hodgson, M.C., 2695
Hodgson, Maurice, 3032
Hofer, Peter, 1241
Hoffer, Clara, 138
Hoffman, George J., 1808, 1809, 1810, 1811
Holdsworth, D.W., 3346, 3474, 3475
Holloway, G.F., 3596
Holm, B., 3292
Holmes, J.L., 1303
Holmes, Marjorie C., 3642, 3643
Holmes, N.B., 3347
Holmgren, Eric J., 2150A, 2151, 2483

Holt, S., 2907
Holton, R.H., 634, 3161
Honic, E., 3393
Hood, M.L., 1576
Hooke, A.J., 3152
Hoover, A.L., 3644
Hope, E.C., 538
Hopkins, E.S., 539, 540
Hoppenrath, I., 3116, 3348
Hopwood, Victor G., 2908
Horan, John W., 2153
Horn, M., 734
Horrall, S.W., 1064, 1065, 1065A
Horsfield, B., 3033
Horvath, Maria, 847, 3645
Hosie, Inez B., 2484
Hossé, H.A., 1577
Hostetler, John A., 848, 2300
Houghton, J.R., 2485, 2604
Hourticq, L., 41
Housego, I.E., 2544
Howard, F.W., 3477
Howard, Henry, 793, 3349
Howard, Irene, 2776, 2909, 3476
Howard, Joseph Kinsey, 914, 915
Howard, Victor, 3183
Howath, M., 3645
Howay, F.W., 42, 247, 2777, 2778, 2779, 2780
Howell-Jones, G.I., 2781, 3350, 3350A
Hromnysky, Roman, 337
Hubitcz, E., 1242
Huel, R., 3478
Huel, R.J.A., 248, 735, 1743, 1744, 1958, 1959, 1960, 1961
Hughes, Katherine, 2382
Hughes, M., 2066
Hughes, S., 983
Hull, V.L., 2214A
Hulmes, F.G., 2301
Hume, D., 841
Humphries, Charles W., 2910, 3275, 3276, 3351
Hunt, P.R., 3034
Hunter, A.A., 1578
Hunter, A.T., 1066, 1962
Hunter, B.F.C., 1161
Hunter, Murray T., 2782
Hurd, W. Burton, 43, 541
Hurley, K.C., 1593
Hutchings, C.J., 1304, 1471
Hutchinson, Gerald, 736
Hutchinson, H.K., 3277
Hutchinson, R., 1433, 1579
Huyshe, G.L., 942
Huzel, B., 1580

Ignatiuk, G.P., 139
Imrie, John M., 2383
Inderwick, Mary E., 2486
Ingles, Ernest B., 542
Inglis, A.I., 1305
Inglis, G.B., 249
Inglis, J., 2865
Innis, Harold A., 428, 429, 543, 544, 649, 650, 849
Ireland, W.E., 2783, 2784, 3035, 3352
Ironside, R.G., 2020, 2434, 2534
Irvine, William, 338, 339
Irving, John A., 340, 2302, 2303, 2304, 2305
Irwin, D.D., 1963
Irwin, Jane, 2911
Irwin, L.B., 430
Isbester, A.F., 850
Istvanffy, D.I., 2384, 2435
Iutcovich, M.J., 1243
Ivanisko, H.I., 3352A
Iwaasa, David B., 2215

Jackman, S.W., 1745, 2785, 3036, 3037, 3038
Jackman, W.T., 431
Jackson, Gilbert E., 545
Jackson, James A., 1162, 1163, 1306
Jackson, John N., 3646
Jackson, M., 1746
Jackson, W., 2215A
Jaenen, C.J., 737
Jahn, H.E., 1164, 1243A
Jameson, G.B., 1067, 1964
Jameson, Sheilagh S., 738, 2306, 2385, 2386, 2605, 2606, 2607, 2607A
Jamieson, F.C., 984, 2487, 2696
Jamieson, Stuart Marshall, 651, 2903, 3173, 3185, 3186
Jarray, G.L., 41
Jenness, Diamond, 250, 251, 2216, 2912, 2913
Jennings, John, 252, 2217
Johannson, P.R., 2786
Johns, H.P., 2787, 3039, 3040
Johnson, A.N., 546
Johnson, Arthur H., 2387
Johnson, Charles W., 547
Johnson, D.B., 2565
Johnson, Edward Philip, 3117
Johnson, F. Henry, 2914, 2915, 3278, 3279, 3280, 3281
Johnson, G., 253, 254, 1068
Johnson, Gilbert, 1701, 1747, 1927, 1928
Johnson, J.K., 341
Johnson, L.P.V., 2307
Johnson, M., 2308

Johnson, P.R., 3041
Johnson, Patricia M., 3353
Johnson, R.A., 3042
Johnson, Ronald C., 2488
Johnson, T.A., 1382, 1581
Johnston, A., 548
Johnston, E., 3485
Johnston, P.A., 2608
Johnston, Richard, 229, 230
Jonasson, J.A., 916, 917, 918
Jones, H.I., 549
Jones, J. Michael, 2788
Jones, O.D., 2697
Jones, R.L., 1165
Jordan, Mabel E., 2218, 2219, 2698, 2789 3187, 3354, 3355
Judy, J.W., 2436
Jupp, Ursula, 3597

Kalbach, Warner E., 140
Kalman, H., 3479
Karass, K.P., 2437
Kavanaugh, Martin, 1166
Kaye, B., 851
Kaye, V.J., 1069
Kealey, G.S., 843
Kealey, L., 843
Keddie, G.R., 3644
Kelly, L.A., 892
Kelly, L.V., 550
Kelly, Nora, 44, 45, 3282
Kelly, William, 45
Kemp, H.D., 1167
Kemp, V.A.M., 1070
Kennedy, D.R., 652
Kennedy, Howard Angus, 985, 986, 987
Kennedy, J.H., 3357
Kennedy, J.J., 1748, 3356
Kennedy, N.J., 2609
Kennedy, Orvis A., 2309
Kennedy, W., 3480
Kensit, H.E.M., 141
Kent, R.H., 1582
Kenvyn, R., 3481
Kenward, J.K., 2310, 2525
Kerfoot, Denis E., 3188
Kerr, D.P., 3482
Kerr, Don, 2106
Kerr, Donald, 1583
Kerr, J.B., 2916
Kerr, James, 2790
Kerr, John R., 2388
Kerri, James N., 1584, 2542
Kew, M., 3637
Kidd, Thomas, 3358

Kiewiett, C.W., 2791
Kilvert, Barbara, 3359
King, A., 2025
King, Carlyle, 1965, 1966
King, George B., 739
King, Mona S., 2699
King, T.P., 1307
King, W.L.M., 2917
Kinnaird, G.J., 988
Kipling, Rudyard, 2543
Kirk, D.W., 551
Kirk, L.E., 1967
Kirkconnell, Watson, 1244, 1434, 1585
Kirkwood, F.B., 1749
Kitto, F.H., 1168, 1702
Kizer, Benjamin, 46
Klassen, H.C., 47, 75, 852, 2610, 2611, 2612, 2613, 2636
Klassen, Peter George, 1434A
Klenke, M., 3483
Klinck, Carl F., 853
Klippenstein, D.H., 2389
Klippenstein, L., 142, 1245, 1277
Kloppenborg, A., 3484, 3485
Klymasy, R.B., 255, 256, 854
Knight, Rolf, 855, 2918, 2919
Knill, William D., 2220
Knowles, Eric, 2107, 2116
Knowles, Janet, 1884
Knowles, Stanley, 342
Knox, H.C., 1169
Knox, Paul, 3189, 3190
Knuttila, K.M., 1812A
Koch, E., 1586
Koenig, D.J., 3043, 3044
Koester, Charles B., 856, 1071, 1750, 1812
Kohl, S.B., 112
Kojder, A.M., 1968
Kolehmainen, John Ilmari, 2920
Kopas, C., 3360
Kopas, L.C., 3045
Kovach, J.J., 1703
Kovacs, M.L., 143
Krawchuk, P., 1246, 1587
Kreutzweiser, Erwin E., 943, 1704
Kristianson, G.L., 3046
Kristjanson, G.A., 1275
Kristjanson, L.F., 2026
Kristjanson, W., 1247
Kroetsch, R., 2154
Kuch, Peter, 48
Kupfer, G., 2552, 2700
Kuthan, G., 3486
Kuz, T.J., 1588
Kyba, J.P., 1813, 1814
Kydd, M.W., 257

Laatsch, W.G., 2220A
Lai, Chuen-Yan, 2921, 2922, 2922A, 2923, 3598
Lai, H., 2701
Laing, F.W., 2792, 3118
Laing, G.A., 1435, 1589
Laing, Hamilton M., 552
Lalonde, André, 989, 1072, 1073
Lam, Y.L.J., 1409
Lamb, B., 3487, 3488
Lamb, James E., 1170, 1344A
Lamb, R.E., 919
Lamb, W. Kaye, 432, 2793, 2794, 3191, 3489
Lambrou, Y., 2924, 3490
Landa, M.J., 1250
Lane, Marion, 3192
Lang, A.H., 653
Langstretch, T. Morris, 49
Langton, H.H., 990
Laponce, J.A., 3047, 3491
Large, R.G., 3361, 3362
Larmour, J., 991, 1074
La Rose, H., 2702
Lash, H.N., 2713
Latiff, A.H., 1578
Lattimer, J.E., 553
Laughland, A., 554
Laut, P., 1884A
Lautt, M.L., 740
La Violette, Forrest E., 2925, 2926, 2927
Laviolette, G., 258
Lawrence, Joseph C., 3193, 3194
Lawrence, M.C., 2614
Lawrence, V.H., 2390
Lawton, A., 1969, 2027, 2108
Lawson, Elsie, 1436
Layton, Monique, 2928
Leacock, Stephen B., 50
Le Chavellier, Jules, 992
Lecompte, Edouard, 1251
Lee, C.L., 3599
Lee, Carol F., 2929
Lee, D.T.H., 2930.
Lee, Lawrence B., 555, 2221, 3119
Lee, T.R., 2438, 2703
Leechman, Douglas, 3120
Leechman, J.D., 259
Leeson, W. Roy, 2795
Legasse, Jean H., 1248, 1249
Legge, A.D., 1171
Lehmann, Heinz, 260
Lehr, John C., 143A, 2221A, 2222, 2223, 2224, 2225
Leigh, R., 856A, 2882A, 3437

Leitch, Adelaide, 1885, 3121
Le Neveu, A.H., 3492
Leonoff, C.E., 1751
Lenz, K., 794
Leppard, H.M., 2391
Leslie, W.R., 1172
Lester, G.A., 2225A
Levadie, M., 1252
Léveillé, J., 1529, 2564, 2667, 3426
Levin, A., 2615
Lewis, Claudia, 2931
Lewis, Maurice H., 2489
Liddell, K.E., 2155, 2156, 2796
Lim, H.S., 2109
Lindal, W.J., 1437, 1752
Lines, K., 3600
Lingard, C.C., 1075
Lioy, M., 3494
Lipset, S.M., 1815, 1816
Lipton, Charles, 654
Little, A.D., 1383
Liversedge, Ronald, 741, 3195
Lloyd, Trevor, 1173
Lochhead, Douglas, 857
Logan, H.A., 655
Logan, H.T., 3283, 3284
Lohrenz, Gerhard, 261
Lonergan, S.G., 556
Long, J.A., 2311, 2312
Long, P.S., 557
Loosmore, T.R., 3048, 3196
Lopatin, I.A., 3495
Lord, G., 1529, 2564, 2667, 3426
Lort, J.C., 3601, 3638
Lort, R., 2932
Lowe, P., 1384, 1590
Lower, J.A., 433, 2797, 2798, 3197
Lowther, Barbara J., 3647
Lozowchuk, J.W., 1999
Lucas, Fred C., 1591
Lucow, W.H., 1438, 1592
Ludditt, W., 3363
Luk, L.W.C., 1753, 2110
Lunn, Jean, 858
Lunsden, J., 1076
Lunty, A.J., 1593
Lupton, A.A., 2392
Lupul, M.R., 1077, 1078
Lusty, Terrance, 920
Lussier, A.S., 289
Luxton, E.G., 2157
Lycan, Richard, 144
Lyle, G.R., 1079, 1754
Lyndell, Honoree B., 2799
Lyons, C., 3198

Lyons, John E., 1970, 1971, 3285
Lysenko, Vera, 262
Lysne, D.E., 2490

McAdam, Eben, 2226, 2227
McAfee, A., 3496
McAllister, J., 1308
McAra, Peter, 2067
McArton, D., 1439, 1594
MacBeth, M.E., 1309
MacBeth, R.G., 51, 52, 434, 1080, 1253
McCabe, James O., 2800
McCaffy, E., 3602, 3603, 3604
McCaig, James, 2158
McCandless, Richard, 3199, 3497
McCann, L.D., 795, 2704, 3605
McClung, Nellie, 343, 742, 743
McConnell, R.S., 2705
McCormack, A.R., 344, 656, 657, 796, 1310, 1311, 1595, 3049
McCormick, David, 1312
McCormick, James Hanna, 2028
McCourt, E.A., 744, 859, 993, 1705, 1886
McCracken, J.W., 2029, 2030
McCracken, K.W.L., 2706
McCracken, Melinda, 1596
McCrea, R.L., 1816A
McCrorie, James Napier, 1887, 1888
McCrossan, R.G., 53
McCutcheon, Brian R., 345, 1313, 1314
McCutcheson, M.K., 2031
MacDonald, C., 1817, 1972
MacDonald, D.I., 1472
McDonald, H.L., 2032, 3498
McDonald, Hugh, 2439, 2707
Macdonald, John, 2491
MacDonald, K.J., 3050, 3364
MacDonald, Mary Christine, 2129, 2130
McDonald, M.L., 3365
MacDonald, N., 3499, 3500, 3501, 3502, 3503
Macdonald, Norman, 145
McDonald, R.A.J., 3504
Macdonald, R.H., 2032
MacDonald, R.I., 558
McDonald, R.J., 1081, 1973
MacDonald, Robert J., 2228, 2492
MacDonell, R.A. 2229
McDougall, J.L., 435, 860, 1974
McDougall, John, 944
McDougall, R.J., 3505
MacDowell, G.F., 1385
MacEwan, Grant, 54, 55, 56, 57, 58, 263, 264, 436, 559, 560, 561, 562, 563, 564, 565, 566, 745, 2230, 2231, 2232, 2313, 2616, 2617, 2618, 2619, 2620
McEwen, Tom, 2933
MacFarlane, R.O., 1174, 1254, 1597
McFeat, Tom, 2934
McGeer, Gerald G., 3506
McGeer, Pat, 3051
MacGibbon, D.A., 437, 567, 658, 2393
McGill, A.S., 3507
MacGill, E.G., 2935
McGilloary, C.L., 2708
McGinnis, D., 2394, 2621, 2622
McGlashan, S., 2719A
McGovern, P.D., 3200, 3508.
McGowan, D.C., 2033, 2034
McGown, A.F., 2277, 2421
McGregor, D., 3509
McGregor, D.A., 3510
MacGregor, James G., 59, 2159, 2233, 2234, 2395, 2709, 2710, 2711
McGugan, Angus C., 2493, 2494
McGuire, B.J., 3366
McGusty, H.A., 2235
McHenry, D.E., 346
MacInnes, C.M., 2160
MacInnes, Tom, 2937, 3511
MacInnis, Angus, 2936
MacInnis, Grace, 347, 2936
McIntosh, R.G., 2544
McIntosh, W.A., 2314
McIntyre, A., 1175
McIntyre, L., 3648
McIntyre, M.L., 2236
MacKay, D.R., 3201
McKay, R.J., 265
McKee, W.C., 3512, 3513
McKechnie, N.D., 3202
McKelvie, B.A., 2801, 3367
MacKenzie, J.K., 568, 608
McKenzie, K.S., 2938
McKenzie, M.T., 2495
MacKenzie, W., 509
Mackie, M., 2237
Mackie, Victor J., 1176, 1929, 1930
McKillop, A.B., 1315, 1598, 1598A, 1599
McKillop, W., 3203
McKinlay, F.M., 2315
MacKinnon, C.S., 3368, 3606
MacKinnon, T.J., 3204
Mackintosh, W.A., 60, 146, 569, 659
MacKirdy, K.A., 2802
MacLachlan, Morag, 3122
McLaurin, C.C., 746
Maclean, Hugh, 438, 1975
McLean, R., 2496

MacLean, Una, 2316, 2497
McLean, W.J., 994
MacLennan, D.A., 1444
McLeod, D.M., 1082, 1976
McLeod, D.R., 1386
MacLeod, G.P., 1316
MacLeod, J.T., 1931
McLeod, Keith A., 1818
MacLeod, M.A., 1600, 1601, 1602
McLeod, N.L., 2498, 2623
Macleod, R.C., 348, 1083, 1084
MacLeod, W.B., 570, 660
McMenomy, Lorn E., 1976A
McMillan, C.J., 2440
MacNab, F., 2803
McNab, K.M., 2499
McNaught, K., 349, 350, 351, 1387, 1603
McNay, Diane, 3286
MacNeil, Grant, 3205
McNeill, Leishman, 2624
MacNutt, Ola, 2307
McPhail, L.R., 3369
McPherson, A.E., 2035, 2036
MacPherson, C.B., 2317
MacPherson, Ian, 60A, 661, 661A, 661B, 747, 796
MacPherson, L.G., 1604
McPherson, W.J., 571
McQuarrie, A.H., 2318
McQueen, R., 662
MacRae, A.D., 2161
McRaye, W.J., 1255
McWilliams, Margaret, 1177

Macoun, J., 1085, 1178
Madsen, R.P., 2319
Maerz, L.P., 2500
Magrath, C.A., 2162, 2441
Mahaffy, A.W., 572
Mahon, W.C., 2068
Mailloux, I.D., 2712
Makovski, L.W., 3514, 3515
Makowski, W.B., 266
Mallea, J.R., 861
Malliah, H.C., 2320
Mallory, J.R., 352, 2321, 2322
Malycky, A., 862, 863, 864
Mandel, E., 61, 748
Mann, William E., 2501
Manning, E.C., 2323
Mansell, R.L., 2454
Maranchuk, Michael H., 267
Maranda, E.K., 2939
Marchak, Patricia, 3287

Mardon, H.L., 1388
Marken, Jack W., 865
Markson, E.R., 921
Marlatt, D., 2940
Marlyn, F., 2713
Marlyn, J., 1606
Marriott, H., 3123
Marshall, L.G., 1977
Martin, Chester, 62, 147, 353, 439, 945
Martin, G.R., 3043
Martin, John, 2238
Martin, M., 3043
Martin, Mayor, 2069
Marton, E.G., 2324
Marunchak, M.H., 1257
Masson, J.K., 2325, 2545
Masters, D.C., 1389, 1607
Mather, B., 3370
Matheson, M.H., 2037, 3371
Matravolgyi, T.A., 2070
Matters, Diane, 2288, 3516
Matthews, G., 105
Mawson, T.H., 2071, 2625, 3517
May, Ernest G., 2626
Maxwell, J.A., 354, 355, 1317, 2804
Mead, W.J., 3203
Medovy, H., 1258
Megill, William J., 1180, 1932
Mellis, G.W., 2038
Menzie, E.L., 3124
Menzies, June, 1819
Menzies, M.W., 573
Mercer, E.B., 3052
Merrill, L.I., 1258A, 1754A
Metcalfe, J.H., 1473
Metcalfe, William H., 1474
Métin, Albert, 2805
Meyer, Ron H., 3649
Mika, Nick, 440, 995
Miller, C., 996
Miller, D., 3372
Miller, F., 3053, 3518, 3519
Miller, J.R., 1318
Miller, James A., 2326, 2502
Milligan, Frank A., 1319
Mills, Harry, 2240
Mills, J.C., 575
Milnor, A.J., 1820, 1821
Minden, Robert, 2941
Minghi, J.V., 2941A, 3519A, 3520
Minifie, James M., 148, 749
Minter, Ella S.G., 866
Mitchell, E.B., 63, 797
Mitchell, George, 1608
Mitchell, H., 575

Author Index 283

Mitchell, Howard T., 3206
Mitchell, Ken, 64, 750
Mitchell, N., 3521
Mitchell, R., 1609
Mitchener, E.A., 356, 357, 1086
Mitchinson, Wendy, 714
Mohamed, A.M., 1822
Mohan, E.M., 2627
Moir, G., 1181
Moir, John S., 751
Molyneaux, Marianne M., 2503
Moneo, G.W., 109, 814, 2039
Monk, H.A.J., 3402
Monu, E.D., 1475
Moodie, D.W., 851
Moogk, Peter N., 3522
Moon, Robert, 1706
Moore, George A., 1390, 1391
Moore, W.H., 441
Morgan, E.C., 149, 1087, 1088, 1089, 1978
Morice, A.G., 752, 753, 946, 1090, 2806
Morissette, Pierre, 1823
Morley, A., 3523
Morley, Marjorie, 1682
Morley, Terrance, 3054, 3055, 3207
Morman, James B., 576
Morris, J.L., 1182
Morris, Keith, 442
Morris, Philip Alvin, 2942
Morrison, A.S., 1440
Morrison, E.C., 2628
Morrison, H.M., 150
Morrison, J.W., 577
Morrison, P.N.R., 2628
Morrison, W.R., 1091
Morrow, E.L., 754
Morrow, J.W., 2546
Morse, E.N., 2943
Morton, A.S., 65, 151, 268, 1979
Morton, Desmond, 997, 998, 999, 1000
Morton, James, 2944, 3056
Morton, W.L., 66, 67, 68, 152, 358, 359, 360, 361, 362, 867, 868, 947, 947A, 1183, 1184, 1185, 1186, 1187, 1188, 1336, 1441, 1442, 1610
Moser, Charles, 2945
Mosher, S.P., 3289
Motherwell, W.R., 1092
Mott, M.K., 1259, 1611
Mowers, Cleo W., 2547
Mozersky, K.A., 755, 798
Mulvaney, C.P., 1001
Munday, J.G., 2946
Munro, G.R., 3237
Munro, J.A., 2947

Munro, John M., 3057
Munsterhjelm, Erik, 1889
Murchie, R.W., 578, 2140
Murphy, E.F., 3524
Murray, Jean E., 1980, 1981, 2040, 2072, 2073, 2112, 2113
Murray, Keith A., 3208
Murray, L.H., 1093
Murray, O.B., 799
Murray, S.N., 1345
Murray, Walter, 269
Myers, Gustavus, 664
Myers, T.R., 3607

Nader, G.A., 800
Naipaul, B.M., 1755
Nakayama, T.M., 2948
Namm, R., 3525
Napier, Nina, 3650
Navalkouski, Anna, 2504
Naylor, Tom, 665
Neal, M.W., 2074
Neane, Roland, 3125
Nearing, Peter A., 2505
Neary, Peter, 2870A, 3010A
Neatby, H. Blair, 363, 1982
Neatby, Hilda, 1094
Needler, G.H., 1002, 1003
Neering, Rosemary, 922
Nelles, H.V., 1189, 1392, 2418
Nelson, Denys, 3126, 3373
Nelson, J.G., 69, 70
Nelson, John, 71
Nelson, L., 3209
Nesbitt, J.G., 3210
Nesbitt, L.D., 2365, 2396
Netboy, Anthony, 2807
Neufeld, W., 1475A
Newinger, Scott, 2629
Newman, J.F., 1346
Newman, Peter C., 364
Newton, Norman, 2949, 2950
Nichol, John L., 2114
Nicholson, B.J., 756
Nicholson, L.H., 1095
Nicholson, T.G., 1612
Nicol, E.P., 3526, 3608
Nicoll, Ian M., 2714
Niddrie, J.G., 2239, 2715
Niebel, M.R., 1890
Niwinski, A., 3485
Nodwell, L.M., 2608
Nordegg, Martin, 666
Normandeau, Louis, 1004

Norrie, K.H., 153, 667, 668
Norris, John, 2951, 2952
North, G., 3211
Northrup, Minnie, 365
Nursey, W.R., 1522

O'Brien, Robert W., 2952A
Ockley, B.A., 2716
Oddie, Emmie, 580
Ogden, R.L., 3527
Oglesby, J.C.M., 2808
Ogmundson, Rick, 1319A
Oka, Mike, 2240
Okannesian, P.B., 3528
Oldham, Evelyn, 3290
Oliver, E.H., 72, 757, 1096, 1097, 1707, 1891, 1933, 1984, 1985, 2041
Oliver, Frank, 2717
Oliver, Thelma, 3058
O'Malley, M., 1613
O'Neill, P.B., 1986, 2075
Oppen, W., 827
Orlikow, L., 1320
Ormsby, Margaret A., 2809, 2810, 2811, 2812, 2813, 2814, 2953, 3059, 3060, 3061, 3127, 3128, 3129, 3130
Orr, A.D., 3212
Osborne, K., 869
Osing, Olga, 3375
Osler, E.B., 923
Oster, J.E., 758
Osterhout, S.S., 2954

Page, Donald M., 759
Page, J.E., 1614
Page, James, 870
Painchaud, Robert, 760, 1615
Palmer, H., 154, 155, 2241, 2242, 2243, 2244, 2245, 2327, 2739
Palmer, T.J., 270
Palmer, Tamara, 2327
Pammett, J.H., 312
Panting, G.E., 1347, 1348
Parker, Ian D., 3062, 3063, 3064
Parnell, C., 1098, 2718
Parr, J., 1616
Parrott, Michael, 2442
Partridge, E.A., 366
Partridge, Richard S., 1392A
Pascoe, J.E., 2042
Pashak, L.B., 2328
Passmore, F., 1987
Paterson, D.G., 3214

Paterson, T.W., 3376
Patillo, R.W., 3529
Paton, J.A., 3530
Patricia, M., 2151
Patterson, A.E., 1443
Patterson, E. Palmer, 271
Patterson, F.J., 3377, 3531
Patterson, R.M., 3378
Patterson, R.S., 2506
Pattison, M., 2115
Patton, Harold S., 367, 581, 582, 583
Paul, A.H., 73, 1892, 1893
Paulsen, F.M., 272
Paustian, Shirley I., 2131
Payton, W.F., 1988
Peach, John S., 2630
Peacock, Kenneth, 273, 274
Peake, Frank A., 2508, 2719, 2815, 3291
Pearce, William, 1005, 2163
Pearl, Stanley, 924
Pearse, Chas R., 2443
Pearson, D.F., 2816
Peck, D., 669
Peddie, Richard, 2631
Peel, Bruce, 761, 871, 1708, 1709, 2116, 2132, 2740
Peet, J. Richard, 670
Peitchinis, Stephen G., 2632
Pelletier, Emile, 1260
Pendakur, V. Setty, 3532
Pennanen, Gary, 275
Penner, Norman, 1393
Penny, N.L., 1261
Pentland, H.C., 671, 872
Pépin, C.L., 2548
Percira, C.P., 1262, 1617
Perry, Fraser J., 2633
Perry, G. Neil, 3131
Persons, Heather, 3533
Peter, Karl, 276
Peters, B.F., 2397
Peters, J.E., 3215
Peters, Victor J., 277, 1263, 1264
Peterson, Alex E., 1015
Peterson, C.W., 584, 672
Peterson, Lester R., 2955
Peterson, T., 1321
Pethick, Derek, 2956, 3534
Pettipas, K., 1265
Peuker, T., 3533A
Philip, C.R., 2634
Philip, Catherine, 2507
Philip, L., 861
Phillips, A.D., 1476
Phillips, B., 585

Phillips, Gordon C., 1477
Phillips, P.A., 673, 674, 675, 1394, 1618, 3216
Pick, Harry, 1756
Pierce, R.J., 2246
Pigeon, Louis Philippe, 2164
Pillsbury, Richard W., 2858
Pilton, J.W., 3610
Pinno, Erhard, 1989
Piper, C.B., 586
Piper, J., 2117, 2118
Pitt, Dale L., 3217
Pitt, E.L., 2247
Plaskett, J.S., 2817
Platt, A.W., 2365
Playfair, W., 3535
Plunkett, T.J., 1619
Podmore, D.R., 2719A
Poelzer, Irene A., 1099, 1757
Pogue, B.G., 2818, 3379
Pohorecky, Z.S., 1710, 1758
Pollard, J.R.A., 443
Pollard, W.C., 156, 2398
Pomeroy, E.M., 587
Ponich, M.H., 278
Ponting, J. Rick, 238A
Poole, Colin, 2165
Porritt, E., 676
Porteous, J.D., 3380
Porteous, Neil, 2957
Porter, Richard P.R., 3536
Potrebenko, Helen, 2248, 2249
Poulin, J., 873
Powell, T.J.D., 1711
Powers, J.W., 2076
Powrie, T.L., 1894
Pratt, A.M., 1190
Pratt, D.F., 1620
Pratt, J., 2635
Pratt, L., 2444
Preston, J.A.V., 1006
Preston, R.A., 874
Prevey, C.F., 2399
Priestley, Norman F., 2400, 2401
Pritchard, F.B., 1478
Pritchett, John P., 1191
Proudfoot, B., 2402
Proverbs, T.B., 3044
Puchniak, S.A., 948
Putman, Ben, 1895

Quigley, Leo R., 1349
Quo, F.Q., 2312

Raby, S., 1100, 1759, 2403
Radecki, Henry, 279
Ralston, Keith, 2763, 2958, 3218, 3219, 3652
Ramsay, Alan, 1621
Ramsey, A.B., 2959, 3220, 3221
Ramsey, Bruce, 2819
Rankin, Harry, 2960, 3537, 3538
Ranson, E.J., 1622
Rase, W., 3533A
Rasmussen, Linda, 74, 762
Rasmussen, Lorna, 74, 762
Rasporich, A.W., 75, 76, 157, 280, 2636
Ravenhill, Alice, 2961
Ravis, D., 2119
Ray, M.V., 281
Rea, J.E., 77, 763, 1323, 1324, 1325, 1395, 1623, 1624, 1625, 1626
Read, S.E., 2820
Ready, W.B., 1326
Ream, P.T., 2549, 2550
Redikopp, H.I., 1192
Reece, J., 1266
Rees, Ronald, 1896, 2120
Reese, N.A., 2077
Reesor, B.W., 1934
Reeves, B.O.K., 2637
Reeves, C.M., 3132
Regehr, T.D., 444, 445, 446, 447, 448, 449, 875, 1193, 1396
Rehmer, L.W., 1935
Reid, A.N., 1101, 1102, 1103, 1104, 1105, 2079
Reid, David J., 3222, 3223
Reid, Escott M., 1825
Reid, Helen R.Y., 307, 3007
Reid, L.V., 450
Reid, Richard Gavin, 158, 159
Reid, R.L., 677, 2962
Reid, W., 3292
Reid, W. Stanford, 282
Reimer, Derek, 2821
Reimer, P., 892
Rendell, Alice, 2043
Resnick, Philip, 3065, 3190
Reynolds, A., 2551
Reynolds, G.F., 1627
Rich, S. George, 1628, 1629, 1630
Richards, J.H., 78, 1712, 1713, 1714, 1715
Richter, J.J., 3133
Richtik, James M., 160, 1193A, 1194, 1267, 1350, 1351, 1630A, 1631
Rickard, Bruce, 589
Rickard, T.A., 2822
Ricou, L.R., 764, 765

Ridd, D.G., 1007
Ridd, John E., 949
Riddell, R.G., 79
Riddell, W.A., 1991
Ridge, Alan D., 2250
Ridout, Denzil G., 1479
Riis, Nelson A., 3134, 3381
Rizui, A.A.B., 3382
Robert, G.R., 2329
Roberts, A.F., 3284
Roberts, D.J., 3066
Roberts, L.E., 2251
Roberts, Sarah Ellen, 2404
Robertson, A.E., 3539
Robertson, Heather, 80, 161, 283, 1352
Robertson, R.W.W., 950
Robertson, Terry, 1874
Robertson, Thomas B., 1632
Robin, Martin, 368, 678, 2823, 2824, 3067, 3068
Robinson, A.C., 1480
Robinson, B.W., 1633
Robinson, I.M., 3383, 3384
Robinson, J. Lewis, 2825, 2826, 3385, 3540
Robinson, Leigh Burpee, 2963, 3386
Robinson, M.E., 1480, 2080, 3611
Robinson, M.Z., 766
Rodenhizer, John, 3293
Rodney, W., 369, 2827
Rodwell, L., 1897, 1992, 2044, 2045
Roe, F.G., 81, 82, 451, 590, 591, 2405
Roehle, R.G., 592
Roemer, M.I., 1993, 1994
Rogge, J.R., 1397
Rohner, Evelyn C., 2964
Rohner, Ronald, 2964
Rolland, Walpole, 2509
Rollins, Philip Ashton, 593
Rolph, William K., 1716, 2330
Romanowski, E.T., 1633A
Rome, D., 2965
Rondeau, Clairs, 1898
Rorem, C.R., 1899
Roscoe, A.A., 1195
Rose, R.T., 2720
Rose, W.J., 1353, 1481
Rosenberg, L., 1268, 1634, 2081
Rosender, J.M., 1649, 1685
Rosenthal, H.M., 3387
Ross, D.S.G.; 1398
Ross, Hugh R., 1327
Ross, M., 2082, 3069
Rostecki, R.R., 1635, 1636, 1637, 1638
Rothery, Agnes, 3224, 3541, 3612
Rowan, M.L., 1269

Rowand, Evelyn, 1008
Rowat, D.C., 312
Rowe, K., 1482
Rowe, P.A., 1639, 1640
Rowntree, G.M., 452
Roy, Patricia E., 2827A, 2828, 2966, 2967, 2968, 2969, 3225, 3226, 3227, 3228, 3229, 3542, 3543, 3544, 3545, 3546, 3547, 3613
Roy, R.H., 83, 1000, 1009, 2829, 2830, 2831, 2832, 2833, 2834, 2835, 2836, 2837, 2838, 2970, 2971, 3230
Royce, Marion V., 767
Rubin, M.W., 1826
Rudnyckyj, J.B., 1196, 1641
Ruff, Norman J., 3070
Ruggles, R.I., 1208
Rumball, W.G., 1444
Rumley, Dennis, 3071, 3519A, 3520
Rumsey, F., 3231, 3388
Runnalls, F.E., 3389, 3390
Russell, E.T.P., 1717, 2121
Russell, N.C.H., 1197
Russell, P.A., 1827, 1828
Russell, R.C., 162
Russenholt, E.S., 1642
Ruth, R.N., 1445
Rutherford, J.C., 594
Rutherford, P.F.W., 84, 801
Ruzicka, S.E., 3614
Ryan, John, 1270, 1271, 1354, 1355
Ryder, Dorothy E., 826
Ryder, N.B., 285

Saarinon, T.F., 2638
Sage, Walter N., 85, 2779, 2839, 2840, 2841, 2842, 3072, 3073, 3074, 3548, 3549
Sahir, A.H 1901, 1902, 1903
St. John, R.M., 3391
St. John, S.T., 1904
Sampson, W.R., 3135
Sanders, D., 815, 2972
Sanderson, James F., 286
Sandhu, K.S., 2972A
Sandison, James, 3294, 3550
Sanford, T.M., 3075
Saper, Arthur M., 1398A
Sarjeant, W.A.S., 2100, 2103, 2123
Savage, Candace, 74, 762
Savage, R.L., 453
Sawatzsky, A.A., 2252
Sawatsky, H.L., 1273
Sawchuk, J., 1272
Saywell, John T., 370, 371, 3076, 3077, 3078, 3232

Scace, R.C., 85A
Scawn, D.R., 2331
Schieder, Rupert, 2973
Schimnowski, F.M., 1274
Schlichtmann, H., 1905, 1906
Schofield, Emily M., 2974
Schofield, Frank Howard, 1198
Scholfield, E.O.S., 2780
Schultz, Earl L., 2510
Schultz, Harold J., 2332, 2333, 2334, 2335 2336
Schurman, D.M., 3392
Schwartz, C., 1719, 2336A
Scott, A.D., 3233
Scott, D., 3393
Scott, J.J., 3634
Scott, Jack, 3234, 3235
Scott, M.M., 1684
Scott, W.G., 2721
Scott, William, 3294A
Scott, W.L., 287
Scratch, John R., 2337
Seaborne, Adrian A., 1760
Seager, Allen, 2445
Sealey, D.B., 288, 289
Sealey, G.D., 679
Seaman, H.S., 1199
Secretan, J.H.E., 454
Seldon, J., 163
Selman, Gordon R., 3295, 3296, 3297
Selwood, H.J., 1631, 1643, 1643A
Senior, Norman, 2843
Serfaty, Meir, 2338
Serra, J., 3394
Shandro, P.A., 2253
Sharp, E.F., 1275
Sharp, P.F., 86, 164, 165, 166, 372, 595, 877, 1108
Shaw, P.C., 2254
Shaw, W.T., 1446
Shearer, Ronald A., 680, 3215, 3236, 3237
Sheikh, Z.A., 1644
Shelton, W.G., 2844, 3079
Sheps, M.C., 1833
Shera, John W., 1010
Sherman, Paddy, 3080
Shibata, Y., 3653
Shipley, Nan, 290, 1483, 1645
Sherdahl, R.M., 1834
Sherriff, A.B., 1907
Shook, L.K., 768
Short, R.B., 1400, 1646
Shortt, Adam, 87, 1109, 1110, 3238, 3615
Shulman, N., 300
Shute, A.J., 2722

Shutt, F.T., 596
Siamandas, G., 1647
Siddigue, M., 2122
Siegal, Joy H., 2979
Siegfried, N.R., 1399
Siemens, A.H., 2844A, 3136
Silver, A.I., 925, 1111
Silverman, P.G., 2845, 3239
Sim, V.W., 1484
Simeon, Richard, 373
Simms, E.F., 1447
Simon, Frank, 2511
Simpson, George W., 167, 1720, 1721, 1995
Sinclair, Gordon, 1485
Sinclair, Peter R., 374, 1835, 1836, 1837, 2339
Sinclair, Sylvia, 3551
Sindlinger, T.L., 455
Sinton, Robert, 1761, 1762, 2083
Sisler, W.J., 1648
Skelton, O.D., 456
Sloan, Robert W., 88
Sloan, W.A., 3240, 3299, 3395
Sloane, D.L., 1649, 1685
Smart, John, 3654
Smeltzer, M.F., 1763
Smerek, John, 238
Smiley, Donald V., 1838
Smillie, E.E., 291
Smith, Allison, 1996
Smith, B.E., 3081
Smith, B.R.D., 3082, 3083, 3396
Smith, C.E., 1356
Smith, Charles W., 3655
Smith, D.B., 2975, 3397, 3656
Smith, David F., 375, 376, 377, 878, 1792, 1793, 1794, 1839, 1840, 1841, 1842, 1843, 2101, 2340
Smith, Denis, 378, 379
Smith, Dwight L., 879
Smith, Ian, 2846
Smith, M.M., 2341
Smith, M.W., 2976
Smith, P.D., 2342
Smith, Pamela J., 2046
Smith, Peter J., 89, 802, 2639, 2640, 2641, 2642, 2723, 2724, 2725
Smith, W.G., 168
Smyly, C., 3616, 3617
Snidal, D.J., 1401
Snider, E.L., 2552
Snyder, H.M., 2726
Somuyiwa, M.O., 1357
Sorby, T.C., 3618
Soules, G., 3552

Spafford, D.S., 1844, 1845, 1846, 1847, 1866
Sparby, Harry T., 2512
Specht, Allen, 2847
Spector, David, 597, 879A, 879B, 879C, 1112, 1402, 1650
Spence, Thomas, 1200
Spencer, J.E., 1908
Spencer, L.O., 598
Spinks, J.W.T., 1997
Sproule, A.F., 2255
Sproule-Jones, Mark, 3084, 3085, 3398
Spruce-Sales, Harold, 3428
Spry, Irene, 169
Stabler, J.C., 802A, 1113
Stacey, C.P., 90, 1011
Stadel, C., 1486
Stahl, John, 599
Stainer, John, 2848
Stainsby, D., 3486
Stalker, A., 803
Stamp, R.M., 782, 2513, 2643, 2644
Stanbury, W.T., 2886, 2977, 2978, 2979, 3300, 3399, 3400, 3401
Stanley, George Douglas, 2514
Stanley, George F.G., 91, 170, 292, 293, 293A, 294, 880, 926, 927, 928, 929, 930, 931, 932, 933, 951, 1012, 1013, 1014, 1015, 1114, 1201, 2343, 2645, 3086
Stanton, J.B., 1276
Stead, Robert J.C., 171, 2166, 2646
Steck, W.F., 2123
Steed, Guy F.P., 3553
Steele, C. Frank, 2256
Steele, S.B., 1115, 2084
Steen and Boyce, 1487, 1488, 1489, 1652
Steen, J.E., 1651
Steen, P., 2719A
Steeves, Dorothy, 3087
Stegner, Wallace, 91A
Steininger, F., 1764
Stelter, Gilbert A., 804, 881, 882
Stephens, D.G., 769
Stephenson, A.T., 2553
Stephenson, G.P., 457
Steven, Paul, 842
Stevens, G.R., 458, 459
Stevens, Leah, 3241, 3554, 3555
Stevens, R.C., 172
Stevenson, D., 3399
Stevenson, J.A., 1848
Stewart, A., 600, 1358
Stewart, Alistair M., 1448
Stewart, George, 601
Stewart, J., 3402
Stewart, J.R., 2980

Stewart, Keith J., 681
Stewart, W.R., 1116
Stewart, W.W., 1849
Stich, K.P., 173
Stinson, L., 1328, 1653
Stock, A.B., 602
Stokes, E.B., 2647
Stone, G.M., 1998, 2085
Stone, Leroy O., 174
Stout, C.H., 2446
Strange, H.G.L., 603
Straaton, K.V., 2981, 3556
Stratton, P.R.V., 3557
Strayer, B.L., 92
Strom, T., 2648
Strong-Boag, Veronica, 379A, 769A, 2256A
Strongitharm, B.D., 3403
Stuart, Duncan, 604, 605
Stuart, J.A.D., 1202, 1359
Stuart, K., 1117
Studness, C.M., 175
Stutt, R.A., 1909
Sugimoto, Howard H., 2982, 2983, 2984
Sumida, R., 2985
Suski, J.G., 2727
Sutcliffe, J.H., 1403
Sutherland, N., 3088
Sutley, Zack T., 93
Sutyla, C., 883
Swain, H., 3519A
Swainson, D., 94
Swanson, W.W., 176, 472, 606
Swindlehurst, E.B., 2401, 2406
Swyripa, F.A., 884
Symes, O., 607
Symington, Fraser, 295
Syrnick, John H., 1449

Tagashira, K., 1999
Taggart, J.G., 608
Taillon, Louis-Oliver, 1450
Takla, E.F., 2649
Talbot, F.A., 460
Talbot, L.D., 1654
Tallant, Clive, 2047, 2048
Tanghe, R., 885
Taraska, E.A., 2447, 2650
Tarasoff, K., 296, 3558
Tatreau, Bobbie, 2849
Tatreau, Doug, 2849
Taylor, G.W., 3242
Taylor, Griffith, 2850
Taylor, Harry, 3404
Taylor, John H., 805, 806

Taylor, K.W., 1678
Taylor, L., 2525
Taylor, L.D., 3559
Taylor, M.G., 1850, 2000
Teit, James, 2986
Telford, Gertrude S., 2001
Telmer, F.H., 2448
Tennant, Paul, 3024, 3089, 3243, 3405, 3453, 3560, 3561
Tetreault, Alexis, 2407, 2408, 2409, 2410
Thair, P.J., 609
Théoret, A.E., 1360
Theron, J.D., 1655
Thibault, Claude, 886
Thiessen, H.W., 610
Thirnbeck, A.R., 2167, 2410A
Thomas, C.T., 1203
Thomas, J.J., 686
Thomas, Jean McC., 1118
Thomas, L.G., 177, 887, 1119, 2344, 2345, 2411, 2651, 2728
Thomas, Lewis H., 95, 96, 178, 380, 611, 888, 934, 1016, 1120, 1121, 1122, 1123, 1124, 1125, 1126, 1127, 1128, 1765, 1851, 1852, 1853, 1910, 2002, 2003, 2086, 2124, 2346
Thomas, Lillian Jean, 1403A
Thomas, Paul, 1451
Thompson, John H., 97, 381, 612, 1452, 1453, 1656
Thompson, L.R., 461
Thompson, M.E., 777
Thompson, N., 462
Thompson, R.L.B., 2004
Thompson, W.P., 2005, 2006
Thompson, W.T., 1129, 1657
Thomson, Georgina H., 2412, 2413
Thomson, James S., 2007
Thorarinson, S.A., 1658
Thorner, T., 2515, 2652
Thornton, James E., 3302
Tiessen, Hugo, 613, 2125
Timlin, M.F., 179
Timms, P.T., 3562
Tims, John W., 2516
Tippett, Maria, 2851, 3303, 3304
Tiveton, D.J., 382
Todd, J.B., 952
Toews, J.G., 142, 1277
Tollefson, Edwin A., 1854, 1855, 1856
Toombs, M.P., 2008
Toren, E.P., 3443
Torhjelm, Gary Douglas, 2554
Touchie, Rodger, 2852
Trace, H.D., 2449

Tracie, C.J., 297, 1766
Treleavan, G.F., 3408
Trémaudon, A.H., 298, 953, 954, 955, 956
Tremblay, M.A., 614
Trofimenkoff, S.M., 98
Troper, Harold Martin, 180, 181
Trosky, O.S., 778
Trotter, B., 615, 2087
Trouth, N.S., 2653
Turek, Victor, 1278
Turenne, R.E., 1329
Turnbull, I.D., 1490, 1659
Turnbull, Jean, 3657
Turner, Allan R., 1130, 1722, 1857, 1858, 1911, 1912, 2009, 2088, 2134A
Turner, C. Frank, 299
Turner, John Peter, 1131, 1132, 1133
Tuttle, C.R., 1660
Tyler, E.J., 616, 779
Tyman, John L., 182, 183, 184
Tyre, Robert, 1767, 1859, 1936, 2010, 2089, 2126
Tyrrell, J.B., 1204

Ujimoto, K.V., 2987
Ulmer, A., 3408A
Underhill, F.H., 383, 2791, 3244
Unger, Gordon, 1860, 1861
Usher, Jean, 2988, 2989, 3305
Utley, James A., 3137

Valentine, V.F., 1768
Valee, F.G., 300
Vallée, Lloyd L., 1877
Vanderhill, B.G., 185, 186, 187, 1205, 1361, 2168, 3138
Van Klaveren, Adrie, 3398
Van Tighem, Frank, 2258
Van Vliet, H., 617
Varnals, D., 3306
Vaughan, W., 463
Venables Alex., 1491
Vidal, H.V., 1454
Villa-Acre, Jose, 2169
Villeneuve, P.Y., 2989B, 3408B
Vincent, D.B., 1661
Vogelesang, R.R., 2414
Voisey, P.L., 99, 807, 2259, 2347, 2654
Vrooman, C.W., 3139

Waddell, Douglas, 1662
Waddell, J.M., 1492

Author Index

Waddell, W.S., 384, 2348
Wade, F.C., 808, 3409
Wade, G.M., 464
Wade, Mason, 100
Waggoner, M.A., 1862
Wagner, J.F., 1769
Wagner, Philip L., 2989C
Wahn, J.D., 1723
Waines, W.J., 101, 385
Waite, W.H., 2010A
Waites, K.A., 3090, 3308, 3563
Walbran, John T., 2853
Walchuk, W., 2729
Walden, F.E., 3621
Walden, P.S., 3410
Walhouse, F., 3564
Walker, Bernal E., 2517
Walker, D., 1492A, 1663
Walker, James, 2260
Walker, John F., 3245
Walker, J.W., 889
Walker, M., 3622
Walker, R.R., 3091
Wallace, R.C., 1206, 1404
Walter, M., 2854
Warburton, T.R., 3092, 3623
Ward, N. Lascelles, 2990
Ward, Norman, 386, 1863, 1864, 1865, 1866, 2091, 2349
Ward, Tom, 2655
Ward, W. Peter, 1134, 2991, 2992, 2993
Wargo, A.J., 3246
Warkentin, J.H., 102, 103, 104, 188, 1207, 1208, 1279, 1280, 1362, 1363, 1364
Warner, D.F., 387, 957
Warren, John, 2450
Warrian, P., 687, 843
Wasylow, W.J., 1770
Waterfield, D., 3247
Waterson, E., 618
Watson, Edward, 1771
Watson, K.F., 2555
Watson, Robert, 1209, 1210, 1211
Watt, A.B., 2730
Watters, Reginald Eyre, 2855
Watts, Alfred, 2856
Watts, C., 1664
Waywitka, Anne B., 2261, 2415, 2416, 2451, 2452, 2453
Weadick, Guy, 2656
Weaver, Emily P., 1455, 2092
Weaver, John C., 809, 810, 2731
Weaver, S.M., 815
Webster, Daisy, 3093
Weeks, Kathleen S., 2857

Weightman, Barbara A., 2994
Weinard, Philip, 2417
Weir, D.A., 2995
Weir, G.M., 780, 781
Weir, J.R., 3411
Weir, T.R., 105, 1281, 1365, 1405, 1665, 1666, 1667
Weir, Thomas K., 811
Wellwood, R.J., 3658
Welsh, R.H., 2995A
Weppler, D.M., 3094
Wertenbaker, T.J., 106
West, Edward, 619
West, George E., 1668
West, Karen, 2556
Westcott, F.J., 688
Westmacott, M.W., 388, 465
Weston, G., 3565
Weston, Phyllis E., 2518, 2519, 2657, 2658
Wetton, C., 1772
Whalen, Hugh J., 2350, 2351
Wheatley, J., 690
Wheeler, Anne, 74, 762
Wheeler, R.Z., 3106
Wheeler, S., 620
Whetten, N.L., 812
Whetter, D., 3566
White, C.O., 1937, 1938, 1939, 1940, 2049
White, Howard, 2996
Whiteley, A.S., 189
Whiteside, Dan, 890
Wibois, Joseph, 107
Wichern, P.H., 1669, 1670, 1671, 1672
Wickett, S.M., 1135, 1136, 3412
Widstoe, John A., 621
Wilbur, Richard, 389, 3095
Wilcox, A.G., 2262
Wild, Ronald, 2997, 3366
Wilgus, W.J., 466
Wilkie, D., 3595
Williams, C.B., 850
Williams, David R., 2998
Williams, J. Earl, 2520
Williams, Merton Yarwood, 1493, 2858, 2859
Wilmot, Fred, 1673
Willmott, Donald E., 621A, 1913, 1941, 2127
Willmott, W.E., 2999, 3000, 3413
Willms, A.H., 2352
Willms, A.M., 301
Willows, A., 1282
Wilson, Alan, 2860
Wilson, E., 3567
Wilson, J., 1330, 1914
Wilson, J. Donald, 782, 3001
Wilson, J.G., 1456

Wilson, J.W., 3624
Wilson, L.A., 2453A
Wilson, L.J., 2521
Wilson, Thomas E., 2263
Wilton, Sidney, 1494
Winkler, H.W., 1406, 1495
Winter, George R., 3139A
Wiseman, Nelson, 1331, 1678
Wolcott, H.F., 302
Wolfe, S., 1775
Wonders, William C., 2170, 2264, 2732, 2733, 2734
Wong, C.S.J., 2522, 2659, 2735
Wong, W.H., 1283
Wood, E.H., 108
Wood, Kerry, 1137
Wood, Louis Aubrey, 390
Wood, W.D., 892
Woodcock, George, 303, 935, 1017, 2861, 3002, 3625, 3659
Woodcock, I., 3625
Woodland, Alan, 3414
Woods, D.S., 1457
Woods, H.D., 1407
Woods, J.J., 3140
Woodsworth, Charles J., 3003
Woodsworth, J.S., 190, 813, 3248, 3568
Woodward, Frances, 2862, 3660, 3661, 3662
Woodward, J.S., 391
Woodward-Reynolds, K.M., 3415
Woolworth, Nancy L., 1284
Worley, R.B., 3096
Woycenko, Ol'Ha, 304
Woychuk, J.K., 2736
Wright, A.J., 3309, 3310, 3416
Wright, J.F.C., 305, 691, 1724, 1725, 1726, 1727, 3004

Wright, J.M., 3626
Wright, Norman E., 1212
Wright, Paul, 3249
Wright, R.W., 2454
Wynne, R.E., 3005, 3006

Yackulic, G.A., 622, 2265, 2455
Yarham, E.R., 3569
Yates, S.W., 1915
Yauk, T.B., 1679
Yeates, M.H., 1612
Yerburgh, R.E.M., 3250
Young, Charles H., 306, 307, 3007
Young, Cy, 3417
Young, E.M., 3570
Young, G.A., 3571
Young, George, 1213
Young, J.H., 3237
Young, R.C., 2031
Young, R.E., 3572
Young, T.C., 2266
Young, Walter D., 392, 393, 2093, 3097, 3098
Younge, Eva B., 718
Yule, Annie I., 1916
Yuzyk, Paul, 1285

Zahradnitzky, G.L., 467
Zakuta, Leo, 394
Zaslow, M., 893
Zenter, H., 308, 783
Zieber, G.H., 2660, 2661, 2737
Zides, Murray, 2050
Ziegler, Olive, 395, 784
Zimmerman, C.C., 109, 814
Zirnhelt, D., 3089, 3560

Organization, Institution, and Serial Index

Alberta Historical Society, 260
Alberta History, 253
Albertan Geographer, 254
Anglican Church Archives of British Columbia, 258
Archives de l'Archdiocèse de Saint-Boniface, 256
Archives of the Canadian Rockies, 257

British Columbia Forest Products Limited Archives, 258
B.C. Geographical Series, 263
British Columbia Historical Association, 260
B.C. Historical News, 254
BC Studies, 254
British Columbia Telephone Company Archives, 258

Canada West Foundation, 260
Canadian Frontiers of Settlement, 261
Canadian Mennonite Brethren Archives, 256
Canadian Plains *Bulletin,* 254
Canadian Plains Research Center, 259
Canadian Plains Studies, 262

Fort Steele Regional History Library, 258

Glenbow-Alberta Institute, 259
Glenbow-Alberta Institute Archives and Library Research Centre, 257

Historical and Scientific Society of Manitoba *Transactions,* 253

Jewish Historical Society of Western Canada, 259

Kamloops Museum and Archives, 258

Legislative Library of Alberta, 257
Legislative Library of British Columbia, 258
Legislative Library of Manitoba, 255
Legislative Library of Saskatchewan, 256
Lutheran Central Synod Archives, 256
Lutheran Missouri Synod Archives, 256

Manitoba Historical Society, 260
Manitoba Pageant, 253
Maritime Museum of British Columbia, 258
Medicine Hat Historical Foundation, 257
Mohyla Institute Archives, 256

Newest Review, 254

Oblate Archives of Alberta-Saskatchewan, 257

Prairie Division, Canadian Association of Geographers, 259
Prairie Forum, 253
Provincial Archives of Alberta, 257
Provincial Archives of British Columbia, 258
Provincial Archives of Manitoba, 255

Red Deer and District Archives, 257
Red River Valley Historian, 254
Red River Valley Historical Society, 260
Research Centre for Canadian Ethnic Studies, 260
Royal Canadian Mounted Police Museum, 256

Saskatchewan Archives, 256
Saskatchewan History, 253
Saskatchewan History and Folklore Society, 260
Saskatchewan Power Corporation Archives, 256

294   Organization, Institution, and Serial Index

Selkirk College Archives, 258
Simon Fraser University Archives, 258
Sir Alexander Galt Museum, 257
Social Credit in Alberta: Its Background and Development, 261

Ukrainian Canadian Archives, 257
Ukrainian Cultural and Education Centre Archives, 256
United Church Archives (Alberta Conference), 257
United Church Archives (B.C. Conference), 258
United Church Archives (Manitoba Conference), 256
United Church Archives (Saskatchewan Conference), 256
University of Alberta Archives, 257
University of Alberta—Special Collections, 257
University of British Columbia—Special Collections, 258
University of Calgary—Special Collections, 257
University of Manitoba Archives, 256
University of Saskatchewan Archives, 257
University of Victoria—Special Collections, 258

Vancouver Maritime Museum, 258

Western Canadiana Publications Project Newsletter, 254
Western Canadian Journal of Anthropology, 253
Western Canadian Studies Conference Proceedings, 262
Western Division, Canadian Association of Geographers, 259
Western Geographical Series, 262
Western History Group, Canadian Historical Association, 259